Second Edition

Content Area Reading and Learning

Instructional Strategies

Diane Lapp
James Flood
Nancy Farnan
San Diego State University

Allyn and Bacon
Boston • London • Toronto • Sydney • Tokyo • Singapore

Series Editor: Virginia Lanigan
Editorial Assistant: Nihad Farooq
Manufacturing Buyer: Aloka Rathnam
Marketing Manager: Kathy Hunter
Editorial-Production Service: Electronic Publishing Services Inc.
Cover Administrator: Suzanne Harbison

Library of Congress Cataloging-in-Publication Data

Content area reading and learning : instructional strategies / [edited
    by Diane Lapp, James Flood, Nancy Farnan. — 2nd ed.
        p.   cm.
    Includes bibliographical references and index.
    ISBN 0-205-18893-1
    1. Content area reading.   2. Reading (Secondary)   I. Lapp, Diane.
II. Flood, James.   III. Farnan, Nancy.
LB1050.455.C66   1996
428.4'07'12—dc20   95-33569
                                                                          CIP

Printed in the United States of America

10 9 8 7 6 5 4   99 98 97 96 95

Contents

Preface

This is a working textbook. It provides students with maximum interaction with the information and strategies discussed in each chapter. Each chapter begins with a Think before Reading Activity, includes one or two Think while Reading Activities, and ends with a Think after Reading Activity. Each type of activity is clearly marked with a box around it to assist the teacher and students use of these as catalysts for thinking and discussion. These activities present questions and scenarios designed to integrate students' previous knowledge and experiences with their new learnings about issues related to content area reading, literacy, and learning. The many strategies and instructional ideas contained in each chapter often serve as a basis for the activities, frequently requiring students to use the strategies in their answers.

In addition, a graphic organizer and chapter preview begin each chapter. Chapters are designed to offer readers a genuine overview of concepts and ideas contained in each one. The graphic organizers, particularly, can be used by students as a framework around which to begin constructing knowledge on topics of literacy and learning across content areas.

Why a book about content area reading and literacy? Unfortunately, when the topic of reading is introduced to content area specialists, it is often met with perplexed stares. Most content area specialists believe that any reading related instruction is the work of the English teacher or the remedial reading teacher. Content specialists also often believe that their students are not interested in their subject area, are not learning enough about it, and are not reading the assigned material. Reasons for these concerns were studied in 1977, in "How Content Teachers Telegraph Messages Against Readers" in *The Journal of Reading*, Volume 20, pp. 646–648, by B. J. Rieck, who reported the findings of a study in which English, science, social studies, mathematics, physical education, art, and home economics teachers participated. Although published over two decades ago, insights from this survey are reflective of concerns in many content area classrooms today. In his survey, Rieck asked teachers:

1. Do you require reading in your course?
   97 percent responded *yes*, 3 percent responded *no*
2. Do most of your students read their assignments?
   58 percent responded *yes*, 42 percent responded *no*

Rieck, in attempting to understand the *why* of these responses, further asked approximately three hundred students from the 42 percent of teachers who responded *no*:

1. Do you like to read?
   52 percent *yes*, 38 percent *no*, 10 percent *no response*
2. Do you read your assignments in this class?
   15 percent *yes*, 81 percent *no*, 4 percent *no response*

Isn't this perplexing? Why do students who like to read not feel the need to read their assignments?

3. Do your tests cover mainly lecture and discussion or reading assignments?
   98 percent lecture and discussion, 2 percent reading

Perhaps teacher behaviors are suggesting that there is no real need to learn from the textbook.

4. Are you required to discuss your reading assignments in this class?
   23 percent *yes*, 70 percent *no*, 7 percent *no response*

If completion of the textbook assignments is not needed for success on tests or classroom discussion, students may not be motivated to read.

5. Does your teacher give you purpose for reading or are you only given the number of pages to read?
   95 percent pages, 5 percent purpose

It appears that although teachers may want students to read textbooks, they do not know how to integrate lecture, discussion, and textbook reading.

6. Does your teacher bring in outside material for you to read and recommend books of interest for you to read?
   5 percent *yes*, 95 percent *no*

It seems that relationships between topics presented in content areas and real-world situations are not being modeled through experiences that say "lifelong reading of expository materials is important."

7. Does your teacher like to read?

20 percent *yes*, 33 percent *no*, 47 percent *don't know*

Isn't it interesting that although 52 percent of the students responded that they like to read, 80 percent of them do not credit their teachers with being readers? And isn't it interesting that after spending approximately two hundred classroom hours together, it isn't obvious to them that books are important to their teachers?

Rieck concluded:

> Out loud, teachers are saying: "I require reading in this course. All students are to read the assignments. Students are to read X number of pages from the textbook." However, their nonverbal attitude says to students: "You really don't have to read the assignments because you aren't tested on them and probably won't have to discuss them. You should read X number of pages but there is no real reason to do so. Reading really isn't important. Outside reading is of little value in this class. My students will have no way to tell whether or not I like to read" (p. 647).

We propose that this attitude still prevails because the majority of secondary teachers received little if any instruction in how to integrate reading into their teaching plans. Many teachers believe they must "cover their material" and that covering the material is unrelated to good instruction or to reading. Secondary teachers often feel that they are specialists and that heavy reliance on the text somehow reduces their knowledge of the content area.

We agree that secondary teachers must be content area authorities, but we believe they must be more than that. They also must be able to use instructional strategies to ensure that all students learn content area concepts and learn to apply these concepts to real-life situations. Where written materials are involved, we believe that teachers, as instructional specialists, must know how to help students use the reading strategies that they will need to comprehend and learn.

This text has been designed to provide content area teachers with strategies that will help them teach their chosen fields of expertise. Section one, *Content Area Reading: An Overview*, contains two chapters which provide, respectively, a look into the history of content area reading and insights into today's state-of-the-art perspectives.

Section Two, *The Teacher and the Text*, contains four chapters which explain the need for content specialists to understand text-related strategies that will make their roles as teachers of a particular discipline more effective. Also explained in this section is the complexity of the structure of content area textbooks.

Section Three, *The Students*, contains four chapters which illustrate the emotional, cognitive, and psychological development of the adolescent. Also emphasized are the ways in which adolescents learn.

Section four, *The Instructional Program*, contains thirteen chapters which provide instructional examples and strategies for teaching all of the content areas. Also included in this section are chapters which explain how to use literature to introduce and expand content area reading, how to integrate reading, writing, and thinking strategies throughout content area subjects, and how to effectively use computers in content area classes.

Section five, *Model Programs*, contains six chapters which address the curricular issues of classroom management, cooperative grouping, and assessment. Also included are examples of exemplary secondary classrooms and programs.

This text, *Content Area Reading and Learning: Instructional Strategies*, addresses instructional issues and provides classroom practices that will enable all secondary teachers to do an even better job of sharing the joy of their subject area by ensuring that their students develop both content concepts and strategies for continued learning. The goal of this text is to help content area specialists model, through excellent instruction, the importance of lifelong content area learning.

The editors would like to acknowledge the excellent contributions made to this text by all the authors. In addition, we would like to thank those who helped in varying ways with the production, especially Sheila Felber, a teacher of Language Arts and Reading in the Chula Vista, California School District; Dr. Linda Lungren, Magnet/Technology Resource Specialist with the San Diego Unified School District; Dr. Ricardo Cornejo and Dr. Lynne Thrope, content area literacy educators; Kelly Goss and Michelle LeTourneau, graduate students and beginning teachers. Thank you. We would also like to thank Robert Curley of San Jose State University and Suzanne Robbins of Lock Haven University for their reviews of this edition. To all of you and to every other teacher and professor who has attempted to address content area reading and language arts issues, we applaud you!

Content Area Reading: An Overview

C h a p t e r *1*

Content Area Reading

A Historical Perspective

MARY W. OLSON   ERNEST K. DISHNER

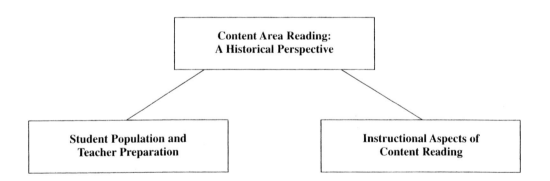

Think before Reading Activity

If a time travel machine took you back to the early 1900s and made you a high school student once again, what do you think your day in a public high school would be like? What might your experiences be? Describe the students and teachers. How do your teachers teach, what do you think your homework will be tonight? What subjects are you taking, and how do you think they will help you as an adult in 1910 or so? Note a few imaginary experience on the lines below.

Where do you live?

_____

_____

_____

What are you and your friends like?

_____

_____

_____

What happens in a typical school?

_____

_____

What is contained in the school curriculum?

_____

_____

What are the educational beliefs of the teachers?

_____

_____

_____

Activity 1–1

This chapter traces the development of content reading from the early 1900s to the present time. The chapter contains a description of the school population before 1925 and the changes that have occurred in that population over eight decades, and discusses how the school population affected the preparation of teachers, specifically their preparation related to content reading. The chapter then chronicles teachers' use of content reading strategies and the change in the materials used for content reading instruction. Next, the chapter considers the history of three critical areas in content reading: the initiation of reading-to-learn instruction; the debate between subject specific reading skills versus generic reading skills; and recommendations on how to study. Finally, the chapter provides a summary and a conclusion for future student needs based on the information in the chapter.

Content area reading and learning is not a new concept in the professional literature. As reading developed into an area of study (generally credited as beginning with Cattell's 1886 eye movement study), interest in and research about content reading grew into what has become one of the most researched and discussed aspects of the reading field. In fact, even prior to 1925, educators had investigated various aspects of what we now call content area reading. In the Twenty-Fourth Yearbook of the National Society for the Study of Education (NSSE), Part 1 (Whipple, 1925, pp. 1–2), William S. Gray, the then dean of the College of Education at the University of Chicago, provided the first formal perspective on the relationship between reading and other school subjects, or what is now considered content reading and content reading instruction.

> As a means of gaining information and pleasure, it [reading] is essential in every content subject, such as history, geography, arithmetic, science, and literature. In fact, rapid progress in these subjects depends in a large degree on the ability of pupils to read independently and intelligently. It follows that good teaching must provide for the improvement and refinement of the reading attitudes, habits, and skills that are needed in all school activities involving reading.

In this chapter, we will trace the development of the notions of content reading and content reading instruction from the early 1900s to the present time. First, we will describe the changes in student profiles across this period that to some degree have prompted the growth in content reading preparation for teachers. Second, we will chronicle teachers' use of content reading instructional practices and the changes in the materials used for content reading instruction. Finally, we will consider the history of three critical areas in content reading: (1) the initiation of reading-to-learn instruction; (2) the debate between subject-specific reading skills versus generic reading skills as descriptive of content reading; and (3) the recommendations on studying, or reading-to-learn skills. We chose this organization for the chapter because it considers the context in which content reading and content reading instruction occurred across the twentieth century, as well as the evolution of three important aspects of content reading. In addition, we believe preservice and inservice teachers need a sense of perspective for this area of study; that is, it is our belief that an understanding of the past provides important background information for understanding present practice and future solutions.

Student Population and Teacher Preparation

An examination of figures from the U.S. Bureau of Census reveals some startling facts about the changing patterns and growth of the U.S. public school population during this century. In 1900, of the approximately 15.5 million students attending our public schools, only 0.5 million, or 3 percent, of that number attended high school (Stinnett, 1974). In contrast, approximately 27 percent of the 47.9 million students attending K–12 schools in 1992 were enrolled in grades 9–12. That is, while our nation's total school population increased 200 percent during those 90 plus years, the population of our secondary schools increased from 0.5 million students to 12.8 million (U.S. Department of Education, 1993).

Significant advances within the testing movement in the early 1900s led to the development of standardized reading tests which made it possible to compare the reading performance of various individuals and groups. In an early study, Gray (1916) compared the reading comprehension scores as measured by the Gray Silent Reading Tests of students in grades 2 through 8 in thirteen U.S. cities and found significant differences in reading performance across the sites; an even greater difference of achievement was noted when comparisons were made between the best and worst schools within each school district.

Countless other studies of reading achievement throughout the 1920s and 1930s led to the conclusion that many students in the nation's secondary schools were reading disabled. In the late 1930s and early 1940s, several reading methodology texts for secondary-level classroom teachers were published (Center & Persons, 1937; Strang, 1940; Bond & Bond, 1941), and almost without exception, these textbooks included reviews of studies that documented the reading problems of secondary-level students. In sum, the growth of the numbers of students who continued schooling to the high school level coupled with the reading difficulties of many of those students led to increased preparation of teachers in reading instruction, particularly content reading instruction at the secondary level.

Generally, reading teachers ascribe to the notion that every teacher has a responsibility to assist students in "reading to learn." The preparation of teachers in content reading, however, had a fairly slow start, given the early recognition of the importance of being able to read and learn information in the content areas. For example, today the minimum requirement of a bachelor's degree as a prerequisite for a teaching certificate is well established. In the not too distant past, however, this was not the case. Between 1900 and 1920, not a single state required that teachers earn a bachelor's degree to teach in its elementary schools, and only ten states required secondary teachers to hold undergraduate degrees (Stinnett, 1974). In the 1919–1920 academic year, 54 percent of our nation's classroom teachers had less than a high school education or the equivalent. By 1950, twenty-one states required bachelor's degrees for elementary certification and forty-two for secondary certification, and it was not until 1974 that all states required, as a minimum, a bachelor's degree for all teachers (Stinnett, 1974).

The major impetus to teacher preparation in content reading instruction occurred during the late 1950s and early 1960s with a study (Austin & Morrison, 1961) jointly sponsored by the Carnegie Corporation of New York and by the Graduate School of Education at Harvard University. The goal of the study group was to determine how U.S. colleges and universities prepared elementary teachers of reading and to recommend improvements in the preparation. One important finding reported by the researchers was that although the focus of many undergraduate reading methods courses was on the primary reading program, the intermediate-level skills, especially study skills and critical reading in the content areas, were often ignored or, at best, covered superficially. An important recommendation that impacted content reading was "that the basic reading instruction offered to prospective elementary teachers be broadened to include content and instructional techniques appropriate for intermediate and upper grades" (p. 145). Additionally, the research team noted the importance of the development of reading skills beyond the elementary level and, therefore, recommended "that a course in basic reading instruction be required of all prospective secondary school teachers" (p. 147). These two recommendations sought to affect teacher preparation in content reading at both the elementary and secondary levels. Finally, the survey revealed three vital areas—critical reading, study skills, and grouping practice—in which college reading methods instructors perceived a need for more empirical data. Thus, the researchers recommended that additional study be conducted in these areas.

In the spring of 1974, a follow-up to the earlier 1961 study was funded by a grant from Temple University. Of the three recommendations related to content reading in the original study, the suggestion that the elementary reading methods courses be broadened to include content and instructional techniques appropriate for intermediate and upper grades received the most positive response in the follow-up study. Morrison and Austin (1977) further reported a significant increase in required reading course work for teachers in training.

In a later study, Farrell & Cirrincione (1984) noted that thirty-two states had instituted requirements in reading for prospective secondary teachers, but by the beginning of the 1990s, only twenty-nine states had retained the requirement (Mastain, 1991). Regarding the recommendation that additional experimental research be initiated in the areas of critical reading, study skills, and grouping practices, only 22 percent of the respondents indicated that such research was "in effect" (Morrison & Austin, 1977); however, reading researchers were to respond to these recommendations during the 1980s.

Content Reading Materials and Strategies

This section considers the materials recommended for content reading instruction, content reading strategies educators recommend teachers use, and their actual use by teachers.

Instructional Setting: Materials/Content

Materials used for content reading include a variety of texts, such as school books, pamphlets, journals, reference books, magazines, and manuals. Subject area textbooks, however, are the most visible and prevalent classroom resource used by teachers to present content. Because reading teachers have consistently recognized the textbook as an important determinant of successful content learning, in this section we will examine how the ideas and beliefs about textbooks or "text-type" reading materials have changed.

Initially, educators classified content area resources as "work-type" reading materials and were chiefly concerned with the physical characteristics of the material. Called the "hygienic requirements of printed materials" by Whipple (1925), these concerns were of serious interest to researchers and educators and included

> style of type; legibility of different letters of the alphabet; length of line; distance between the lines; size of type; thickness of the vertical strokes of letters; spacing of words and letters and the space between the vertical strokes of letters; color of type; color and texture of paper; color of pictures; and size of book. (p. 191)

It was not until the late 1950s and the 1960s, however, that educators began definitively to describe content reading materials in terms of organizational patterns within both narrative and expository texts (Niles, 1965; Shaw, 1958; Smith, 1963, 1965; Strang, McCullough, & Traxler, 1967). Thus, for nearly forty years, leaders in reading focused considerable attention on surface and visual features of reading materials and only cursory attention on text type or internal text structures as variables that could cause comprehension difficulties.

A little recognized, but important article by Phillip Shaw (1958) in *The Reading Teacher* signaled a shift of pedagogical emphasis from superficial, mostly cosmetic concerns about texts to rich research areas that included interest in the internal structure of both narrative and expository texts (Mandler & Johnson, 1977; Stein & Glenn, 1979) and in strategies to teach these structures to students (Beck, Omanson, & McKeown, 1982). Shaw's "Rhetorical Guides to Reading Comprehension" not only identified text types and distinctive rhetorical guides within each type but also claimed that students who learn rhetorical devices as writers will recognize them as readers. He further argued that this information should be directly taught, not left for readers to acquire through experience (e.g., through wide reading).

Shaw notwithstanding, it is Niles (1965) who is most often credited with a program to teach awareness of text structure by showing students how ideas are organized in patterns, such as enumerative, sequence, cause-effect, and comparison and contrast. Herber (1970) amplified this trend by emphasizing organizational patterns of expository text and stressing their importance to comprehension. The conceptual difficulty of content books was another aspect of the text that researchers recognized early on. Gray (1937) and Uhl (1937) cautioned educators of the limitations of readability formulas to determine text difficulty.

Evidence of a further shift away from the surface elements of reading materials is the joint resolution by the International Reading Association and the National Council of Teachers of English on readability. The major thrust of the joint resolution is to eschew the wide use of readability formula as the *only* determinant in the text-to-student match. "Many factors enter into determining the readability of materials," the resolution reports, "including the syntactic complexity of sentences, density of concepts, abstractness of ideas, text organization, coherence and sequence of ideas, page format, length of type line, length of paragraph, intricacy of punctuation, and the use of illustration and color." In addition, the resolution states: "student interest in the subject matter plays a significant role in determining the readability of materials."

Think while Reading Activity

In this section the authors discuss two slogans used in conjunction with content area teaching and learning. They are:

1. "Every teacher is a reading teacher"
2. "Every teacher teaches students to learn from texts"

Before reading this section of the chapter note your thoughts and feelings about these two slogans. After reading check your thoughts to see if they've changed or expanded.

_____

_____

_____

_____

_____

Activity 1–2

Recommended Content Reading Strategies

In an early study described by Gray (1925), 250 grade 4, 5, and 6 teachers in New York and Louisiana were surveyed to determine how their students used reading in the preparation of their assignments in content subjects (or work-type reading). The ten most frequently listed purposes included "associating ideas read with previous experience, finding answers to thought-provoking questions, finding the author's aim or purpose, finding the most important idea of a paragraph or selection, selecting important points and supporting details, drawing valid conclusions from materials read, selecting facts which relate to a problem under consideration, judging the validity of statements, discovering problems for additional study, and remembering and reproducing what is read" (p. 16). It is important to note that the recommendations for teachers to help students successfully read content materials, particularly expositions, were simply to encourage wide reading (Whipple, 1925; Gray, 1937; McCallister, 1936) or to require a second reading of the material (Yoakam, 1922).

During the 1960s and 1970s, Harold Herber and his doctoral students at Syracuse University designed and implemented a series of significant research studies specifically focused on content reading instruction (Herber & Sanders, 1969; Herber & Barron, 1973; Herber & Vacca, 1977). More recent and notable is the work of professionals associated with the Center for the Study of Reading at the University of Illinois and the research faculty at the Institute for Research on Teaching at Michigan State University, whose efforts include research on reading and learning from content texts.

Teachers' Use of Content Reading Strategies

Despite recommended content reading strategies being extensively described in content reading methodology textbooks and requirements for content reading courses in teacher preparatory programs (Conley, 1992; Roe, Stoodt, & Burns, 1991; Vacca & Vacca, 1989), it is difficult to determine the degree to which teachers actually use content reading strategies in their classrooms. Many undesirable teaching practices described by Gray (Whipple, 1937) were still being used widely in the early 1960s (Austin & Morrison, 1963), for example, reading instruction provided as a discrete subject with little or no reading instruction in the content areas. Despite efforts to encourage all teachers to use content reading strategies, Early (1957, p. 7) stated:

> Authorities agree that every teacher should be a teacher of reading, but they point out that this desirable goal is far from being achieved, largely because subject-matter teachers lack training in reading methods.

Olson and Rosen (1967) identified the content teacher's reluctance to teach reading skills as the major problem in the development of reading programs at the secondary level and suggested that many teachers probably see no reason to change. They further speculated that teachers might very well be confused by the slogan "every teacher is a reading teacher." In a survey of the attitudes of middle and secondary teachers toward teaching reading in the content areas, Singer (1979) reported much more acceptance for the perspective that "every teacher teaches students to learn from texts" than he did for the more traditional slogan.

In an extensive study of elementary reading instruction utilizing teacher questionnaires, interviews, and observations, Austin and Morrison (1963) noted a discrepancy between what teachers said they did and what actually occurred in the classroom. They concluded that other than the development of subject-matter-related vocabulary, "there was only limited evidence that reading skills were being taught in the content areas" (p. 50). In a later study, Durkin (1978 & 1979) echoed that conclusion and observed that intermediate-level social studies periods were viewed by teachers as a time to cover content and have children master facts.

Gee, Olson, and Forester (1989) surveyed 1,124 subscribers to the *Journal of Reading* to determine how widely U.S. schools have implemented content reading programs and to discover factors which encourage and hinder development of such programs. Although teachers believed content reading programs would improve student learning, approximately 63 percent of U.S. schools have not considered developing such programs. Conditions associated with schools with successful content reading programs include all teachers sharing responsibility for reading instruction, strong administrative leadership, effective inservice, and time and budgets to support the program.

There is a growing awareness that content reading strategies should begin in the early years of children's education because children need to develop proficiency with simple expository texts so that they will be able to confront successfully information in content textbooks in the later grades. Primary grade teachers have identified six strategies they find helpful for young children as they learn to read content material: previewing vocabulary/concepts; using manipulatives (maps, pictures); retelling what they read; summarizing what they read; visualizing what they read; and brainstorming notions related to a topic (Olson & Gee, 1991). This suggests that some use of content reading strategies does occur at the primary level.

Three Aspects of Content Reading Instruction

Reading gains more and more importance as students progress through the grades because content teachers expect them to master the information of their subject areas, a task that requires students to study or "read to learn." The notion of studying has been broadly defined to include habits and attitudes that are conducive to study, such as creating a quiet place, having a specific study time, and even buying your own book so that you might mark it freely (Crawford, 1928). On the other hand, Smith (1963) offered a more restrictive definition of studying, arguing that studying involves those "skills used when there is intention to *do something with* the content read" (p. 307). More recently, studying or reading to learn is defined as an event that requires performing "identifiable cognitive and/or procedural tasks" (Anderson & Armbruster, 1984, p. 657).

In this section, the following three concerns about reading and studying content materials will be traced from the early 1900s to the present time: (1) when to initiate studying instruction; (2) whether reading and studying are subject specific or generic; and (3) how to teach students to read and study content material.

Initiating Reading-to-Learn Instruction

Providing instruction in reading-to-learn or how-to-study strategies has generally been initiated at and restricted to secondary schools. Prior to 1910, studying consisted mainly of the preparation of oral recitations that students had memorized. However, by around 1910, the educational emphasis was shifting from oral reading and oral recitations to silent reading, which was seen as a necessary ingredient for studying and as a method with great potential for improving reading abilities (Flemming & Woodring, 1928; Young, 1927). Thus, rather than rote memorization of facts, students now had to interpret, evaluate, learn, and recall the author's message, which it was believed they did more effectively if reading silently and rapidly (Gray, 1919; Whipple, 1925)—a condition more easily achieved by children in the later grades than the early grades.

Concurrent with the change from an oral to a silent reading emphasis, educators began to perceive students as deficient in study skills (McMurry, 1909). Although McMurry did not directly link studying to reading, his examples and recommended study techniques indicated that studying was synonymous with "reading to learn."

The shift of emphasis from oral reading to silent reading and students' lack of study skills may have influenced Gray (1919) to urge that training students to read and study effectively should begin in the first year of elementary school; nevertheless, both notions came to be linked with the term "content reading" (Gray, 1947, 1952) and to be restricted primarily to secondary schools. In fact, at the elementary level, content reading instruction today seems to be limited for several reasons, even though primary teachers can identify instructional practices as effective in helping children read content material (Olson & Gee, 1991). For instance, children read mostly from basal readers whose selections are primarily fiction (Anderson, Hilbert, Scott, & Wilkinson, 1985); furthermore, children rely on teachers' oral presentations of content information rather than on reading (Armbruster, et al., 1991) because reading content text is particularly difficult for them.

Think while Reading Activity

An early research study about reading and learning by McMurry was discussed in the section you just completed ("Initiating Reading-to-Learn Instruction"). He stated that in 1909 educators had begun to perceive students as deficient in study skills. Do you think McMurry might say the same about today's students or would he have another opinion? Write your thoughts here.

_____

_____

_____

_____

_____

_____

Activity 1–3

Subject-Specific or Generic Reading Skills

Gray's (1919) tally of teachers' responses to how their students used reading suggested that the reading behaviors needed in each content area differed from subject to subject. Of significance, however, is the question whether reading skills are generic to all content area reading or whether reading skills are content specific (Moore, Readence, & Rickelman, 1983). Some content reading methods books contain separate sections on reading in each subject (McCallister, 1936; Olson & Ames, 1972; Roe, Stoodt, & Burns, 1991; Singer & Donlan, 1988). Conversely, other textbooks treat content area reading skills as generic to all subject reading (Brunner & Campbell, 1978; Vacca & Vacca, 1989; Bond & Bond, 1941; Herber; 1978; Readence, Bean, & Baldwin, 1992). The question remains unresolved because research is inconclusive as to the merits of one position over the other.

Teaching Study or Reading-to-Learn Skills

Generally, the reading behaviors subsumed under work-type reading in the early 1900s are the same behaviors classified as reading and study skills today. These include identifying the author's main points, interpreting and evaluating information, locating information (dictionary, encyclopedia, and map skills), reading graphic aids (charts, tables, and graphs), increasing rate of reading, following directions, and organizing information (summarizing, outlining, notetaking, and underlining).

The notion of students' previewing what was to be read and setting purposes for their reading has an early history in education (McMurry, 1909; Wrenn & Cole, 1935; Yoakam, 1928). Consistent with early recommendations by educators, Robinson (1946) created SQ3R (Survey Question Read-Recite-Review) as a systematic and succinct strategy to motivate students and to help them control their own studying or learning routines. He advocated previewing the material to be learned and setting purpose questions before actual reading. Students then read, recited answers to the questions, and reviewed the text. Robinson's strategy spawned a number of variations such as EVOKER (Explore, Vocabulary, Oral reading, Key ideas, Evaluation, Recapitulation) (Pauk, 1963), REAP (Read, Encode, Annotate, Ponder) (Eanet & Manzo, 1976), and SQRQCQ (Survey, Question, Read, Question, Compute, Question) (Fay, 1965), all of which are independent strategies that specifically direct students on *how* to study and learn information from text material.

By the late 1940s, the interest in reading and studying had begun to decline. From 1948 to 1957, the first twenty volumes of *The Reading Teacher* contained only five articles under "Study Skills" (Summers, 1969). This represented only 0.6 percent of the total articles published. Even when articles on "rate" and "reading in the content fields" were included, only fifty-two articles, or 6 percent of the total number published specifically focused on these topics.

More recently, interest in reading to learn and studying (Anderson & Armbruster, 1984) has revived somewhat, probably because of the research conducted on comprehension at the Center for the Study of Reading. Specifically, the organizing skills (i.e., summarizing, outlining, notetaking, underlining) have enjoyed attention from researchers who investigated studying as one aspect of reading (Day, 1980; Bretzing & Kulhavey, 1981; Harris, 1990; Nist & Kirby, 1989).

Reading and studying with a specific purpose have had a prominent place in the education literature since emphasis shifted from oral reading to silent reading. Initially, some educators urged teachers to begin teaching youngsters to read and study content material in the primary grades; however, contemporary content reading instruction, if it occurs, usually does so in intermediate grades and only occasionally in the secondary schools. Some educators believe reading and studying skills are generic and applicable in any subject area. Others view subject areas as having reading and study skills specific to each subject. How to teach students to read and study content material enjoyed much attention between 1909 and the early 1940s, but then waned. However, interest has revived, often under the banner of "reading to learn."

Summary and Conclusion

The significant growth in the U.S. public school population, especially at the secondary level, was described, as were the reading abilities of school children. The preparation of teachers to provide instruction in content area reading was noted along with content area materials, strategies, and teacher use of those strategies over this century. We also traced the history of three critical areas in content reading: when to start reading-to-learn instruction; the status of subject-specific reading skills versus generic reading skills as being

---

Think after Reading Activity

The authors of this chapter provided an overview of content area reading instruction from the 1900s through today. Attending school today is really different than it was in the early 1900s. Based on your experiences and what you've read in this chapter, list five ways you think content area reading instruction has changed.

1._____

2._____

3._____

4._____

5._____

Are there any ways that it hasn't changed?

_____

_____

_____

_____

_____

Activity 1–4

descriptive of content reading; and the skills involved in reading to learn. We now conclude with an observation of what we see as a grave problem in the effort to help children read to learn.

Although the general school population growth pattern decreased in the late 1970s and through much of the decade of the 1980s, an even more dramatic change in our school population is occurring. A review of available data suggests that enrollments are once again increasing and that, as a result of linguistic and cultural differences and/or poverty, the current and future student population will present new challenges to educators. Heavily concentrated among the economically disadvantaged, minority groups, immigrants, and non-English speaking families, these students comprised at least 30 percent of our school population in the mid 1980s (Levin, 1985), and that percentage will likely continue to increase through the remainder of this century.

Disadvantaged youngsters have always been part of our public school system, but it was not until the 1960s that specially designed programs beyond the traditional curriculum were developed and implemented on a large scale. Compensatory education programs, federally funded under Title I of the Elementary and Secondary Education Act of 1965 and its successor, Chapter I of the Education Consolidation and Improvement Act of 1981, have had modest success (Burton & Jones, 1982); however, even with increased funding levels, compensatory education programs alone will fail to solve the educational problems of our disadvantaged youth. Only through the improved education of teachers and administrators at both the preservice and inservice levels can we hope to improve the reading and learning skills of our youth, particularly in content areas. The amount and diversity of content material increases significantly as children grow older, mandating sound and effective improvements in content reading instructional practice before we will realize a truly literate society.

Content Area Reading

The Current State of the Art

THOMAS W. BEAN   *JOHN E. READENCE*

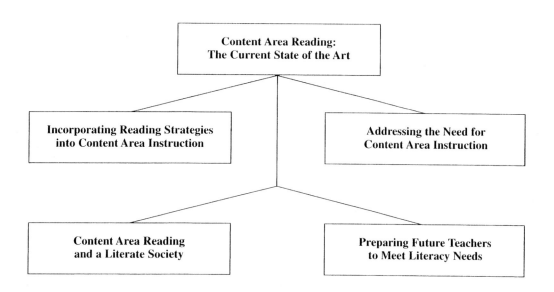

Think before Reading Activity

Think back to your high school years. What strategies or activities did your teachers use to help you understand your textbooks?

_____

_____

_____

_____

_____

If your college professors taught you additional study and reading strategies or activities, jot down what they were.

_____

_____

_____

_____

_____

Activity 2–1

Content area reading, the process of guiding students' comprehension of challenging texts and supplemental materials in history, English, science, and other subject areas, has grown rapidly in the last twenty years. In this chapter we address a number of issues concerning content area reading that have emerged in recent years along with some future projections. We have organized the chapter around four key questions: (1) Why is there a need for content area teachers to incorporate reading strategies into their instruction? (2) To what extent is American education addressing the need for content area reading instruction? (3) Does content area reading assist the development of a literate society? (4) What are some future projections for accomplishing the task of preparing teachers to meet our literacy needs?

Why Is There a Need for Content Area Teachers to Incorporate Reading Strategies into Their Instruction?

At least three aspects of reading at the secondary level strongly suggest a need for content area teachers to incorporate reading strategies into their instruction: a change in instructional emphasis from learning to read to reading to learn; a change in the nature of instructional texts as students advance through the grades; a recent change in curricular emphasis that corresponds to our growing use of technology.

Oral language activities and story reading encourage literacy in the early grades. The probability of success in these early learning-to-read activities is high. But by about grade 4, a fairly dramatic shift in the purpose for reading occurs. In *Stages of Reading Development* (1983), Jeanne Chall of Harvard University charts the peaks and valleys that naturally occur as a student moves toward advanced literacy. Chall regards grade 4, her stage 3, as a crucial transitional stage in which a student moves somewhat abruptly from learning to read in friendly narratives into reading to learn with expository texts. Increased reading in expository prose parallels the growth of our technological society and a concomitant change in the level of reading proficiency required for success in such a society. Chall views stage 4, high school reading ability, as a *minimal* level of proficiency for our technological age.

> Just 40 years ago, an 8th-grade reading level was typical of people 25 years old or over, and that was considered above the standard of minimal literacy. Today, the average is an 11th to 12th-grade level. Although it means a much higher reading ability, it probably has about the same relative value as an 8th-grade level had 40 years ago. (Chall, 1983, p. 3)

Our recent emphasis on guiding students' comprehension and moving them toward independent learning from text is clearly needed. A good many students will flounder without adequate teacher guidance in reading complex texts in fields such as science and social studies. This is especially true if our goal is to prepare our students for the challenging reading demands of a technological age. Thus, the role of the content area reading course has become even more crucial because the nature of content reading demands teachers who are well versed in a repertoire of strategies that enhance students' comprehension of challenging texts. Indeed, certain characteristics of content textbooks sometimes place students at a disadvantage. Content teachers need to be well grounded in the analysis and evaluation of texts they select.

Textbooks in history, science, and other content areas continue to improve, but the process is a slow one. The problems inherent in many of these texts make it important for teachers to have a systematic means of analyzing and evaluating text characteristics that are likely to influence students' comprehension. Ideally, a subject area text should be challenging while adhering to principles of good writing and organization (Herber, 1984). Fortunately, the process of text analysis is an integral part of most content area reading classes offered in the United States for preservice teachers (Farrell & Cirrincione, 1986).

Singer (1992) developed a text evaluation instrument designed to help content teachers assess their texts along the dimensions of organization, explication of ideas, conceptual density, metadiscourse (i.e., places where the author "talks" to the reader), and instructional devices. Other text evaluation instruments can be found in various methods texts for content teachers (e.g., Readence, Bean, & Baldwin, 1995). What are some of the potential problems with content texts?

One problem is that facts and their relationships may be expressed in a text without any indication of their importance. It is a rare textbook that specifies *why* a student might want to know the information being introduced (Bransford, 1984). For example, in mathematics, knowing that numbers have square roots may be important for passing a test, but the real significance or usefulness of the knowledge is rarely explained. Students are quick to grasp the level of involvement a text demands and adjust their efforts accordingly. For example, Smith and Feathers (1983) found that students in social studies could ignore reading assignments and still perform reasonably well. They were able to listen for text information from the teacher.

When students do engage with a text in social studies they are confronted with an organizational structure that compartmentalizes information (Bean, Sorter, Singer, & Frazee, 1986). They are likely to read a chapter on the Colonial Revolution in America followed by a test. Then they may read a chapter about the French Revolution followed by another test. Asked to describe some salient stages of revolutions in general or to predict the progression of an unfamiliar revolution, they are at a loss. Texts that compartmentalize information encourage a "read and memorize" strategy rather than integration and application of ideas. Most content area courses devote time to solving some of these problems through teacher intervention using three-level study guides and other comprehension strategies aimed at extending students' thinking into the realm of real-life problem solving.

This national interest in developing students who can think creatively and use powerful electronic technology including computers, telecommunications, and video displays underscores the need for content area reading instruction that incorporates these factors. A 1986 report by the Carnegie Forum on Education and the Economy pointed out that our past emphasis in classrooms on routines such as reading the text and answering rote memory questions on a test was adequate for a factory-based society that capitalized on routines. However, much more creativity will be required of students and teachers in today's and tomorrow's knowledge-based society. The report states:

> The focus of schooling must shift from teaching to learning, from passive acquisition of facts and routines to the active application of ideas to problems. That transition makes the role of the teacher more important, not less. (p. 45)

The implication for preservice and inservice courses designed to prepare content area teachers for this challenging role is clear. Professors must model the process of higher-

---

Think while Reading Activity

Think about the instruction you received throughout your school years in the content areas. What can you infer from these experiences about the assumptions your former teachers must have made about you as a textbook reader? Were they correct or not? Please discuss.

_____

_____

_____

_____

_____

_____

Activity 2–2

order thinking within those classes, placing students in collaborative problem-solving groups and providing assignments that require analysis and creativity. Future teachers who experience this process are more likely to approach their own teaching in a similar fashion.

Our knowledge-based society relies increasingly on telematic means of communication spanning tremendous distances in space and time. Subject area teachers should become well-versed in simulations and activities that tap the interactive power of micro-computers and videodisk technology (Lewis, Radziemski, Blanchard, & Mason, 1992; Provenzo, 1992). Given the challenges to educate secondary students for higher-order thinking and telematic communication now and in the future, the implementation of content reading programs becomes even more necessary.

To What Extent Is American Education Addressing the Need for Content Area Reading Instruction?

Content Reading Programs

Content reading programs are based on the notion that all students are required to learn from a variety of texts throughout their schooling. In order to learn successfully with these texts, students must be exposed to a variety of reading and learning strategies that will help them meet the demands of coping with the new vocabulary, concepts, and text organization they will encounter. Reading is taught functionally as the skills and processes needed to learn from text are integrated with the learning of content (Readence, Bean, & Baldwin, 1995). Thus, students become the center of the curriculum rather than the skills to be learned or the subject to be mastered.

Although content reading programs seem to be the most beneficial to students in terms of preparing them to comprehend and critically read their daily textbook assignments, a remedial reading model unfortunately seems to dominate schools, particularly at the middle and secondary levels. Readence, Bean, and Baldwin (1992) suggested that a number of misconceptions about reading instruction in general may account for this. These beliefs are inconsistent with our current knowledge of learning in content classrooms for the following reasons.

First, even adult readers can be faced with a learning-to-read situation if they encounter a text that is foreign to their experience. The situation is analogous to younger readers with newly encountered text material. Second, content texts present inherently different text organizations than basal readers and also present heavier vocabulary and concept loads. Basal readers, on the other hand, have more similar text organizations (predominantly story-type) and gradually introduce new words and concepts to students. Thus, to say the processes involved in learning from basals and content texts are identical is a meaningless argument. Third, as previously discussed, remedial reading programs focus on skill dificiencies. It cannot be expected that what students learn in these classrooms will readily transfer to reading in subject-matter texts.

Finally, teachers should consider themselves as facilitators of students' textbook learning. It is their job to see that students interact with text at a high level of understanding through a judicious use of reading and learning strategies. Unfortunately, it has been documented that teachers see themselves more as information dispensers. For instance,

Hinchman (1992), in a qualitative study of secondary teachers' plans and conceptions of reading, found that teachers consider reading as a means of covering the course content. Reading was viewed as a way to dispense information, rather than as a means to read and learn from the textbook.

In an update of state teaching credential requirements conducted by Farrell and Cirrincione (1984), they explored three key questions: Is a reading methods course required for certification in grades 7 through 12? To which content areas does this requirement apply? How is the requirement met?

Farrell and Cirrincione (1984) reported that 31 states and the District of Columbia had a reading requirement for all content area teachers at the secondary level. In addition, five states had the same requirement for English/language arts teachers, but no requirement for other academic fields. There is a good deal of diversity by state, best seen by examining selected states. California, for example, requires a content reading class for all academic fields (social studies, science, English, math) but not for art and physical education. In reality, most of these students also take a class as they are pursuing authorization to teach in mainstream academic fields such as social studies, in addition to their credential in art or physical education. In contrast, Maryland specifies that only English and social studies teachers are required to take the content reading course, and the state of Maine had no requirement in content reading at the time of Farrell and Cirrincione's survey. There has been a steady increase in the development of these requirements to include teachers from all academic areas.

The increase in state requirements for preservice teachers to take a content reading course suggests that we are addressing this need. However, the great majority of teachers in secondary schools earned their credentials at a time when content reading classes were not required for single-subject certification. How are we addressing their needs?

Fortunately, educators realize that to maintain the impetus of content reading at the preservice level and reorient the teaching techniques of existing teachers, it is necessary to provide inservice education and staff development for content teachers. Recognizing the need for continuous professional development and given the fact that there are few resources available to guide inservice education for content teachers, the International Reading Association published a monograph appropriately titled *Inservice Education for Content Area Teachers* (Siedow, Memory, & Bristow, 1985). This text provides a basic model of inservice education with accompanying descriptions and examples of inservice sessions and references to articles and books illustrating the use of various content reading strategies. Most contemporary staff development efforts span three to five years, recognizing that change takes time. In the past, content teachers were often the victims of brief, one-shot inservice sessions held in a large group auditorium setting during sixth period. Clearly, little can be accomplished in such an impersonal atmosphere.

Guskey (1986) proposed a model for staff development that should guide this process, especially where content area teachers are concerned. Guskey argues that traditional staff development efforts mistakenly begin by trying to alter a teacher's beliefs and attitudes. He regards this approach as futile because teachers' beliefs and attitudes are influenced primarily by their students' successful achievement. Because of this fact, Guskey recommends starting with a strategy-based focus aimed at altering teachers' classroom practices in small increments. If, for example, students' learning improves as a result of a content teacher's use of a three-level study guide in science, then that teacher is likely to embrace a content reading philosophy. Guskey's review of the research in changing teacher beliefs and attitudes supports this alternative model. Positive teacher beliefs were significantly related to their students' achievement gains as a result of experimenting with a new strategy.

Reading educators have been involved in helping content teachers with staff development projects in learning from text throughout the country. For example, Singer and Bean (1988) described three model programs and their operating procedures: an intern model, an inservice model, and an evolutionary model.

The *intern model* was based on the notion that placing interns, trained in a content reading philosophy, into content area teaching situations to develop model classrooms could provide the impetus for improving the instruction of all teachers in the school. Their role was to share their expertise in content reading with other teachers by serving as consultants within the school. They were given released time during the school day to work

---

Think while Reading Activity

In the following pages the authors discuss three model staff development programs for content area teachers: an intern model, an inservice model, and an evolutionary model. As you read, *summarize* each model. Then reflect on the model you think is the most effective for long-term change in a school.

Intern Model:

_____

_____

_____

Inservice Model:

_____

_____

_____

Evolutionary Model:

_____

_____

_____

Your own reflections about a long-term change model:

_____

_____

_____

Activity 2–3

with other teachers on implementing content reading strategies. The program centered on demonstration of the various content strategies by the interns and consultation with teachers to help them utilize the same strategies in their own classrooms. Although it took the greater part of the school year for the interns to develop rapport with their faculties and gain credibility as content reading specialists, the program was eventually effective in disseminating new information on learning from text to other teachers.

The *inservice model* was a school district program using intensive, long-range inservice as the basis for implementing a content reading philosophy. Instead of sporadic, one-shot inservice efforts, a three-year project of planning and demonstration of content reading strategies was instituted; in this way potentially scores of teachers and hundreds of students were influenced by the sustained effect of the program. A primary assumption that guided the training sessions associated with this model was the need for teachers to directly experience learning from text strategies before they could be expected to apply the strategies themselves. Thus, two-week summer workshops were used as a means to acquaint teachers with the strategies, coupled with the need to actively experience their usage and then experiment with them in small-group settings. In this way the participants were able to develop a resource handbook of sample lessons exemplifying the appropriate use of a variety of vocabulary and comprehension reading and learning strategies. In turn, these handbooks served as the basis for staff development sessions carried on throughout the academic year. The initial evaluation of the project revealed that, slowly but surely, the content reading strategies were becoming part of the teacher's natural repertoire of instruction. Again, the key to the perceived change in teachers' instructional habits was long-term sustained efforts on the part of the school district and its teachers to provide a better learning atmosphere for the students.

The *evolutionary model* was a small-scale approach to staff development at the individual classroom level. It involved a single teacher in the planning, development, and applied research stages of learning from text over a period of three years. Additionally, the teacher involved in the project was relatively naive about content area reading. Through the process of engaging in a series of applied instructional experiments, a number of benefits have been noted. First, the teacher-researcher has increased his repertoire of appropriate instructional strategies. Second, the students have become the direct beneficiaries of this instruction. The students have become actively involved in the teaching and learning strategies as the teacher has attempted to move the class from dependence on him for their learning from text to self-reliance and independence in their own learning. Finally, this model has paved the way for other teachers to take notice of the new techniques used. This has not come about through administrators suggesting that other teachers pay attention to this learning from text approach; rather, the students have acted as ambassadors with other teachers by using the strategies they learned in studying in their other classes. As a consequence, other teachers have seen that these strategies can be useful in helping students learn from text.

Both beginning teacher preparation and staff development programs in content area reading are continuously improving. Their impact on students' learning and achievement seems promising, but we need to collect more systematic evaluative data on how teachers adapt content strategies and the relative impact of these procedures on students' achievement.

Does Content Area Reading Assist the Development of a Literate Society?

Some studies at the secondary level suggest that content area reading strategies have an impact on reading achievement and perhaps literacy in general. For example, grade 10 students in a world history class who were taught a summarization system and a procedure for graphically displaying text concepts (graphic organizers) during two consecutive semesters achieved significantly better test and written recall scores than their peers using traditional outlining (Bean, Sorter, Singer, & Frazee, 1986). During the following year, some of the students spontaneously transferred that knowledge about how to construct a graphic organizer to the task of studying their biology text. This anecdotal information implies that content area reading strategies may well have a long-range impact on students' literacy.

In another study spanning a semester, we taught grade 10 world history students how to construct graphic organizers in conjunction with an options guide, a form of study guide designed to encourage concept generalization and prediction (Bean, Sorter, Singer, & Frazee, 1986). Students used the strategy initially in small groups and later individually. On an essay test asking students to delineate the stages of a revolution and predict events in a revolution which they had not yet studied, students who received this instruction significantly outpaced their peers (who used traditional outlining and whole-group discussion).

Although it is not within the scope of this chapter to review the growing body of research on content area reading, this developing database, albeit limited by the absence of a large-scale longitudinal study, shows a generally positive influence on students' achievement in complex material. In addition, our society will continue to define "literacy" at increasingly higher and more demanding levels, making it imperative that content teachers have a well-developed repertoire of theories and strategies.

Projections for Accomplishing the Task of Preparing Teachers to Meet Our Literacy Needs

Although any number of predictions about the future are possible, and may even be risky, we will venture a few predictions of our own. Some of our immediate needs concern the increase in academic requirements for most high school students. Teacher preparation in content area reading will take on increased importance with a concomitant need to renew knowledge on a regular basis. In addition to conventional credentialing programs, we can expect to see more certificate offerings for teachers who need to return to post-bacalaureate classes to sharpen their instructional skills in content area methodology. This emphasis on helping all students, including those destined for work rather than college, should foster a greater interest in funding long-range research exploring promising strategies.

We can expect technology, particularly in the form of multimedia interactive videotext presentations, to play an increasing role in students' learning. Content area reading courses will evolve to model pedagogically sound ways of integrating learning theory and technology. Distance learning tools that allow students to communicate with library databases and other students using electronic mail spanning national and international boundaries will change our current notions of learning from texts.

As teacher training programs require increasing sophistication on the part of their students, with career ladders that require continuous learning, we can expect to see more action research being conducted in the ecologically valid setting of the classroom. Graduate study will become an increasingly important requirement for advancement in the teaching profession.

Already the distinction between content area reading and elementary reading is beginning to blur. In many graduate programs, both secondary and elementary reading specialist candidates take a content area reading class. Many of the concepts and strategies introduced are applicable in the early grades.

Finally, the integration of reading and writing in most content area reading classes is a trend that will continue. Newer methods texts in content area reading devote increasing space to writing as a bridge to understanding and reflecting on texts.

In summary, creative teachers will make dull, unfriendly texts readable through lessons that integrate the various content areas such as art, music, science, social studies, and English. Teachers will become increasingly sophisticated in their use of multimedia technology in constructing lessons. Content reading classes for preservice and inservice teachers encourage experimentation with cooperative grouping structures and the use of technology. Since these classes are on the rise as a requirement for a credential in most states, the future looks bright.

Think after Reading Activity

If you could speak to one of your former content area teachers, what would you relate to him or her about the ideas you've read in this chapter?

_____

_____

_____

_____

_____

_____

_____

Activity 2–4

The Teacher and the Text

C h a p t e r *3*

The Role of Textbooks and Trade Books in Content Area Instruction

DIANE LEMONNIER SCHALLERT   *NANCY LEE ROSER*

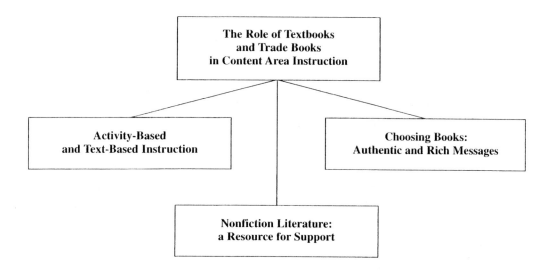

Think before Reading Activity

Think about the experiences you have had reading content area texts. What were they? Think about a time when you tried to read a content-specific book that you didn't have much content knowledge of, e.g., computer manual, construction manual. How did you do? What would have helped you to more easily read it? Write your answers below.

_____

_____

_____

_____

If you are able, pair with another person in your content area to share your experiences. Ask about theirs. Then reflect individually and note some common areas related to the use of content area texts that emerged from your discussion. See if this list can be expanded as you read this chapter.

_____

_____

_____

_____

_____

_____

_____

Activity 3–1

For the last twenty years or so, there has been an interesting dichotomy between what teacher educators recommend about how science and social studies should be taught and what has been the prevailing practice in classrooms. Teacher educators have emphasized inquiry and discovery modes and have deplored expository and text-based instruction. By contrast, teachers have generally remained wedded to their textbooks and to instruction that gives students a relatively passive role. To this debate, reading researchers bring a view of reading as an active, meaning-making activity that resembles hypothesis testing and problem solving. In this chapter, we present the case for three arguments: (1) that teacher educators present a more balanced approach between activity-based and text-based instruction so that they can provide guidance to future teachers in how to use text and written materials; (2) that reading materials, including content textbooks, that present authentic and rich messages be chosen, even if their use must then be supported substantially by teachers; and (3) that teachers look to nonfiction "trade" literature for children and young adults as a resource for that support. It is our hope that these insights will persuade all teachers to enliven and enrich their instruction with the use of broadly chosen written materials. Such a result, we think, is crucial if the curriculum is to have a major role in fostering a citizenry that can read intelligently about scientific and social/political topics.

For reading researchers, an interest in content area textbooks is quite natural. Of course, we are also likely to be interested in broader issues of instruction, but the textbook is a particularly obvious and relevant focus point. It is not surprising that reading research relevant to content area instruction has dealt with issues such as how well-written are the textbooks made available to students during their science or social studies lessons, how well-prepared from their reading instruction are the students to deal with their content textbooks, and how successful are content teachers in guiding their students' understanding of textbook assignments. The chapters in this volume exemplify these general topic categories.

On the other hand, content area experts—those who identify themselves as discipline experts and who train elementary and secondary content area teachers—hold a different view of the textbooks associated with their fields. For the most part, we find that content area experts have a generally negative view of reading as a source of learning about a topic, even though many of them write textbooks and nearly all of them use textbooks in their own college-level instruction. In methods courses, learning science by reading is proclaimed to be a poor, and in the extreme, a shameful cousin to learning science from hands-on experiences. In the other content areas, the use of textbooks is discouraged as well because they are seen as mere transmitters of expert knowledge to passive novices.

Such a view can seem surprising when juxtaposed against reading researchers' views of reading as a complex, active process that challenges the reader to marshall personal

---

Think while Reading Activity

Let's pretend that the content area steering committee at your school has a meeting this Thursday to determine the future direction for your school in your specific content area. Three teachers are scheduled to address the committee: an activity-based teacher, a text-based teacher and you, an advocate of a balanced approach. As you read the next section, jot down a few notes and be prepared to briefly state how you would address your colleagues to explain the importance of a balanced approach between text-based and activity-based learning.

_____

_____

_____

_____

_____

_____

_____

Activity 3–2

resources to construct sense from print. Because we know that it is easily possible to learn by reading and because reading about science and social studies topics can be quite enjoyable, we take it for granted that students also can learn from and enjoy text. From this perspective, it would not make sense to deny students reading as a source for learning about science and social studies.

In the rest of this chapter, we want to make three points related to the role of reading in content area classrooms. First, we argue that in preparing future content area teachers, teacher educators should consider altering their current views of text. We believe that a different balance is needed between activity-based and text-based instruction, one in which reading is given more credence for learning. Second, we examine some paradoxical characteristics of content area textbooks: too often they suffer from being too dense, yet they lack the elaborative content needed to help readers make sense of the topics presented; and too often, although their prose is uninteresting and pointless in that it lacks an authentic point of view and sense of author intent, it nevertheless includes seductive details that grab attention from major points. Finally, we remind content area teachers and reading specialists of some important but often neglected resources. We argue for the use of trade literature, by which we mean printed *nontextbook* materials, across the curriculum and offer suggestions for locating these resources.

Achieving a Balance Between Text-Based and Activity-Based Learning

The overwhelming message that today's teachers encounter as part of their content area methods courses is that students learn when they are actively involved. Thus, teachers have been taught to plan hands-on activities, to include as much discovery and inquiry in their curriculum as they can muster, and not to rely on text-based instruction because it is often the lazy way out.

The message teacher educators present to prospective teachers is reinforced by what appears in their textbooks associated with social studies and science methods courses. In an earlier survey we conducted of more than a dozen popular methods texts, we found very little space devoted to helping teachers think about how to use the students' textbooks in their instruction. With a few exceptions, they did not discuss the topic at all or gave it an average of five pages out of 400. Whenever the topic was mentioned, nearly half of the discussion addressed limitations and problems associated with text-based instruction. In the most current methods textbooks, we do detect some change. It is still true, however, that student teachers are generally counseled away from text-based instruction toward more real-world, experience-based learning and hands-on activities.

It is easy to understand and appreciate this view held by content area experts. The conventional recommendation has a legitimate basis in that it stems from the fear that instruction will revert to the mundane, such as turn-taking oral reading and assigning underprepared students pages from the text with questions to be answered in complete sentences. Such practice is deplored generally by education experts but most vehemently by content area educators. Although they quickly agree that some text-based instruction may be necessary and need not take the form of their worst-imagined scenario, content area experts find it hard to believe that science learned exclusively from reading could lead to any kind of deep, personal appreciation of content. To understand the problem from the perspective of the science or social studies expert, imagine the contrast between reading a museum guidebook, even a very well-crafted and beautifully illustrated one, rather than visiting the special exhibit itself. The greatest concern of the content area expert is that instruction will become solely dependent upon a passive form—the textbook.

Are these fears grounded? Unfortunately, the answer seems to be yes. Despite what teachers are taught in their methods courses, surveys of what goes on in science and social studies programs at the elementary and secondary levels reveal that the textbook is most often a major, if not the only, component of instruction (Harms & Yager, 1981). In reaction, experts increase their emphasis on activity-based instruction and disparage textbooks even more vociferously.

We offer a different approach for consideration. Using textbooks does not have to mean that learning is passive, because reading does not have to be passive. In current descriptions of reading, the reader is necessarily and continually involved as the primary contributor to meaning. The reader is said to "construct" a meaning, not "interpret" a message and certainly not to "receive" one. Construction, a term that reading experts use interchangeably with comprehension, depends substantially on the knowledge the reader brings to the text. Guided by one's purpose for reading and the social conditions that apply, one builds a personal rendition of the message intended by the author. Under conditions in which the student wants and is able to comprehend deeply an author's message, reading is as active as thinking or problem solving.

What this might mean is, first, that what is often presented as the ideal method of instruction is also the ideal way of ensuring that students understand what they read. When teachers use modeling, demonstrations, experimentation, inquiry, and provide real-world experiences for their students, they are helping develop the knowledge frameworks to make reading meaningful. What content area experts advocate is exactly what reading experts advocate—personalized linkages as bridges to new understandings. That is, learning always starts with what the learner already knows.

However, there is a second implication from current research on textbook use, one that might require content area teachers to make some adjustments in how they teach. Connections between classroom activities and text content need to be more aggressively identified (Schallert, Alexander, & Goetz, 1985, 1987). Teachers need to realize how much influence they have over the kind of understandings students can develop from reading their textbooks. If there is one area in great need of improvement in the education of future content area teachers, it is in encouraging them to be as innovative and active as guides to textbook reading as they are in other components of instruction. It is the teacher, not the textbook, who is responsible for guiding the process of learning, even of learning from the text.

Additionally, we want to assert that helping students learn how to read science and social studies is a proper goal in its own right. Much press has been given recently to literacy in general, and to scientific literacy in particular. In all that has been said in the name of literacy, it is clear that there is no consensus about exactly what the term encompasses. We would like to add our view to the debate. We believe that goals for literacy should include an attitude toward, knowledge about, and some skill in dealing with the written word. For the more specific kinds of literacy such as scientific literacy, we believe that reasonable educational goals include students feeling comfortable in using printed material as a source of information, knowing how to find what they might need in print and how to evaluate properly its veracity and value, and understanding the special kinds of discourse they encounter.

A junior high school student we know named Jay needed information on centrifugal and centripetal forces to write a report for his science class. Having checked the resources at home and finding lots of information on centrifugal force but not enough on centripetal force to help him with the point he wanted to make in his report, he asked his mother to take him to the library. Once there, he quickly found the *Encyclopedia of Physics* and opened the huge volume to the proper page. As his mother sat beside him laboriously trying to understand the beginning of the entry, she noticed that his eyes were already down the page. When she asked how he had got so far ahead of her (how he had so quickly skimmed the information on centrifugal force and had found the section he needed), Jay answered simply, "I'm good at reading science."

Teaching Content with Poorly Written Textbooks

One reason content area experts criticize text-based instruction is that they remember how deadly textbook prose can be. They know that obscure, incoherent, dense, impersonal sentences can quickly kill an interest in a topic. Even in the most recently published textbooks, which are generally quite good, such sentences, and sometimes whole passages and chapters, are easy to find (Anderson & Armbruster, 1984; Armbruster, 1984; Beck, McKeown, & Gromoll, 1989).

Reading researchers have not taken any more kindly to textbook prose. Most recently, they have pursued two puzzling phenomena. The first refers to a certain style that results from the fact that textbook authors take their goal to be "to cover all relevant topics" rather than to explain fully a few well-chosen points. A particularly incisive analysis of social studies textbooks is provided by Beck, McKeown, and Gromoll (1989), who demonstrate how a textbook's presentation of content can at the same time be dense and also lack the necessary elaboration to make sense of the many topics that are introduced. Connections are left out, details that would allow a reader to understand the distinctions being presented are eliminated, nontechnical but imprecise vocabulary is used. What is often missing is the essential example or explanation that would help a novice reader understand why a particular detail with its associated technical term is being mentioned. For example, in one high school biology textbook that Schallert and Tierney (1982) examined, a description of the reproductive system of the male frog ends with the short simple sentence, "During the breeding season, the thumbs of the male frog are enlarged." Having discussed in great detail where sperm cells are first produced and the names of the different places to which they travel on their way out of the frog, the authors never tell how the thumbs (on the hands? which hands? do frogs have hands?) are used. The fact, though likely to be remembered by students because of its own, unique connotations and imageability, is not connected to anything else.

A second phenomenon associated with textbook prose that reading researchers are currently exploring is the paradoxical effect of interest on learning from text. On the one hand, perhaps because textbook authors are so concerned with their task of mentioning all the necessary topics, they seem to forget to make their prose interesting and to shy away from expressing any particular point of view toward their topic. Textbook language easily takes on a didactic, impersonal tone, the expression of a reasonable, all-knowing intellect, removed from any emotional commitment to the topic or to the audience.

Take for example the methods textbooks mentioned earlier that we surveyed. We know how strongly content area experts deplore text-based instruction, yet these methods texts, on the whole, remained remarkably unemotional in their presentation of the pros and cons of text-based instruction. True, the cons were allowed to be the last word on the topic, but even when presenting the dangers of text-based instruction, the discussion was balanced and cautious. We saw none of the impassioned plea we heard in the voices of the content area teacher educators we interviewed. A student teacher reading one of these texts could easily come away with a vague impression that all methods were fine, although one of them, text-based instruction, simply was not discussed to any great extent. How much more interesting textbooks would become if their authors assumed that they should have a point of view in their writing.

Further, textbooks often include an inappropriate use of material meant to interest students but that acts more as a siphon of attention away from the important content being presented. Research on interest as a variable has revealed an intriguing puzzle. As one would suspect, when learners are interested in what they are reading, whether because they have a longstanding interest in the topic or because the author has crafted a presentation that arouses interest in most readers, they learn and remember the intriguing information. However, what is interesting about interest is that it can actually undermine readers' ability to learn the more important information presented in a text by drawing readers' attention away from important but less enticing information (e.g., "Nelson first distinguished himself by blockading Toulon, a port city on the coast of France, and capturing Corsica) to unimportant but fascinating tidbits (e.g., "During that battle, Nelson's right arm was badly mangled up to the elbow"). (The examples are from Wade & Adams, 1990; see also Garner, Gillingham, & White, 1989; Wade, Schraw, Buxton, & Hayes, 1993). Content textbooks make frequent use of display principles that are aimed at breaking up the print by including anecdotes and details in colored, offset boxes. The concern we have with this practice is that readers may find themselves seduced by these details and get only a fragmented understanding of the disciplinary view of the topic.

These observations would certainly seem to support the recommendation to use textbooks as little as possible in content area classrooms. The problem is that we know that teachers *do* rely extensively on their textbooks and yet provide little in the way of guidance to help students overcome the shortcomings of textbook prose. Many excellent suggestions discussed in other chapters in this volume are worth trying in order to help students deal with pointless and content-impoverished texts. In addition, we recommend that teachers share directly with their students the literature, resources, and references, that *they* use or that *they* have enjoyed in finding out about a topic. True, these materials may be judged as above the students' ability to understand them were they to tackle them on their own.

Think while Reading Activity

What if you were asked by your principal to help develop an up-to-date list of trade books to support the content area textbook in your field. Please review what you're reading in this chapter to determine what criteria you would use to develop this list.

_____

_____

_____

_____

_____

_____

_____

_____

Activity 3–3

However, we are suggesting that with some help from teachers (and parents where appropriate), these resources may be particularly effective. The essence of this suggestion is that adults support young people's introduction to material that is authentic and good but perhaps too difficult for students to deal with independently.

To content area teachers, we offer the reminder that they can influence textbooks by taking seriously their role in textbook selection. Much of the content and format of textbooks is determined by traditions that publishing companies have come to believe sell books. When teachers demand books that are written more coherently, in a style that is more human, more approachable, and with enough information to pique and satisfy the curiosity of students who are increasingly sophisticated about the world they live in, then authors of texts will receive more latitude and write better textbooks.

Using Trade Books across the Curriculum

Content specialists do not need to be reminded to ensure the accuracy and authenticity of the texts they provide for students. What may be less apparent is the abundance of choices of text that can support and extend their teaching. Today, there are more informational trade books covering more topics with more breathtakingly beautiful formats than ever before. That which characterizes excellence in general literature also characterizes excellence in informational books: good writing, authority in source, quality illustrations, and durable construction. In addition, the best informational trade books have particular characteristics that allow them to serve specific teaching functions: they provide in-depth information on specific topics; they can provide more up-to-date and timely treatments than slower-to-produce textbooks; they are often written in a rich, personal style. Finally, we value the variety of trade books available because a range of books ensures that all readers in a classroom, regardless of reading level, have something to read related to the topic of study and are not blocked from the advantages of acquiring information through print.

Moss (1991) argued five reasons for the inclusion of nonfiction trade books in content area classrooms:

1. Teachers can more readily individualize content area reading instruction through the use of nonfiction trade books.
2. Nonfiction trade books have both content and visual appeal.
3. Nonfiction trade books provide in-depth information on particular content area topics ranging from people to places to scientific processes.
4. Nonfiction trade books often contain information arranged more logically and coherently than in content area textbooks.
5. Nonfiction trade books, because they are published every year, are more current than content area textbooks.

Although all these points are valuable ones, at least two bear repetition. First, regardless of the grade level of the students, content area teachers can enrich their teaching by incorporating trade books—including informational picture books—in their classrooms (see Neal & Moore, 1992). The quality, design, and richness of the best trade literature can help to clarify, organize, extend, and enrich instruction. Science writer Eugene Garfield (1984) admits that whenever he has difficulty understanding a scientific phenomenon, he goes in search of a children's book on the topic. More than a few high schoolers have had their interest in American history piqued by the style and wit of Jean Fritz, who makes such historical figures as Sam Houston and Pocahontas alive and human without sacrificing accuracy in the telling, and many students have grasped difficult concepts because of the handles provided by children's science writer Seymour Simon through such texts as *Storms* (1989) and *Our Solar System* (1992).

The second point that needs underscoring is that provision of a variety of texts means that all students, just as adult readers, can read what they like, what they choose, and that which answers *their* questions. Content classrooms, with all the pictures, regalia, media, and equipment they contain, are enriched further when stocked with trade literature (Guzzetti, Kowalinski, & McGowan, 1992). Trade books, specialized magazines, and newsletters in the classroom setting serve the same functions as they do in the adult world—as sources for information, verification, substantiation, and clarification—but also for discovery, access to other times and places, and most of all, for pleasurable learning because good informational print can make for a good read.

Huck, Hepler, and Hickman (1993) offer a set of recommendations for the selection of trade books to support knowledge growth in the content areas that are applicable across age and ability levels. They suggest that teachers select books that:

- attract attention to the topic
- let students browse and explore content
- have read-aloud possibilities
- provide independent reading at varying levels of difficulty

- are basic references
- contain enough information for in-depth study
- have a limited focus for very specific interests
- guide activities and experiments
- can be readily compared
- introduce new perspectives or connections
- accommodate new and extended interests

Keeping informed about the more than 73,000 books for children that are currently in print, and that are added to at a rate of about 6,000 books per year, means (1) resolving to stay in touch with an informed librarian, (2) browsing new titles in libraries and bookstores (including specialty bookstores for children and young adults), and (3) monitoring reference sources that list relevant new publications. For example, "Notable Children's Trade Books in the Field of Social Studies" appears in the April issue of *Social Education.* "Outstanding Science Trade Books for Children" appears annually in a spring issue of *Science and Children.* Each list is prepared by content specialists in cooperation with the Children's Book Council. In addition, the topical listing *Subject Guide to Children's Books in Print* is updated yearly and available in public libraries (Cullinan, 1989), as are general selection aids such as *Horn Book Magazine, School Library Journal, The Bulletin of the Center for Children's Books,* and *Booklist.* We provide more specific references below (see Huck, Hepler, & Hickman, 1993, for a complete listing):

> *Science Books and Films.* Published five times yearly by the American Association for the Advancement of Science, 1333 H St., NW, Washington, DC, 20005.
>
> *Appraisal: Science Books for Young People.* Quarterly reviews of science and technology books for children and young adults. Available from the Children's Science Book Review Committee, 36 Cummington St., Boston University, Boston, MA 02215.
>
> *Outstanding Science Trade Books for Children* and *Notable Children's Trade Books in the Field of Social Studies.* Available from the Children's Book Council, 67 Irving Pl., New York, NY 10003.
>
> *Kobrin Letter.* Reviews informational books and is published ten times yearly by Beverly Kobrin, Editor, 732N Greer Rd., Palo Alto, CA 94303.
>
> *Science and Children.* Includes a monthly review of science books. Available from the National Science Teachers Association, 1201 16th St., NW, Washington, DC 20005.
>
> *Science and Technology in Fact and Fiction: A Guide to Children's Books* (1990). DayAnn M. Kennedy, Stella S. Spangler, and Mary Ann Vanderwerf. Includes reviews of 350 fiction and nonfiction books for young children through elementary grades. R. R. Bowker, 245 W. 17th St., New York, NY 10011.
>
> *The Museum of Science & Industry Basic List of Children's Science Books.* Bernice Richter and Duane Wenzel. Includes annotations for 1400 trade books in science. American Library Association, 50 E. Huron St., Chicago, IL 60611.

E for Environment: An Annotated Bibliography of Children's Books with Environmental Themes (1992). Patti Sinclair. Offers books with focus on ecology, endangered species, and the environment. R. R. Bowker, 245 W. 17th St., New York, NY 10011.

Best Science Books and A-V Materials for Children: Selected and Annotated (1988). S. M. O'Connell, V. J. Montenegro, & K. Wolff. Annotations for materials published between 1982 and 1988. American Association for the Advancement of Science, 1333 H Street NW, Washington, DC 20005.

American History for Children and Young Adults: An Annotated Bibliographic Index (1990). Vandelia VanMeter. Reviews books published between 1980 and 1988. Libraries Unlimited, P.O. Box 263, Littleton, CO 80160.

World History for Children and Young Adults (1991). Vandelia VanMeter. (See address above).

Index to Collective Biographies for Young Readers, 4th ed. (1988). Karen Breen. R. R. Bowker, 245 W. 17th St., New York, NY 10011.

Another source for excellent, approachable, and timely information is periodical literature. We refer here to the many magazines on special topics that are available for audiences of all ages. Secondary-level students enjoy and benefit from such magazines as the *Smithsonian, National Geographic, Discover,* and *Odyssey.*

Our point in this section has been that learning from reading does not have to be restricted to learning from textbooks because a wealth of informational trade books are available on many concepts encountered in the content areas. As a final point, though it may not need to be mentioned, we want to remind content area teachers that there are excellent pieces of fiction, poetry, and other literary genres as well that can enrich or act as an intriguing introduction to particular concepts in science, history, even math. Although we chose not to mention particular examples of such noninfomative texts and how they can be linked to content information, we are clearly in favor of using any resource to intrigue, make coherent, explain, enliven, and connect concepts the students are learning in their content classes.

Conclusion

To summarize, we have argued that content area instruction should include a different and more important role for print-based learning. In our first section, we presented the case for reading as an active, problem-solving process that is very much influenced by teachers' attitudes toward the text and the type of task assignments they give related to the text. We also argued for content-specific literacy as a worthy educational goal. Second, we discussed some characteristics of textbooks and suggested ways in which content area experts can help improve them. Finally, we suggested that classrooms be enriched with the many resources available in the form of trade literature relevant to the content areas.

Before we close, we have two final points to make. The first is that we do not want to be misunderstood as supporting a return to text-based instruction, at least not in the way that such instruction typically is realized. We are advocating increasing the role of good text materials used in creative and stimulating ways. To a return to typical text-based instruction, we say no. To the use of good books used well, we say yes.

Our second point, lest it somehow slip by unnoticed, is that, above all, teachers should use texts that they themselves love. Students are quick to notice the attitude that teachers have toward the text materials they assign in courses and are likely to form the same opinion of those materials. Of course, not all useful materials will be wholly attractive. We think it is very important that content area teachers find at least some text materials that they can fully appreciate and that they introduce these to their students. We know that most of these students as adults are likely to have their only contact with the topics presented in content area classrooms through reading, and we believe it is important that they have a positive attitude toward such reading. Otherwise, we fear little information about the wonders of the natural and social world will reach them.

Finally, to end on a more positive note, we would like to recount one more experience with Jay, the junior high school student we introduced earlier. One night, as Jay was putting the final touches on the robot he was making for a science project, his mother asked him how he could have made such a clever little machine. He replied, "Ingenuity and *Boys' Life*." We were struck by how aptly he had represented the argument we are making here: many past hands-on experiences tinkering with motors and electrical wiring had given him the skill and confidence, the ingenuity as he called it, to attempt to construct the robot. The magazine article had provided him with the plans, information, and suggestions he needed. Ingenuity and text together had made the robot possible.

Think after Reading Activity

Refer back to your answers in the Think before Reading Activity and write a brief statement about whether you think the common themes you discussed with your group support or conflict with the ideas presented in this chapter. What changes would you make?

_____

_____

_____

_____

_____

_____

_____

Activity 3–4

C h a p t e r 4

Understanding the Readability of Content Area Texts

EDWARD FRY

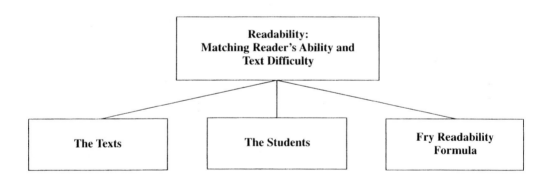

Think before Reading Activity

Think about all of the times you've thumbed through books in a bookstore. What criteria did you use to select those you've chosen? What makes a book hard for you to read?

_____

_____

_____

_____

_____

_____

_____

Activity 4–1

A reader's ability to enjoy a selection, willingly read, and learn from a text depends in part on the match between the reader's ability and difficulty of the material. In this chapter a readability formula, its use, and benefits will be presented. Using this formula, it is possible to select texts which have a close match between the reader's ability and the difficulty of the text.

Teachers frequently ask their students to read an article, a chapter in a textbook, or sometimes a whole book. When they do this they usually expect three things:

1. The student will enjoy the reading experience.
2. The student will continue reading the whole assignment.
3. The student will learn something so that he or she will be able to discuss the reading assignment in class, answer questions based on the assignment, summarize the reading assignment in his or her own words, and relate the information gained to other knowledge or other subjects.

If the student is to accomplish these three things, there must be some match between the student's reading ability and the reading difficulty of the material. To choose a far-fetched example, it is not reasonable to expect someone with grade 3 reading ability to be able to read an article in the *Encyclopedia Britannica* and (1) enjoy reading it, (2) continue reading it, or (3) learn much from it. It doesn't much matter if that student is in grade 3 with normal reading ability or a senior in high school with grade 3 reading ability.

Students in any class in any school come with a range of abilities that are greatly influenced by their prior experiences. Many are average, some a little above average, some a little below average, a few way above average, and a few way below average. In every class you teach, the students will have a range of reading ability—every single class. How big is that range? In a typical grade 9 it could easily range from grade 4 to grade 12 reading ability, with most students being in the grade 8 to 10 ability range. Is this shocking? No, it is just normal and it is the result of many factors that will be addressed in this chapter and in Chapter 5.

Another important thing you need to know is that reading matter also has a difficulty range. Some material is hard to read and some material is easy to read. You don't have to be much of a student of English literature to figure out that Hemingway is easier to read than Faulkner. Now, when you say that Hemingway is easier to read than Faulkner, you are probably basing that on your own experience. You might even say that you are basing it on subjective judgment. There is nothing wrong with subjective judgment, we all use it all the time; but the problem is that sometimes it is not too accurate. So, while subjective judgment as to the difficulty of an article or a chapter is useful, it is often not too accurate or, as we might say in testing, it is not reliable (the score jumps up and down or is not consistent).

Readability Formulas

Is there a better way of finding out the difficulty of an article or a book? One way that we will propose is by the use of a readability formula.

A readability formula is an objective way of measuring the difficulty of any article, chapter, or book. In fact, it is so objective that it can even be done by a computer. But it can also be done by any teacher with just a little bit of training or willingness to follow directions. We will show you how by using a simple graph (Fry, 1977). See Figure 4–1. You will be able to take any article or chapter and assign a grade level of difficulty to it, not perhaps with complete accuracy, but with more accuracy than by just using your subjective judgment. Not only that but you will get reliability, which means that any other teacher using the same formula on the same passage will come out with the same grade level.

Why do you want to assign a grade level to your reading assignment material? Because of "1, 2, 3"—(1) student pleasure, (2) willingness to continue reading, and (3) learning from printed material, when you match the student's reading ability with the material difficulty. Most of the time when you want a student to understand that chapter in a history book, or you want the student to be able to discuss a science article or complete reading a novel, you'd better pay some attention to matching the reading material with the student's reading ability.

There are over 1,000 published articles on readability (Klare, 1984), and here are some of the ways they have validated readability scores. By taking a large group of students and varying the difficulty level of several passages, some of the following things have been demonstrated:

1. Comprehension. As the difficulty increases, comprehension scores fall. In other words, students learn more when the material is easier or, perhaps, when the match is better.
2. Oral reading errors. As the difficulty increases, more oral reading errors occur. You can easily demonstrate this yourself. Give a student two passages, one easy and one hard, and count on your fingers the number of oral reading errors.

3. Inclination to continue reading. If the passage is better matched to the student's ability, there is a tendency for the student to read longer, or not stop in the middle. Related studies in journalism show that newspaper readers tend to read articles that are not too difficult.

4. Correlation with other methods. A readability formula tends to correlate with other formulas and methods of judgment. Different formulas tend to rank a range of books in the same order of difficulty, though there is some variance in assigning exact grade levels. One method of estimating readability is to have trained observers compare a new passage with a set of standard passages. Readability formulas tend to rank the different books the same as trained comparative judgment (but readability formulas don't need trained observers or the relative slowness and subjectivity of making comparisons).

One source of opposition to readability formulas is that they are sometimes misused as writing guides. Because formulas tend to have just two major inputs—word length or difficulty, and sentence length—some authors or editors have taken just these two factors and modified writing. They sometimes end up with a bunch of short choppy sentences and moronic vocabulary and say that they did it because of a readability formula. Formula writing, they sometimes call it. This is a misuse of any readability formula. A readability formula is intended to be used after the passage is written to find out for whom it is suitable. It is not intended as a writer's guide.

Content of Readability Formulas

How do readability formulas work? Most of them have two major inputs: a semantic factor (meaning) and a syntactic factor (grammar). Both of these factors are measured by surprisingly simple methods.

The semantic factor is measured by word difficulty, and word difficulty is judged by word length. In the case of the readability graph in Figure 4–1, this factor is measured by the average number of syllables per 100 words (the more syllables, the more long or difficult words). You count out 100 words in a sample, then count the number of syllables in that 100 words. This measure is based on Zipf's principle (he was a linguist who postulated that the more frequent or common a word, the shorter it is). It doesn't always work because there are short difficult words, for example, "tyro," and some long easy words, for example, "beautifully." But if you take at least three 100-word samples, you will find that usually Zipf's principle works and that the exceptions get lost in the average.

The syntactic factor is measured by an even easier direct objective input. You simply take the average number of words in a sentence. The logic here is that longer sentences have more complex syntax (grammar). In practice, this means that you just count the number of sentences in your 100-word sample.

Next you take these two inputs, (1) the average number of syllables in three 100-word random samples and (2) the average number of sentences per 100 words, then enter these into the graph, and you have an estimated grade level.

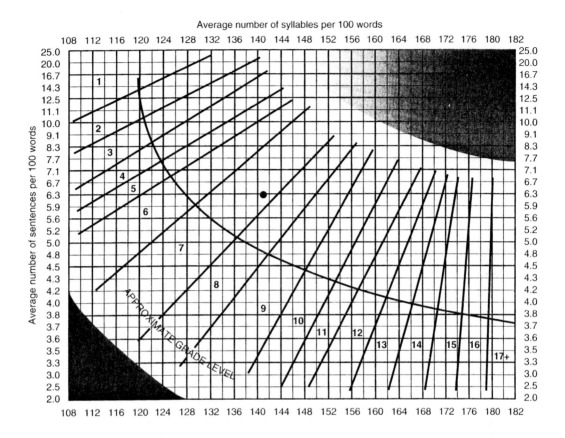

DIRECTIONS: Randomly select three 100-word passages from a book or an article. Plot average number of syllables and average number of sentences per 100 words on graph to determine the grade level of the material. Choose more passages per book if great variability is observed and the book has uneven readability. Few books will fall in gray area, but when they do, grade level scores are invalid.

Count proper nouns, numerals, and initializations as words. Count a syllable for each symbol. For example: "1945" is 1 word and 4 syllables and "IRA" is 1 word and 3 syllables.

EXAMPLE:	SYLLABLES	SENTENCES
1st Hundred Words	124	6.6
2nd Hundred Words	141	5.5
3rd Hundred Words	158	6.8
AVERAGE	141	6.3

READABILITY: 7th Grade (see dot plotted on graph)

FIGURE 4–1   Graph for Estimating Readability—Extended

Source: Edward Fry, Rutgers University Reading Center, New Brunswick, NJ 08904.

Think while Reading Activity

Based on the information about readability in this chapter, what might you as a teacher do to help your students enjoy reading and also learn from a textbook in your content area? As you read this chapter, note the factors that affect readability—how well someone can read a textbook.

_____

_____

_____

_____

_____

_____

_____

_____

Activity 4–2

Incidentally, there are a dozen or more other formulas that use slightly different inputs and calculation. Two of the best known are the Spache (1953) for grades 1–4 and the Dale-Chall (1988) for grades 4–12. Both of these use an unfamiliar word count to measure the semantic factor. An unfamiliar word input is the number of words not on a common word vocabulary list. They both use sentence length for a syntactic factor. These inputs are then entered into an algebraic formula using constants and some simple calculations to obtain the grade level of a passage.

Other Considerations

Be careful not to confuse "readability" with "legibility." Readability is the difficulty of the article. It predicts what level of reading ability is needed by the reader in order to "1, 2, 3"—(1) enjoy, (2) continue reading, and (3) learn or have good comprehension. Readability can be guessed at (subjective judgment), or it can be more accurately predicted by using a readability formula. Legibility is but a minor visual appearance factor in readability. Legibility has to do with the quality of the handwriting or the size of the type. One common error in judging the difficulty of children's books occurs when the publisher does not change the story but merely sets it in larger type when he wants to sell the book to younger children. Setting a book in larger type doesn't do much for true readability.

Another confusing factor is "interest level." The subject matter might be interesting for a poor or young reader, but if the readability is too high then "1, 2, 3" won't occur. For example, Mark Twain's *The Adventures of Huckleberry Finn* is interesting for students in grade 3 or 4, but the readability is about grade 8, so basically the normal grade 3 or 4 student can't read it. However, it is a great book to read to children.

An exception to this "interest level" discussion is that if motivation is extremely high, the student will read at a much higher than normal readability level. We see this happening all the time in high school when a student with grade 4 reading ability reads the driver's license manual that has grade 9 readability. But usually that same student can't muster up that kind of motivation for a biology textbook or an English literature reading assignment.

Establishing the difficulty (readability) of a book or article can help a teacher in making effective and pleasurable reading assignments. It might even cause the teacher to make differentiated assignments so that the poorest readers and the best readers in a class are not expected to read the same amount or the same difficulty of materials.

Teachers often serve on textbook selection committees, and knowing the readability (difficulty expressed in grade level) should be one factor in the selection process. There are many other factors in textbook selection, such as appropriate content, interest, format, illustrations, and teachability.

Think after Reading Activity

Choose two texts, one easy and one hard. They can be textbooks, short stories, news articles, or any other text that you might use in your classroom. Check the readability using Fry's Readability Formula.

Book 1	Passage 1	Passage 2	Passage 3	Average	Grade Level
# of syllables					
# of sentences					

Book 2	Passage 1	Passage 2	Passage 3	Average	Grade Level
# of syllables					
# of sentences					

Based on these readability scores, what conclusion can you draw about these texts. Do you think you've determined the total difficulty level or should other criteria be considered? What role does the reader play in this interaction? What two factors are measured by this formula? What else would you need to consider about your students for the texts you've selected?

_____

_____

_____

_____

You'll need to keep a copy of the selections you used for this activity for an activity in the next chapter.

Activity 4–3

Readability formulas are not infallible. They have a standard error of measurement, just like tests of students' ability. The standard error for grade level scores of readability is about (+ or –) one grade at the elementary level and about two grades at the senior high level, but they have the advantage of greater reliability or consistency and greater objectivity than the subjective opinions of different teachers and librarians.

More importantly, having even a little experience at doing a readability formula opens up the whole concept of different difficulties of various reading materials. Teachers have always known that some books are harder to read than other books. Readability formulas are simply a more scientific refinement of this concept. The formulas are not perfect, but neither is subjective opinion.

C h a p t e r 5

Considerate Texts

BONNIE B. ARMBRUSTER

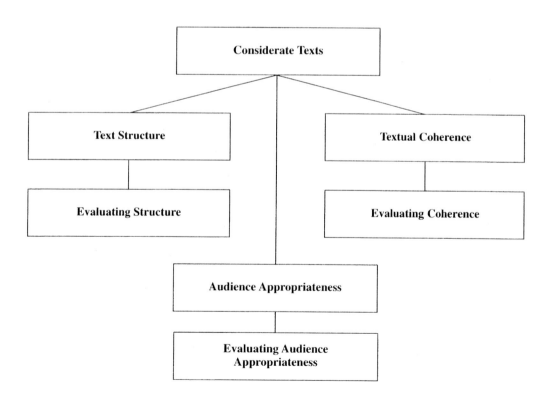

Think before Reading Activity

Using one of the texts from the Think after Reading Activity at the end of the previous chapter write down three to five things in addition to syllables and sentence length that you believe make the selection easy to read. (You will also need this text for the Think after Reading Activity at the end of this chapter.)

1. _____
2. _____
3. _____
4. _____
5. _____

What makes the chapter difficult to read?

_____
_____
_____
_____
_____
_____
_____
_____

Activity 5–1

In school learning situations, content area textbooks are the most common form of informational text. It is these texts to which the idea of "considerate text" is most commonly applied.

"Considerate text" is text that facilitates comprehension and learning from reading. The purpose of this chapter is to explain what makes text considerate, or conducive to comprehension and learning. By applying the information in this chapter, teachers will be able to make informed decisions about selecting and using informational texts in the classroom.

A "considerate text" is a text that facilitates comprehension and learning from reading. The notion of considerate texts applies primarily to expository, or informational text, in which the author's main purpose is to help the reader acquire new information from reading. In school learning situations, content area textbooks are the most common form of informational text. (See Anderson & Armbruster, 1984, and Armbruster, 1984, for earlier discussions of considerate textbooks.)

Why should teachers know about considerate text? First, teachers need to understand that *in*considerate text is one reason many students have difficulty learning from reading (e.g., Applebee, Langer, & Mullis, 1989). Second, teachers should know what makes text considerate so they can make more informed decisions about selecting and using informational text in the classroom.

Because reading is a complex process in which meaning is constructed from the interaction between features of the text and resources of the reader students can have difficulty learning from reading for many reasons. Some reading problems are attributable primarily to the reader. For example, the student may lack appropriate background knowledge to learn from reading, including knowledge of the structure and syntax of informational text, the specific topic covered by a text, or the cognitive and metacognitive strategies needed to learn from reading. Other characteristics of readers that affect comprehension and learning include motivation, interest, purpose, and perseverence. In addition to problems attributable primarily to the reader, the interactive/constructive view of reading implies that the text itself can be a problem. The way a text is written can influence comprehension and learning, both negatively and positively.

The purpose of this chapter is to explain what makes text considerate, or conducive to comprehension and learning. The notion of considerateness covers aspects of text other than those measured by readability formulas. To repeat, the information in this chapter is designed to help teachers identify text features that may cause problems in comprehension and learning, as well as to make more informed decisions about selecting and using informational text (especially content area textbooks) in the classroom.

The three sections that follow discuss three somewhat overlapping features of text that have been suggested by research to contribute to comprehension and learning, and thus to considerateness: *structure, coherence,* and *audience appropriateness.* Each section defines the feature, briefly discusses the research supporting its importance, and provides suggestions for how to evaluate the considerateness of text with regard to that feature.

Structure

Definition

Structure, or organization, refers to the system of arrangement of ideas in a text and the nature of the relationships connecting the ideas. Structure is determined by the author's purpose and the content to be communicated. A few basic text structures, which appear to capture fundamental patterns of human thought, have been identified by rhetoricians, linguists, and psychologists. These basic structures are the building blocks of informational text.

Among the most common structures are description, comparison and contrast, temporal sequence or process, cause and effect, and problem and solution. *Description* is a simple listing of descriptive information about a concept. This structure may include the definition of a concept (its defining attributes) and examples. Description is very common in content area textbooks. For example, a social studies textbook might describe various tribes of Native Americans, while a science textbook might define and enumerate types of simple machines. *Comparison and contrast* describes similarities and differences between two or more concepts. For instance, various geometric forms might be compared and contrasted in a mathematics textbook, and male-female anatomy might be compared and contrasted in a health textbook. *Temporal sequence or process* conveys a series of events, steps, or processes over time. An explanation of how a bill becomes a law or instructions on how to change a tire would follow this structure. A *cause and effect* structure conveys a causal relationship among ideas or events. Explanations of phenomena in the social and natural sciences (for example, explanations of erosion or the fall of the Roman Empire) are often communicated through cause and effect structures. *Problem and solution,* which may be a subset of cause and effect, conveys a causal relationship between a problem and its solution. Many events in history, such as migrations, wars, and social reforms, as well as issues in the areas of health or science-technology-society, are often cast in the form of problems and solutions.

These structures are rarely found in "pure" form in text. Rather, structures are often embedded in, and interleaved with, other structures. For example, a unit on the Civil War might have a top-level problem and solution structure, but within that structure are likely to be comparisons and contrasts between the North and South, descriptions of people and places, and temporal sequences discussing battles.

Research Evidence

Considerable research over the past two decades indicates that structure, or organization, has an important effect on learning from text. The bottom line of the research evidence is that the better organized the text and the more apparent the structure to the reader, the higher the probability that the reader will learn from reading (e.g., Bartlett, 1978; McGee, 1982; Meyer, Brandt, & Bluth, 1980; Richgels, McGee, Lomax, & Sheard, 1987; Taylor, 1980, 1982). The implication for considerate text is that it should be clearly and logically organized, and the organization should be salient.

Guidelines for Evaluating Structure

Evaluating the considerateness of texts with regard to structure involves evaluating several layers of organization, from the global organization of the text as a whole to the local organization of sections and even paragraphs.

Perhaps the easiest way to evaluate global organization is to examine the structure as conveyed by headings and subheadings organized as an outline. Does the outline reflect an accurate and logical sequence and hierarchy of content? For an entire textbook, the table of contents might suffice for a first pass at evaluating global organization. However, because tables of content usually include only chapter titles, they are generally not detailed enough to reveal structural problems. Therefore, it may be necessary to construct an outline of the headings and subheadings of individual chapters or a sample of chapters. In my experience, making a quick outline of chapter headings and subheadings has revealed problems of illogical subsumption (such as including a section on wind and water erosion within a chapter on glaciation) or inconsistent treatment of topics (such as presenting the potentially confusable animal groups of reptiles and amphibians in a single section, while birds, mammals, and fish are discussed in separate sections).

In addition to evaluating the structure as revealed through the hierarchical organization of headings and subheadings, it is also important to evaluate the salience of the structure—how apparent it is to the reader. One way structure can be made salient is through *signaling*—aspects of text that indicate or emphasize structure.

Signaling takes several forms. One type of signaling can occur in the introductions and summaries that accompany units, chapters, and sections. In considerate texts, introductions give the reader a good overview of the content and structure of the information to follow. In this way, readers are given a full statement of the organizing framework before they encounter the text proper.

Introductions in the form of learning objectives can also signal structure. For example, after reading the following introduction, readers know to expect the content to be organized as cause and effect, description, and comparison and contrast:

In this chapter, you will learn

- *what causes weather changes*
- *three main types of clouds*

Summaries signal structure by recapitulating the organization of main ideas. For example, in the following partial summary, statements of main ideas signal the structure of the text used to develop those ideas:

Key Ideas:

- *Waves, currents, and tides cause the movement of ocean waters*
- *Features of the ocean bottom include mountain ranges, plains, slopes, deep trenches, and canyons*

Another form of signaling is titles or headings that suggest structure, such as "How Sound Travels," or "Causes of the Boxer Rebellion." A third type of signaling is pointer words and phrases that are associated with particular structures. For example, "similarly" and "in contrast" signify a comparison and contrast structure, while "because," "therefore," and "as a consequence" denote a cause and effect structure. A fourth type of signaling is in the form of typographical cues, such as bullets to indicate a list of features in a description or definition, and numbers to indicate a sequence or process.

A second major way text structure can be made salient is through accompanying graphic representations of content that visually convey the structure. For example, a web or concept map can depict description, a table or matrix represents comparison and contrast, and a flow chart captures a sequence or process. Figure 5–1 gives an example of a concept map that depicts the organization of this chapter. When graphic representations of structure accompany text, they help highlight the underlying organization.

In summary, considerate texts are organized clearly and logically. In addition, the structure is made very obvious through signaling or through accompanying graphic representations.

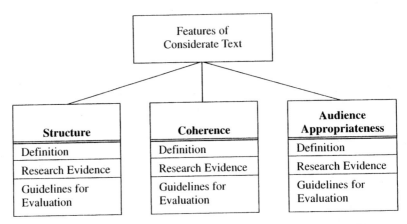

FIGURE 5–1   Concept Map Showing the Structure of This Chapter

Coherence

Definition

Coherence refers to the extent to which events, concepts, or phenomena are logically and clearly explained. A considerate text includes only information that is important and relevant to developing concepts or explaining events and phenomena, and this information is clearly explicated in a way that makes apparent its significance. In texts that are considerate with regard to coherence, readers should not have to expend much cognitive effort inferring, organizing, or constructing relationships among ideas.

Think while Reading Activity

While reading this chapter explain some of the additional factors that affect text friendliness (readability). Don't forget to think about the role of the reader.

Activity 5–2

Research Evidence

Several studies have examined the influence on comprehension of aspects of text related to coherence. Baumann (1986) demonstrated that texts revised to contain explicit statements of main ideas led to greater recall than texts with implicit main ideas. Some other text elements related to coherence have been shown to have a negative effect on comprehension: ambiguous references (Frederiksen, 1981); lack of explicit or clear relationships between events (Black & Bern, 1981; Kintsch, Mandel, & Kozminsky, 1977; Marshall & Glock, 1978–1979; Pearson, 1974–1975; Stein & Nezworski, 1978), and inclusion of irrelevant information (Schank, 1975; Trabasso, Secco, & van den Broek, 1984). One kind of irrelevant information is "seductive details" (Garner, Gillingham, & White, 1989)—information that is interesting but unimportant.

Guidelines for Evaluating Coherence

Several text features can contribute to considerateness with regard to coherence, as suggested by the research cited above. One feature is the salience of main ideas. In considerate texts, main ideas are explicitly stated. Explicit main ideas appear in prominent places such as introductions and summaries, headings, and topic sentences at the beginning of sections and paragraphs. Main ideas should not be buried in the middle of paragraphs or left to be inferred by the reader.

A second way to promote coherence is that all information in the text should be clearly connected to the main idea. In considerate text, all content contributes to and supports the development of the main idea. Considerate texts avoid "seductive details"— those interesting tidbits of information that tend to be memorable but unimportant. An example of a seductive detail occurs in most accounts of the building of the American transcontinental railroad—the fact that Governor Stanford missed the spike and hit the rail when he tried to drive in the final, golden spike (Armbruster & Anderson, 1984). Although interesting and memorable, this detail hardly contributes to an understanding of why and how the transcontinental railroad was constructed and what effect it had on westward expansion.

A third way that texts can be coherent is through the logical ordering of events and ideas. For example, events should generally be ordered from first to last, and supporting evidence should typically be presented from most to least important. Causes need to be linked with effects, and problems with solutions.

A fourth feature contributing to coherence is the obvious relationship between events and ideas. Relationships such as cause and effect, sequence, and contrast should be made explicit in the text (for example, through the use of conjunctions such as "because," "then," or "but") rather than left to be inferred by the reader.

Clear references to preceding concepts are a fifth feature related to coherence. In considerate text, pronouns are unambiguous, and references to previous concepts and events are direct and explicit. For example, it is often preferable to repeat exact references such as "the Abolitionists" rather than use the pronoun "they," and precise terms such as "World War II" rather than vague terms like "the war," especially if there is any possibility of confusion about the referent.

Think while Reading Activity

Using the text you used for the Think before Reading Activity, skim it to see if there are any sections that lack coherence. Explain why you've chosen them. Rewrite one of the statements so it is a considerate text as defined by Armbruster.

_____

_____

_____

_____

_____

_____

_____

Activity 5–3

A final feature related to coherence is smooth transitions between topics. In considerate text, transition statements such as summaries and overviews provide closure for topics that have already been discussed and set expectations for subsequent information, including how it is related to what came before.

Audience Appropriateness

Definition

Audience appropriateness refers to the extent to which the text matches the target readers' probable knowledge base. In developing new concepts and explaining events, considerate texts build on the background knowledge readers are likely to have. Considerate texts elaborate new concepts sufficiently to be meaningful to readers and to facilitate learning.

Research Evidence

The constructive theory of reading implies that what the reader brings to the text is critical to comprehension. Many kinds of prior knowledge are involved in constructing meaning, but the main one of concern to this discussion of audience appropriateness is topic knowledge, or "the intersection between one's prior knowledge and the content of a specific passage" (Alexander, Schallert, & Hare, 1991, p. 334).

Guidelines for Evaluating Audience Appropriateness

One important aspect of text related to audience appropriateness is conceptual density, or the number of new concepts introduced per unit of text. In general, the denser the conceptual load, the more difficult the text (Kintsch & Keenan, 1973; Kintsch, Kozminsky, Streby, McKoon, & Keenan, 1975). Considerate texts, therefore, say a lot about a few ideas rather than a little about many ideas. Concepts are elaborated and explained thoroughly enough to be understandable by the target audience, considering their likely topic knowledge.

This aspect of considerateness is frequently violated in content area textbooks because publishers try to provide an encyclopedic coverage of the topic. By sacrificing depth for breadth, textbooks often fail to explain concepts and clarify the relationships among ideas in a way that matches the topic knowledge of the intended audience.

Texts are also audience appropriate when they make wise use of the readers' likely topic knowledge. Considerate texts build on existing knowledge. For example, considerate texts define new terms by using only words and concepts that are likely to be familiar to the reader. Defining *igneous rocks* as rocks formed from magma is not considerate if the readers do not know what magma is. Considerate texts use examples and analogies that are understandable, believable, and relevant to the audience. For example, it is not considerate to define *haciendas* by comparing them to Southern plantations before the Civil War if the reader is unlikely to be familiar with the characteristics of antebellum Southern plantations. When necessary, considerate texts also address incorrect prior knowledge that readers may bring to the text. Misconceptions can be very resistant to change. Therefore, the authors of considerate texts seriously consider readers' ways of thinking. They try to overcome problems with incorrect prior knowledge by refuting common misconceptions (e.g., Maria & MacGinitie, 1987; Marshall, 1989). Considerate texts also present explanations in different ways that make explicit the differences between naive and expert conceptions.

Conclusion

Within an interactive, constructive view of reading, the reader plays a major role in comprehension and learning. However, reading is not entirely reader based; the text also influences the process. Informational text is considerate to the extent that it optimizes features determined by research to facilitate comprehension and learning. Extending beyond word difficulty and sentence length—the objective, quantifiable features measured by readability formulas—the notion of considerateness encompasses structure or organization, coherence, and audience appropriateness.

The notion of considerate texts is important to teachers in the content areas because the nature of the materials their students read will greatly affect classroom instruction. If students cannot understand their textbooks, for instance, the teacher will either need to present the content in an alternate mode or spend considerable time helping the students read to learn.

Teachers can benefit from knowing about considerate text when making day-to-day instructional decisions. For example, teachers can anticipate when students are likely to encounter difficulties in learning from reading and compensate by providing extra assistance (for example, study guides) or supplemental or alternative modes of instruction (for example, substituting a more considerate text, showing a videotape, or conducting a supplemental demonstration). Also, teachers informed about considerate text may be more

Think after Reading Activity

Using the same selection from a content area text that you used in the opening activity, reevaluate it based on the following criteria discussed by Armbruster.

Structure:

_____

_____

_____

_____

Coherence:

_____

_____

_____

_____

Audience Appropriateness:

_____

_____

_____

_____

Role of the Reader:

_____

_____

_____

_____

Conclusion:

On a scale of 1 to 5, evaluate the text you chose on a continuum of whether it is considerate (1) or inconsiderate (5).

Circle one: 1   2   3   4   5

Briefly explain your evaluation:

_____

_____

_____

Activity 5–4

sensitive to the kinds of difficulties students encounter when reading, and thus be more able to provide optimal assistance.

Evaluating text for considerateness can be difficult, however. One problem is that adults often have difficulty assuming the perspective of the students who will be reading the text. Evaluators need to be quite sensitive to the characteristics of the target audience. Or, even better, representatives of the target audience—students—should be the ones to evaluate texts for considerateness.

Evaluating texts for considerateness can be time consuming. Determining the appropriateness of structure, coherence, and audience appropriateness takes time because it requires a careful, thoughtful reading of the text. Simply flipping through a textbook will not reveal the kinds of problems associated with inconsiderateness.

Despite the problems associated with evaluating text for considerateness, an appreciation of text features related to considerateness can help teachers help students learn from reading. The purpose of this chapter has been to foster an awareness of reading materials as an important aspect of reading and learning in the content areas.

Chapter 6

Identifying and Teaching Text Structures in Content Area Classrooms

STEPHEN SIMONSEN

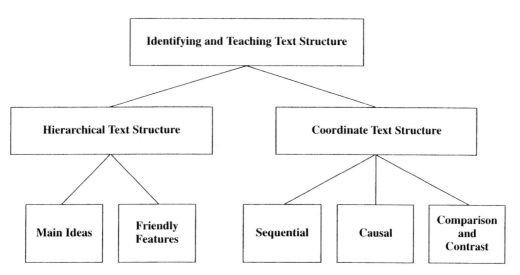

Think before Reading Activity

Content area teachers often bristle at the suggestion that, in addition to being math, science, and social studies teachers, they also have to be reading teachers. What is your response to this? You briefly thought about this in Chapter 1. Reflect on your initial response and see if you now have an expanded view.

_____

_____

_____

_____

_____

_____

_____

_____

Activity 6–1

Many content area teachers are tempted to forsake assigning expository text in favor of presenting material in more alluring media: videos, slide shows, lectures, field trips, guest speakers, and audio tapes (Stewart, 1989). And why not? The material needs to be taught, and students often avoid assigned reading (Smith & Feathers, 1983), or do not adequately comprehend expository text.

However, research suggests that students gain more information from expository text than from the other media when the text is assigned as a primary source of information and the teacher provides instruction in how to comprehend it (Chall, Jacobs, & Baldwin, 1990). Under these circumstances, students are more likely to read assigned text (d'Ydewalle, Swerts, & De Corte, 1983), show more gains in reading than do other students (Chall, 1983), and continue reading and learning effectively after graduating (Dahlberg, 1990). In short, for optimal learning, now and later in students' lives, content area teachers must assign expository text and provide instruction in comprehending it.

How do you, a content area expert who may have expected to teach subject matter and let reading take care of itself, teach comprehension of expository text? You need two tools: a recognition of the various types of expository text structure, and for each type, a few basic strategies for teaching comprehension.

This chapter will familiarize you with expository text structures. The first half describes the two most common types of hierarchical text structures: list, which comprises most textbook chapters, and journalist, which encompasses newspaper articles and short magazine articles. The second half presents the three most common types of coordinate text structures: sequential, causal, and comparison and contrast, which reside in instruction manuals, reviews, and short expository texts and are embedded in longer texts. The description of each text type is accompanied by suggestions for pertinent comprehension strategies that require little expertise and take no appreciable time away from teaching your content area.

Hierarchical Text Structures

Resembling the flow chart of some top-heavy corporation, hierarchical texts contain one or more main ideas, each elaborated on with supporting details. Experienced readers use their knowledge of this hierarchical structure to locate main ideas and distinguish them from supporting details, so that comprehending and recalling the text is far easier (Conlin, 1992).

List Structure

List structure, used in most textbook chapters and long news stories, resembles an outline: an introduction that states the theme, and a body partitioned into one section for each main idea. Each section opens with its main idea, then elaborates on it, sometimes dividing the elaboration into subsections. (See Figure 6–1.) This chapter, with its introduction stating the importance of text structure, two sections on families of text structure, and subsections describing particular family members, is written in list structure. By elaborating on each main idea separately, list structure provides a tremendous advantage with complex content, such as chemistry, auto mechanics, and government, because readers can concentrate on one main idea at a time and understand each fully before going on to the next (Weisburg and Balajthy, 1987).

Teaching Comprehension of List Texts

Helping students comprehend list texts is a two-step task. First, you must teach them to locate the few select main ideas that stick out in list texts, or else the students will get mired in monstrous swarms of facts far too numerous to remember (Schwalm, 1990). Next, you can help students learn to build those main ideas into patterns, trends, or larger concepts, so they will rely less on rote memorization and more on higher levels of thinking to understand the material (Clarke, Martell, & Willey, 1994).

Locating Main Ideas. Christensen's (1967) generative model of the paragraph is being revisited by some researchers to help students distinguish main ideas from supporting details in paragraphs and list-style chapters (Simonsen, 1992; Schwalm, 1990; Day, 1980).

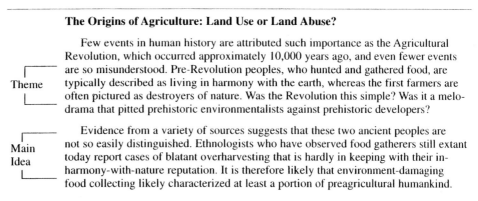

The Origins of Agriculture: Land Use or Land Abuse?

Theme — Few events in human history are attributed such importance as the Agricultural Revolution, which occurred approximately 10,000 years ago, and even fewer events are so misunderstood. Pre-Revolution peoples, who hunted and gathered food, are typically described as living in harmony with the earth, whereas the first farmers are often pictured as destroyers of nature. Was the Revolution this simple? Was it a melodrama that pitted prehistoric environmentalists against prehistoric developers?

Main Idea — Evidence from a variety of sources suggests that these two ancient peoples are not so easily distinguished. Ethnologists who have observed food gatherers still extant today report cases of blatant overharvesting that is hardly in keeping with their in-harmony-with-nature reputation. It is therefore likely that environment-damaging food collecting likely characterized at least a portion of preagricultural humankind.

FIGURE 6–1 List Text
Source: Steve McWilliams, Professor of Anthropology, College of the Desert.

What is the generative model of the paragraph? Consider the top-down nature of the following paragraph:

> Glaciers, despite their barren, stationary appearance, support many kinds of life. Fish thrive in the rivers of ice melt that flow underneath. Ice worms tunnel through the surface and eat pollen that blows in from nearby forests. Flowers sometimes bloom in the dust that collects on the edges. Some of these ice flowers grow as high as four feet.

You probably noticed that the first sentence is the broadest; as the topic sentence, it introduces the topic of life in a glacier. According to Christensen (1967), each paragraph must have one broadest sentence, which he calls a level 1 sentence. You probably noticed also that the next three sentences, the ones about fish, ice worms, and flowers, are more specific, and each provides detailed information on the level 1 sentence's topic of life in a glacier. Christensen's model labels these level 2 sentences because they are more specific than the level 1 sentence and each elaborates directly on the topic raised in it.

The last sentence provides yet more specific information on flowers, which were introduced not directly in the level 1 sentence, but in the preceding level 2 sentence. Christensen's model labels this one a level 3 sentence because it is more specific than the level 2 sentences and elaborates directly on information raised in one of them.

In short, generative paragraphs contain multiple levels of generality: one level 1 sentence and any number of sentences at higher levels. The higher the level, the more specific the sentence. Sentences at each level elaborate specifically on a topic raised in a sentence at the preceding level.

How do you use the model to teach detection of main ideas in paragraphs? As many as 75 percent of the paragraphs in textbooks contain a level 1 sentence (Smith & Chase, 1991). Therefore, in a prereading exercise, you can select important paragraphs from a chapter and point out the level 1, 2, and 3 sentences and their interrelationships, reminding your students that level 1 sentences contain the main ideas (Schwalm, 1990). When a paragraph does not include a level 1 sentence, you can deduce the main idea by generating a likely level 1 sentence. As students learn to identify levels of generality from your modeling, they may be placed in groups of three or four during in-class reading and assigned to take notes jointly by writing down both recognized and generated level 1 sentences (Day, 1980).

You can teach students to detect main ideas for an entire list-style chapter with a directed reading activity in which you draw an analogy between a level 1 sentence and the chapter introduction and title, between level 2 sentences and headings, and between level 3 sentences and subheadings. Within sections of chapters, you may draw analogies between level 1 sentences and introductory paragraphs, and between level 2 sentences and the elaboration that follows (Simonsen, 1992; Schwalm, 1990).

Building Main Ideas into Concepts.   Unfortunately, the very advantage of list structure, the isolation of main ideas so that they can be learned and understood one at a time, also means that they are often presented as atomized bits of information without reference to their roles in a larger pattern, trend, or process (Martorella, 1990).

Fortunately, bottom-up graphic organizers can solve this drawback of list structure by grouping the isolated main ideas in ways that reveal relationships, patterns, and concepts. Clarke (1991) suggests assigning one of several visual aids for students to fill in while reading, depending on how the information needs to be reorganized. If the text's separation of main ideas confuses the sequence of events, students can be assigned to record those events in their natural order on a time line. When list texts scatter related measurements across several sections, students can cluster the measurements in bar graphs. Finally, when objects of a comparison are separated by too much intervening information, circle diagrams encourage students to group the differences and similarities close together. (See Figures 6–2A through 6–2C.)

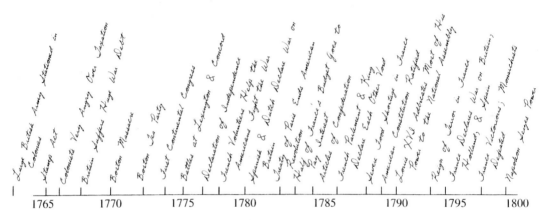

FIGURE 6–2A Time Line

Chapters 15 and 16: The American and French Revolutions. As you read these chapters, write the important events diagonally above the years in which they occurred.

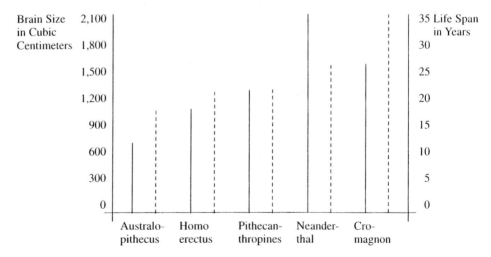

FIGURE 6–2B Bar Graph

The passage on human evolution provides incidental information on the brain sizes and estimated life expectancy of each of our ancestors. As you read, graph the brain size of each ancestor with a solid line and the estimated life span with a broken line.

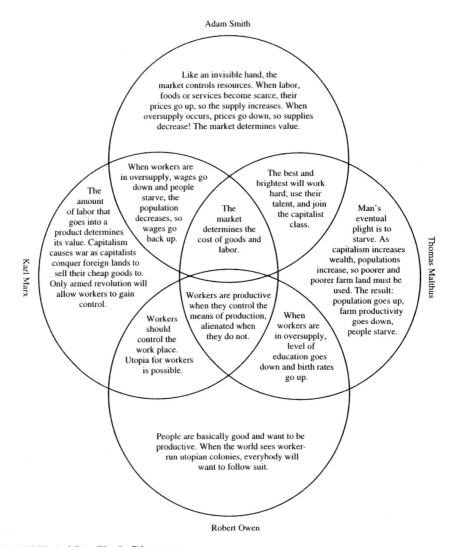

Adam Smith

Like an invisible hand, the market controls resources. When labor, foods or services become scarce, their prices go up, so the supply increases. When oversupply occurs, prices go down, so supplies decrease! The market determines value.

When workers are in oversupply, wages go down and people starve, the population decreases, so wages go back up.

The best and brightest will work hard, use their talent, and join the capitalist class.

The amount of labor that goes into a product determines its value. Capitalism causes war as capitalists conquer foreign lands to sell their cheap goods to. Only armed revolution will allow workers to gain control.

The market determines the cost of goods and labor.

Man's eventual plight is to starve. As capitalism increases wealth, populations increase, so poorer and poorer farm land must be used. The result: population goes up, farm productivity goes down, people starve.

Workers are productive when they control the means of production, alienated when they do not.

Workers should control the work place. Utopia for workers is possible.

When workers are in oversupply, level of education goes down and birth rates go up.

Karl Marx

Thomas Malthus

People are basically good and want to be productive. When the world sees worker-run utopian colonies, everybody will want to follow suit.

Robert Owen

FIGURE 6–2C   Circle Diagram
As you read the chapters on Adam Smith, Karl Marx, Thomas Malthus, and Robert Owen, fill in the circle diagram to show where they agree, disagree, and stand alone.

Adapted from Clarke (1991).

Friendly Features of List Text
If you are considering adopting one of several textbooks with similar readability levels, you may be able to select the most comprehensible one by checking for explicit headings and subheadings. Since list text contains carefully separated main ideas, explicit headings and subheadings that identify main ideas and display their relationships can greatly aid

comprehension (Grant & Davey, 1991). What are the traits of explicit headings and sub-headings? First, differences in capitalization, markings, indentation, boldfacing, or print underscore hierarchical relationships between ideas. Second, they must appear frequently enough to identify all pertinent concepts. Third, they should name precisely the processes, facts, or terms to be learned (adapted from Santa, Havens, & Harrison, 1989; Britton, Glynn, Muth, & Penfield, 1985).

Journalist Structure

Used in short and medium-length newspaper and news magazine articles, journalist structure is a simple two-block design, with all main ideas crowded together in brief opening paragraphs and all supporting details following later. (See Figure 6–3.) Usually, the front page of a newspaper is laid out so that the main ideas of articles are printed on the first

Tight funds don't stop schools from balancing budget

By CHRISTINE MAHR
The Desert Sun

Main Idea #1

RIVERSIDE — Despite little or no increases in state funding, Riverside County's 23 school districts managed to balance their budgets and maintain adequate reserves for 1994–95.

Main Idea #2

Spending plans in all of the districts—including the valley's Palm Springs Desert Sands and Coachella Valley unified school districts — were approved by Riverside County Superintendent of Schools Dale Holmes.

Under a state law that took effect in 1992, all county school superintendents must approve or disapprove every district budget by Aug. 15.

Supporting Details for Main Idea #2

Budget approval especially is significant this year because, for the fourth consecutive year, districts receive the same or slightly less funding per student than last year, said Jerry Kurr, the county office of education's assistant superintendent of administration and services.

"Generally, the districts are being very responsible in how they're handling their finances," Kurr said.

Because of inadequate funding, districts have had to make major changes in their operations and services to adjust for increasing costs from inflation and additional state and federal requirements, Kurr said.

Many districts reduced spending by increasing class sizes and reducing staff through attrition, he said.

Supporting Details for Main Idea #1

The three local districts avoided major cuts this year, but in the past several years made significant cuts, including reductions in student transportation and elimination of staff positions.

Coachella Valley Unified, along with two other county districts — Perris Union High School District and Val Verde Unified — operate under financial recovery plans adopted by their school boards.

FIGURE 6–3   Journalist Text
Copyright 1994 by *The Desert Sun.* Reprinted by permission.

page, and the details are presented in the continuations of the articles on later pages. This pattern allows readers to read the beginning of an article and quickly gain an understanding of the event, then decide whether to turn the page and read on for more detail or go on to another article (McCombs, Son, & Bang, 1988).

The two-block design of journalist structure is easily diagrammed on a chalk board, overhead projector, or handout. (See Figure 6–4.) The diagram advises students to look for all main ideas in the opening paragraphs, and for elaborative details in the body (adapted from Barnett, 1984). The diagram also provides directions and slots to guide students in taking their own notes while reading (Armbruster, Anderson, & Meyer, 1991). In a foreign language or English as a second language class, this diagram helps students anticipate the location of information, which provides additional cues for understanding the language (Anderson, 1985).

Main Ideas

Each of the first two paragraphs contains a main idea for the article. Write each one in your own words in the box.

1.

2.

Supporting Details

Paragraphs three through five contain facts and statistics that give more information on the second main idea. Write two that you think are important in your own words in the box.

1.

2.

Paragraphs six through nine contain facts and statistics that give more information on the first idea. Write two that you think are important in your own words in the box.

1.

2.

FIGURE 6–4   Block Diagram of Journalist Text
Adapted from Barnett (1984).

Think while Reading Activity

A friend of yours is in another academic discipline. He or she has asked you to share some of the content of this course. You have decided to share this chapter with your friend. One reason you've made this decision is because this chapter is written in list structure style. Using the examples found in Figures 6–1 and 6–2 (A–C), develop a graphic organizer that will help your friend understand why this course is important for teacher education majors.

_____

_____

_____

_____

_____

_____

_____

_____

_____

_____

_____

Activity 6–2

Coordinate Text Structures

Distinct from hierarchical structures, coordinate structures do not segregate main ideas and develop them in isolation like twins separated at birth. Rather, in more lively form, coordinate structures expose the relationships between the ideas or reveal the patterns they comprise. Some coordinate passages narrate processes, such as how and why volcanoes erupt, revealing how each event in a chain precedes or even causes the next; others dig up interesting points by making comparisons, such as alerting the reader to what finds can be made at "junker" versus "gourmet" garage sales. In all events, coordinate texts either sequence steps or group traits to compare ideas, objects, places, or people of roughly equal importance (Conlin, 1992). This section will introduce you to three common coordinate structures, sequential, causal, and comparison and contrast, and suggest how to help your students comprehend them.

Sequential, Causal, and Comparison and Contrast Structures

Sequential text reviews an event, describes a process, or gives directions by sequencing the steps in their naturally occurring order. The advantage of this structure is clarity; the sequence provides a plot or scaffolding that aids recall and supplies context for the information (Conlin, 1992). Examples of sequential topics are incidents in the Watergate scandal, stages of sleep, and how laboratory rats are conditioned into pressing a lever when a light flashes. Causal text is very similar, also sequencing steps in their naturally occuring order, except that each step causes the next, and steps more often are simultaneous (Conlin, 1992). Examples of causal topics are the effects of an increase in the money supply, why cold fronts sometimes bring tornados, and what started global warming. Texts are both sequential and causal when some steps are caused by their predecessors, but others merely follow their predecessors. (See Figure 6–5.)

Comparison and contrast text reveals the differences and similarities of two or more objects, places, events, or ideas by grouping their traits for comparison. The advantage of this structure is learning through analogy; the more readers learn about one thing, the better they will understand the other (Joyce & Weil, 1986). Comparison and contrast structure comes in two styles.

The block style first describes one thing in its entirety, and only then describes the other thing in its entirety. This style is very comprehensible because the reader does not need to divert attention to following transitions from one thing to the next. It is most effective in descriptive text, such as depicting the desert before and after irrigation, or the appearance of gold versus pyrite in the bottom of a pan.

The alternating style, like two bickering attorneys, volleys back and forth, describing the things trait by trait. It is preferable to the block style when there is more factual information than the reader could reasonably be expected to recall from one block while following the comparisons in the next. For example, a passage comparing and contrasting the functioning of brains and computers may first describe how both handle parallel processing, then how they store information, and then how they retrieve it (Langan, 1989). (See Figure 6–6.)

The Oldest Highway in the United States

The oldest highway in the United States is not the Camino Real, the Santa Fe Trail, the Chisolm Trail, or the Appalachian Walkway. These trails, old as they are, are youngsters compared to the oldest: The Natchez Trace, connecting what are now Natchez, Mississippi, and Nashville, Tennessee.

The trace winds and twists through the woods between these cities, without bridges. It climbs down canyons and up hills, and is seldom wide enough to let three horses by at the same time. Even today it is not paved, and only one city, Jackson, Mississippi, crosses its path. The trace is an astonishing 10,000 years old. What could have created it and kept it alive today?

About 8,000 B.C., North America had many large animals that migrated freely. Without cities in their way, many of them roamed in large herds, destroying trees and cutting trails. Ground sloths, mastodons, and buffaloes often retraced old routes they had trampled through the woods. This is how the Natchez Trace got its start, as a series of trails cut by animals. Native Americans hunted the animals on these trails. Over time, Native Americans connected the trails so they could follow the animals further from home.

Meanwhile, these connected trails opened up trade between tribes. We have evidence of objects traveling over 1,500 miles from one tribe to another. Thus, the trace also served as a commercial link.

FIGURE 6–5   Sequential-Causal Text

A Review of Color Purple

The Color Purple, originally a novel by Alice Walker and, more recently, a motion picture produced by Steven Speilberg, is set in the early 1900s. Celie, a young black girl raped by her father and forced to marry Mr. _____, struggled with her husband's beatings and humiliation throughout her life. The film and novel differ immensely in one aspect: the portrayal of Celie's strength. In the movie, her strength is often an outwardly physical reaction or act of courage, whereas in the book her strength is within herself.

The novel portrays Celie as a depressed woman with no identity and barely a reason to live. She is so abused by men, the system, and society that she finds herself not feeling anything. The only time that Celie would speak to Mr. _____ in the novel was when spoken to, and even then she still would have been slapped for talking back. This depicts Celie as a stoic. Even though she experiences such hardships and pain, she endures it bravely. She shares her pain only with God.

The film, however, allows Celie more of a life of her own. Once she stands up to Mr. _____ and threatens to cut his throat with a knife. Often, Celie goes out without him. These activities give Celie an opportunity to be herself. They also hint that Celie is occasionally brave enough to act without considering Mr. _____. Thus, the movie does not allow as much pity for Celie as the novel does.

Walker portrayed Celie as emotionally solid enough to carry on and patient enough to forgive Mr. _____. Speilberg painted Celie's strength physically. She was firm enough to stand up for herself when necessary and brave enough to take chances.

FIGURE 6–6   Comparison and Contrast Text
Sally Ann Brierly, College of the Desert, Palm Springs, Ca.

Teaching Comprehension of Coordinate Text

With graphic organizers, you can help students follow the sequence of events or grouping of traits in coordinate text (Armbruster, 1989). Summary graphic organizers provide a pictorial overview of the text's structure and summary of key information for preparation before reading (Joyce & Weil, 1986). In guided note taking, the text's structure is pictorially represented also, along with blank slots in which to write in information while reading (Armbruster, Anderson, & Meyer, 1991). Also, you can encourage your students to analyze the text's sequencing or grouping with top-down graphic organizers (Henry, 1993; Clarke, 1991).

Summary Graphic Organizers
The structure and content of a coordinate passage to be read can be summarized graphically and presented on a chalk board, overhead projector, or handout. With this peek ahead at the content, students' prior knowledge of the topic is activated before they read so they can comprehend the text more thoroughly by connecting it with what they already know. In addition, now knowing the structure, students can free their attention from discerning the structure of the text and instead center on its content (Dunston, 1992). Two types of summary graphic organizers represent coordinate text well. Sequential and causal texts are portrayed by flow charts, containing a box for each event, and each box contains a brief summary of the event. Comparison and contrast texts of both types are portrayed very well with Venn diagrams, in which similar points appear in the overlap, and disparate ones appear in the areas of the circles outside the overlap (adapted from Clarke, Martell, & Willey, 1994). (See Figures 6–7A and 6–7B.)

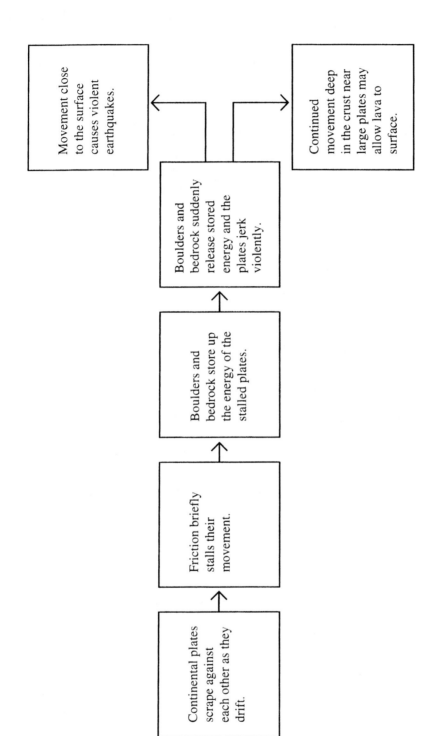

FIGURE 6–7A Flow Chart for Causal Text

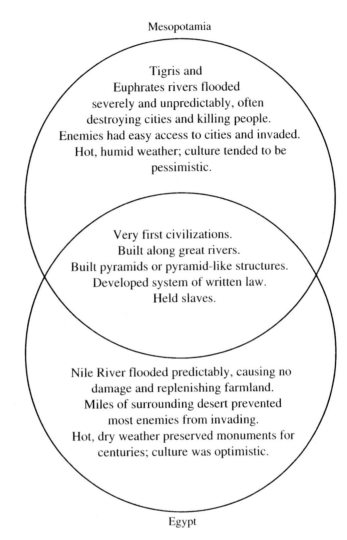

Mesopotamia

Tigris and
Euphrates rivers flooded
severely and unpredictably, often
destroying cities and killing people.
Enemies had easy access to cities and invaded.
Hot, humid weather; culture tended to be
pessimistic.

Very first civilizations.
Built along great rivers.
Built pyramids or pyramid-like structures.
Developed system of written law.
Held slaves.

Nile River flooded predictably, causing no
damage and replenishing farmland.
Miles of surrounding desert prevented
most enemies from invading.
Hot, dry weather preserved monuments for
centuries; culture was optimistic.

Egypt

FIGURE 6–7B   Venn Diagram for Comparison and Contrast Text
Adapted from Clarke, Martell, and Willey (1994).

Guided Note Taking Using Block Diagram Guides

Block diagram guides look exactly like summary graphic organizers, except for one major difference: you have left the boxes or circles empty. Their purpose is to serve as a pre-reading guide to acquaint students with the text structure, help students comprehend the text by signaling when main ideas are looming, and develop note-taking skills. In a pre-reading exercise, review the guide, explain how to use it, and describe the text structure. Then, while reading, students fill each box or circle by scribbling in one- or two-sentence

---

Think while Reading Activity

In this section of the chapter, the author talks about coordinate text structures, which help the reader understand the relationships between the ideas and patterns in the text. One of these structures is called a flow chart. After you read the selection in Figure 6–5, create a flow chart for it. You can find an example of a flow chart in Figure 6–7A. Use it to help you make your own.

How did making this chart help you understand the relationship between ideas and patterns in the selection your read?

_____

_____

_____

_____

_____

Activity 6–3

---

summaries of the main ideas (adapted from Armbruster, Anderson, & Meyer, 1991; Armbruster, 1989).

Try these steps to prepare block diagram guides for a sequential or causal text:

1. Draw a box for each significant step or trait in the passage. If you give handouts, be sure that each box is big enough for students to scribble in one or two sentences.
2. Label each box with a brief title that characterizes one of the steps. Be sure that your titles follow the text's sequence.
3. Connect the boxes with arrows to underscore the sequence.

Try these steps for comparison and contrast text:

1. Trace a circle for each thing to be compared and allow for sufficient overlap. (Compact disks are often the right size.)
2. Label each circle with a brief title that characterizes the thing it represents.

Reexamining the Facts with Top-Down Graphic Organizers
Since coordinate texts often pursue only one angle on sequencing or grouping, unwary readers may forget to question whether other credible angles are possible with the same information. To this end, as postreading exercises, top-down graphic organizers can goad

students into questioning the author's angle and perhaps even constructing a different angle, so thinking occurs at such higher levels as analysis and evaluation (Henry, 1993; Clarke, 1991).

Top-down graphic organizers take a main idea or conclusion from a passage and encourage readers to take a detailed look. Henry (1993) suggests extracting a key word that relates directly to a main idea or pattern in a text and directing students to copy the word, circle it, and draw arrows pointing out from the circle. At the end of each arrow, the students write a word or phrase that sums up what they know about the key word. Next, when ready, students free write, incorporating some of their own words and phrases from the ends of the arrows. The exercise requires six to ten minutes and is designed to let students tap into their emotions about what thay have read, discover their own opinions about the topic, and analyze the passage critically.

Clarke (1991) suggests drawing a pair of scales, each scale with room for five phrases. Students are encouraged to write statements expressing agreement with the text on one side, and problems, questions, or reservations on the other side, then judge which side weighs the most. Class discussion and argumentation is a booster for this activity, especially in early trials.

Friendly Features of Coordinate Text: Cohesive Ties

Cohesive ties (see Table 6–1 for examples) clarify relationships between sections of coordinate text by separating and sequencing, identifying causal relationships, and signaling similarity or disparity. However, some publishers omit cohesive ties to shorten sentences and lower estimated readability levels, which ironically can render the text less comprehensible (Martorella, 1990; Clark, 1986). Consider this comparison and contrast passage:

> When shopping for a classical guitar, look for traits that distinguish it from a country guitar. To aid your technique, the neck should be about a half inch thicker and about 25 percent wider than the neck of a country guitar. Your fingers should move up and down and reach back and forth across the neck easily when you practice scales. The body should be made of thin hardwood rather than the thick hardwood that country guitars need to support wire strings. Thin hardwood produces a more delicate sound.

The passage contains isolated chunks of information, and their relationships are unclear. Now consider the same passage with no changes except the addition of three cohesive ties: *two, first* and *second:*

> When shopping for a classical guitar, look for *two* traits that distinguish it from a country guitar. *First,* to aid your technique, the neck should be about a half inch thicker and about 25 percent wider than the neck of a country guitar. Your fingers should move up and down and reach back and forth across the neck easily when you practice scales. *Second,* the body should be made of thin hardwood rather than the thick hardwood that country guitars need to support wire strings. Thin hardwood produces a softer sound.

TABLE 6–1 Cohesive Ties for Coordinate Text

Sequential and Causal Cohesive Ties

First	Second	Third
One	Two	Three
Next	Subsequently	Consequently
Later	Meanwhile	Simultaneously
Consequentially	So	Then
Afterward	Again	Therefore
Last	Finally	Now

Comparative and Contrastive Cohesive Ties

However	But	On the other hand
Then again	On the contrary	In contrast
And yet	So did	So too
Also	Similarly	In addition
The same is true for	And	Both
Too	Indeed	Whereas
First	Second	Third
One	Two	Three

The cohesive ties clarify the passage by (1) alerting the reader to anticipate two important pieces of information, (2) allowing the reader to more easily sort out the two important traits from the rest of the text, and (3) implicitly identifying the rest of the text as elaboration of the two main points. Your intuition as a reader and awareness of cohesive ties are probably the best guides to gauging the comprehensibility of coordinate passages.

Think after Reading Activity

Refer back to your answer for the Think before Reading Activity in Chapter 2. Can you add to your answer by considering the pitfalls some students are likely to encounter when they read in content area textbooks? Consider how the information in this chapter might prevent someone from falling into one of those pitfalls. Jot down your ideas here.

_____

_____

_____

_____

_____

_____

_____

_____

Activity 6–4

Conclusion

Although they are beyond elementary school and many are reading at or above grade level, your students still have a long way to develop as readers. The expository text you assign to them is more difficult and probably far different from anything they have read before. Therefore, the responsibility falls on you to teach them to comprehend this brave new material in your content area. By identifying the structure of the text you assign—list, journalist, sequential, causal, or comparison and contrast—you can select appropriate strategies to teach comprehension without taking appreciable time away from teaching your content area.

The Students

The Students

Who Are They and How Do I Reach Them?

NANCY MARSHALL

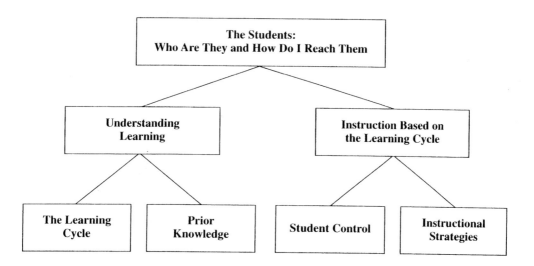

Think before Reading Activity

What's one of the easiest things you remember learning? What factors made it so easy? While reflecting on this learning experience, note any characteristics that can be transferred to a classroom situation.

_____

_____

_____

_____

_____

_____

_____

Activity 7–1

This chapter is written to answer two interrelated questions: (1) Why is there a conflict between student interests and curricular requirements, and (2) How can teachers prevent this conflict? To answer these questions, a model of the learning process is presented as the basis for understanding the role of the student in the classroom. The second part of the chapter focuses on instructional strategies that are based on the learning cycle.

The central message of the chapter is that good instruction builds student desire to learn by showing students that they already know something about the topic and helping them relate new information to what is already known. Far from making teaching more difficult, this kind of instruction actually makes content area classrooms more positive and academic.

I can teach either the curriculum or the students. They are worlds apart.

The students need to learn practical skills, not the advanced theory that is required by the course syllabus. If I teach them what they need, I'll be fired for failing to do my job. If I teach the program, no one will pass the course. It's hopeless.

These are typical comments made by teachers when responding to the question, "What is the biggest problem you face when teaching your subject area?" These comments show they are aware that teaching content for which the students are not ready is inappropriate, and that teaching only what the students want to learn is equally inappropriate. Thus, teachers find themselves caught in a no-win situation: one in which neither students' needs nor curricular demands are met, a situation that often leads to student misbehavior and to teacher burnout.

This situation does not need to occur. Students and curriculum should not be adversaries. Students can succeed in learning course content.

Think while Reading Activity

As you read the next section, "Understanding Learning," use this drawing of the learning cycle to jot down new information as you read it. As you complete this activity, reflect on your own learning process and how this information can help you become a better student.

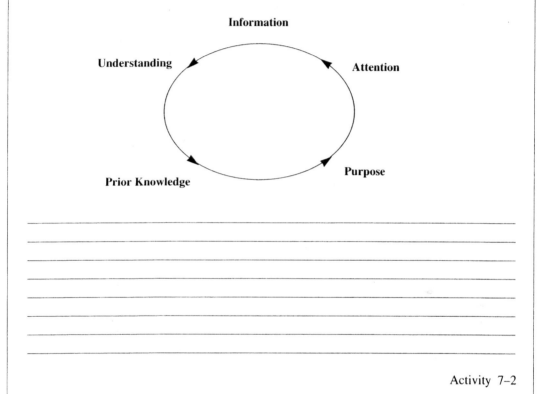

Activity 7–2

Understanding Learning

Instruction should begin and end with students. This means that the teacher's understanding of students should form the basis of all instruction. To understand students, one must understand the way people learn, including the effect of earlier learning experiences on students' attitudes and willingness to become involved in new learning. To begin with, learning is not passive accumulation of information. It does not flow from textbook or teacher to the student along a one-way street. Instead, it is an interaction between the student and the information. This means that learning is controlled as much by experiences students bring to the learning situation as it is by the way the information is presented. This

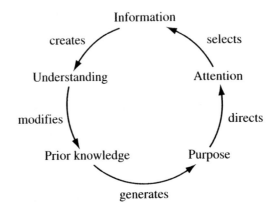

FIGURE 7–1   The Learning Cycle

view of learning, sometimes called *schema theory* (Anderson, 1977), can be pictured as a continuous cycle, like that shown in Figure 7–1.

To understand this figure, it is easiest to begin with *prior knowledge*. Since all new learning is based on existing knowledge, the previous experiences of the students are central to the complete cycle. Furthermore, prior knowledge helps create reasons for learning or not learning. Depending on *purpose* for learning, attention is directed differently. The student either attends to the new information or does not. *Attention* is limited; we cannot pay attention to everything in a new situation. For learning to be efficient, therefore, attention must be directed to the most important *information*. Once the information is encountered, it needs to be *understood*. This occurs when the learner makes connections between new information and prior knowledge. In this way, all new learning is a composite of new information and students' existing understanding. Finally, to be able to use new information as the basis of subsequent learning, students must use the new understanding to *modify* existing knowledge; this is done by either adding it in directly or by revising previous understanding. The modified prior knowledge can then be used to direct subsequent learning.

This view of learning puts considerable emphasis on the role of the student and requires the teacher to take students' prior knowledge into account when planning and delivering a lesson. When this is done, learning is likely to occur; when it is not, learning will result by chance rather than by intention. Thus, it is important for the teacher to be able to identify the state of students' prior knowledge.

The Nature of Prior Knowledge

Prior knowledge is everything the student has ever thought or experienced. It includes prior exposure to the topic and to the way the topic is organized. It also includes school experiences. All these affect students' willingness to participate in new learning. This is shown in Figure 7–2.

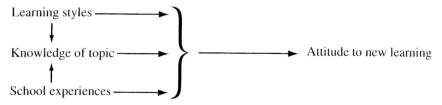

FIGURE 7–2   Types of Prior Knowledge

Learning Styles

Every person is born with the ability and the desire to learn, but different people learn in different ways. Some of us seem to be able to take isolated pieces of abstract information one at a time and use these to build up an understanding of the whole. Others seem to be more comfortable when first seeing the whole picture concretely and then breaking it into its component pieces. The first group has been called *abstract/sequential learners,* and the second group has been called *concrete/holistic learners.* In addition, some people are *logical* thinkers; they are able to make connections among ideas for reasons that they can articulate. Others are *intuitive;* they can make connections among ideas that are often creative and difficult to explain. These two dimensions of thinking can be combined to make a picture of common learning styles, like that shown in Figure 7–3.

According to Kolb (1984), the *abstract/logical* thinker is a problem solver and decision maker who tends to have control over personal emotions and to use language to define and delineate abstractions. The *concrete/logical* thinker is a risk taker, an impulsive person who learns from others and by trial and error and who uses language to help in the difficult synthesis process. The *abstract/intuitive* learner is excellent at synthesis tasks, is good

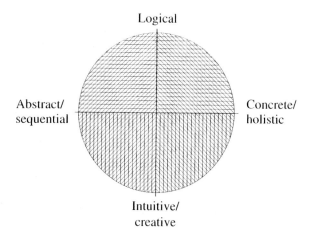

FIGURE 7–3   Model of Student Learning Styles

at planning and organizing, is less concerned with practical considerations than with theoretical consistency, and is not good at relating to people. This learner tends to use language to control others. Finally, the *concrete/intuitive* learner is imaginative and can view a topic from many points of view. This person learns best from direct experience and uses language to express self.

All of us can think both sequentially and holistically and can function both logically and intuitively, but we tend to be more comfortable with some ways of thinking than with others. Unfortunately, schooling stresses only one way of thinking: the logical, sequential way (McCarthy, 1981). We offer students pieces of information and expect them to be able to synthesize them into a logical whole. Some students can do this easily and others cannot. Certainly, the more holistic learners tend to be the ones who end up in special programs like compensatory education and learning disabilities classes (Perfetti, 1985).

Knowledge of Topic

One can learn if there is no relevant prior knowledge with which to relate new information (Wilson & Anderson, 1985). Most of us have had experience trying to learn new information when we did not have the needed prior knowledge. I certainly did. The first course I took in computer programming was one in which the instructor assumed that all the students had some knowledge of elementary calculus; I had not. As a result, the concepts that the instructor used to explain the new content were meaningless to me, and I dropped the course.

This demonstrates the problems that can occur when prior knowledge is inconsistent with information to be learned. It also demonstrates an important rule of teaching: For learning to occur, the teacher has to start with the students' existing understanding and build from there. This prior knowledge does not need to be about the topic directly, but it does have to be relevant to the topic. For instance, most students do not have the experience of living in foreign countries, yet they can learn about the governments of these countries if they have some knowledge of governmental structure and can make comparisons among the various governmental systems.

Even with knowledge relevant to a topic, new learning can be difficult. This tends to happen when direct, personal experience is in conflict with the concepts to be taught (Marshall, 1986). For example, a group of grade 4 and 5 students read a passage from a social studies book on the responsibilities of children at home and at school (Marshall, 1982). The authors of the text were careful to eliminate any sexual stereotyping in their presentation by using examples of boys helping in the kitchen and girls in yard maintenance. Yet the students insisted that the major ideas presented were that boys should mow the lawn and girls should do the dishes because "This is the way we do it at home."

Teachers must address initial misconceptions directly and repeatedly in order to overcome them (Roth, Smith, & Anderson, 1984). One way to do this is to make a network of students' existing knowledge before new learning and then to change the network as new information is encountered. In this way, misconceptions are addressed directly and new learning is modeled concretely.

Determining Prior Knowledge

The point being made here is that school learning can be easy or difficult for students, depending on how well lessons match their background. Thus, it becomes the responsibility of the teacher to determine the level and kinds of prior knowledge that students bring to the learning situation and then to use this information as the basis for planning and delivering the lesson. One way to do this is to use the following questions as the basis of planning content area lessons.

1. What do the students need to know before they can learn this topic? (Develop a test of the needed prior knowledge. If it exists, the lesson can extend from there. If it is incomplete or nonexistent, the lesson must begin with instruction about the missing elements of prior knowledge.)
2. How is the information organized? Can I make a diagram of the way the pieces of information fit together? (You should be able to. Such diagrams should be presented to the class before new learning to help the holistic learners and again after new learning to help the sequential learners.)
3. What are the connections between existing knowledge and new information? (Specify these and then help the students make these connections by using concrete examples and by using the diagram as models of how old and new information fit together.)

The Rest of the Learning Cycle

So far, we have limited our discussion to one part of the learning cycle, prior knowledge. Clearly, learning is not limited to prior knowledge or no one would ever learn anything new. To get a more complete understanding of the learning process, a brief discussion of each of the other elements of the cycle follows.

Purpose for Learning

The best students are usually interested in learning course content because they want to know the information. Unfortunately, not all students are this motivated, and without a rational purpose for engaging in the learning situation, little learning is likely to occur because students will not pay attention. Purpose is even more subtle than this, however, because people with different purposes for learning actually remember different kinds of information (Prichert & Anderson, 1977). Therefore, a good lesson must contain activities that cause the students to *want* to learn the relevant new information in the lesson.

One way to do this is to point out discrepancies between different ways of understanding a topic. For instance, some students believe that whales and dolphins are fish because they live in the water, whereas others believe they are mammals because they have lungs. If this difference is brought out as part of activities designed to elicit relevant prior knowledge, it can be used to set a tone of inquiry for the lesson. Students can then be instructed to look for information about the way scientists distinguish between the various vertebrates. This kind of purpose setting is relevant to students because they will want to know who is right; it is relevant to the content because learning major concepts is an important part of all courses.

Paying Attention

As stated at the beginning of this chapter, attention is limited (LaBerge and Samuels, 1985). We are physically unable to attend to all stimuli that our senses receive every second. Just try, for instance, understanding three or four simultaneous conversations. No one can. The moment we tune into one conversation, we lose track of another.

This is equally true when dealing with information in a course. No one can pay equal attention to all the information found on a page in a textbook or covered in a minute of a lecture (Smith, 1981). Instead, we select the information to which we attend with the hope that what we select is the important information being presented. Attention is directed to those concepts with which we are already familiar (LaBerge & Samuels, 1985) and to those that meet our purposes for learning (Prichert & Anderson, 1977). When learners have the necessary prior knowledge and relevant purposes for reading, they are more likely to pay attention to important information (Anderson, 1982).

Teachers should direct student attention to the most important information. This can be done through the use of study guides, prequestions, or direct suggestions, such as "Pay attention to the characteristics that scientists use to classify the vertebrates." If all the information is important, the students need to be exposed to it repeatedly, each time paying attention for a different purpose.

New Information

Information can be presented so that it is easy or difficult for students to understand. This is true for lessons delivered by teachers and for textbooks. Textbooks written to facilitate learning have been called *considerate text* (Armbruster, 1984). The characteristics of considerate text are discussed in Chapter 5 in this book.

Constructing Meaning

Once the student has attended to new information, it must be related to existing knowledge for it to be meaningful. In other words, the meaning that a student ends up with is a combination of prior knowledge and new learning (Anderson et al., 1977). When the two are similar, learning is relatively easy. When they are dissimilar, new learning is likely to be rejected and existing understanding is likely to remain unchanged.

The best way to prevent this from happening is to be sure that all students have the needed prior knowledge with which to relate new learning. However, it is also possible to help students construct appropriate meaning after the new information has been introduced. To do this, the teacher must address initial misconceptions directly and show the students why their initial understanding is incorrect, and then relate the corrected understanding to the new learning.

Modifying Prior Knowledge

When students have understood the new information, there is one more step to be completed before learning is complete. This part of the learning cycle requires the student to move beyond understanding the new information in the context in which it was presented; instead, the student must be able to apply the new ideas in situations that were not presented as part of the lesson. Only when new information can be used in new situations have students truly gained control over the course content.

A network seems to be ideal at this point in a lesson because it can function as a concrete representation of the processes of *assimilation* and *accommodation* (Piaget, 1952). Assimilation is adding new information to existing knowledge. It is modeled by simple elaboration of an existing network. Accommodation is a more difficult process because it requires that students make changes in existing knowledge to make it more consistent with new information. It is modeled by redesigning the network, coming up with new concepts and relationships when needed and eliminating those that are no longer necessary. It is the process of accommodation that is modeled when the teacher addresses students' initial misconceptions and corrects these during the course of the lesson.

Instruction Based on the Learning Cycle

Clearly, learning is a complex set of processes that occurs most efficiently when all its component processes are taken into consideration. Equally clearly, different processes need attention at different points in a lesson. Figure 7–4 shows the best times to focus on each process.

Before students are introduced to new concepts, they should think about what they already know and come up with purposes for learning. This is the time to be sure that all

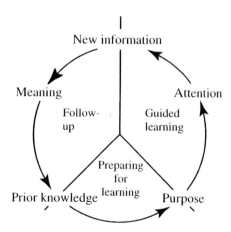

FIGURE 7–4 The Learning-Instructional Cycle

students do have relevant prior knowledge and that they have no misconceptions that could interfere with efficient new learning. It is also the time to point out inconsistencies in existing knowledge or to challenge elements of that knowledge in order to provide relevant purposes for interacting with the new information.

To aid the students while learning, their attention should be directed toward the important new information. The important information will vary depending on the purpose for reading, and this may mean that students need to interact with new information repeatedly, each time attending to a different subset of information. When students attend for different purposes, they must then pull the information together. This is part of the process of constructing meaning.

Promoting Student Control over Learning

This does not mean that the teacher is always supposed to tell students what to think about before new learning, provide them with purposes for reading, tell them what to attend to, and tell them how to relate new to old information. In fact, this would be doing the students a disservice. Students need to learn to use these processes for themselves so that they can become self-directed learners. Consequently, the best lessons are those that help the students move toward independence. The instructional activities that have been most successful in teaching students how to learn factual information (Anderson & Armbruster, 1984) are discussed next.

Networking
Networking, also known as semantic mapping, is appropriate in the preparation and follow-up parts of a lesson. In the preparation step, networks of existing knowledge can be used to help put existing student knowledge together so that it can be used as a framework for new learning. Furthermore, inconsistencies in prior knowledge can be noted easily in networks, and these can be used as a source for developing relevant purposes for learning. Networks after new learning help students integrate new information into a whole and then to relate new and old concepts. They are especially valuable instructional tools to use with holistic learners.

Self-Questioning
Self-questioning is an excellent strategy to help direct attention to relevant new information. Students who use this technique well can develop questions relevant to a particular subtopic or topic and then use the questions as the basis of note taking. However, most students do not know how to develop good questions, so teachers need to help them learn how to do this. One technique that improves student self-questioning is reciprocal teaching (Palincsar, 1984). Another successful technique is the use of explicit instruction in how to develop good questions. Again, the teacher is responsible for beginning the lesson and developing questions. The difference is that the teacher then goes on to explain the reasons for asking the specific questions rather than others. As the lesson progresses, students take

over the responsibility for developing the questions and for explaining their reasons for developing the specific questions. The steps in explicit instruction (Roehler & Duffy, 1984) for teaching students to develop questions include:

1. explaining how and why to ask good questions
2. demonstrating how to frame good questions and the reasons such questions are good
3. leading students as they try to develop good questions
4. slowly withdrawing support from students
5. giving them many opportunities to use self-questioning when reading content area materials

Summarizing
Summaries function like networks because they present the major ideas in relationship to each other. They differ from networks in that the information is presented in sequential prose rather than holistically and visually.

Teachers need to help the more holistic/visual students to develop summaries. One way to do this is to use a follow-up network to organize the ideas and then to show students how to use the network as the source of information to be included in the summary. Going directly from a network to a written summary is difficult because the organization of the information is very different. However, if one first turns a network into a formal outline (which is sequential and verbal but does not require complete sentences to express ideas) and then uses the outline to create the written summary, the summary tends to flow more easily from the students.

Value of Study Strategies
All three of these study strategies have one thing in common: They require students to integrate new information with existing knowledge. In other words, they require active student participation in new learning. The products differ, but the need for students to shape new learning to meet desired goals runs through all three.

Instructional Activities

Many instructional activities help students learn content as they move through the learning cycle and simultaneously help students develop the study skills needed for successful learning. The procedures for three of these are briefly presented here. All three contain similar strategies, yet all three differ in terms of the intensity of instruction.

Reciprocal Teaching

Palincsar's (1984) reciprocal teaching strategy has been developed to promote self-directed, content area learning. Reciprocal teaching is a series of steps that are first used by the

Think while Reading Activity

Three instructional activities are discussed in this section: Reciprocal Teaching, ARC, and PONDARRS. As you read, summarize each and note how you might use each in your classroom.

Reciprocal Teaching

   Summary

   _____

   _____

   _____

   Classroom Implementation

   _____

   _____

   _____

ARC

   Summary

   _____

   _____

   _____

   Classroom Implementation

   _____

   _____

   _____

PONDARRS

   Summary

   _____

   _____

   _____

   _____

   Classroom Implementation

   _____

   _____

   _____

Activity 7–3

teacher and later by students who act as the teacher during part of a lesson. Regardless of the person who acts as teacher, the following steps are used:

1. Anticipate any problems that may exist in learning the new information. Problems can occur with vocabulary, unexpected concepts, misconceptions, and so on.
2. Read a brief amount of text or otherwise interact with the new information in an attempt to eliminate the possible problems.
3. After reading, summarize the part of the text read, pointing out the major concepts.
4. State the main idea of the section of the text.
5. Ask a question about the passage for someone else in the group to answer.

Reciprocal teaching is best conducted with a small group of students and is most appropriate for students who have serious problems learning in the more normal ways. It is a teacher-intensive procedure that requires much time to be spent on small pieces of text so that students learn the material thoroughly and so they learn procedures intended to direct future learning.

ARC

Another such procedure is ARC (Vaughn & Estes, 1986), which stands for anticipation, realization, and contemplation. The focus of the *anticipation* part of the lesson is on using existing knowledge as the basis of predicting the kinds of information to be encountered in new learning. This prediction activity is much like self-questioning in that it sets a purpose for learning and helps students use existing knowledge to direct attention. The *realization* part of the lesson occurs as students interact with the new information. It can be thought of as reading in order to confirm or reject the predictions made before encountering the new information. The *contemplation* part of the lesson occurs after new information is encountered and is used to help students pull information together. Vaughn and Estes describe a number of different activities for each part of the ARC lesson, all of which should lead to improved learning and to student-directed learning. Because a number of different activities can be used in the ARC lesson, it is the most flexible of the three procedures presented here. It is probably best for students who do not need the structure and constraints of reciprocal teaching.

PONDARRS

The third procedure is PONDARRS (Marshall, 1981), a process that is intended to be done with a whole class over a complete unit of instruction. It is time consuming, but it is also the most complete of the three procedures outlined here. The steps in PONDARRS follow:

Preparation for Learning

1. Elicit the *P*rior knowledge of the students relevant to the topic to be learned.
2. *O*rganize the prior knowledge generated in the first step into a *N*etwork or similar visual representation.

Guiding Learning

3. Preview a section of the text or lecture to identify the specific subtopic to be presented.
4. Develop questions based on prior knowledge and concepts expected to be encountered in new learning.
5. Read or listen to Answer the questions. Discuss answers and relate them to questions.
6. Revise the network by adding in new information about the subtopic and reorganizing parts of the network when needed.
7. Repeat steps 3 through 6 for each part of the new information being presented.

Follow-Up

8. Reorganize the network, which has now become very complex and detailed, into a simpler, clearer picture of the students' current understanding of the topic.
9. Create a formal outline from the finalized network.
10. Write a Summary of the topic by developing a sentence for each of the major sections of the outline.

PONDARRS can be used as a whole lesson or in pieces. Its primary strength seems to lie in the continued use of the network throughout all parts of the sequence, but the self-questioning and summarizing steps also help the students.

The Value of Study Strategy Lessons

Lessons like these take instructional time away from the content area information at the beginning of the school year. However, the overall benefits of the lessons include learning and, in the long run, increased speed of learning. Thus, over the academic year, there will be no decrease in the amount of content area information covered, and student performance should increase.

Conclusion

At the beginning of this chapter, several questions were raised about conflicts that can develop between the content to be taught and the desires and interests of the students. The chapter has been an attempt to demonstrate that conflicts need not occur. When teachers take students' existing knowledge of the topic and their preferred ways of learning into account, student learning will improve and subsequent willingness to participate in other learning situations will increase. Teachers who have made use of the instructional strategies summarized in the last section tend to produce comments like the following when answering questions about their attitudes toward their teaching situations:

> Once the students understood what to do, they actually became interested in the lesson. They learned more also.

The networks really helped students understand the content and made them interested in the lesson. Once they learned how to use networks, they began to use them on their own with remarkably positive results.

The biggest difference I noticed was that the students no longer resisted instruction. In fact, they were enthusiastic about participating in the lessons. And their test results proved how successful their learning was.

Think after Reading Activity

A teacher is quoted in the conclusion of this chapter as saying, "The biggest difference I noticed was that the students no longer resisted instruction. In fact, they were enthusiastic about participating in the lessons." Relate how you think the information in this chapter helped that teacher and his or her students.

_____

_____

_____

_____

_____

_____

_____

_____

Activity 7–4

Chapter 8

Engaging Students' Interest and Willing Participation in Subject Area Learning

MARTHA RAPP RUDDELL

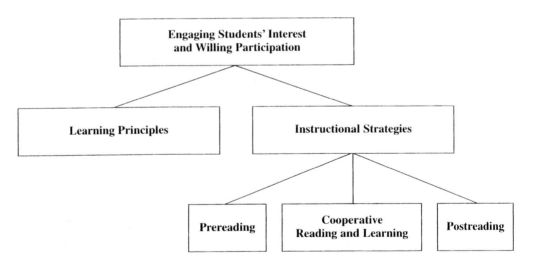

Think before Reading Activity

Thinking back to your days in elementary, middle, or high school, recall which class or classes most engaged your attention and interest. On the lines below, explain what made these classes memorable.

_____

_____

_____

_____

_____

_____

_____

_____

Activity 8–1

This chapter discusses how to activate students' interest and purposeful involvement in learning. Three principles guide the discussion: (1) learning occurs most rapidly and efficiently when new concepts and information build on what is already known; (2) the easiest way to gain and hold students' interest and attention is by engaging them in intellectually rich activities that require problem solving, language interactions, and active participation; and (3) personal identification with and investment in an activity increases and sustains learner persistence and productivity. Specific instructional strategies based on these principles and application of those strategies in various subject areas are presented.

Content area teachers are a unique and diversified group. by inclination and training, we are historians, scientists, athletes, and musicians first, and teachers second. This is not to say that we are not dedicated teachers, but rather to acknowledge that we began with a special interest and talent in a given area, increased and refined our abilities through additional study, and somewhere along the way realized that we wanted to communicate this knowledge and interest to others. We take special pleasure in knowing that we have, in some way, been influential in young people's lives, and we have a strong responsibility for the success and achievement of all students—those who are not like us as well as those who are. Our challenge is to design and implement instruction that promotes interest and involvement where no ready-made interest exists.

Webster's *New World Dictionary* (Guralnik, 1978) defines "interest" as "a feeling of intentness, concern or curiosity about something." In the classroom, and within the context of teaching and learning, interest could be thought of as "manifest curiosity" (A. Manzo, personal communication, 1974)—curiosity that is visible in the attitude and participation of eager, engaged students. Any discussion about how to develop student interest in content subjects must ultimately focus on the question, "How do I stimulate this feeling in my students?"

The purpose of this chapter is to present various instructional approaches for increasing student interest and involvement in learning. A basic premise of the chapter is that although all subject areas are not equally interesting to all students, sound, well-developed instruction that engages students in an interesting process will, to a large degree, override that variation. Critical also is that learning subject area content is our primary goal, and further that subject area textbooks and texts of all types are major sources of information in our classrooms. Instruction designed to enhance interest must therefore account for both the instructional goal (learning content) and the instructional medium (textbook reading).

Learning Principles

Three learning principles serve as the philosophical basis for the instructional strategies presented in this chapter.

Learning occurs most rapidly and efficiently when new concepts and information build on what is already known. Schema theorists (Anderson, 1985; Bransford & Johnson, 1972; Rumelhart, 1984), educators, and others (Newman, 1991; M. Ruddell, 1993; Tierney & Pearson, 1992) have long emphasized the critical role of prior knowledge in learning. Sadoski and his associates (1992) propose further that "concreteness," or ease of imagery, plays a central role in achieving connections between students' prior knowledge base and the comprehension and recall of text. Abstract representations in text thus appear to be considerably more comprehensible when instruction provides opportunity for imagery that assists students in making these important linkages.

The easiest way to gain and hold students' interest and attention is by engaging them in intellectually rich activities that require problem solving, language interactions, and active participation. Over seventy-five years ago, John Dewey (1910) formulated the steps of discovery learning: (1) identification of a problem (a "felt difficulty"), (2) location and definition of the problem, (3) suggestion of possible solutions, (4) reasoning to determine the implication of possible solutions, and (5) observation and testing of hypotheses leading to acceptance or rejection of solutions. Interestingly, the discovery learning approach is markedly similar to the teaching strategies for problem solving and creative thinking that emerged in the 1970s (Covington, Crutchfield, Davies, & Olton, 1972; Davis, 1973; Torrance & Myers, 1974), and shares many characteristics of the cooperative and collaborative learning models of the 1980s and 1990s (Bayer, 1990; Sharan & Sharan, 1986; Slavin, 1990).

Common to the discovery, problem solving and creative thinking, and cooperative learning instructional models is collaborative effort by students as they engage in language interactions to arrive at socially negotiated meanings (Vygotsky, 1986). Along the way, three important cognitive operations serve to lead students toward problem solution. *Divergent thinking,* the search for many solutions, occurs as students brainstorm possibilities. This is followed by *convergent thinking,* the search for the best solution through the processes of evaluation and judgment, the hallmarks of critical thinking (Russell, 1956). Throughout, *question asking* is preeminent as students seek solutions; in fact, the task itself begins with a question: "What is the problem here?" These three cognitive operations, divergent thinking, convergent thinking, and question asking, mediated by group and language interactions, provide the basis for many intellectually rich learning activities in classrooms.

Personal identification with and investment in an activity increases and sustains learner persistence and productivity. In his model of affect in the reading process, Mathewson (1994) suggests that such variables as attitude, motivation, affect, and physical feelings influence the reading process. Rosenblatt (1994) refers to reader stance in relationship to text and the highly individualistic meaning that each reader constructs. Goodman (1985, p. 830) further notes the influence of reader intent:

> consider the effect on comprehension of the intention of each of these readers: (1) a professional proofreader reading for typos, (2) a teacher reading a students' assignment, (3) an editor reading the text for potential publication, (4) a critic reviewing the text (5) a student reading the text as a class assignment.

Think while Reading Activity

In the beginning of the chapter the author states, "The easiest way to gain and hold students' interest and attention is by engaging them in intellectually rich activities." As you read this chapter there will be several effective instructional strategies. Choose one from each group. Describe two ways each strategy engages student interest.

Prereading Strategy

_____

(name of strategy)

Cooperative Learning

_____

(name of strategy)

Postreading

_____

(name of strategy)

_____

_____

_____

_____

_____

Activity 8–2

Generalized from reading and comprehension to all learning, these ideas suggest that, whether consciously or unconsciously, learners make a decision to learn (or not to learn) and approach learning with specific intent that influences both the outcome of instruction and their willingness to persist; this is evident in the wide variation we see in student interest and participation in daily classroom activities. Activities that encourage personal identification and investment in learning have a positive effect on the decision to learn, intention, persistence of the learner, and the outcome of learning (Davidson, 1982; Haggard, 1982, 1986a; Ruddell, 1992, 1993).

Instructional Strategies

These three principles discussed above, which highlight the importance of prior knowledge, collaborative problem solving activities, and student investment in learning, serve as the basis for the instructional strategies we will discuss in the remainder of this chapter. Keep in mind that these activities are simply representative samples, or exemplars, of the type of instruction suggested by the principles upon which this chapter is based, but certainly not the only ones available. The literature abounds with many more. The following discussion describes prereading learning strategies, cooperative reading-learning strategies, and postreading learning strategies.

Prereading Learning Strategies

The *Content Directed Reading-Thinking Activity* (Content DR-TA) (Haggard, 1985; Ruddell, 1993) requires that students work in pairs or small-group teams. The teacher asks teams to work together to list everything they know about a general topic. For example, the teacher might say, "List everything you know about mammals." Students have seven to eight minutes to work while the teacher observes their progress and listens in, from a distance, to see what kind of information is being exchanged. After lists are complete, the teacher announces the specific topic of the reading assignment and asks students to predict which items on their lists they might expect to find in the text. The teacher says, "Today we're going to read about marine mammals. Go back to your list and put a checkmark by anything that you think will be in the reading. Add any new ideas that you might have." Student teams review their lists for two or three minutes, marking items they predict will appear in the text and adding new ones. The teacher assigns the reading and asks students to put an X by items on their lists that they find in the reading. When everyone has finished reading, discussion focuses on how well students predicted what information would appear in the text and on additional new information. This is followed by discussion of major concepts and implementation of additional learning activities.

Langer's *PReP* strategy (1982) is highly similar to Content DR-TA. Intended as a small-group or whole-class activity, it starts with the teacher saying, "Tell anything that comes to your mind when I say _____ [mammal]." Student's free associations with the target word are recorded on the board. Then the teacher asks, "What made you think of _____ [each student's response to the first question]?" After these responses are discussed, the teacher says, "Based on our discussion, have you any new ideas about _____ [mammals]?" Following this, students are ready to read or learn new information about the topic of study.

Both Content DR-TA and PReP are deceptively simple instructional strategies; they are, in fact, elegant solutions to the problem of how to prepare students for learning. In each, students have opportunity to recall and examine prior knowledge, gain information from one another, and develop hypotheses regarding the nature of the information to be learned. Because each requires verbal interaction, the teacher gains access to what students already know (and do not know), and the students themselves gain information from one another. The nature of the initial task ("List everything you know about _____." "Tell anything that comes to your mind when I say _____") brings students' prior knowledge base into concrete terms, thus setting the stage for linkages between their prior knowledge and new information. These, and other instructional strategies, for example, Carr and Ogle's KWL Plus (1987), are highly adaptable to various classroom settings and instructional goals, as demonstrated by the following example.

Jane, a teacher in a combined grade 4 and 5 classroom, spent considerable time preparing for a unit on Native American cultures. She collected numerous reference books from the library and carefully planned reading assignments, class projects, and an introductory lecture and discussion. When she announced to the students that they were going to start a unit on Native American cultures, the students assured her that they "learned all that last year." Altering her plans radically, Jane suggested to the class that if they already knew everything there was to know about Native American cultures, perhaps this information should be recorded. She divided the class into groups, supplied each group with butcher paper and marking pens, and asked the students to write everything they knew about Native American cultures on the paper. While groups worked, she piled the reference books in the center of the room, and she directed students' attention to the books when the lists were complete. Jane speculated that there might be some information in the books that was not on any list and asked students to choose a book, return to their group to verify information on the group list, and add any new information found in the reference books. In subsequent whole-class discussion, groups presented their finding and formulated topics for group research projects. Thus, a very successful unit on Native American cultures was launched.

Steps for Planning and Teaching Content DR-TA and PReP

Content DR-TA

1. Ask student teams to list everything they know about a general topic (e.g., sharks, addition, the Mississippi River).
2. Announce the specific topic (e.g., varieties of sharks, adding 3-place numerals, lessons of the Mississippi).
3. Ask students to predict what information on their lists will appear in the text and to add any new ideas to their lists.
4. Have students read the assignment and note how well they predicted what would appear and what they added.

5. Lead a short discussion about what students knew before they read and what new information they found ("How well did you predict?" or "What were some of the things you knew before we read? What are some new things you found?").

PReP

1. Decide what key concept you wish to focus students' attention on before reading the story or text.
2. Choose the stimulus word, picture, or event to focus students' attention on the topic. Prepare any materials you need to prepare.
3. Prepare your stimulus question (e.g., "What do you think of when I say 'friendship'?" or "What comes to mind as you look at this picture?").
4. Record students' responses on the chalk board as they respond to the stimulus question.
5. After children have responded, point to specific responses recorded on the chalk board and ask individuals, "What made you think of this when I said '[initial stimulus question]'?"
6. Extend the original question. "Based on our discussion, do you have any new ideas about [concept]?"
7. Guide students into the reading. "Our story is about . . .; what do you think we might find in the story?"

Cooperative Reading-Learning Strategies

Cooperative reading-learning activities require three conditions. First, activities must have students working in pairs or small-group teams toward clearly articulated goals. These goals may be determined through teacher decision, students decision, or a combination of the two. Second, students need to sit at tables or group desk arrangements with free access to resource materials so they can work together with the least amount of noise, movement, and confusion. Third, working arrangements and procedures must be structured to increase student efficiency and decrease problems. For example, rules establishing the number of people who can be out of their seats or at a given resource area at a time set limits to the amount of classroom movement while at the same time instilling a sense of responsibility in students. In activities requiring communication between groups, a sensible strategy is to have each group select a representative who may visit other groups to transmit or receive needed information. In this way, the cooperative learning classroom environment is open and supportive, rather than closed and prohibitive (Hudgins et al., 1983); at the same time, it is structured with clear guides for student behavior (Ruddell, 1993).

The *Group Reading Activity* (GRA) (Manzo, 1974; Manzo & Manzo, 1990) divides responsibility for initial learning and presentation of topic information among five or six small groups in the classroom. The teacher determines the divisions (e.g., in the marine mammals unit, the subtopics may be baleen whales, toothed whales, eared seals, earless seals, otters) and assigns a topic and corresponding textbook reading to each group. Additional resources are available in the room. Groups must determine what is the most important information in the reading, and how that information can best be presented to the rest of the class. Presentation options include written summaries and outlines, oral reports, panel discussion, plays, and multimedia presentations. Toward the end of group deliberation, the teacher selects one member of each group to visit another group in the role of critic. Each group outlines their idea to the visiting critic, who provides feedback and additional ideas for the group to consider. After critics have returned to their original groups, plans are revised and presented to the teacher, who assists in the final planning. Groups then do the requisite preparation and present the information to the class. After presentations, students are encouraged to "speed read" the material for which they were not responsible, and the class, with teacher guidance, decides what areas of the unit need further reading and study and makes arrangements for follow-up.

The *Creative Thinking-Reading Activities* (CT-RA) (Haggard, 1978, 1979, 1980; Ruddell, 1993) are short, ten- or fifteen-minute warm-up activities for increasing students' problem solving and critical-creative reading abilities. Standard creative thinking tasks (e.g., product improvement, unusual uses, What would happen if?) are used for small groups of students (or partners) to generate as many solutions as they can. For example, groups might be asked to list as many ways they can think of to improve school desks. Then using a single criterion (e.g., Which improvement do you think would be most useful?), groups select one, or combine several, of their ideas to arrive at a final answer (one of my groups decided that school desks should have hydraulic lifts so that the student in the back of the room could see as well as those in the front). Group answers are then shared with the whole class. This type of thinking and problem solving is transferred to content-specific reading and learning by the simple expedient of the teacher reminding students to "use your CT-RA kind of thinking" as they address such issues as finding the solution to urban crime, or how to measure volume, or unravel the mysteries of ancient Egypt.

The Group Reading Activity and Creative Thinking-Reading Activities, as other such cooperative learning approaches, for example, Jigsaw Grouping (Aaronson, et al., 1978; Slavin, 1990), Group Investigation (Sharan & Sharan, 1986), and Collaborative-Apprenticeship Learning (Bayer, 1990), emphasize group problem solving as a central aspect of learning. In each, students share information and expertise, interact with one another, and work through ideas collaboratively; through the processes of divergent thinking and speculation, question asking, convergent thinking, and evaluation and judgment, they negotiate toward solutions.

Doug, a student teacher, chose to introduce a marine mammal unit by bringing to class skeletons and skeletal parts of marine mammals he had collected. Student groups were given one of the skeletons, an information card to assist in its identification, and numerous resource books. Students were asked to assume the role of biologists and to work together to identify the animal, its characteristics, and its life habits. As groups worked, Doug circulated among them, assisting and giving guidance when needed. Initial findings were then presented to the class, and ideas for further group study presented.

Steps for Planning and Teaching GRA and CT-RA

GRA

1. Determine the material to be studied and the lesson or unit objectives.
2. Divide the reading material into four, five, or six topic sections.

3. Establish four, five, or six cross-ability and cross-status groups; the number of groups should correspond to the number of topic sections established.
4. Assign one topic section of the reading material to each group; each group is to determine (1) what is the most important information in the section, (2) what other information is needed to understand the topic, and (3) how the group can best present the topic to the rest of the class.
5. Appoint one student critic from each group to go to another group to listen to that group's plan for presenting its material to the class.
6. Allow time for the student critic to make constructive recommendations.
7. Consult with each group regarding its plans for presentation.
8. Allow time for presentations to be finalized.
9. Have groups present.
10. Conduct full-class discussion for further clarification and research or project ideas.

CT-RA

1. Design or adapt from published materials creative thinking tasks in the categories of "What would happen if [houses could fly, we had eyes in the backs of our heads, everyone in the world spoke the same language, numbers meant something different every day]?" "Think of all the unusual uses you can for [any common object—paper clip, brick, shoe]" and "How would you improve [school desks, soda cans, teddy bears]?"
2. Develop with students the rules for brainstorming:
   a. Think of as many ideas as you can.
   b. No criticism of any ideas—even your own.
   c. Go for freewheeling thought—the wilder the idea the better.
   d. Build on others' ideas and combine ideas when you can.
3. Give students the creative thinking task (only one) and allow five minutes for brainstorming.
4. Share ideas in large group.
5. Announce single criterion for students to evaluate and select an answer; for example, "Which of your unusual uses do you think is the wildest?" or "How would you market your new, improved teddy bear?"
6. Share these responses.
7. Find opportunities in subject learning instructional events to have students use their "CR-TA thinking" to solve problems.

Postreading Learning Activities

The *Group Mapping Activity* (GMA) (Davidson, 1982) is a means for students to record their personal response to literature or to organize content information after reading. In the GMA, students are directed to "Map your perceptions of what the story (or chapter) was about," and allowed time to develop maps in whatever way they choose. Maps are then shared with the class and discussed regarding individual student's views of the materials read and choices for representing that information in his or her map. Student maps are therefore not right or wrong, but rather personalized statements of students' understanding of main ideas, relationships, and important information in text. Haggard (1985; Ruddell, 1993) suggests that maps developed for subject area study be shared first with partners in a discussion of how each partner organized her or his map and why that organization was chosen. Partners are then responsible for assuring that both maps, regardless of organizational plan, contain sufficient information to serve as guides for continuing and future study.

Maps are particularly useful for response to daily reading assignments and may grow and change as new reading provides additional information about a given topic. They serve also as useful prewriting aids and as the basis for instruction in such skills as outlining, summarizing, and stating main ideas. More importantly, they provide opportunity for intense discussion in which "students ask each other about various elements in their maps, agree with shared interpretations of the passage, or disagree with various interpretations. Students challenge one another, and their questions and responses represent high levels of critical thinking" (Davidson, 1982, pp. 55–56).

The *Vocabulary Self-Collection Strategy* (VSS) (Haggard, 1982, 1985, 1986a; Ruddell, 1992, 1993) is intended to foster long-term vocabulary growth and promote the acquisition and development of the language of academic disciplines (Ruddell, 1993). After reading, student teams (partners or small groups) identify words or terms in the reading assignment which they wish to learn or know more about. Each team nominates one word or term and tells (1) where they found the word, (2) what they think it means in this context, and (3) why they think the class should learn it. The teacher also nominates a word. During class discussion, words are put on the board, defined first from context and group knowledge, and then, if needed, from any references available. A final list is established by eliminating duplicates and words already known. Chosen words are then redefined and written with definitions in vocabulary journals or entered on maps (Haggard, 1985; Ruddell, 1993). Words not chosen for class study may be recorded by students who wish to learn them.

Various follow-up activities support and increase students' learning of their VSS words. These activities should (1) allow students to use new words in a meaningful way, (2) allow students opportunity to associate new words and concepts with their own experience, (3) develop associations with other words, (4) develop higher-level thinking skills, (5) lead students to many different resources, and (6) acknowledge the social nature of learning (Haggard, 1986b; Ruddell, 1993).

Semantic Mapping (Johnson, Toms-Bronowski, & Pittelman, 1981; Dyer, 1985; Heimlich & Pittelman, 1986) is an activity that has students in groups record all their associations with a given word (e.g., "government"). When ideas run out, students then group their associations into categories, label the categories, and develop a semantic map showing the original word and its relationship to the categories and associations. *Word Treasure Hunts* (Haggard, 1986b) direct students to "Find out everything you can about the word _____. Check several resources, ask your friends, ask your parents or others." Information collected is brought back to the group, shared, compiled and mapped.

Semantic Feature Analysis (Johnson, Toms-Bronowski, & Pittelman, 1981; Anders & Bos, 1986; Pittelman, Heimlich, Bergland, & French, 1991) presents vocabulary words and associated words and features on a grid (see Figure 8–1). Students working in groups

ILLUMINATION	Heat Producing	Beamed	Fluorescent	Incandescent
Flashlight				
Sunlight				
Candle				
Streetlamp				
Headlight				

FIGURE 8–1   Semantic Feature Analysis: Illumination

indicate which features and words match by marking a plus (+) in intersecting squares and a minus (–) for those that do not. Following this, students are invited to add to the words and features lists, and complete the exercise with the additions. Further discussions may be stimulated by replacing the yes-no (+/–) coding with "always," "sometimes," "never" criteria using additional coding symbols.

The value of GMA and VSS, and other such postreading strategies—for example, Question/Answer Relationships (QAR) (Raphael, 1986)—is the very strong personal identification with learning that students develop. *Their* ideas and response to text are validated; *their* words become central to class study of a unit or topic. The enthusiasm generated by personal investment in and commitment to learning is quite real and highly contagious. Almost without realizing it, students become captivated by the process and willingly exert greater effort and energy on the product. This may not happen immediately; students, from the most avid to the most reluctant, are all too used to copying literal responses and the shortest definition possible from textbooks and dictionaries. When confronted with activities that require active response and personal choice, they don't believe: They don't believe there really is not a "right" or "wrong" way to map; they don't believe their nominated words will really be used for the class vocabulary list. The antidote to this reaction is time and perseverance.

Katherine was a teacher with a high-track grade 11 English class. She decided to introduce VSS in that class because she felt those student would be receptive to it. As part of a reading homework assignment, she asked students to select a word they wanted to learn or know more about from the text to nominate for a class vocabulary list. Fewer than half the class brought words the next day. Discussion was desultory, at best. The following week,

---

Think while Reading Activity

Semantic feature analysis is a great vocabulary strategy. It helps students learn to develop associations between words. Please complete the semantic feature analysis included in this chapter (see Figure 8–1). Then complete the chart below.

Modes of Transportation				
	Gas Powered	Your Choice	Wheels	Your Choice
Car				
Motorcycle				
Canoe				
Your Choice				

Activity 8–3

---

with another story, she made the same assignment; everything changed. Almost all the class chose words, discussion was enthusiastic, and debate over the class list was lively. By the third assignment, she had the full support and participation of the entire class.

Steps for Planning and Teaching GMA and VSS

GMA

1. After the reading, ask children to construct maps. Use the following means to clarify the mapping task:
   a. "A map is a diagram of what you think the chapter (or text) is about. There is no right or wrong way to map. You may use words, shapes, or pictures on your map."
   b. Show dummy maps (maps you've made up in advance), saying, "A map may look like this . . . like this . . . or like this."
   c. "Do not look back at the text while you're mapping. You may look back at it later."
2. Have students display maps "so we can see how different they are."
3. Ask students to share their maps by telling how they mapped and why they chose to do it that way. Use prompts and questions to clarify and extend their thinking.

VSS

1. After reading (or other learning event), ask student groups to find a word or term that they would like to know or learn more about. Students are to be prepared to:

    a. Identify the word or term in context
    b. Tell where they found it
    c. Tell what they think the word or term means
    d. Tell why they think the word or term should be on the class vocabulary list

2. Accept word nominations with discussion of possible meanings and reasons for learning (*a* through *d* above). Encourage extension and refinement of meanings through collaboration and pooling of information.
3. Nominate the word you wish to have on the list and supply all of the requisite information (*a* through *d* above).
4. Narrow the class list to a predetermined number (if needed).
5. Refine definitions as needed for each word or term.
6. Direct students to record the final list words and definitions (as developed in class discussion) in vocabulary journals, on maps, or where you wish.
7. Develop VSS lesson activities for reinforcement.
8. Provide time for students to complete lesson activities assignments.
9. Incorporate vocabulary items into an end-of-unit or spelling test as appropriate.

Conclusion

The prereading, cooperative, and postreading learning strategies presented here are all intended to increase student interest in learning and to encourage the manifest curiosity that comes with internal motivation and need to know. These activities derive from the three learning principles cited earlier: (1) learning occurs most rapidly and efficiently when new concepts and information build on what is already known; (2) the easiest way to gain and hold students' interest and attention is by engaging them in intellectually rich activities that require problem solving, language interactions, and active participation; and (3) personal identification with and investment in an activity increases and sustains learner persistence and productivity. The manner in which each activity satisfies these learning principles is summarized in Figure 8–2. The components of each activity are listed; the principles applicable to each component follow in bold print. Please note that in each component, significant language interactions occur.

These activities share three additional characteristics worth mentioning. First, they represent an approach to teaching in which the learner, rather than the teacher, is the central focus of instruction. This does not suggest that the teacher assumes a passive role. Quite the contrary. The teacher's role is highly active: planning instruction; establishing the structure necessary for successful implementation; observing, assisting, and guiding students and groups as they work; and assessing and adjusting the process on a daily and possibly minute-to-minute basis to meet instructional and classroom needs. In the meantime, it is students who are talking, exploring ideas, examining questions, looking for answers, and making decisions.

The effectiveness of such an approach is evident in the quality of learning and enthusiasm it generates. Teachers often find it difficult to interrupt small-group discussions to move students on to another stage of the process. Conversation and debate continue well beyond the stipulated time period, and often outside the classroom itself. When that hap-

Content Directed Reading-Thinking Activity (Content DR-TA)

1. Listing everything known about a general topic — **Prior knowledge.**
2. Predicting items that will be in text about a specific topic — **Problem solving;**
   Investment in learning.
3. Marking ideas while reading — **Investment in learning.**

Prereading Plan (PREP)

1. Free association with topic — **Prior knowledge.**
2. Reasons for associations — **Investment in learning.**
3. New ideas about topic — **Problem solving.**

Group Reading Activity (GRA)

1. Small-group reading and discussion — **Prior knowledge.**
2. Deciding what information is most important — **Problem solving; Investment in learning.**
3. Determining mode of presentation — **Problem solving; Investment in learning.**
4. Presenting ideas to critic and making revisions based on critic's advice — **Problem solving;**
   Investment in learning.
5. Determining areas for further study — **Problem solving; Investment in learning.**

Creative Thinking-Reading Activities (CT-RA)

1. Brainstorming many solutions — **Prior knowledge; Investment in learning.**
2. Choosing best solution — **Problem solving.**
3. Application of solution to problem — **Investment in learning.**

Group Mapping Activity (GMA)

1. Individual mapping after reading — **Prior knowledge; Investment in learning;**
   Problem solving.
2. Sharing and discussing maps — **Investment in learning; Prior knowledge.**

Vocabulary Self-Collection Strategy (VSS)

1. Nomination and context definition of words — **Prior knowledge; Investment in learning.**
2. Selection of class word list — **Investment in learning; Problem solving.**
3. Refining definitions and follow-up vocabulary activities — **Problem solving.**

FIGURE 8–2   Instructional Activities and Learning Principles

pens, when students do not want to stop learning, we have indeed made magic happen in the classroom. We have captured students' interest and the energy it creates and transformed it into self-directed learning.

A second characteristic shared by these strategies is the high level of support provided for all learners. This support is evident in the emphasis on peer interaction in small-group and partnership settings, where students "have substantial opportunity to speculate, raise questions, try out new ideas, or 'not know' something in a safe, cooperative environment" (Haggard, 1985, p. 209). In essence, it allows rehearsal time before the solo performance of saying something smart in front of thirty other people. Support is also provided by provision in these activities for students to use a wide variety of learning resources beyond the designated classroom text; thus, students are able not only to find materials suited to their own particular interest and achievements levels, but also to perceive how such materials and books are central, rather than supplementary, to the curriculum as a whole (Ruddell, 1993). Support for learning, through cooperative effort and use of wide resources, yields much more learning opportunity for many more students and is particularly valuable in classrooms where language, cultural, and other kinds of diversity are the norm. Important also is that this support, in itself, increases students participation and interest in learning.

The third characteristic shared by the strategies presented in this chapter is their simplicity; all of them are marked by relatively few directions, steps, or constraints. Certainly, each has a general flow of instruction, but within that, flexibility exists for adaptation to a wide variety of classroom needs, student abilities, and teaching styles. This feature is significant. In his research on the "influential teacher," Robert Ruddell (1980) found that high school students place high value on good teaching. When asked to identify teachers who had been influential in their lives and indicate the nature of that influence, 47 percent of student responses fell into the category Quality of Instruction. Subsequent studies (Ruddell & Haggard, 1982; Ruddell & Kern, 1986) found that these influential teachers, characterized by their students as good teachers, represented many different teaching styles. Ruddell and Kern (1986, pp. 145–146) conclude:

> There is no one "best way" to teach, but rather, there are many ways of implementing effective instruction. . . . The teacher needs to be thought of as an *active decision maker,* not as merely a performer of isolated techniques. In order to make felicitous decisions, a teacher needs to be sensitive to the student's prior knowledge and belief, aware of the classroom dynamic, and flexible in both establishing goals and implementing plans appropriately.

The simplicity of the activities presented here not only allows but encourages flexibility and adaptation. Specific strategies may be used singly or in a variety of combinations. For example, a teacher might wish to initiate instruction with PReP, lead directly into a Group Reading Activity, and follow up with Vocabulary Self-Collection; or, he or she could combine Content DR-TA with the Group Mapping Activity and VSS. CT-RAs may be implemented with any content-focused problem; those using the stem "What would happen if?" are applicable to any subject area. Further, these instructional strategies may be used with various media (films, videotapes, lectures, demonstrations) simply by engaging the class in an event alternative to reading. These strategies are robust. Not only are they amenable to wide variation in mode and method of implementation, they yield large results with relatively little expenditure in planning time, resources, materials development, and change of classroom routine.

In the final analysis, it is we, as teachers, who provide the critical instruction that links students' lives with the subject matter so meaningful and important to us. When we do not do this, we must understand what Smith and Elliott (1979, p. 23) make so poignantly clear:

> Our subject area . . . has not been singled out by the students as the [area] in which they are refusing to be interested. They are refusing it on exactly the same basis that they would refuse to be interested in denture cream, retirement plans, or support hosiery. They are not willing to spend their time and energies on things for which they see not real-life transfer or payoff.

The instructional strategies we have discussed demonstrate real-life transfer to students by engaging their prior knowledge base, involving them in collaborative problem-solving situations, and encouraging personal investment in learning. The emphasis on problem solving through cooperative effort encourages student interest and willing participation in the learning event. This in turn results in real learning and accomplishment for all students in all subject areas. That, then, is the payoff—the internal gratification that such accomplishment brings, not only to students but to teachers as well. Use of these strategies and the many others like them makes learning—and teaching—interesting, exciting, and ultimately, worthwhile.

Think after Reading Activity

Design an instructional activity based on one or more of the strategies presented in this chapter. Select one that you believe will engage students' attention and interest in a concept, idea, or piece of information associated with your content area. (You might want to collaborate with a partner from another content area in order to create an interdisciplinary lesson.) Briefly outline the activity.

Content Area:

_____

_____

_____

Information/Concept/Idea:

_____

_____

_____

Activity:

_____

_____

_____

_____

Rationale:

_____

_____

_____

_____

Activity 8–4

Context for Secondary Reading Programs

CARL SMITH

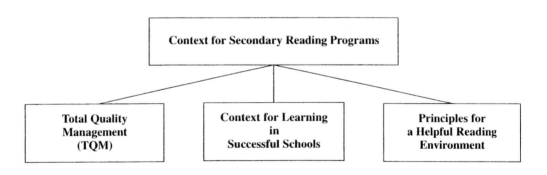

Think before Reading Activity

Your neighbors are thinking about sending their child to a high school you really think is terrific. This might be a real school you attended or one you dream about. What characteristics make it outstanding?

_____

_____

_____

_____

_____

_____

_____

_____

Activity 9–1

How do successful schools approach their jobs differently from other schools? This chapter presents results of a study conducted in twenty-three successful schools. In this study, parents, students and others identified characteristics that they judged as significant contributors to the success of their schools. These characteristics are analyzed and applied to a context for secondary reading programs.

Total Quality Management

This chapter is not about school management, or if it is, only by coincidence. Rather, it is about principles of behavior for those who participate in successful schools. When seen from the perspective of recent management theory, much of what is described in this chapter fits into an approach called "Total Quality Management." Originally publicized through the writings of Deming (1987) and Garvin (1988), Total Quality Management is a philosophy that focuses on the needs of customers and on the achievement of quality-oriented objectives. In this philosophy, customers include coworkers, as well as those people who pay for services. If we applied those terms to the school environment, our customers would be students and parents as well as our teacher colleagues (Bunstingly, 1992; Fruston, 1992).

The attitudes reflected in the successful schools described here show a concern for all participants in the learning environment. Students, of course, are the primary recipients of the school's educational services, but teachers and parents are important customers, too. One of the major principles of Total Quality Management is that all participants in the enterprise need information, and they all need to feel that they are contributing valuable energy to the school's outcome. This principle reminds the teacher to open the learning circle to other teachers and to parents.

If a school creates a context for learning that clearly involves students, parents, and all teachers in a cooperative enterprise, it enhances the possibility that all parties will achieve some of the results that they seek. Most of the balance of this chapter reviews the characteristics of successful schools in order to derive operating principles that can guide others who wish to create a context for effective learning.

Students as Beneficiaries

He turned this school around with a single directive: *Prove that what you want to do is for the benefit of the student.*

That's as close to magic as you're going to get—turning a school around with a single directive. But in a study of effective schools, the parents and teachers of one New York school said the principal had worked that magic. He had turned their school from a mediocre high school to a recognized, highly effective school with one directive over a five-year period. When he met with teachers and parents soon after assuming the principal's role, he said: "I will change courses, reorganize programs, find staff and money—it doesn't matter. But first you must prove to me that what you want to do will benefit your students."

He did not waiver in his resolve. No matter the proposal, his first (and sometimes his only) statement was: "Prove that it will benefit the students." By doing that, he created a small revolution in the school. He turned everyone's attention to the reason for schooling—to benefit the learning of the boys and girls in the school. The atmosphere and the academic results in that high school were a major tribute to that principal's ability to focus attention and to his persistence in sticking to his resolve.

Context for Learning in Successful Schools

Highly successful schools seem to approach their job differently from other schools. We can infer that difference from the responses of parents, teachers, and students in successful schools who were asked to label the causes of success in their schools (Smith, 1986). What emerges from their responses is a sense of community rather different from what most of us experience in the schools where we work. Let's examine the causes identified by parents, students, and teachers and apply them to a context for a secondary reading program. For each of these groups we will list their top four or five causes and give examples of what they meant in some schools.

The schools in the study were located in urban, suburban, and rural areas of various parts of the country. In small groups of six to eight, participants responded to the general question "What do you think causes the success you have in this school?" Respondents then fed ideas to each other. They were encouraged to agree and to disagree with the comments of their peers and to try providing specific examples of what caused them to agree or to disagree with a statement about a cause of success. In that way, generalizations were supported or defeated by concrete examples.

Parents Analyze Success

Although it may be assumed that parents see schools primarily through the eyes of their children, parents who participated in the interviews also participated in some way in the school program. They were PTO officers, classroom volunteers, and members of curriculum committees. When asked what caused the success of their schools, their most frequent responses were:

1. My child likes to go there.
2. In this school we have choices.
3. The school provides regular communication.
4. We have a well-organized administrator.

My Child Likes to Go There

Liking to go to school is a symptom of what goes on in the school. Their children wanted to go to the successful school they now attended. The reasons: they were treated with respect; they felt like individuals; teachers were concerned with their well-being and their personal interests in addition to their academic pursuits. It may seem a bit far-fetched to list "liking to go" as the number one cause, but parents saw that as a sure indicator of the school's success. In their own way, parents were saying that the school knew how to interest boys and girls in the life of the school community—no small feat.

We Have Choices

When parents have the sense of making choices regarding school, clearly something different has happened. Because the typical public school situation ties students to an assigned school and to assigned teachers, parents' feelings that they could choose among alternatives reflect the variety of ways that they participated in the decision making regarding their children. Those alternatives included being able to select the school they wanted, selecting the teachers they preferred, and participating in curriculum decisions.

Their sense of choice was also associated with being on curriculum committees and being able to discuss course choices with department heads and with counselors along with their children. It meant being able to make schedule adjustments when something did not work out, whether based on a pupil-teacher conflict or a decision that the course was not beneficial. One feature that secondary parents felt was particularly helpful was the opportunity to make appointments with teachers and counselors during times set aside for choosing courses. They felt that gave them a chance to discuss the specific needs of their children and to ask for assistance in working out those needs.

Regular Communication

Even the secondary schools in this study were praised for the regular communications they had with the home. Not only did these schools mail home monthly newsletters that included departmental or school activities, but teachers in these schools were encouraged by policy to inform parents when their child had made some significant progress. In one school, teachers were provided with "happygram" postcards that they mailed to parents to let them know the good news.

GOOD NEWS!

Dear Parent:

Henry's recent paper on the elections showed a nice sense of organization, something he's been working on. I am pleased and thought you would want to know.

Sincerely,

Teacher

Those schools also had a communication policy that worked in favor of problem cases. As problems began to emerge, they were confronted as early as reasonable. Problems that involved drugs, truancy, or other serious infractions were quickly referred to school officials for action.

Well-Organized Administrator

Parents praised administrators for maintaining firm and fair discipline, running a good meeting, knowing what's going on in the school, and bringing together department heads or teachers to meet with parents when the teachers' knowledge and participation would be helpful.

Students Analyze Success

Students, from their own perspective, gave some causes for success similar to those of their parents, but they also listed different ones.

1. School isn't boring.
2. There is a sense of order.
3. We have good books and materials.
4. The teachers like kids.
5. Kids help each other.

It Isn't Boring

Students' most frequently mentioned cause—it isn't boring—is similar to the number one item on the parents' list. Students in highly successful schools saw their school as different from others they had attended or knew about. In successful schools, students engaged in project work and were challenged to compare their textbook readings with readings from other books. Teachers helped students see why their work was important beyond the classroom. The last comment fits nicely with Kounin's characteristic for an effective teacher—one who makes the routine of the classroom seem real (1982).

A Sense of Order

Only a few students in the study emphasized the value of strong discipline when speaking of a sense of order in their schools. In one large urban school, however, students listed discipline and a safe environment as their number one cause for success. Most other students gave examples of the help they received with academics:

> In this school we know what it takes to succeed.
>
> Teachers give us clear guidelines for each course.
>
> If we have problems, we get help.
>
> Teachers let us in on the secrets.
>
> Teachers show us what to do instead of just telling us to do it.

Some of these comments by students will seem more integrated when joined with reactions from teachers in these same schools; the revealing aspect of students' comments is that they not only recognize order and direction, but also list it as one of the primary causes for success of their school.

We Have Good Books

Students in these schools praised their books and materials. They felt that they had better books and materials than students in other schools, but in fact, they had similar textbooks and library books as might be found in a large percentage of schools in the country. In other words, teachers made the books in these schools seem better.

Teachers Like Kids

Parents said the same thing. What students recalled about their teachers is that they took a personal interest in them. Teachers discussed students' ideas about their subjects. They remembered and talked about things that were going on in students' lives outside the classroom.

Students Help Each Other

As students analyzed their schools, the attitudes expressed by students for one another was the fifth most frequent cause for success. Their comments reflected a sense of friendliness, but more than that. There were also numerous illustrations of one student helping another. Perhaps more teachers in these schools formed peer tutoring groups or cooperative learning groups. At least students commented on feeling comfortable working with classmates both in and outside the classroom.

Think while Reading Activity

Smith states that "The attitudes reflected in the successful schools . . . show a concern for all participants in the learning environment." One component of a successful school is regular school-home communications. Suppose that you are lucky enough to work in such a school. Review what you've read so far in this chapter and begin to draft a short letter below to your students' parents that (1) gives some news information about your class and (2) invites parents in any way they choose to support the school-home connection.

Complete your draft as you read further in the chapter.

Dear _____ :

_____

_____

_____

_____

_____

_____

_____

_____

_____

_____

Activity 9-2

Teachers List Causes of Success

Just as there were similarities and differences between the causes listed by parents and those listed by students, so there are similarities and differences in the causes of success identified by teachers. Teachers operate on the inside of the system and have a better sense of the planning and relationships among various levels of personnel in the school. They thus have the opportunity of assigning causes of success from a different perspective from parents and students. Their top five causes were:

1. We cooperate and share ideas.
2. Parents cooperate.
3. We have common goals and materials.
4. We are given freedom to explore new ideas.
5. Our administrator is very supportive.

When the desires and backgrounds of many teachers are put together, it may seem impossible to arrive at agreement on priorities for instruction and human respect, but some schools do accomplish that end. Two schools in the survey said they "agreed to agree." They decided the only feasible way they could make significant progress was to agree on three or four priorities each year and to monitor their progress toward achieving those priorities. "We agreed to agree on three!" After they selected the top three priorities for the school, they could then pursue their own personal priorities. First, though, they pursued the common goals of the school. Setting goals and priorities in a democratic fashion is also a basic principle in the philosophy of Total Quality Management.

Freedom to Explore New Ideas

Everyone wants freedom, especially in the United States where the very word demands reverence. Some readers may have predicted that personal freedom would be the number one cause of success. If fairy godmothers granted wishes, probably most teachers would ask for the freedom to do what they desire in their classrooms, but teachers in this survey recognized an important nuance in their vision of freedom. Their analysis of the cause of success revealed that they were indeed free to explore new ideas—as long as those ideas were for the clear benefit of the child. The principal described at the outset of this chapter might be held as the role model for other school personnel in this study.

Freedom in these schools was dependent on teacher cooperation, parent cooperation, and adherence to common goals and materials. It was freedom to help children grow within a common plan, within a community base. The textbook and the common goals of the faculty constituted a base from which students and teachers could explore ideas, wherever they saw a clear benefit.

Supportive Administrator

Other studies of successful schools have put the school administrator at the head of the list of reasons for success (Edmonds, 1982). After looking at administrative differences between high-scoring schools and those with lower scores, these studies concluded that the principal or the chief administrator was central to successful performance. Teachers saw it differently.

It was not organizational ability or the curriculum leadership of the administrator that teachers saw as causes of their school's success. In fact, some of them commented about other schools where they had taught under well-organized principals, where the principal frequently discussed curriculum and paid much attention to it, but they did not consider those other schools particularly successful. They lacked some of the other ingredients that we have been discussing here: teacher cooperation and common goals agreed to by the faculty. These teachers then turned the cause in a slightly different direction. It was not the organization of the principal that was critical. It was his or her support of the common effort of the school. The true cause here, they said, was a supportive administrator.

When administrators show respect for the objectives of teachers, parents, and students, they see their leadership role as one that involves supporting the personnel instead of merely organizing or pushing certain curriculum plans. That attitude creates a sense of community where everyone learns and works together. Teachers, parents, and administrators all concern themselves with helping students. They work cooperatively to help students grow, and in the process they also learn and grow.

Principles for Successful Learning

If we were to review the causes listed by students, parents, and teachers, we would find in them the principles for successful learning, no matter what the subject. Let's extract from the list of causes those principles that seem most applicable to reading at the secondary level. One might contend that all of them are applicable because they all contribute to a healthy learning environment, but it will be most beneficial for us to examine those over which teachers exercise a high degree of control.

From all the causes listed by students, parents, and teachers, one could abstract three principles to guide the classroom teacher in creating a helpful context for reading instruction. Those principles are related to motivation and interest, goals and order, and mutual support.

1. The reading context should capture the interest of the students and encourage active participation.
2. It should be clear to the student what the objectives are and that those objectives can be met in an orderly fashion.
3. Reading and learning should be conducted in an atmosphere of mutual support that involves parents, teachers, and administrators, as well as students.

Interest and Motivation

As important as this principle is, one almost hesitates to list it first because motivation is so often confused with bells and whistles. Students do not need to read adventure comics in order to think reading is stimulating. Students in the study thought their books and materials were good because their teachers and perhaps their parents made those books appear to be special. They communicated their own excitement about the contents of books. Students became interested because the books were available for solving problems and for developing projects. They often worked in teams to explore the ideas that appeared in the books, so their image of reading was not passive; they were active participants in the process of learning.

Visits to these schools expanded the image of activity. Even though textbooks were the usual starting points for a discussion, other books were brought into the picture. Students were asked to build a bridge between ideas in books and ideas in their minds. They were asked to solve issues that were raised in their text by exploring the answers in other books and magazines. What made these classrooms interesting was the stimulating thought that was taking place, not the difference in the materials that were available.

Certainly teachers and parents want their classrooms to be as bright and motivating as possible. Video materials, computers, magazines, as well as the traditional textbooks should be resources for learning and for learning to read more effectively, but all these materials could be present and the students would still fall asleep and rate the class as boring. Just as teachers want the freedom to explore new ideas, so do students. Just as teachers saw a responsible connection between freedom and their obligation to their students, so can students see that their own long-term interest and their present motivation need to be tied to responsible objectives. Otherwise, motivating activities are titillating but unsubstantial.

Goals and Order

Although it may be surprising that students recognize the need for order in the classroom, they expressed their desire for order in successful schools. Naturally, that sense of order was related to goal-setting activities that the faculty engaged in, but the faculty of these schools did not set goals and then hide them under their jackets. They communicated these goals to the students and showed them how to reach them. "They let us in on the secrets."

If students and teachers are working cooperatively to learn, then both have to know the objectives of learning. That means teachers and students have to discuss frankly what they want to achieve. It means that teachers help students understand the objectives for learning and the systems for reaching their goals. In reading secondary textbooks and related materials, those goals might include techniques and strategies for handling descriptions, complicated directions or formulas, persuasive essays, and so on. Also, these goals would fit into the more pertinent goals of solving problems that arise in reading subject-matter material.

Mutual Support

The notion of collaboration receives considerable attention in education, but the concept should not be limited to students working together. Teachers, parents, and administrators also require mutual support as they work for the benefit of students. It is especially important that they approach their task in a spirit of collaboration. That attitude and effort should be high on the agenda of adults who work with students at the secondary level.

An attitude of cooperative effort among parents, teachers, and administrators becomes workable when these adults keep students as the focus of their efforts. For some teachers and administrators, this means a deliberate effort to draw parents into the work of education and to establish an unmistakable policy that parents too are responsible for their children's learning.

Conclusion

Just as a philosophy of Total Quality Management in the business world opens the eyes of workers to see their internal as well as their external customers, successful schools do the same thing. The successful school understands that superior outcomes do not result from the intense work of one teacher working with one superior student. The successful school is one that helps students, teachers, and parents feel that they are all successful. They serve each other as providers and as customers in the school environment. That sense of school quality, of school success, arises from a commitment by all parties to help one another. They start with common goals, share information, accept their individual responsibilities, and feel the reward of mutual respect. In that kind of context, content reading will thrive—as will all sorts of other learning.

Think after Reading Activity

The intent of the information in this chapter is to help you reflect on the context for effective schools. Perhaps you found yourself comparing your own educational experiences with the successful schools discussed in this chapter. Hopefully some of your own experiences were catalogued here. Look back on your list from the Think before Reading Activity and add any other effective educational practices that you were introduced to as you read this chapter.

_____

_____

_____

_____

_____

_____

_____

Activity 9–3

C h a p t e r *10*

Students Acquiring English

Reading and Learning

ELEANOR W. THONIS

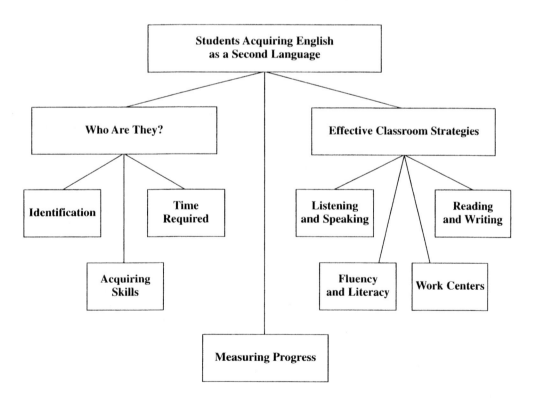

Think before Reading Activity

Assume that you have just been hired to work in the school district that was your number one choice. As you meet your students you realize that many cultures and languages are represented. Thinking about your students, you realize your primary concerns are (1) to find out who these students are and (2) how best to teach them. On the lines below, jot down five things you might do to determine your students' current levels of language development.

1. _____

2. _____

3. _____

4. _____

5. _____

Activity 10–1

There are critical questions that must be answered if educators are to provide appropriate curriculum and instruction in reading for students who are not native speakers of English. The purpose of this chapter is to address the following issues: (1) Who are the students acquiring English as a second language and how can they be identified? and (2) How can curriculum and instruction most effectively meet the literacy needs of these students?

The intent of this chapter is to review several issues concerning reading instruction for students who do not speak English as their first language. In classrooms of the United States, these students are usually referred to as *bilingual students*. Despite language differences, they are expected to comprehend and to express ideas presented in oral and written English. Students whose native language is not English must function at a high level of language competence in order to manage the content of courses required in secondary schools. Many of these students do comprehend easily and do respond successfully. Many others, however, are unable to do so. These are the students whose school records are filled with the sad statistics of poor achievement, retention in grade, and early dropout. Among the questions that confront individuals who have the responsibility for educating limited English speaking students in grades 7 through 12 are these:

Who are the students acquiring English as a second language?

How are they identified?

When should they begin a reading program in English?

How can they best acquire the requisite reading and writing skills?

What time is needed to develop skills?

What are some effective classroom strategies?

How can student progress be measured?

These questions represent only some of the concerns that challenge teachers of students who are not native speakers of English. The complexities inherent in teaching students who are going through their adolescent years are great. When the dimensions of language differences and cultural diversities are added to this responsibility, the complexities increase in geometric progression.

Who Are the Students Acquiring English As a Second Language?

Second language students who have been casually labeled bilingual are very diverse in their language and literacy competencies. No single description applies to all students. Some students will be fluent in their home language only, but unable to read and write it. Many students will have strong backgrounds of knowledge and skills obtained through education and experience in their own countries. Other students will have enjoyed few educational opportunities in their homelands. A small group of students will appear to demonstrate adequate control of oral English but will continue to encounter serious difficulties in written English. A large number of secondary students will have partially developed both the language of the home and the language of the school. These students may also have some reading and writing abilities, but the levels of skill development are insufficient for success in school. There are enormous differences among students who carry the designation bilingual, a term that, to be useful, must be more precisely defined. Students acquiring English as a second language may possess strong potential for fluency and literacy in two languages. However, the extent to which such potential is realized depends on their educational opportunities at home, in their communities, and at school.

As the resources, time, talent, and personnel permit, teachers and administrators should look very carefully beyond the bilingual label of their students. Before planning a reading program for these students, educators need to ask:

How well does the student speak his or her own language?

What is the level of reading and writing skills in the home language?

What is the school history of the student, including attendance, achievement, languages, and rate of school transfer?

What language is usually spoken in the home?

What are the reading and writing skills of the student in English?

Is the student's achievement level commensurate with his or her age and development?

How well is the student able to manage content in the various secondary subject areas offered in English?

Other personal variables of health, intelligence, maturation, interest, and self-esteem should also be considered. The present strengths and future promise of the students must be considered if their language and literacy needs are to be understood.

The expectation is that students beyond grade 7 will use English language and literacy skills, previously acquired, to carry content in subject-matter courses encoded in English. However, large numbers of students in grade 7 are still attempting to understand, to read, and to write. The assumption that students can acquire oral English, that they can master the writing system, and that they can then use these skills in school subjects designed for native speakers of English is an unreasonable one. Second language students cannot apply skills they have not yet acquired. Furthermore, they cannot learn a new language and use it to carry content at the same rate as English speakers who have enjoyed thousands of hours of English language opportunities at home, in the neighborhood, and at school.

These students have great need for support and assistance. They require specific programs to nurture listening, speaking, reading, and writing in English. Given the differences among students in the many personal and educational facets of their experience, no single plan of reading instruction will address the needs of all of them. However, modifications in instruction can make the knowledge and skills of English more accessible. These adaptations of the curriculum should be developmental in nature, not remedial. Students who do not possess sufficient fluency and literacy in English should be considered as students with the need to acquire new skills, rather than as students who need compensatory efforts for their deficiencies and deficits.

How Are the Students Acquiring English As a Second Language Identified?

For many students, the teacher does not need a formal assessment to know that they speak a language other than English. Their speech may be minimal and their limited production of oral English heavily accented with the sounds and intonation patterns of their native language. The careful ear and eye of a competent teacher is the best instrument to identify them. It is important, however, for the teacher to listen and to observe second language students over a reasonable period of time in order to judge their language competence. Such students may be reserved or shy and not wish to talk much at first. After an initial observation that may alert the teacher to the presence of second language students in the classroom, other information must be gathered.

Among the several instruments available to determine language status are (1) language assessment scales, (2) language dominance instruments, (3) reading achievement tests, (4) writing skills evaluation, and (5) cultural variables reviews.

Language assessment scales are intended to measure the student's ability to hear and to discriminate among the phonemes of English, to demonstrate the knowledge of words, to use the syntactical patterns, and to produce relevant information in comprehensible form.

Language dominant measures are arranged to present the same or similar items in two languages. The instrument may contain oral and written forms of both languages, and the scores on both sets of items are compared. The stronger score purports to represent the language in which the student can best function.

Language achievement tests are almost always tests of written language. They may contain a reading section with items on vocabulary and comprehension, a section on usage and grammar, and subtests on spelling, capitalization and punctuation. They are norm-referenced measures that have been standardized on a population of English-speaking students.

Assessment of students' writing skills may be of two kinds. The first is a multiple-choice format that directs students to select the correct or best response. The incorrect items may contain grammatical mistakes, faulty word usage, or sentence fragments. The assumption is that students who score well on such tests are proficient in written expression. The second kind of evaluation consists of obtaining a sample of the students' writing. Students write one or more paragraphs in response to a specific stimulus called the *prompt*. Their writing efforts are then scored according to a scoring rubric that contains a detailed description of an acceptable sample of written English. A review of the cultural and language variables may offer additional information that impacts on the student's performance.

The extent to which the students' language and literacy skills in the native language are assessed is dependent on the resources and personnel available in the schools. For example, when there are large numbers of Chinese speakers as in San Francisco or many communities of Spanish speakers as in New York, then schools may find it practical and possible to conduct the assessment of students in both English and in the native language. More significant than the gathering of information is the use of the data. After students have been identified and some of their educational strengths and needs have been determined, a reasonable plan must be made to promote reading and writing skills in English.

When Should a Reading Program in English Begin?

Ordinarily, a discussion of beginning reading centers on the concept of reading readiness. For older students, it may be safely assumed that maturation has already been accomplished. Normally, high school students have learned to listen, attend, observe, and discriminate. Spatial awareness has been developed and motor control established. This is the course of growth for students of any language. For this reason, older students may be counted on to bring these background abilities to the reading of English and to demonstrate strong preparation for the task, with the exception of their ability to hear the sounds and patterns of English. Too, if they have learned to read in another writing system, they may need to adjust their spatial orientation to print. For example, Farsi and Hebrew are read right to left; Japanese is read top to bottom and right to left; Chinese is read top to bottom and left to right. Nonetheless, older students who have some degree of literacy in their own language are ready to read English as soon as they begin to control simple structures and develop a basic vocabulary. They can read that which they understand and express orally.

Some students are unable to read in their own language, and in spite of reading instruction in English, are functionally illiterate. They may have not learned to read and write in their native language and may not have had success in learning to read or write in the second language, English. Almost all the subject matter beyond the elementary years is presented in lectures and textbooks. The burden of processing English speech and print increases as the students move along through the junior and senior high school years. For these students who have failed to read efficiently before they come to the secondary schools, a cautious introduction to reading English should be planned. The preparation minimally should include (1) discussion of the subject matter to be read, (2) introduction of vocabulary relevant to content, (3) presentation of connecting or qualifying words necessary for comprehension, (4) identification of specific skills needed to complete the reading assignment, and (5) expression of confidence in the student's ability to become successful readers.

How Can They Best Acquire the Requisite Skills?

Reading and writing are skills, and skills are best acquired through practice. The more students read, the better readers they become. For students reading in a second language, their practice must be arranged to focus on the specific knowledge and skill demanded by the subject matter. To read mathematics, students must understand the concepts and computation process. They must comprehend the abstractions expressed in mathematical symbols and in words. They must acquire the specialized vocabulary of the problems to be solved. The teacher may guide the practice by (1) asking the students to pick out words they do not know; (2) identifying what is given, what is needed, and what must be done to complete the problem; (3) illustrating the use of tables, graphs, diagrams, if relevant to the solution; (4) organizing the sequential steps and working them through one at a time; and (5) checking for the students' comprehension of the problem-solving process.

It is helpful for second language students to restate information in their own words. The teacher may ask for a definition of terms: What is an *estimate, equivalent* or *place holder?* Students may be asked to state what the problem is about. This question calls for them to find the main idea. Ask students to select the information they will need to solve the problem. They will have to search for the essential and nonessential details. Encourage students to formulate the question to be answered. They will practice drawing a conclusion. Practice in these reading skills applied to the mathematics textbook and materials improves the students' language and study habits as well.

To read science texts, the second language English students must learn a technical vocabulary that is very difficult in any language. They need to recognize that reading in science is generally accomplished at a slower, more thoughtful pace. As in the materials of mathematics, science textbooks contain many references to abstract ideas. The text is usually heavily weighted in diagrams, charts, tables, and graphs. Teachers may guide the practice in reading science by (1) helping students develop orderly thinking strategies, (2) outlining steps necessary to follow a science experiment, (3) encouraging precise understanding of scientific terms, (4) preteaching the specialized vocabulary, and (5) reducing the amount of material to be read at one time. Students will bring greater comprehension to the ideas as written if there has been ample opportunity to talk about the content of the material first. The teacher may arrange for students to participate in the science experiments themselves, measuring, estimating, observing, and finding the equipment needed. As these activities are provided, oral language is being extended, and the framework necessary for reading comprehension is being built. The use of films, filmstrips, video, and pictorial material can greatly enhance the comprehensibility of science lessons. The teacher may show a film or a sound filmstrip with the sound turned off. The teacher may then do the narration in a lower register, using shorter sentences, simpler structures, and easier vocabulary. When the film is over, students can ask questions, discuss the content, and clear up any misunderstandings.

To read social science textbooks and workbooks, students must learn to sort through an enormous amount of material. They need to know how to find specific information without having to read each word on a page. They need to improve their reading rate in order to cover the required content. The specialized vocabulary of the social sciences is full of abstractions: republic, demographics, aristocracy, capitalism. The temporal words that signify order and sequence are essential for following events and identifying *when* they occurred: latter, prior, finally, then. The subtleties of meaning may be given in connective words, for example, *but, if, since, although.* The spatial terminology provides clues to *where* the action is taking place, for example, fifty-second parallel, latitude, hemisphere, bush. Teachers may improve students' reading skills in the social sciences by (1) giving concrete examples of abstract concepts; (2) asking for the identification of relevant details; (3) reducing structural complexities to simple statements; (4) helping students find new meanings for familiar words; (5) dividing very long sentences or passages into smaller ones; (6) providing specific instructions in idiomatic usage; (7) stressing the thinking skills of evaluation, synthesis, and analysis; and (8) giving opportunities to compare and to contrast the past with the present.

Teachers will want to take time to introduce the textbook to the students so that they can find their way around in it. In addition to the parts of a book with which the students may already be familiar, (e.g., title page, table of contents, and glossary), point out any features that are special, such as chapter headings, prereading questions, and bold print to highlight key ideas.

To read literature and to enjoy its beauty to the fullest, students must be encouraged to reflect on concepts of human behavior. They need to appreciate the range of human emotions and to have an awareness of personal needs. As students read various literary genres, they grow in their understanding of universal themes and the commonalties among people of different cultures. Teachers encourage students to deepen their love of literature and to improve in the ability to read it by (1) teaching rich and subtle meanings of words in a variety of contexts; (2) stretching the multiple meanings of words; (3) developing the understanding of figurative language; (4) reviewing concepts of story structure; (5) using cognitive mapping as a strategy for vocabulary growth; (6) presenting concepts of setting, character, plot, and theme; and (7) offering a generous variety of literary forms.

To ensure success, teachers must plan to provide the background information, the *schemata,* that students will have to use as they read. The concepts, vocabulary, idioms, and story structure should be talked about and well understood on an oral basis as students deal with the written content. The teacher may use real objects, pictures, pantomime, gestures, and other devices to ensure meaning. Students may be encouraged to role play or to dramatize parts of their material. Dialogue between characters may be memorized and acted out in class. Often the teacher will want to read exciting or difficult passages to the students and allow the students the full enjoyment of beautiful, authentic language.

What Time is Needed?

Time is a very critical variable in planning successful programs for students acquiring English as a second language. These students need time to develop a background of experiences in an English-speaking milieu. They should have extended time in activities that help them communicate with other students and with their teachers. Because there is not enough time to acquire the skills in English first and then use such skills in learning subject matter, these students are best taught to read in the various content courses. They must, however, have a program designed especially for them. An instructional plan intended for native speakers of English has a pace that is too rapid, a sequence of skills that is inappropriate, and a set of objectives that is unrealistic.

Students need time to do the following:

Acquire the sounds, structures, and vocabulary of oral English.

Develop the background of information labeled in English.

Practice a variety of techniques that help them to recognize unfamiliar words.

Receive directed instruction in the strategies that improve comprehension.

Avoid the premature introduction to written text for which little or no preparation has been made.

Use their native language skills for transfer to English whenever applicable.

Think while Reading Activity

As you read this chapter you're going to be thinking about many strategies and issues that are related to students who are acquiring English as a second language. Complete the following chart as you read.

Strategies for General Use	Listening and Speaking Strategies	Reading and Writing Strategies

Activity 10–2

What Are Some Effective Classroom Strategies?

Teachers who serve second language students use classroom strategies that seem to work best for them. The following strategies are offered for the consideration of teachers.

Seat the student close to the front of the room where directions and instructions may be given with fewer distractions.

Speak naturally, but slowly, to allow for comprehension to develop.

Use a lower register, that is, shorter sentences, simpler concepts, and fewer multi-syllabic words.

Support content area instruction with visual material such as pictures, diagrams, stick figures, and drawings.

Provide manipulative materials whenever possible to make mathematics and science lessons meaningful.

Do not call on the student for a lengthy response. Elicit one-word or gestural answers when appropriate.

Avoid correcting errors of pronunciation, structure, or vocabulary. Accept the student's effort, or if necessary, state the response correctly without comment.

Do not expect mastery of language or the accuracy of an native-English speaker.

Assign a dependable classmate to assist whenever additional directions are needed to follow through on assignments or seat work.

Allow time for silence for taking in the new melody, rhythm, and rhyme of English.

Provide a climate of warmth and caring.

Listening and Speaking

Listening is the students' first language skill. Students come to school with many thousands of hours of listening to the language around them and have learned to make sense of the speech community into which they have been born. To some extent, many high school teachers may assume that the ability to listen develops easily along with growth. They may also discover that listening is a complex process and that a large number of today's students are poor listeners.

A few suggestions for teachers on improving the conditions for listening are these:

Encourage the students to focus their attention on the speaker.

Give the students a reason for listening.

Keep listening activities within reasonable attention spans.

Remember that it is difficult to sustain attention when the students do not share the language of the teacher.

As the teacher plans lessons to help students become better listeners, the expected responses should be free from the burden of long verbal answers. To check the students' attention and comprehension, the teacher may ask for gestural responses such as raising hands, nodding yes or no, clapping, holding up cards, or signaling in some way. These nonverbal interactions are especially productive for non-native speakers of English.

Suggested strategies, many of which are appropriate for all students, not just for second language students, are as follows:

> Have students predict from a title what the reading selection is about. After reading, have them validate their predictions.

> Use Total Physical Response (TPR) for a few minutes at the end of a class session to practice vocabulary introduced in a previous lesson—substitute nouns, adjectives, or verbs (see Asher, 1977).

> Introduce new topics by determining what students may already know about the subject using the KWL technique. (What do you *know?* What do you *want* to know? What have you *learned?*).

> Express interest and pleasure in the student's native language. When appropriate, ask how an expression or a point of view can be stated in the student's language.

> Plan discussions of different subjects that provide for diverse points of view. Help students learn to listen, to wait for the speaker to finish, to look at the group, and other suitable behaviors.

> Include traditional literature in listening to fables, folktales, myths. Search for the many commonalties that exist across cultures and languages.

> Use the biographies of heroes and heroines from several cultures to explore the values and beliefs of others.

> Teach students ways to identify a theme, to summarize the cultural influences, and to recognize how culture influences the ways people behave.

> Assign book talks in small groups for practice in speaking.

> Give students enough time to prepare, to develop, and to share their work, oral or written.

> Provide for opportunities where the teacher can confer individually with a student to advise or to help the student polish the language.

When students come from homes where languages other than English are spoken, teachers are eager to have these students become proficient in English. They may try to hasten the students' progress through the natural progression from silence to fluency. Stages of second language development have been identified as follows: (1) The pre-production level in which students are silent. They respond in gestures and actions. Lessons focus on listening comprehension of connected discourse and building a receptive vocabulary; (2) the early production level in which verbal responses are limited to one or two words and speech attempts represent that which students have heard and understood; (3) the speech emergence level in which students speak in greater length and can express ideas in simple structures, and (4) the intermediate fluency level in which students engage in conversation and can function effectively in appropriate reading and writing activities.

Reading and Writing

The purpose of this section is to describe some of the ways that reading instruction may be used in classrooms for second language students. These students present different levels of competency in written English. They may be (1) able to write one or two words, (2) comfortable in writing simple sentences, or (3) confident in creating paragraphs. At the word level, students may benefit from keeping an important word notebook, taking words in dictation, and copying content area words of interest and relevance. When students are capable of writing sentences, they may be encouraged to write a brief description of someone in their family, combine two short sentences into longer ones, take dictation of sentences, and read sentences written by classmates. As students grow in the skills of written expression, they may practice by writing a brief report of a personal experience, summarizing a sporting event, reviewing an item from the newspaper, or giving a description of a favorite person. They may also enjoy working in small groups to proofread the work of others or to write a collaborative paragraph to follow a beginning sentence.

Use the language experience approach that is based on the learner's experiences in his or her language. As students encounter experiences in their own surroundings, they may think and talk about them. What they have said, others may write. Then, because they are the very thoughts and words of the students, they can understand what someone reads to them. Ultimately, students may read these written forms themselves. This approach may be a group process in which a class may participate, or it may be an individual one between a student and the person who invites the student's thoughts and words. This practice is considered an excellent way to begin for students who are not native speakers of English.

Read, read, and read to students often, from all kinds of written connected discourse—books, magazines, pamphlets, letters, notices, memos, and stories. Make print media a very important feature of the class environment.

When pictorial material is used, talk about contents of pictures, emphasizing key words from the lesson. Write essential phrases on the chalk board; have students copy what has been written; use choral reading of the material written on the board.

When short anecdotes relevant to the day's lesson are provided, demonstrate meanings through gestures, real objects, and pictures. Prepare a ditto sheet of the anecdote; have students read together; ask students to circle words that were difficult; review these words in subsequent lessons.

When short poetry selections are enjoyed, stress the rhythm and rhyme of the poem. Read one or two lines; ask students to recite the lines together; repeat lines and encourage students to memorize them. Write lines on the chalk board; read the lines together as a class; have students copy in notebooks; continue to convey meaning in pictures, gestures, or with real objects; talk about the poem.

If there is a lending library with pictorial material and easy to read books, encourage students to take them home. Have students report briefly on what they have read, write on chart paper what the students say, and encourage students to read a sentence or two that they have enjoyed.

Building word files of a vocabulary of importance and interest to students, promotes their organization skills. Ask each student to keep a notebook. Write on the board the words that are important to students as they express them. Have students add their personal work alphabetically in their notebooks.

When using a textbook, read to students some of the difficult passages; check for comprehension frequently, and divide them into short, manageable segments. Assign literate mentors to students who are preliterate or illiterate; encourage silent not oral reading activities; use the resources of the school library and media center.

Written language supports oral competence and expands dimensions for learning. Speaking and writing are both expressive forms of language behavior. They are developmentally interrelated and proceed naturally in a language-rich environment. As writing becomes an expected activity each day, students grow in their abilities to express their thoughts and to put them in written form. When students share their writings, their efforts are appreciated and validated as important. Beginning writings may not be graded, marked, or evaluated for form. As opportunities for writing continue, skills improve with the teacher's guidance and encouragement.

As practice in written expression is given, these early attempts improve naturally. An important feature of writing in a classroom described as a literate environment is the frequency. When a regular time is set aside for students to write, and when the teacher supports these written attempts with little or no commentary on correctness, the students write more.

Use a drawing or illustration as a stimulus for writing something, even one word. The writing may be done by the teacher, a classroom volunteer, or an English-speaking student. Encourage original writings. Offer help as requested, but tell the students that they do not need to wait until help is given. They should be urged to create in writing the inventions of their own minds. Reassure the students that their thoughts and ideas are the most valuable features of their work, and that together, the teacher and the students will review and edit it in order to produce the conventional forms.

Introduce journal writing and make the use of journals part of frequent writing opportunities. The content of journals may vary with the changing purposes for writings: personal, curriculum specific, or subject-matter interests.

Work Centers

The teacher may wish to arrange a part of the classroom in work centers. These centers have specific purposes and contain the materials necessary for the activities. Centers may be reading, listening, or writing work sites, or they may be a combination of all of these. Centers should be stimulating, creative, and interesting to the students as they enjoy many language and literacy experiences.

A Listening Center is generally an arrangement to provide listening activities for a small group of students, usually six or eight. There is a recorder or tape player for the small group to follow along with a minimum of directions from the teacher. Centers have the advantage of offering on tape a story that a student may have missed because of absences. They may also allow some students the opportunity to hear a story again and follow along independently. While the listeners listen, the rest of the class may be very productively immersed in the other language and literacy activities available in the classroom.

Think while Reading Activity

A variety of effective strategies for teaching students who are acquiring English as a second language are discussed in this chapter. You have read about some of them. The author describes several more throughout this section. As you complete your reading, list five effective strategies below.

Effective strategies:

1. _____
2. _____
3. _____
4. _____
5. _____

Elaborate on one strategy here:

_____
_____
_____
_____
_____
_____
_____
_____
_____

Activity 10–3

In a Library Center the teacher brings together magazines, books, pictures, catalogs, and newspapers. These materials are organized well and are readily available to the students. The center suggests a quiet, businesslike atmosphere among a comfortable chair or two and a work table. The bulletin board has announcements and posters that tell the students about the work center.

A Homework Center may offer extra direction to students who have need of help, providing time and space to get started on homework when the day's assignments have been completed, and teaching students how to organize their time and materials. This center may be open for only a part of the day and may be staffed by cross-grade tutors or volunteers. One of the major purposes is to assist students in improving their study habits.

The Authors' Center may contain paper and other writing materials that provide for writing and creating finished work. This center also has materials for illustrating, binding, or decorating the final product.

Centers are but a few of the work sites where students and materials may be brought together for specific language and literacy experiences. Centers will vary according to the space available and the configuration of the classroom. They will also vary with the nature of the curriculum and the interests of the students. Some of the characteristic of effective centers are these:

> Materials are accessible for individual work, or for small groups.
>
> Materials include the many kinds of print with which students are already familiar: product labels, logos, or signs.
>
> Storage space and containers for putting things away are essential.
>
> Equipment, such as computers, listening posts, or other technological supports, must be safely and securely located in convenient places.
>
> Centers are clearly labeled to convey their purposes.
>
> Use of centers allows for the amount of traffic going through them on a daily basis.
>
> Time at a center is fairly allocated to accommodate the participation of all students.
>
> Rules to control schedules, cleanup, and behavior should be few but enforced fairly.

Integrating Fluency and Literacy

For the purpose of presenting the characteristics of a literate environment, the receptive language skills, listening and reading, and the expressive language skills, speaking and writing, have been placed in separate contexts. Language development and use, however, are not happening in isolation. They are interdependent, interrelated, and mutually supportive. Students who are not native speakers of English demonstrate a variety of skill levels in both oral and written English. To accommodate student diversities, teachers must be imaginative and flexible in providing for these differences. Some suggestions follow.

> To insure comprehension, make every possible use of gestures, voice stress, emphasis, objects, pictures, and pantomime as lessons are presented.
>
> To achieve real communication, encourage conversations, role playing, questioning, discussions, and other opportunities to send and to receive actual messages.
>
> To allow for the individual differences in readiness to produce speech, recognize that not all the students will respond orally at the same time. Allow as much listening time as they may need.
>
> To encourage teachers to guide the lessons in ways that are comfortable, provide suggested comments, questions, and recommendations only. Teachers need to feel free to add, to change, or to omit as they and the materials interact with their students.
>
> To meet objectives for preproduction, production, and thinking skills, teachers appreciate that, although the activities are at times mentioned separately, listening, speaking, reading, writing, and thinking are not separate mental activities. Classroom lessons involve multiple language skills, but not all children need to overtly demonstrate them at the same time and in the same manner.

Other Strategies

Sheltered English is an approach that modifies the teaching of content areas in English. Students who are having difficulties in reading textbooks that have been written for native-English speakers are offered adaptations with these specific changes:

Instruction focuses on one or two essential concepts.

Lesson objectives are few and state exactly what students are expected to do.

Vocabulary is always put in meaningful context.

Lessons begin with an exploration of what students bring to the lesson (their schemata).

Teachers examine the materials carefully to determine readability, text features, and other factors relevant to comprehension.

Instruction offers activities that build meaning from the text.

Students put thinking, language, and literacy skills together in an integrated program that is comprehensible.

How Can Progress Be Measured?

Students will show whether they are making progress by their day to day performance in their classes. The teacher is the best observer of such progress or its absence because the teacher has a regular opportunity to appraise the students' work, their participation in class, and their attitude toward the subjects. In addition to observations by the teacher, personal interviews to discuss with the students their perceptions of how classes are going are useful and revealing. Teacher-made tests designed to measure specific skills provide solid information as well. Standardized instruments prepared for administration to native speakers of English may have only limited usefulness in establishing levels of achievement or in showing change as a result of instruction. The data obtained on such tests must be interpreted cautiously and should be supplemented with other information that teachers have collected. There is no one best way of measuring progress. Informal assessment may include samples of students' work, observations completed by the classroom teacher, checklists describing language competence in a variety of social contexts, and other evidences of growth in language and literacy proficiencies.

Conclusion

This chapter has reviewed some of the critical questions that concern teachers who are working with students who are not native speakers of English. The challenge for teachers is that of guiding students to listen, speak, read, write, and think in English so that they can cope with the speech-print connections. The task is complicated by the constraints of time, complex subject matter, and differential backgrounds of students in secondary schools. The expectation that all second language students can acquire English and use English as instruments for learning, within the span of the time available, may be unrealistic for many of them. There has been an effort to describe the students, to caution teachers about student diversities, and to recommend specific instructional strategies for improving classroom instruction. Students acquiring English as a second language share the same needs of all students of any language. They need a safe, supportive classroom, a comprehensible curriculum, a reasonable amount of time, and appropriate materials. Above all, they appreciate teachers who enjoy them and celebrate their diversity.

Think after Reading Activity

Design an activity based on one or more of the strategies presented in this chapter that you believe will help non-native English speakers understand the lessons in your curricular area. (You might want to collaborate with a partner from another content area in order to create an interdisciplinary lesson.) Briefly outline the activity.

Content Area:

_____

_____

Information/Concept/Idea:

_____

_____

_____

Activity:

_____

_____

_____

Rationale:

_____

_____

_____

Activity 10–4

The Instructional Program

Chapter 11

The Content Area Teacher's Instructional Role

A Cognitive Mediational View

LAURA R. ROEHLER

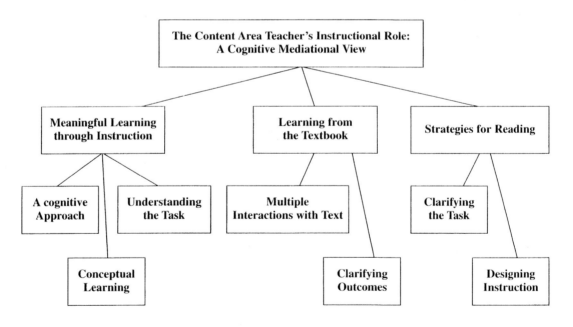

Think before Reading Activity

Does this statement ring true to your ears? "Read the following chapter and answer the ten questions at the end." What's wrong with this picture?

_____

_____

_____

_____

_____

As you read this chapter, take some notes on how you would rewrite this refrain.

_____

_____

_____

_____

_____

_____

_____

                                                    Activity 11–1

This chapter (the first edition of which was co-authored by Gerald Duffy) emphasizes the content area teacher's instructional role. Two fundamental aspects of instruction are emphasized, the way the academic task is understood by the teacher and the students and the interactions that accompany the task. Students actively construct meaning from the experiences in their environment. That is, students cognitively mediate the classroom experience, and what they ultimately learn is a result of what the task and the subsequent interactions cause them to conclude about the experience. What defines the experience in subject-matter areas is the task pursued and the subsequent interactions about that task. This chapter describes how to apply the instructional factors of task and interactions as a framework for making decisions about how to use textbooks and associated reading strategies.

Content area teachers pass on the knowledge of specific academic fields. Traditionally, this process is guided by two assumptions: that the major way to learn an academic subject is to read about it and that the textbook is the source of content area knowledge. For instance, Goodlad (1983) found that teachers expected students to read and study outside of the class, largely without teacher preparation or assistance. Hence, content area reading becomes important.

However, learning the knowledge of an academic field requires more than passively receiving bits of knowledge from a book or a teacher. The goal is for students to build meaningful conceptual understandings about the content, as opposed to engaging in the rote, arbitrary, and verbatim recitation of facts. Consequently, content area learning requires more than a textbook, because the textbook represents the author's meaning and the student will construct a slightly different understanding (Pearson & Tierney, 1984). Therefore, the teacher's instructional role is more than following the textbook and explaining it to students (Wade, 1983).

Given that students in subject-matter classes should construct meaningful understandings of the content, this chapter describes the content area teacher's instructional responsibility. It provides a description of the ingredients essential for instruction that results in meaningful conceptual learning, a description of the textbook's role, and a description of the role that reading techniques and strategies play.

A Cognitive View of Content Area Learning and Instruction

Traditionally, content subjects have been taught in accordance with three principles: (1) the student is a blank tablet to be written on or an empty container to be filled, (2) the teacher (or the textbook) is the authority that dispenses knowledge, and (3) the instructional process consists of students absorbing the information that the teacher or textbook presents. Hence, it is not unusual to find content area teachers assigning textbook chapters, conducting question and answer sessions about the chapter, and then giving tests. With this kind of instruction, some students do not learn the material at all or learn it only for short periods of time, usually just long enough to pass the end-of-unit test. Typically, they memorize isolated pieces of content material, storing them in a nonorganized way. Seldom do they develop conceptual frameworks about the content or develop meaningful linkages among concepts. Rarely do they see any usefulness for the information they have memorized.

Think while Reading Activity

While reading the chapter, jot down a few notes that help clarify for you the definition of cognitive mediation.

_____

_____

_____

_____

_____

_____

_____

_____

Activity 11–2

A Cognitive View of Learning

For content area teachers to help their students develop organized, useful, and meaningful conceptual understandings, the traditional passive view in which students remember isolated information must be replaced by an interactive, cognitive view involving five characteristics. Conceptual learning occurs when meanings about content area knowledge are (1) gradually constructed, (2) by the learners, (3) through a series of interactions with the content, (4) with new information integrated with old information, (5) so that the result is conscious awareness of what is being learned, when it will be useful, how to use it effectively, and its value.

This interactive, cognitive approach puts a different light on content area learning. Because learning is constructed gradually, understandings develop over time, not in a single experience. Because it is constructed by the learners, students must actively participate in the learning as opposed to being passive recipients of knowledge. Because it occurs by integrating new knowledge with old knowledge, students must have opportunities to combine instructional content with what is already known and generate restructured understandings. Finally, because it must result in students' conscious control, metacognitive awareness and reasoning rather than memorizing answers becomes the focus.

Consider an example. Assume that a high school economics teacher teaches a set of lessons on the characteristics of capitalistic, socialistic, and communistic governments in order to develop outcomes in which students understand the strengths and problems of the three types of governments. The lessons are taught over three weeks to allow students to gradually construct understanding; students engage in a series of interactive oral and written conversations with the teacher, the text and each other, leading to their active participation as they talk, write, and do. They integrate old knowledge into new knowledge using a chart on which descriptions of economic systems are developed. The lessons start with the creation of a chart like the one in Figure 11–1. The chart is divided vertically into two sections labeled strengths and problems. The two sections are divided into three parts and labeled capitalism, socialism, and communism. As the strengths and problems emerge from conversations, they are added to the chart. Throughout the lessons, the chart is regularly revised and updated. Discarded strengths and problems are kept for periodic review. A teacher guides the interactions so students develop awareness about how economic systems help us understand why there is conflict between countries with different types of government.

A Cognitive View of Instruction

When learning is viewed in this way, instruction is no longer a matter of dispensing textbook information to passive learners. Instead, it is a process of intentionally orchestrating the classroom environment so that students are helped to construct the concepts specified by the curriculum. The teacher does this by assessing the students' understandings about the topic, their valuing of the topic, and their background experiences that relate to the topic. The teacher also assesses the context material to see how well it matches the expertise of the students. Then the teacher develops lessons that provide the support students need to learn and the challenge that students need to internalize the knowledge. This inter-

	Strengths	Problems
Capitalistic Government		
Socialistic Government		
Communistic Government		

FIGURE 11–1   A Chart for Constructing Content Area Knowledge

nalization becomes learning. The instructional process has two important ingredients. The first is to understand the task in order to explain it (Doyle, 1984), and the second is the creation of opportunities for students to interact with the content so that over a period of time they construct the intended meaning (Duffy, Roehler, Meloth, & Vavrus, 1986; Pearson, Roehler, Dole, & Duffy, 1992).

Understanding the Task

The task students engage in during content area instruction is a major determinant of what they learn. The teacher defines the task by deciding what outcomes are being met and what academic experiences students should have. For instance, when content area teachers routinely assign textbook chapters and the questions at the end of the chapters, the task is defined as getting correct answers to questions and not as learning the major concepts undergirding the content area. Consequently, students learn to provide answers to questions; they do not necessarily construct the larger conceptual understandings associated with the content and how these relate to their lives. Consequently, how the teacher defines the task is crucially important in determining what students learn from content area instruction. For instance, a teacher had decided to develop a unit on how people from everywhere had created the United States. Her guiding question was, "How did the cultures contribute to the development of the USA?" Her goals were to develop positive attitudes about the diversities of the many cultures that contributed; to develop awareness and understandings about the similarities and differences of the contributing cultures and our present nation; and to enable students to develop compare and contrast strategies, library research strategies, and conversation strategies. Using these outcomes and guiding question, the teacher created tasks that caused the students to focus on developing understandings rather than tasks that may have caused students to remember isolated answers to questions.

The Interactions

Once the task is understood, students' learning is further influenced by the interactions they have with the content as they pursue that task. Each time students interact with content, they restructure their mental understandings about it. That is, new knowledge about the content is combined with their old knowledge, and a new meaning is constructed. Assuming a consistently defined task, the more likely it is that the desired understanding will ultimately be developed.

Interactions take two forms. One is verbal interaction, the conversations between teacher and students typically associated with class discussions. The nature of the verbal interactions during discussions of academic content, particularly what the teacher communicates as being important, significantly influences what students learn. For instance, when a teacher's talk during a discussion emphasizes and rewards instant answers as opposed to hypothesis generation, students come to understand that memorization rather than reasoning is valued.

The second kind of interaction is the activities students engage in while pursuing a task. For instance, an activity sequence in which the interactions consist of reading a text chapter followed by taking a true or false test carries one kind of message about what meaning students should construct; reading a textbook and engaging in a debate in which the interactions focus on the validity of the information contained in the textbook carries another kind of message about what meaning students should construct.

In sum, instruction must include many interactions between students and content. These can take the form of multiple opportunities to interact verbally with the teacher through discussion, multiple opportunities to engage in activity sequences such as role playing, or a combination of the two. During such interactions, students modify their understandings, restructuring them as they integrate the new experience with the old. If each successive interactive opportunity is consistent with the task as defined by the teacher, students gradually construct a meaning consistent with the desired outcome.

The Teacher and Student as Cognitive Mediators

When teachers provide a clear understanding of task with multiple interactions, content area instruction becomes a process in which both teachers and students engage in cognitive mediation (Winne, 1985). That is, both the teacher and student combine instructional experiences with their current understandings and create new understandings. Students, for instance, come to the instructional situation with accurate or not so accurate conceptions about the content to be learned. When confronted with a task and multiple interactions about that task, students make a series of interpretations about what they are supposed to learn. Simultaneously, the teacher comes to the instructional situation with the intention of developing in students specified outcomes. When presented with students' reaction to the assigned tasks and to subsequent interactions, the teacher interprets these reactions and decides what needs to be done next instructionally. That is, the teacher, like the student, mediates the instructional experience, shaping it through an understanding of the outcomes that are being developed and deciding what needs to be done next to reach those outcomes.

Consider an illustration in which a science teacher is trying to get her students to understand why grass seeds planted in the dark sprouted and began growing even without light (Roth, Anderson, & Smith, 1986). The following interactive exchange between teacher and students, in which the teacher wants students to understand that the cotyledon provides food for the germinating plant, is a good example of cognitive mediation. In the first verbal exchange, one student said that light was not the answer; he understood from the information in the lesson that light was not the source of food. The teacher mediated the student's response and provided explanation to help him understand not only that light was not the food but also what the food could be. The student interpreted the teacher's elaboration and stated that "water and stuff" kept the plant alive. In an attempt to move closer to the correct understanding, the teacher interpreted the student's response again and reworded it as a question, saying, "It already had its food?" With the help of this cue, the student constructed the desired understanding and responded, "It had its cotyledon and everything." The teacher interpreted this response and, wanting to verify that the student understood, asked the student why having a cotyledon was important. The student responded that the cotyledon was the food. The teacher assessed this was an accurate conceptual understanding and positively reinforced the student. In this way, both teacher and students mediated instructional information during verbal exchanges about cotyledons, and the students gradually constructed the conceptual understanding intended by the teacher.

Summarizing a Cognitive View of Learning and Instruction

The content area teacher's instructional role consists primarily of two things. First, the teacher must understand and explain academic tasks so that students draw the desired kinds of conclusions about what is to be learned. Second, the content area teacher must orchestrate students' interactions with the content, primarily through verbal conversations and activities, in ways that cause students to construct the desired understandings while moving toward the desired outcomes. Because content subjects focus on the development of conceptual understandings (as opposed to factual information memorized for short-term recall), content area tasks and interactions should emphasize conceptual understandings rather than short-term memory tasks; and because students mediate tasks and interactions in unique ways, teachers must be ready to spontaneously help students to modify their understandings in order to construct the desired outcome. This collaborative, recursive negotiation between teacher's and students is the heart of content area instruction.

The Role of the Textbook in Content Area Instruction

The textbook is often the dominant feature in content area instruction, dictating what will be taught (whatever is written in the text) and how it will be taught (by explicating the text). From the perspective of both task and instructional interactions, there are problems with this text-dominated, content area instruction. When the content area task is reading the textbook and answering questions about what was covered, students typically interpret the situation to mean that the teacher values memory for factual material and rote recall of arbitrary pieces of information. Similarly, when instructional interactions focus primarily on feedback for the teacher about the correctness or incorrectness of the students' answers to questions, students get little opportunity to construct conceptual understandings and, consequently, often end up with something other than organized and useful conceptual structures.

How content area teachers approach the textbook is crucial. Rather than using the textbook as a passive dispenser of knowledge and checking to see that students remember that knowledge, teachers must take a proactive stance in understanding and explaining academic tasks and in creating instructional interactions involving the content of the selected book.

Defining Academic Tasks

When assigning academic tasks, content area teachers must first analyze the text to determine what kind of knowledge it provides. Does the book communicate conceptual understandings about the academic content, and does it communicate linkages among concepts in an attempt to create a mosaic of conceptual understandings? Or does the textbook communicate mere facts or, in the case of some content area texts, misconceptions about the content (Smith & Anderson, 1984)? In short, content area teachers must read the book with their students' eyes and try to imagine what understandings students are likely to create as a result of completing the reading assignment. In one sense, teachers use the book as a tool for building bridges between what students know and what they need to know (Conley, 1992). While building those bridges, it is important that the task reflect the outcomes. For example, a teacher wanted to develop his students' understandings about the responsibilities of being a citizen. Specifically, the teacher wanted the students to understand how social understandings that have been constructed over time can be brought to bear on current civic issues and problems. He asked the students to read a segment of an autobiography that described a moral dilemma about stealing while working. He then conducted a conversation with the class about whether they thought the author's behavior was appropriate given the circumstances of his time. The class voted yes or no and then discussed why his behavior was or wasn't appropriate. The outcomes of the conversation were then applied to the riots and looting that have occurred in large cities. This teacher wanted his students to conclude that being a citizen involves facing the dilemmas that occur when people live in groups where injustices happen. He had the students complete tasks that reflected the desired outcomes.

Creating Interactions about Textbook Content

In creating student interactions about the content of the textbook, whether they are verbal interactions or activities, the teacher must ensure first that the interactions focus students on the intended outcomes and, second, that students get multiple opportunities to construct the desired understandings. After a single interaction about the content of a textbook, a student combines what was known before with the newly acquired information, but this first attempt is seldom representative of the desired outcome. Multiple opportunities are necessary for students to gradually construct the understanding. Students need to activate what they know and how they feel about a topic; they need to receive information about the topic through oral or written means; they need to interact with each other about the topic and draw tentative conclusions. All this leads to the development of gradual understandings. These interactions about the content of the textbook can consist of conversations and reflections within a variety of activities that help students construct the understandings the teacher had in mind when planning and explaining the task.

In this view, the textbook is a tool, not the instruction itself, and the teacher is the master of the book, not a technician who uses the book as a pseudo script. For instance, the teacher does not hesitate to supplement the book if the message conveyed is likely to cause students to create an understanding different from the one intended; the teacher views the book as an initial source of information, with the heart of the instruction occurring subsequent to the reading of the text, at which time verbal exchanges and activities help students gradually build the intended understandings.

Examine this example (provided by Betty Yugala, a social studies teacher) of a history teacher who selected World War I as a topic. The outcomes for students included developing greater interest in historical inquiry, understanding and knowing the underlying and immediate causes of World War I, analyzing how all the causes interrelated and stem from any of the major causes of their choice, and formulating hypotheses supported by historical evidence. The teacher defined and explained the task as one in which appropriate attitudes and reasoning processes about World War I content should help the students as they developed hypotheses about the causes of World War I. These attitudes would include suspending judgments about preconceived causes, an openness to explore information, a valuing of multiple points of view, and a willingness to create and consider different hypotheses. The reasoning process would be the identification of unstated assumptions, the notation of relevant ideas, and a careful construction of the causes as opposed to a predetermined set of causes that are then justified during the lessons. The teacher used introductory conversations to develop interest and activate prior knowledge about wars. The conversations focused around the following questions initially. Why do wars begin? Why did the Gulf War begin? What are your feelings about the Gulf War? Was the Gulf War inevitable? Could the Gulf War have been avoided? What is your reasoning for the inevitability of this war or the avoidance of this war? The introductory conversation was gradually interwoven into an explanation of what the task would be, how it would be done, and why it was important. The teacher used think sheets (a step by step guide that focused on how to reason) as a way to develop beginning understandings about the causes of World War I and about how to read the chapter. The following questions were part of the think sheets. What am I trying to do? What are my predictions about the causes of World War I?

What reasoning strategies can I use? What are my conclusions? How will I deal with conflicting data? Are my conclusions and my reasoning making sense to me? To others? After the material was read, the students brainstormed the causes of the war, first in small groups and then as a whole class.

An understanding of the task was further developed as the teacher used two film strips with differing interpretations of the main causes of World War I. Student were taught how to develop scenarios or diagrams about the main causes as several scenarios or diagrams were developed with the whole class from the two filmstrips. Opportunities for students to complete their understandings about the causes of World War I were provided as students worked in small groups to develop group scenarios about the causes of World War I. The teacher and students provided opportunities for cognitive mediations to occur by monitoring (1) each student's understanding of the steps of the task, (2) how problems were solved, (3) pacing and participation, and (4) the group's analysis of their interpretations of the causes. The unit was culminated as all scenarios and justifications were explained to the class and turned in for grading.

Summarizing the Role of the Textbook

The content area teacher's instructional role is not simply to get students to read the book. Rather, in assigning the reading of a book segment, teachers must first clearly state the intended outcomes (the understandings students are to have at the close of instruction and what kind of academic work is likely to result in this understanding) and modify the text-

---

Think while Reading Activity

In the section titled "Creating Interactions about Textbook Content," the author begins by stating that "In creating students interactions about the content of the textbook, whether they are verbal interactions or activities, the teacher must ensure first that the interactions focus students on the intended outcomes and, second, that students get multiple opportunities to construct the desired understandings." Jot down an interaction that might occur in your content area classroom that would accomplish this.

_____

_____

_____

_____

_____

_____

_____

_____

_____

Activity 11–3

book assignment to create an academic task that will help students construct the intended understandings. Second, the content area teacher must create multiple interactions with the book content after the reading of the text because students will mediate a single interaction with the text in ways that may result in partial understandings or even misunderstandings.

The Role of Content Area Reading Techniques

There can be little question about the effectiveness of reading strategies that focus on how to make it easier for students of varying reading abilities to use the textbook profitably. However, they must be applied within an understanding of task and instructional interactions. Simply giving students questions, advance organizers, study guides, or text grammars is of little help because the reading techniques themselves cannot change the conclusions students draw about content area learning. The task and the interactions students engage in while doing the task influence what meaning they will construct about the content. Therefore, the teacher must first understand and explain the task and create successive interactions. Then reading techniques such as questions and study guides can be added to help students read the book and prepare for academic conversations.

Consider the following contrasting situations in which both teachers used a study guide in teaching a series of lessons on the Great Depression. In the first situation, the teacher defined the task as developing understandings of the feelings of failure, insecurity, instability, and helplessness that were typical of those times. To help students gather information about how people felt in the 1930s, a study guide was prepared by having students list typical aspects of their daily lives in the 1990s, which was then used when they gathered information about daily life during the 1930s. In subsequent interactions, groups of students summarized their lists, compared them with those of other groups, and created summary statements about the human conditions of the 1930s. In contrast, another U.S. history teacher who taught the same lessons on the Great Depression defined the task as finding the answers in the text. He constructed a study guide to help students find the answers as they read the textbook chapter. The subsequent interactions consisted of having the students write answers to the end-of-chapter questions. The answers were collected and graded. Although both teachers used a study guide, the differences in the task definition and in the subsequent interactions created a measurable difference in the two instructional situations.

In sum, content area reading techniques such as study guides are not ends in themselves. They must be applied within the larger framework of instruction. Thoughtful content area teachers, therefore, first define the task and create interactions that are likely to lead students to the desired understandings. Only then do they assess the reading involved and decide on reading strategies and techniques, such as study guides, which are helpful in that situation.

Conclusion

Because content area instruction is often assumed to be a matter of getting students to read the textbook, content area reading is likewise often assumed to be a matter of expediting this reading. Both assumptions ignore the fact that the heart of effective instruction is the interpretation students make of the tasks they are assigned and the subsequent interactions they have regarding those tasks. The effectiveness of reading in the content area, therefore, depends first on the degree to which content area teachers define the tasks as ones that will move students toward construction of intended meanings and in terms of desired outcomes and orchestrate subsequent instructional interactions in ways designed to reinforce the intended learning. Employing various content area reading techniques to improve and expedite students' reading of books is of little use without first considering the task and the instructional interactions. Only after these decisions are made can book reading be assigned and specialized reading and study techniques be applied.

Think after Reading Activity

Now that you have completed reading this chapter, briefly contrast traditional instructional routine (an assigned reading section, lecturing, and testing) with the cognitive mediational approach discussed in this chapter.

_____

_____

_____

_____

_____

_____

_____

_____

What are your thoughts about implementing either or both of these in your classroom.

_____

_____

_____

_____

_____

_____

_____

Activity 11–4

Real-World Literacy Demands

How They've Changed and What Teachers Can Do

LARRY MIKULECKY

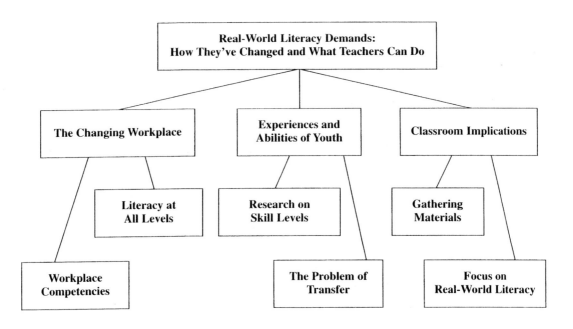

Think before Reading Activity

The subject area you plan to teach is used by adults in the nonschool world. These adults do a good deal of reading and writing related to their jobs and to keep up. This reading is only rarely from textbooks. Alone or with another person from your content area, list the sorts of things someone prepared in your content area might read to:

do his or her daily work

keep up with what is new

plan entertainment and recreational activities somewhat
related to your content area

_____

_____

_____

_____

_____

_____

_____

_____

_____

_____

_____

_____

_____

_____

Activity 12–1

The literacy demands required to thrive in society have changed significantly over the last several decades. These changes are particularly visible in the workplace. NAEP studies of seventeen-year-olds and of young adults indicate that the very literacy skills increasingly required outside of school are the skills many adolescents and young adults lack. Although most teachers should not see their roles as directly preparing students for occupations, teachers can teach students to use literacy to solve realistic problems. This chapter provides information on the changing nature of social and workplace demands, with special emphasis on the new, higher-level basic skills required in the workplace. It concludes with specific suggestions for how teachers can help prepare students for these higher-level literacy demands by integrating more problem-solving, real-world uses of literacy into the reading and content classes they teach.

The Changing Nature of Work

One indication of the changes in literacy skills required to participate in society is the changing nature of work in the United States and other industrialized countries. As new jobs are created and old jobs disappear, new levels and types of basic skills for employment are also created. Increasingly, employees at all levels are expected to perform multiple jobs, keep records to monitor effectiveness, communicate orally and through print, and gather information to solve problems. The U. S. Department of Labor compiles lists of the fastest growing occupations, both in terms of percentage of growth and actual numbers. The fastest growing occupations all call for a good deal more reading, writing, and further training than many high school students currently receive. Even the simplest occupations now often require workers to read instructions and manuals in order to operate equipment, for example, or to follow health department regulations. Although years of training are not required for all new jobs, higher minimum levels of basic skills are required.

Research has revealed the use of reading, writing, and computation in the workplace at a relatively high level. Diehl and Mikulecky (1980) examined one hundred workers from a representative cross section of occupations, ranging from executive vice-president to forklift driver. Only 2 percent of occupations examined required no reading or writing. Time spent reading print, charts, graphs, and computer terminals averaged nearly two hours daily. Mikulecky (1982), in a comparison study of school and workplace literacy demands, found that high school juniors spend less time reading (including homework) than all categories of workers except blue-collar workers.

In addition to facing fairly difficult on-the-job reading and training materials, many high school students are unprepared for how basic skills are used in the workplace. Most of the reading, writing, and computation in the workplace is used to accomplish tasks and make assessments. Rather than reading from a single text, workers must gather information from several sources to solve problems, provide services, and perform tasks. As a matter of fact, Mikulecky and Winchester (1983) and Mikulecky and Ehlinger (1986) have found that the ability to set purposes, self-question, summarize information, monitor comprehension, and make useful notes distinguishes superior job performers from merely adequate job performers.

In 1990 the U.S. Department of Labor instituted the Secretary's Commission on Achieving Necessary Skills (SCANS), an advisory committee on skills necessary for functioning in today's workplace. The charge of this commission was to determine what skills America's schools should be teaching to prepare student's for the current and future workplace. The SCANS advisory committee charges teachers in all classes to develop regular activities that teach students five workplace competencies (U.S. Dept. of Labor, 1991). These activities should teach students to productively use:

Resources—to identify, organize, plan, and allocate resources.

Interpersonal skills—to work with others on teams, teach others, serve clients, exercise leadership, negotiate, and work with diversity.

Information—to acquire, organize, interpret, evaluate, and communicate information.

Think while Reading Activity

Mikulecky characterizes real-world literacy as "the ability to set purposes, self-question, summarize information, monitor comprehension, and make useful notes." The NAEP and SCANS data summarize how well prepared American students are for real-world literacy. As you read this next section, list what you learn about real-world literacy.

_____

_____

_____

_____

_____

_____

_____

_____

_____

_____

_____

Activity 12–2

Systems—to understand complex inter-relationships and distinguish trends, predict impacts, as well as monitor and correct performance.

Technology—to work with a variety of technologies and choose appropriate tools for tasks.

These competencies are seen as key to most jobs worth having. The commission does not recommend that schools attempt to directly prepare students for particular jobs. It does suggest, however, that students become involved in many more long-term tasks and projects which call for increasingly complex applications of these competencies.

Current Experiences and Abilities of Adolescents and Young Adults

School Demands

Data indicate that most high school students perform little reading and writing related to class work. Data from the 1990 National Assessment of Educational Progress (NAEP) reveal that 60 percent of grade 8 and 56 percent of grade 12 students report reading less than ten pages per day of combined in-school and homework reading, and 70 percent of each group does less than an hour of homework per night, with nearly half of grade 12 students reporting a half hour or less of homework (Langer, J, Applebee, A. Mullis, I. & Foertsch, 1990). Information on student writing is similar: 61 percent of grade 12 students report doing papers longer than three pages in English class less than once a month, and 75 percent report never receiving writing assignments in social studies or history classes (Office of Educational Research and Improvement, 1993). There is less literacy in schools than in most workplaces.

Student Abilities

A reasonable way to judge the effectiveness of current classroom techniques is to assess the abilities of students in school as well as the abilities of young adults who have recently matriculated through school. The National Assessment of Educational Progress has performed several national studies of adolescent reading abilities since the early 1970s and surveyed young adult (21–25 years of age) literacy abilities in the middle 1980s (Mullis & Jenkins, 1990; Kirsch & Jungeblut, 1986). NAEP study authors report that the overall reading performance of 17-year-olds improved somewhat between 1971 and 1988.

Nearly 100 percent of 17-year-olds can read at a *basic* level (i.e., following brief directions and locating facts in simple paragraphs). In 1988, 86 percent of 17-year-olds were able to perform at the *intermediate* level (i.e., recognize paraphrases and reach generalizations). This was an improvement from a generation earlier when only 78 percent of 17 year-olds attained this level. To place this *intermediate* level in perspective, it should be noted that this is the level achieved by the average 13-year-old or grade 8 student. It appears that schools and teachers have succeeded, for the most part, in helping the majority of students to do relatively simple reading such as might be found in simple newspaper articles. It also means that an average class of 17-year-olds still has four or five students unable to recognize paraphrases and draw inferences.

Greater difficulties begin to emerge, however, at higher levels on the national assessment of 17-year-olds. Only about 42 percent of 17-year-olds reach the *adept* level. Student attainment of this level has remained essentially the same since 1971. Readers who achieve at the *adept* level are able to understand complicated literary and informational passages, analyze and integrate less familiar material, and provide reactions to and explanations of the text as a whole. Only 4.8 percent of 17-year-olds in 1988 performed beyond the *adept* level and achieved at the *advanced* level. This percentage of students achieving at the *advanced* level has dropped significantly since 1971 when 6.6 percent achieved at this level.

As with the NAEP data on adolescents, however, wide racial and ethnic differences appear in the young adult data. Though a vast majority of all ethnic populations can accomplish basic literacy tasks, gaps in populations become even wider as the complexity of tasks increases. For example, according to NAEP data it is probable that 22 percent of whites would have difficulty writing a letter to state that an error was made in billing. On the same item, 60 percent of African Americans and 42 percent of Hispanic Americans would be likely to have difficulty. Test data indicate that it is probable that 35 percent of whites would have difficulty following directions to travel from one location to another using a map. On the same item, 80 percent of African Americans and 63 percent of Hispanic Americans would be likely to have difficulty.

The Problem of Low Transfer

It has been the assumption and hope of most educators that, if they could teach students to read one sort of material, they would be able to read all sorts. This assumption has allowed educators to believe that school work using textbooks and school reading materials would easily allow students to succeed with reading demands outside schools.

Teachers can do a great deal to enhance students' abilities to transfer literacy abilities from school to workplace and other nonschool settings. To do this, they must give learners a broad background of reading and writing experiences using a variety of materials and calling for extensive use of those materials in completing tasks and solving problems. The U.S. Department of Labor recommends that:

> The nation's school systems should make the SCANS foundation skills and workplace competencies consistent with explicit objectives of instruction at all levels (U.S. Dept. of Labor, 1992, xv).

The Department of Labor also advises that, to be effective:

> Teaching should be offered in context, that is students should learn content while solving realistic problems. *Learning in order to know* should not be separated from *learning in order to do.*
>
> Improving the match between what work requires and what students are taught requires changing how instruction is delivered and how students learn (U.S. Dept. of Labor, 1992, xvi).

Implications and Ideas for Classroom Teachers

Classroom teachers can never prepare students completely for the literacy demands in the workplace and other nonschool settings. Workplace and other nonschool literacy often involves communicating with others and reacting to various forms of print and graphics. Out of school, readers and writers usually have specific tasks, audiences, and contexts in mind. An initial goal for teachers, then, should be to model a real-world sort of literate interchange with a wide variety of material from newspapers, pamphlets, instructions, forms, announcements, manuals, tables, graphs, charts, advertisements, and correspondence. Reading and writing assignments can call for accomplishing specific tasks. Group tasks can help students learn to ask questions and work cooperatively in the way that adults often must work cooperatively using literacy to solve problems.

Gathering Materials

The first step is to gather materials, and students can share in this.

> Set up visits to agencies and businesses to gather materials and interview personnel managers about on-the-job literacy demands.

Appoint students to write and post instructions to absent students on how to do class assignments. (The teacher can check these for accuracy.)

Involve students in some classroom record keeping and form filling. Applying for classroom jobs is one technique.

Applications of Literacy to Problem Solving

Some assignments should involve application or problem solving, using multiple materials, interacting with others, and using literacy as a means to an end, rather than as a way to produce answers to questions or a product whose only audience is the teacher. These problem-solving uses of literacy are legitimate school uses of literacy that can transfer to the workplace and other nonschool settings.

Students write a letter requesting information on a product or a place they wish to visit.

Students interview three adults about the reading and writing they must do on their jobs. They write a letter to the principal, superintendent, or counselor explaining what one must learn to perform these jobs, or they write a story for the class newspaper or magazine.

Students summarize the main ideas from several different materials they have read on a topic of their choice. They make the summary into a booklet or article a younger or poorer reader could understand.

Students plan to accomplish a goal or a personal dream. This may involve writing letters and using catalogs, maps, advertising, price lists, and reference books. A final businesslike report can outline the resources needed and the steps required to make the dream come true.

Teachers can utilize book clubs or student-run businesses, structuring the activity so students must do the necessary writing, record keeping, and reading to operate the business.

Elaborated Plans Using the SCANS Guidelines

The SCANS guidelines listed earlier can be used by teachers to develop projects which call upon students to practice and improve their abilities in each of the five scans areas (allocating resources, interpersonal skills, analyzing and communicating information, understanding systems, and using technology). Below are descriptions of projects demonstrating how each of the SCANS areas can be developed.

Biology Classes

After reading about the seed germination process, have teams of two or three students set up studies to test the viability of various sorts of seed sold by local stores (grass, corn, flowers, etc.) The point is to compare the same product sold using different brand names and sold by different establishments. The result will be essentially a market report on where the most viable seeds may be obtained. The report could be made available through the school newspaper or even distributed by the establishment that has the best seeds.

Resources

Group would need to decide what it needs in terms of:

Seeds (and money if they aren't contributed)

Space

Time to do experiment, analyze data, write up results

Interpersonal Skills

Group must brainstorm tasks and what must be done (choose seed type, contact stores, gather equipment, etc.)

Need to talk to store managers and other adults to gain cooperation.

Letter writing to companies seeking information about seeds and perhaps contributions.

Information

Gather information on conditions and time for germination

Gather and analyze data on % of viable seeds

Present information in verbal, table, and graphic form

Extra-credit (analyze for statistically significant differences)

Systems

Plan out time-lines of when different tasks must be completed

Devise system to monitor if everyone is on schedule and task

Develop alternate plans when things go wrong (i.e. alternate source for seeds, who picks up on writing if team member is ill, etc.)

Technology

Telephone to contact stores

Calculator to compute percentages

Perhaps computer program for word processing, developing charts, statistical analysis

English Classes

Many professions (e.g., medicine, psychology, various sciences) publish digests and summaries of key articles from journals and books that have appeared recently. Nearly every profession has some professional publications. Have students join in groups associated with particular professions, determine what publications exist for these professions, secure back issues of journals for local employers, and produce digests of key ideas. These can be shared with people who helped secure the journals and written in a style that is more readable for average employees than the full articles themselves.

Think while Reading Activity

The biology and English activities in this section follow the SCANS guidelines. They are both interesting and practical. Pick one activity that you liked. Think about how it would help students develop real-world literacy. Record your thoughts here.

_____

_____

_____

_____

_____

_____

_____

_____

_____

_____

_____

_____

_____

Activity 12–3

Another project would be to have students plan, script, and produce short video-tapes. Topics can range from segments of literature read for class to how-to demonstrations related to preparing for the work-world (e.g., interviewing for jobs, dealing with conflict on the job, pro and con positions on drug testing). Information gathering, reading, note taking, and group planning would all precede the actual planning and scripting of the video. Tapes can be viewed by a panel of community "experts" for comment (either orally to class or after viewing at home).

Mathematics Classes

Using a set of building and landscape drawings from a local contractor have teams of four or five students determine amounts of specific materials and cost estimates for those materials. Each team would be responsible for contacting a different building supplies dealer for determining cost of materials. The result will be a written materials list and cost estimates prepared for the contractor or home buyer. Cost comparisons from different building supply dealers would be a useful outcome of this project.

For another project, students could survey parents, teachers, students, and members of the community about a current topical issue and compile results. Data can be analyzed and presented using a variety of charts, tables, and graphs. Various teams would have responsibility for different portions of the survey. Final products could be class presentations, stories for the school newspaper, and in some cases stories for the community newspaper. Variations can include using software which helps to analyze data and produces graphs. If portions of the survey are done over time, time-line graphs can be involved. Examination of how quantitative information is presented to the public in newspapers can be used as sources for ideas and critical discussions of the different approaches.

Additional Projects

Teachers with whom this author has worked have developed literally hundreds of SCANS activities ranging from school-wide interdisciplinary efforts to operate a recycling program to less ambitious plans for students to take lead roles in planning a field trip. Some of these activities include:

> Figuring out how to buy a car.
>
> Planning a banana split party to demonstrate that you don't need drugs or alcohol to have a good time. (Bring a banana as admission to the party.)
>
> Writing an environmental impact statement for a new highway.

Conclusion

Finding realistic uses of literacy in almost any subject area is really fairly simple. After all, if a subject is worth learning, it is very likely used by people outside of school as well as in school. The pamphlets, magazines, and literacy tasks used by adults who care about a subject are perfect materials and tasks to integrate into school learning. Choosing realistic tasks worth doing usually involves students working cooperatively and using literacy to solve problems in ways required once they leave school. The SCANS guidelines can provide direction for types of activities to develop. More time needs to be spent reading and writing to accomplish such activities and less time passively being talked to.

Think after Reading Activity

With a group of two or three classmates, plan an activity that involves students in literacy and problem-solving activities in each of the areas below. The U.S. Department of Labor Secretary's Commission on Achieving Necessary Skills recommends that students start engaging in such long-term problem-solving activities as early as elementary school.

Student Age Level and Content:

_____

_____

Activity Description:

_____

_____

_____

Describe the way the activity provides learning in each of the following areas:

Resources:

_____

_____

_____

Interpersonal:

_____

_____

_____

Information:

_____

_____

_____

Systems:

_____

_____

_____

Technology:

_____

_____

_____

Activity 12–4

Chapter *13*

Teaching Secondary Science through Reading, Writing, Studying, and Problem Solving

CAROL MINNICK SANTA   LYNN HAVENS   SHIRLEY HARRISON

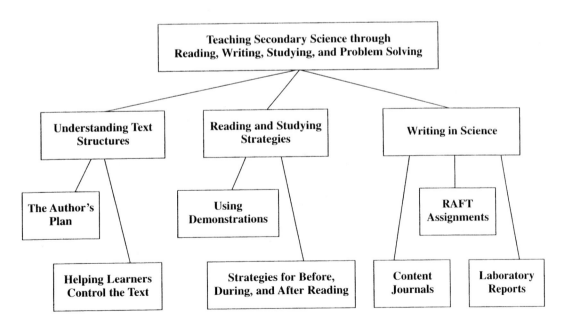

Think before Reading Activity

Think back to the science classes you have taken. What helped you learn and like science? While you're reading this chapter, note the strategies that you might share as a teacher so that someday when your students are asked this question their answer will be ten times as long as yours.

_____

_____

_____

_____

_____

_____

_____

_____

_____

_____

_____

_____

Activity 13–1

For many students, science is a challenging and often confusing discipline. Texts are difficult to read, and students' prior knowledge may be virtually nonexistent. The authors of this chapter discuss these issues and others and offer specific instructional ideas that promote students' reading and learning in science. The chapter describes how to help students read their texts more effectively, how to incorporate writing into a science program in order to enhance student learning and concept development, and how, through using an actual science selection, to develop specific teaching ideas.

The students stare with blank expressions. "Let me ask my question again," the teacher prompts. "Why is it necessary that cells divide? Who can outline the steps in mitosis?" Eyes glass over, papers shuffle, silence stifles. "Well, it appears that I must once again explain the content of your reading assignment." The teacher's frustration rises. Valuable class time is lost to such explanations, limiting the time for involving students in the exploration process of science. Why is it that students seem to learn so little from their reading assignments?

This scene occurs frequently in science classrooms. Students of all levels have difficulty learning science through reading. A common mistake is to assume that students can read science selections independently. Most students arrive at the science teacher's classroom knowing how to read, but few understand how to use reading for learning science content. Given that science texts are used in most secondary science programs, the science teacher faces some unique challenges. Part of the challenge derives from the nature of the content area. Few students have the background knowledge to learn information from science texts. There is too much unfamiliar content for students to grasp without some pre-reading instruction.

Researchers have consistently documented that the amount of knowledge students bring to a reading situation will influence what they learn from the assignment. Recall for a moment an introductory science course you took in college. These courses are among the most difficult because they provide a survey of an entire domain of knowledge such as chemistry or physics. You undoubtedly entered these courses with little background knowledge and had to work exceptionally hard to do well. However, as you began to progress into your major areas, each course began to build on another, and later courses were often easier because you had the background to understand. The problem of experiential background is central for students in grades 7–12 (see Chapter 22).

One challenge is the text itself. Many science texts are not written very clearly (see Chapters 5 and 6). The teacher and students need to take on an editorial role to understand the author's method of presenting information. When students understand how text is organized and written, they can use it more effectively.

Another challenge is the student's knowledge of comprehension and learning strategies. Few students understand how to organize information for learning. Most are able to read their text, but few know how to study and learn from it. All of us can give eloquent lectures and assign reading to students without showing them how to learn. We falsely assume that students can learn how to learn on their own or that it is not our responsibility.

We must continually evaluate our goals as teachers. Do we want students to leave our classrooms with only a collection of facts what will be rapidly forgotten, or do we want them to have a background in science along with the ability to continue learning beyond the confines of our classroom? Instructional goals must be long term.

The content, the text, and the student interact to create instructional challenges for the science teacher. The information presented here will help you understand and meet these challenges successfully. The first portion of this chapter describes strategies for helping students become more aware of text structure so that they can read their texts more effectively. The second portion contains practical teaching ideas based on a sample science selection. These include reading and studying strategies designed for teaching students how to learn science. Part three focuses on writing.

Learning about the Author's Plan

Reading, whether or not it comes from a text, a magazine article, or a nonfiction library book, plays a role in science instruction. For all reading assignments, students need to have an understanding of the author's plan of presentation so that they can use the plan for organizing and learning the information. Once students understand how main concepts are presented, they can begin to use the author's plan to organize information for learning (Slater & Graves, 1989).

Science writing offers students unique challenges. Science authors pack their writing with concepts. Some high school chemistry texts contain an estimated 3,000 words that are unfamiliar to high school students. This far exceeds the words taught in most foreign language classes. Moreover, most scientific writing is plagued with inadequate explanations and extraneous information (Holliday, 1991). Even with these potential difficulties, it is important to teach students that they have some control over their text. The teacher's task is to help students discover how their reading assignments have an organizational framework for learning, even if the author's plan is not altogether effective.

Instruction must progress from teacher demonstration and discussion to guided practice and finally to independent application (see Chapter 11). Begin by showing students how to read the text. Make an overhead transparency of the selection for demonstration. Read the selection aloud and describe how you use the author's clues such as introductory statements, rhetorical questions, bold print, and italics. Underline these clues on the transparency as you read. Talk about how the author develops main ideas and details, and describe the author's style of paragraph development. Point out areas that might cause reader difficulty, such as poorly defined concepts, unlabeled diagrams, and lack of elaboration in explanations. Describe what you do to comprehend and remember the material.

You might begin with a teacher explanation similar to the following:

In order to learn science concepts from a book, nonfiction article, or chapter from a textbook, the first thing to understand is what the author does to help you learn. We are going to figure out the author's plan. What is the author's style of main idea development? Science writers have a plan. If you can figure out the plan, you can use the materials more effectively. Let's read the introduction together. As we read, we are going to make a list of what the author does to help us learn.

Using a transparency of the selection, read the page together and think aloud the author's clues (Pearson, 1985). The conversation might go something like this:

What information is important on this page? Let's read the first paragraph again. What has the author included in the introduction? Is she letting us know what we are going to learn?

What is this author's style of writing? How does she let you know what is important? It seems the author introduces main points through questions. Rhetorical questions are a common pattern of main idea development in science selections. Let's read further. Does the author then answer her own questions?

The conversation continues, and together you build a list of characteristics describing the author's style. Next, you can write the list on the overhead or chart. The list might be similar to the following:

What does the author do to help me learn?

1. Uses introductory or thesis paragraphs.
2. Places main ideas in questions.
3. The author answers these rhetorical questions in the first sentence in paragraphs.
4. The author explains new vocabulary with clear examples.

5. Important vocabulary is in bold print.
6. Pictures and charts are used to explain the vocabulary.
7. The author uses transition words like first, second, and third to write clear explanations.

When reading other selections by the same author, remind students about the author's plan. Most authors have a consistent style of presentation. Then show students how to use the author's plan for selective underlining, building notes, or summarizing.

After you have modelled how to read an assignment, begin releasing more responsibility to students. For example, divide them into groups and make each group responsible for demonstrating their reading of difficult selections. Students also can take on the role of an editorial review board and analyze the strengths and weaknesses of the material. Have each group report their conclusions and come up with suggestions for reading the material more effectively. They may come up with comments such as these: ignore extraneous material, look for main ideas, take notes, and write down questions about unclear ideas. Provide opportunities for students to describe their own reading strategies and to realize the variety of approaches they can call on for comprehension.

Another idea is to have students read the introduction, boldface topics, and conclusions. From this information they can predict and outline the probable text content. After reading, they can revise their outlines. This approach teaches awareness of chapter organization and focuses on how well the author follows through with an organizational plan. Moreover, student committees can take particularly poor sections of the text and revise the material so that it is well written.

Instructional Strategies

As in many science texts, the material we are about to teach on flower reproduction is loaded with vocabulary that is tersely explained with little elaboration. Left to their own devices, most students would have difficulty reading this assignment. Before beginning instruction, have a clear idea about your content goals and make sure students have a notebook or journal for writing.

Let's say that you want your students to learn the following three major concepts in our hypothetical text assignment: (1) the parts of a flower and their functions, (2) variations among flowers, and (3) photoperiodism. Section 1 in the text includes the parts of a flower, and Section 2 describes the variations among flowers and photoperiodism. Because students must know the parts and functions of flowers before they can understand flower variation and photoperiodism, divide the assignment into two sections. Incorporate prereading activities before students read each of the parts. With this in mind, any of the following prereading activities would be appropriate:

Prereading Activities for Parts of a Flower

1. Have a variety of flowers in the classroom (talk to a local florist about saving you flowers that are normally thrown away). Place flower books throughout the classroom. Discuss favorite flowers. Give each student a piece of blank paper. List vocabulary words on the board: stamen, sepal, carpel, receptacle. Working in laboratory groups, students dissect flowers, draw the various parts, list the parts that appear similar in all flowers, and then draw a generic flower with those observed parts. Students predict the function of each part. They write their predictions in their science journal. As they read, they label the parts and write a sentence describing the function. Students read their entries to one another. A class discussion follows in which the teacher reviews the parts and functions of flowers and answers questions. Students revise their journal entries.

2. The teacher draws a generic flower on the board and lists the vocabulary words in chart form. The class brainstorms what they think might be the location and function of each part. They label the parts they know and generate ideas about each part's function. Students then read and revise the chart. After reading, the teacher leads a discussion and fills in the master chart on the board. If there is little information on function in the assignment, students can add information regarding function by examining additional resource materials in the room.

Prereading Activities for Variations and Photoperiodism

1. Write the words "angiosperms," "monocots," and "dicots" on the board. Remind students that they learned the definitions of these words in the last chapter. Lead a discussion until the meanings are clear. Then write the phrases "perfect flowers" and "imperfect flowers." Have students hypothesize definitions for perfect flowers and imperfect flowers and write down in their journals their prediction about their meaning. Ask students to read the subtopic "Photoperiodism and Flowering" and guess what these words mean. Give the students clues by dividing the words photoperiodism into components: photo and periodism. Brainstorm possible definitions for each word part. Again, have them record their hypotheses in their journals. Next, students read and revise their journal definitions.

2. Conceptual mapping, a system for organizing main ideas and details into graphic or pictorial form, works well as a prereading activity. Conceptual mapping instills active comprehension and dynamic discussion. (See Chapter 20.) The teacher writes the word "angiosperm" in the middle of the board or on a transparency. After discussing the meaning of angiosperm, the teacher ask students to brainstorm ways that angiosperms might vary. The prereading discussion is summarized in the form of a map, as in Figure 13–1. The map is similar to an "octopus outline"; the main idea is in the middle and the details radiate out from the hub. After completing the prereading discussion, the students read the selection to learn more about the variation among flowers. Then they revise the map to include information from the selection, as shown in Figure 13–2.

Reading and Postreading Strategies

Some additional ideas for helping students organize information from their reading are selective underlining, two-column notes, and conceptual mapping.

Selective Underlining
Underlining is a powerful tool for processing main ideas if students know how to underline. Novices typically take their magic marker and hemorrhage across the page, underlin-

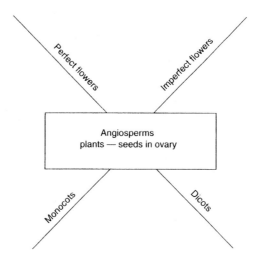

FIGURE 13–1   Conceptual Map

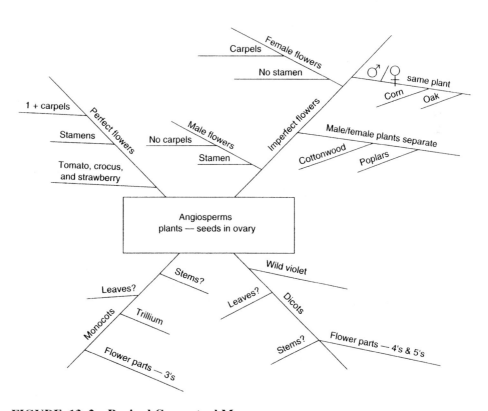

FIGURE 13–2   Revised Conceptual Map

ing practically everything. Underlining has to be taught. Because students cannot write in their text, use consumable materials such as magazine articles, laboratory manuals, and photocopies of reading assignments (Santa & Havens, 1995).

Begin with a demonstration. Photocopy the selection for the students and make a transparency of the assignment. Demonstrate how to underline the material selectively by highlighting key ideas, capturing the essence of the material. Talk aloud, explaining your underlines. Students underline their photocopy as you demonstrate. As you underline, develop guidelines with the class for students to use when underlining on their own. Sample guidelines might include (1) underline key ideas, (2) do not underline a whole sentence, (3) put an asterisk by underlined main points, and (4) make up study questions over main points. Students will need several demonstrations before they can succeed independently.

An intermediary step is to divide students into groups of two or three. Give each group a transparency containing the selection from their reading assignment. Each group selectively underlines the material on the transparency and then presents their underlines on the overhead for class discussion. Once students have success underlining key points and details in their reading, you can begin assigning students to underline assignments on their own.

Two-Column Notes

Two-column notes should be a part of every science curriculum (Santa & Havens, 1995). This form of note taking provides a simple system for organizing information and encourages self-testing. Students learn two-column note taking most easily if they have some instruction in analyzing the structure of their text and in noting main ideas and details through selective underlining. In fact, it is often a good idea to introduce two-column notes with material that students have already underlined.

Make a transparency of a selection. Talk aloud while you demonstrate. Have students divide their paper lengthwise into two columns. As noted in the following example, the left column contains key words naming an essential concept or main idea, and the right portion elaborates on main points. Then, covering the information on the right, students can test themselves using the key words on the left.

Parts of a Flower

Receptacle	Modified stem
Sepals	Leaflike petals and base of flower
Calyx	Made from petals to form protective coating for outer flower
Corolla	All petals together

Male parts of a flower

Stamens	Slender knoblike ends
Anthers	Knoblike ends of stamens
Filament	Thin stalk that supports anther

Two-column notes are particularly useful when the goal is to organize and remember a large amount of information. They also work well for organizing information from videos, movies, and slide presentations.

Conceptual Mapping

Mapping can be used strictly as a postreading activity. Divide students into groups of three or four. Give each group a large sheet of paper and colored markers. Tell them to make decisions about the major ideas in the reading selection and to represent the relationships among ideas in some way. Encourage students to understand that there is not a right way to map an assignment. The only criterion is to represent the essential ideas and their relationships. They can structure their maps using words, phrases, pictures, circles, squares, or whatever they feel best portrays the content. (See Figure 13–3.) The outcome is not nearly as important as the process of discussing content, deciding how to organize the content, and the sheer pleasure of formulating their creations.

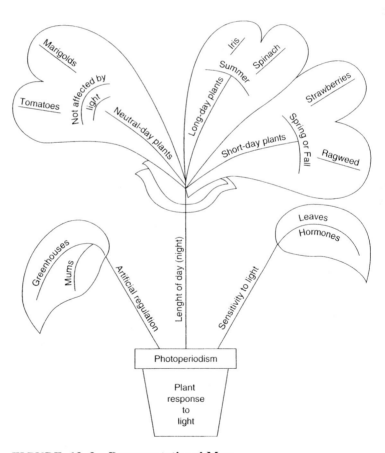

FIGURE 13–3   Representational Map

Think while Reading Activity

The two-column note is a format used for listing and elaborating essential concepts. Let's practice this by completing the two-column note below. Use the information you read in "Learning about the Author's Plan."

Essential Concepts   Elaboration

_____   _____
_____   _____
_____   _____
_____   _____
_____   _____
_____   _____
_____   _____

Activity 13–2

Maps become excellent props for oral presentations and for writing. Because mapping inspires students to organize their thinking, oral reports are usually far superior to those typically presented. Mapping leads readily into writing. Students' conceptual schemes become prewriting tools. The main points depicted in the map become topic sentences in paragraphs, and details evolve readily into supportive sentences.

Writing

Writing is a powerful technique for helping students learn and think critically about science. It forces organization and encourages students to make personal sense of new information by moving learning from a passive, receptive experience to an active, productive situation. Students should have a variety of writing experiences. In this section three types of assignments are presented: content journals, RAFT assignments, and laboratory reports (Santa & Havens, 1991).

Content Journals

Content journals provide students opportunities to write informally about scientific topics without fear of being critiqued by the teacher's red pen. The primary audience is always the writer. At the beginning of the school year, ask students to purchase a spiral notebook that can be kept in the classroom and used for writing two or three times per week. Journals typically are not graded. The teacher may want to collect them periodically, read several of the entries, and award some credit. (Junior high and high school students need this extrinsic motivation.)

Journal writing in science takes a variety of forms. Journal entries work well as part of prereading activities when students write down known information about a topic and make predictions about information in their reading. Students skim their assignment and write about what they think they will learn from their reading. After reading, they revise to include new information. As a postreading activity, students can summarize in one or two sentences their learning during a class period and write a question about any confusions. The next day, the teacher begins class with a discussion of the confusions. Students can also use their journals to summarize information from laboratory investigations and oral presentations.

Students could use journals to record their observations for laboratory reports. Questions and personal reactions to observations are part of journal entries. Because students have opportunities to react freely to their observations, they are better prepared for class discussions.

Journals become tools for developing study skills. Journals serve as reviews for the previous day when students read over their notes and then summarize key concepts. Students also can write down ideas for studying.

RAFT Assignments

These assignments move away from the traditional writing task in which students write an essay for a teacher audience. RAFT stands for role, audience, format, and topic, the key ingredients for making writing assignments (Santa & Havens, 1995). More specifically RAFT means:

1. The role of the writer (Who is the writer?)
2. The audience (To whom are you writing?)
3. The format (What form will it take?)
4. The topic and strong verb (What is your topic and verb?)

RAFT assignments are specific and well focused, which makes writing far more enjoyable to students and more fun for the reader. A writer can take many roles. In biology, for example, you could write from the perspective of a blood cell; the audience could be the other blood cells in the circulatory system. The format might be a travelogue and the topic a description of what happens as you are traveling through the circulatory system. Or you could be a piece of granite being swept over by a glacier stream, and your task as a writer could be to explain to a frog perched on your back how you arrived on the scene.

Writing to audiences who know little about the topic provides a rationale for clear explanations. For example, students can write letters to grade school students explaining scientific topics. The younger children can write back and let the older students know whether or not they have any questions.

The formats for writing vary (e.g., poems, memos, telegrams, editorials, dialogues, letters) and help set the tone for the piece. Having a deer write a letter to tourists pleading to save the wilderness creates a far different tone than having students write on the same topic in the form of a memo. Seldom use the word "write" in your assignments, but incorporate stronger verbs such as "persuade," "convince," and "demonstrate" for focusing the assignment and generating a specific tone.

Think while Reading Activity

RAFT assignments are recommended as a focused way for students to have more fun as readers. Look over the explanation of RAFT assignments again. Try one.

Example | Your Turn

R   Food   R   _____

A   Digestive system   A   _____

F   Love letter   F   _____

T   Why I need you   T   _____

Activity 13–3

The following RAFT assignment is based on the flower selection. You are a pollen grain (role). Explain (format) to a bee (audience) how you should be moved from the stamen to the carpel. Then explain the rest of your travels through the female reproductive parts (topic).

Laboratory Reports

One key component in science instruction is the laboratory experience and its documentation through laboratory reports. Most published laboratory materials offer little help either in executing experiments or in writing reports. Given this situation, how can you make experimenting and report writing an effective learning experience? The first step is to make sure that students understand the steps involved in conducting an experiment. Our first task is to help students learn the scientific method.

Begin with what your class already knows about the topic and arrive at one or two problems or questions that could be investigated. Lead students to recall knowledge relative to laboratory experiences and together come up with educated guesses or hypotheses as explanations. Brainstorm ways to test the hypotheses. Talk about the procedure and materials to test the hypothesis. Once students have completed the experiment, have them go back to their original questions and problem statements. Did their investigation answer their questions? Have them analyze how the information clarified their questions. If the experiment did not answer the questions, ask them to explain why, and come up with alternative ways to examine the issue. Work through many whole-class experiments until students begin to feel comfortable with the problem-solving procedures. Consistently use the same guidelines with each of their investigations until students know how to incorporate the steps.

In addition, show students how to document their investigations in laboratory reports. Begin the process by developing reports together. After conducting an experiment, lead students in writing a model report on the overhead or chalk board. Talk about each part of the report as you write. Once they begin to understand, gradually turn the report writing over to students.

To help with this transition, give students the option of using a framed report form to guide their writing. A framed report assists students by dividing the report into key components and by providing sentence starters and slots for supportive evidence. You may want to use a framed report form similar to the following example to guide students in writing their reports.

LABORATORY REPORT

OBSERVATION: After observing (state something unexplainable), I noticed

_____

PROBLEM (or question): Why does (put observation in the form of a question or
                        problem) _____

HYPOTHESIS: I think _____
                        (refer to the problem or question) is _____
                        An observation that led to this hypothesis is _____
                        I intend to prove _____
                        by _____

MATERIALS: 1. _____
                2. _____
                3. _____

PROCEDURE: (Put in order your plan for proving your hypothesis)
                1. _____
                2. _____
                3. _____

DATA: (Accurate detailed observations of your model and how it
                        works are recorded here. Include visuals such as tables,
                        graphs, mathematical operations, and pictures along with
                        observations.) _____

ANALYSIS AND
CONCLUSIONS: (Examine the problem and your hypothesis. Did your data
                        support your hypothesis? Explain why your results supported
                        or did not support your hypothesis.)

My problem is _____

The results of my investigation are _____

These results may be caused by _____

Therefore, these results did (or did not) support my hypothesis because_____

_____

CLASS CONCLUSION: After the class discussion, we concluded that _____

_____

Once students understand how to include each step of the scientific process in the reports, encourage deviation from the rigors of the preceding format, allowing students more individuality. Framed reports are appropriate only during the initial stages of instruction. Once students have success in writing reports, they should begin writing them on their own. However, insist on well-organized reports that include key components of the scientific process.

Conclusion

In this chapter we have touched upon many ideas to help students become more proficient learners of science. Science content and texts offer students many challenges. You can assist students in meeting these challenges by helping them understand how their text is crafted. Lead them inside and help them unravel the author's plan of presentation. Once students understand how an author has crafted the piece, they can begin using it as a tool for learning.

Before students read, lead them to recall what they already know or might know about the topic at hand, and preteach concepts that might cause difficulty. Then show them how to organize the information for learning. In order to meet the challenges of difficult content and text, students must organize the information in some way. Most of us learn very little by just reading over an assignment, particularly when the assignment is difficult. Selective underlining, two-column notes, and concept maps will help students organize and learn information from their assignments.

Writing informally in journals or more formally using RAFT assignments and laboratory reports helps students become active learners of content. Writing assists students in understanding the complexities of science. Writing forces learners to organize their think-

---

Think after Reading Activity

This Chapter describes several science journal writing activities. Select one of these strategies and describe how, if you were a science teacher, you would use it to facilitate students' reading and understanding of science information and concepts.

_____

_____

_____

_____

_____

_____

_____

Activity 13–4

ing and to evaluate if they have understood a concept. We cannot write about something we don't understand.

In the end, teaching science is a fascinating challenge. Although the rich content is often difficult, it entices students' curiosity. Science provides the stage for exciting teaching and enthusiastic learning. Enthusiastic learners are those who succeed. They know how to learn from their text, think through scientific problems, and write about their discoveries. They leave our classrooms knowing science and knowing how to continue learning when we are no longer available as their guide. They are the products of our thoughtful instruction.

C h a p t e r *14*

Reading in Social Studies

Using Skills and Strategies in a Thoughtful Manner

CHARLES W. PETERS

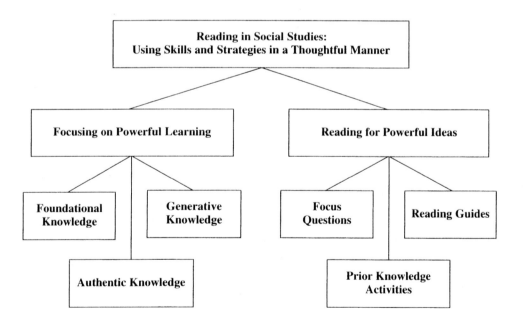

Think before Reading Activity

Every time one turns on TV or opens a newspaper it is possible to hear that today's youth don't have any knowledge of civics. Do you think this is true? How could civics information be presented in a way that makes it relevant to students? Jot down a few ideas.

_____

_____

_____

_____

_____

_____

_____

_____

As you read this chapter, note additional ideas below.

_____

_____

_____

_____

_____

Activity 14–1

The last decade has seen the continuous development and use of reading strategies designed to improve student learning in the various subject areas. They range from activities that activate or assess prior knowledge to activities that facilitate learning from text (Beck & McKeown, 1991; Ogle, 1986; Peters, 1990). Research investigating the overall effectiveness of these strategies is unambiguous—it makes a difference in what and how students go about learning from social studies materials (Camperell & Knight, 1991). From this vantage point, strategy and skill instruction in the social studies is progressing well.

However, there are ominous clouds on the horizon. Although the repertoire of reading strategies has increased, these strategies have not always been used to promote significant and worthwhile understandings. Content is often taught as a parade of disembodied facts that emphasize coverage of large quantities of information. Consequently, reading activities that help students learn thin and superficial information are not helpful; they detract from the primary goal of social studies—promoting civic efficacy (Kaltsounis, 1987; Newmann, 1992; Parker, 1991; Parker & Jarolimek, 1984). The bottom line is that reading activities must be consistent with broad curricular goals and outcomes. If not, reading skills instruction becomes a series of decontextualized activities that do not promote the goals of the curriculum.

It is time that content and process came together. Those who teach social studies cannot ignore what reading research and practice suggest about how to improve learning from text, and reading educators who know about enhancing learning from text cannot avoid the quality of content issue raised by social studies educators. If we are to link reading skills and strategies to important social studies curricular goals, we must keep in mind three axioms: (1) The quality of reading strategies is inextricably linked to the quality of the content; (2) Reading strategies must be selected in a systematic manner; (3) Not all strategies for improving reading comprehension are created equal. This chapter describes the connection between developing and promoting quality learning and how this can be accomplished through reading activities that model thoughtful learning.

Developing more thoughtful reading activities requires two important steps. The first is the identification of the powerful ideas that underlie the content to be learned. Second is the identification of the strategies that promote the learning of powerful ideas. When this is done, reading strategies become tools to help expedite comprehension which do not interrupt the flow of content by introducing unrelated skills. Skills become part of the lesson when they are needed and thus can be used in natural and authentic applications. It is essential that reading activities avoid superficiality by using powerful concepts to form powerful generalizations.

Reinforcing Powerful Learning

Powerful ideas are drawn from *concepts, themes,* and *generalizations* that come from the disciplines that make up the social studies—history, geography, government, and economics. Examples of powerful social studies concepts are change, culture, diversity, justice, and conflict. These concepts can be combined to form themes that are linked to the various disciplines within social studies. Examples of geographic themes are relationships within places and human interaction with the environment. Generalizations drawn from these themes and concepts are the heart of social studies. An example of a generalization is that human adaptations produce both intended and unintended consequences.

An excellent resource for identifying powerful concepts, themes, and generalizations are the various reports published by academic societies, professional organizations, and educational agencies. Some of the more useful are the Joint Committee on Geographic Education (1984), Bradley Commission on History in Schools (1988), Joint Council on Economic Education (1984), Center for Civic Education (1990), and the Center for the Teaching of History (1994). They have published lists of themes for each of the disciplines.

By their nature, powerful ideas and powerful content are integrative and help students form and develop deeper and richer understandings. This is critical for improving comprehension of informational materials such as social studies textbooks. Powerful ideas build knowledge that is the basis of making connections. In addition, they create a network of associations linking new input to prevailing knowledge and beliefs anchored in concrete experiences. As a result, they do not leave students with disconnected bundles of information. When reading activities are thin or superficial, they emphasize coverage of large quantities of fragmented information.

Levels of Knowledge

In order to promote the type of learning that has value and meaning beyond the classroom, social studies teachers must use activities that foster critical reading. Good critical reading skills help foster reflective inquiry, problem solving, and decision making by helping students focus on actual life applications.

To promote this type of learning, reading activities must advance three types of knowledge—foundational, generative, and authentic. These three types of knowledge are important because they serve people well in later academic and nonacademic pursuits by empowering students to move beyond the narrow confines of the classroom.

Foundational knowledge is built by using reading skills and strategies to help students become better at extracting important ideas from the materials, connecting events through causal reasoning, forming more complex conceptual systems, and identifying problems and solutions. Foundational knowledge develops deeper and richer understandings, which move students beyond reproducing the thoughts and ideas of others toward producing new insights for themselves—the creation of generative knowledge.

Generative knowledge leads to the active use of knowledge and skills, because knowledge and skills in themselves do not guarantee understanding. According to Perkins (1992) generative knowledge "does not just sit there but functions richly in people's lives to help them understand and deal with the world" (p. 5). Generative knowledge promotes the use of authentic knowledge.

Authentic knowledge develops when skills and strategies connect information from the text to the larger social context in which students live. Connections are sought between students' lives and the content of social studies, between principles and practice, and between past and present. This type of knowledge requires students to think through concepts and situations, rather than memorize isolated facts to give back on a quiz. Authentic knowledge is used in the actual life applications that the social studies curriculum is designed to prepare students for or in realistic simulations of these application situations.

The Importance of Focus Questions

Reading skills and strategies must contribute to the development of all three types of knowledge. The development of all three types of knowledge is easier to obtain when activities are part of a larger unit of study rather than isolated from one another. To ensure that the activities promote significant and worthwhile learning that is connected and not fragmented, it is a good idea to use a *focus question.* A focus question establishes a clear purpose for reading and learning and helps students connect powerful concepts, themes, and generalizations that are embedded in all three levels of knowledge. In other words, focus questions are not specific questions to be answered definitively by students and then put aside. Rather, they guide instruction by lingering in the back of a teacher's mind while planning lessons, choosing instructional materials, or identifying reading skills and strategies needed to answer the focus question. Consequently, they are problematic and not accompanied by predetermined answers. Nor can they be adequately answered with single words, short phrases, or memorized information. Furthermore, focus questions prevent an overly broad topic that typically serves as a black hole or magnet for large quantities of expository information. Without a focus question there is little motivation or need to think. Question-based units encourage teachers to abandon the role of "knowledge transmitter" and instead assume the role of "inquiry facilitator" (Onosko & Newmann, 1994).

The focus question should be sufficiently challenging to stimulate reflective inquiry. A good focus question has the following characteristics: it is fundamental to the topic of the unit; it refers to an authentic problem, that is, one actually faced by society and not created for academic purposes only; it poses a type of problem that persists over time and place; it requires knowledge drawn from social studies disciplines; and it engages students by being meaningful to them. Examples of focus questions are: How should countries of South Asia address their rates of population growth? Is violence ever justifiable in a democratic society?

The Unit as a Focus

The reading strategies and activities that follow are based on a common unit. First, with the unit as a constant, activities can be systematically linked to a common focus question. This makes it possible to present a range of activities that build deeper understanding as they are strategically used to reference learning that centers on a common topic. Second, it is possible to demonstrate how different levels of reading ability can be addressed in the same unit. Third, by using a unit it is possible to model how all activities are connected and therefore advance all three levels of knowledge.

Because it is important for reading activities to promote the learning of a common set of powerful concepts, themes, and generalizations, the National History Standards were used as a guide in selecting the concepts, themes, and generalizations for a unit on the causes of the Civil War. The theme for the unit is: United States expansion between 1800 and 1861 brought about rapid social, economic, and political change that led to regional conflicts. Some of the powerful concepts associated with this theme are: social, political, and economic conflicts, political compromise, and regional differences. Important generalizations are: economic differences between regions lead to conflict; social differences among groups lead to different political solutions to complex problems. To connect the concepts, themes, and generalizations, two focus questions were created: Should individuals use violence to prevent the enforcement of laws they reject? Was the Civil War inevitable?

The reading activities that follow are designed to help students pull the ideas from their materials so they can form deeper and richer understandings. The first step toward a thoughtful response to the focus questions is making sure students build the necessary foundational knowledge that will permit them to become active, engaged learners.

Using Reading Skills and Activities That Develop Foundational Knowledge

At the foundational knowledge level, reading skills and activities should help students build the requisite knowledge base that moves them to deeper and richer levels of understanding. As research conducted by Spoehr and Spoehr (1994 pp. 73–74) suggests, when historians read they must be able:

1. To imagine themselves in situations unlike anything they are likely to experience.
2. To develop hypotheses about cause and effect, allowing for the possibility that a cause may be quite remote from its effect in time, in category (social, political, economic), or both.
3. To assess how well their hypotheses fit the facts, recognizing that reality is messy and that there will always be counter arguments available that will seem to contradict their hypotheses, and that they must take those counter arguments into account.
4. To define abstractions precisely, and to show how those abstractions, when used and defined by others, have changed their meaning over time.
5. To articulate their own values precisely, making sure that they are positing an opinion and not merely projecting an attitude, and that their conclusions follow logically from the evidence.

What this means is that reading skills instruction must help students make explicit the implicit relationships between important ideas and concepts. This is done by helping students make basic connections between their experiences and the texts they are reading. To ensure that this happens, students need to build on the knowledge they already possess so they can more readily make connections among important ideas. They must also be able to recognize what is in the text and arrange the ideas in meaningful relationships. This is not always easy because students read too quickly over important information without realizing its importance. Finally, students must be able to make new connections and apply what they have learned to new situations. Therefore, these activities should help students pull ideas from the material they are reading so they can engage in historical reasoning, think through cause-effect relationships, use facts to draw conclusions, reach sound historical interpretations, and conduct historical inquiries and research leading to the knowledge on which informed decisions in contemporary life can be based. This type of reasoning is dependent on the ability to construct meaning from the materials students read.

Reading Guides

Reading guides identify explicit skills students need to construct meaning. Reading guides provide a variety of functions. They (1) move students to deeper levels of understanding by helping them organize the information they pull from the text; (2) help students interpret, analyze, and manipulate information in nonroutine ways; (3) show how to use facts to make interpretations and draw conclusions; (4) help students make more complex comparisons that offer insights into complex problems; and (5) help students learn how to anticipate counter arguments, weigh alternative explanations, and understand why one interpretation may be preferable to another.

As the following activities demonstrate, students are shown how to read and think about more complex questions, such as "Was the Civil War inevitable?" Keep in mind that they are only guides and not the required way to answer the question. If students can come up with a better approach, then they should be free to use it. If students already know how to do this type of reading, they don't need the guide. If they don't, they will find the guides useful.

Prior Knowledge Activities

An important reading activity to use at this level is one that assesses prior knowledge. This is critical because without adequate prior knowledge of powerful concepts that are linked to understanding the theme, generalizations, and focus questions, students may struggle through materials failing to make the appropriate connections. Therefore, it is important to obtain some degree of understanding about students' depth of knowledge regarding key concepts.

When assessing knowledge about key concepts, several types of information are important to evaluate. These include: (1) What are the critical or distinguishing characteristics of a concept? For students to be able to distinguish between two or more concepts, they must be able to list the characteristics that distinguish one concept from others. (2) What are examples of the concept? Students who possess accurate knowledge about a concept should be able to provide examples of what it is. (3) Once students can identify critical features of a concept and provide examples, they should be able to write a clear and concise definition. The definition comes after the identification of critical characteristics and examples, because definitions are based on an understanding of these first two categories. What the first two categories model is one way to write a definition that students generate from their own knowledge and not from a glossary or dictionary definition they may not understand. (4) Can students see relationships among concepts? Key to building foundational knowledge is for students to demonstrate how they make connections between key concepts.

The activity presented in Figure 14–1, "Understanding Powerful Concepts," is designed with these categories in mind. Its purpose is to determine whether students possess adequate knowledge about the powerful ideas that underlie the unit on the causes of the Civil War. Since the focus question for the unit deals with powerful concepts such as "conflicts," "compromise," "regional," "inevitability," it is important to determine how much knowledge students have about them before beginning their assigned readings.

Don't be concerned if students cannot fill in all of the categories. If significant numbers are left blank, it may mean that you might have to review or reteach some concepts before beginning the unit. The purpose of prior knowledge activities is not merely to see where differences exist between students and assign a grade, but rather to use that information to make informed decisions about how to proceed with the unit. That is why the activity is administered *before* students begin reading. Students should possess adequate foundational knowledge before they are presented new ideas that build on what they already know.

Concepts	Characteristics of the Concepts	Examples of the Concepts	Connections between Concepts
Conflicts			Conflicts and political compromise
Democratic Values			Regional differences and conflict
Regional Differences			
Political Compromise			Inevitability and conflict
Inevitability			

FIGURE 14–1   Understanding Powerful Concepts

The activity presented in Figure 14–2, "Connecting Powerful Concepts," assesses prior knowledge in a different way. It asks students to provide a concept map of the key terms listed in the activity. The purpose of the concept map is to determine whether students see a connection among powerful concepts, some of which they have seen before and some they have not. Once students have developed the concept map, they must explain their reasoning. If students are to build an integrated knowledge base, then they must be able to connect important concepts and ideas. This activity will let teachers know how students see relationships among important concepts.

There are several critical differences between the activities presented in Figures 14–1 and 14–2. First, in constructing a concept map, students are expected to possess a more detailed understanding of powerful concepts. They must be able to see how multiple concepts fit together into some type of conceptual schema that are linked to the themes, generalizations, and focus questions. It demonstrates the importance of a connected rather than disconnected knowledge, because it is this type of knowledge base that builds powerful conceptual connections. Second, the intent of the concept map activity is to obtain some indication as to the depth and breadth of students' knowledge related to the causes of the Civil War.

Prior knowledge assessment activities like the two described here help students understand how the discipline works—how one justifies, explains, solves problems, and manages inquiry within the discipline. This helps them see the structure and logic of the discipline. This is a critical purpose of the activities.

Reading Activities for Foundational Knowledge

The guides presented in Figures 14–3 through 14–5 show students how to perform the type of reading and reasoning required to pull out major events and link them to the causes of the Civil War, placing these events into a historical problem-solving context so they can extract a lesson that can be applied to a contemporary situation.

Given this purpose of the outcomes, themes, and focus question, an appropriate activity would be one that requires readers to link causally important historical events with their

Concepts	Arrange the terms in the form of a concept map that shows how they are related to one another. Add any additional terms you believe might help explain how they go together.
Civil War States' Rights Federalism Individual Rights Confederation Regionalism Manifest Destiny Industrialization Reformism	
Justification Provide a written summary that explains why you related the terms the way that you did.	

FIGURE 14–2   Connecting Powerful Concepts

Think while Reading Activity

In the beginning of the chapter the author states that there is a concern among educators that too much emphasis is placed on the coverage of insignificant information in social studies classrooms. This results in fragmented and disconnected learning. The author suggests several strategies to help students learn in a thoughtful manner. Below is an example of a causal thinking chart discussed in this section. As you read this section, record your answers and think about how this type of activity can enhance student learning.

Causal Thinking Chart

Event:	*Becoming a Teacher*
Reason:	_____
Result:	_____
Event:	*Majority Rule in South Africa*
Reason:	_____
Result:	_____
Your Turn Here	
Event:	_____
Reason:	_____
Result:	_____

Activity 14–2

reasons and results. The activity in Figure 14–3, "Causal Reasoning," lists important historical events that led up to the Civil War and asks students to identify reasons and results for these events. This activity primarily involves lower-order reasoning. In most cases students are asked to reproduce the thoughts explicitly or implicitly stated in materials they read. The teacher should anticipate a variety of responses. The important thing to look for is whether the responses constitute an acceptable reason that is linked to a plausible result. Since the activity is designed to encourage flexibility in response, a number of responses are acceptable.

An activity like the one presented in Figure 14–3 can be easily modified. If the activity is too difficult, the teacher can provide statements from which students can select the appropriate reasons and results. Or the teacher can provide an event and a reason and see if the student can identify an appropriate result. The critical point is to provide an explicit model for the reasoning involved in exacting the information needed to answer the focus question.

The activity shown in Figure 14–4, "Linking Events Causally," is based on the same reading skills as the previous activity, only it is structured in a more complex manner. In

Event: Publication of *Uncle Tom's Cabin*

Reason:

Result:

Event: Free Soil Dispute

Reason:

Result:

Event: John Brown's Raid

Reason:

Result:

Event: The South views slavery differently from the North.

Reason:

Result:

Event: Plantation owners had most of the political power in the south.

Reason:

Result:

Event: Most Southerners did not own slaves.

Reason:

Result:

FIGURE 14–3   Causal Reasoning

Free Soil Dispute in Kansas

Reason:

Result:

Reason:

Result:

What interpretations or conclusions can be drawn from these events?

People wanted to expand slavery to western territories.

Fighting breaks out in Kansas.

The Kansas–Nebraska Act in passed.

Republican Party is created.

Southerners' distrust of North increases.

FIGURE 14–4   Linking Events Causally

this activity students are given a problem—the dispute in Kansas involving the Free Soil movement—and asks students to demonstrate the causal reasoning involved in reaching a conclusion about the events. Notice that in this activity students have been given support; possible answers are listed at the bottom of the activity. A way to make it more difficult would be to omit these statements or ask students to identify the democratic principles that come into conflict during this dispute.

Activities presented in Figures 14–3 and 14–4 are important because they help students make connections between concepts, events that are needed to construct an argument about the causes of the Civil War. To construct an argument from materials they must read, students need guidance in how to make connections among important events, connections that go beyond superficial understandings to connections that require higher-order thinking. Facts are important in social studies because you need them to form a foundation on which knowledge can develop. This is not just accumulation of facts but discriminating what contributions they make toward making judgments.

The activity presented in Figure 14–5, "Social and Economic Interpretations of the Civil War," requires students to deal with two important perspectives on the causes of the Civil War. After reading several sources they are asked to provide a definition of social and economic causes, indicate the source of the definitions, and then provide two examples that support their definitions. This is followed by a metacognitive question that asks them to explain why the information they provided qualify as examples. This is an important question because this is the first time they have been asked to reflect on the appropriateness of a response. This is an important ingredient in thoughtful learning (Newman, 1990; Tishman, Jay, & Perkins, 1993). This activity also begins to make connections with contemporary events. The idea is that if students understand social and economic factors that contributed to the Civil War, they can find similar examples from events of today. To supply this information means that students must rely on sources other than their textbooks; they must turn to magazines and newspapers. They must think carefully about any example they cite, because they are asked to explain why it qualifies as an example.

The next series of questions requires students to do more synthesizing of information. First, they must compare the similarities and differences between the two perspectives—

Think while Reading Activity

Imagine that you are a social studies mentor teacher at your school. Part of your assignment includes visiting the other teachers to give them suggestions on successful social studies teaching ideas. Yesterday you visited a class and observed that the teacher's instruction could be more effective and the students could be more interested in the assignments. You have concluded that the teacher could accomplish this by relating social studies concepts and facts through reading strategies. This afternoon you are scheduled to talk with the teacher. What are you going to say? Why?

Activity 14–3

Define social causes of the Civil War	Where did you find your definition?	Give two examples of social differences that led up to the Civil War	Why do they qualify as examples?	Give an example from current conflicts, e.g., Northern Ireland, North and South Korea

Define economic causes of the Civil War	Where did you find your definition?	Give two examples of economic differences that led to the Civil War	Why do they qualify as examples ?	Give an example from current conflicts, e.g., Northern Ireland, North and South Korea

FIGURE 14–5   Social and Economic Interpretations of the Civil War

Why does it qualify as an example?	How do social and economic events differ?	How do your observations compare with views presented in your materials?	What other possible interpretations might have been offered?
Why does it qualify as an example?	How are social and economic events similar?		

social and economic—and then compare their observations with that of the views presented in the texts they have been reading. The purpose of this question is for students to see if information in the texts they read is different from what they come up with for their own explanations. Finally, once they have compared their views with that of the various sources they have read, they might be able to come up with other explanations for why the Civil War occurred.

The activities that use reading skills to foster the development of foundational knowledge do a number of things. First, they help readers identify important ideas from text. Second, they help students go beyond surface-level information to form more complex understandings. Third, they introduce the importance of metacognitive reasoning. In the activities that follow, students will move in more direct ways to generate more complex connections—muster evidence, form generalizations, apply concepts, form analogies, and represent knowledge in new ways.

Using Reading Skills and Strategies to Build Generative Knowledge

At the generative knowledge level, reading skills are used to advance higher-order thinking. This is done by constructing reading guides that help students:

1. Solve a problem that cannot be resolved through the routine application of previously learned foundational knowledge.
2. Consider multiple perspectives when analyzing controversial issues related to the interpretation of the causes of the Civil War.
3. Analyze counter arguments that require moving beyond the accumulation of foundational knowledge to using knowledge more discriminatively.
4. Examine events over time to understand the difference between immediate and longer impact of historical events.
5. Understand how facts can be grouped in more than one category (e.g., social, political, economic interpretations).
6. Check the consistency of facts in a stated position.

Students who have problems reading social studies materials and completing tasks that require the use of generative knowledge sometimes have difficulty sorting through the many details and facts associated with important historical events like those surrounding the outbreak of the Civil War. Frequently, this means trying to answer complex questions without possessing the appropriate skills or strategies.

Reading Activities for Generative Knowledge

The reading strategies presented in Figure 14–6, "Comparing Perspectives," model one way to answer the focus question: Was the Civil War inevitable? The reading activity lists important events that led to the Civil War and asks a series of questions designed to examine changing perspectives over time. The activity is divided into two chronological periods

Events	How are the event resolved?	Was there a willingness to compromise?	What is the source of the conflict?	Was there any violence?	Why did people resort to violence?
1. Missouri Compromise					
2. Tariffs					
3. Compromise of 1850					
4. Fugitive Slave Act					
1. Kansas–Nebraska Act					
2. *Uncle Tom's Cabin*					
3. Dred Scott Case					
4. John Brown's Raid					
5. Election of Lincoln					

FIGURE 14-6 Comparing Perspectives

| | Similarities | | Differences | |
	1820–1850	1851–1861	1820–1850	1851–1861
How was the tension resolved?				
Why were people willing to compromise?				
What was the source of the conflict?				
Was violence directly or indirectly associated with the event?				
Focus Question Was the Civil War inevitable? Why or why not?				

FIGURE 14-6 *Continued.*

(1821–1850 and 1851–1861) so students can use the information from their texts to see how responses to these events dramatically changed as time progressed. Hopefully, what the guide helps students see is that by placing historical events into chronological order and then dividing time into two periods, they will discover how time impacts events. The questions that appear at the top of the guide are designed to help students investigate how these historical events were resolved during the different time periods. What the guide models are the types of questions students need to ask themselves as they respond to the focus question.

Notice that certain key questions are repeated on the second page of the activity. This is done to help students who have difficulty making explicit comparisons; the guide helps them organize their ideas. This is an important feature of the guide and should not be overlooked. As students use the guide to organize their ideas, it serves as a prewriting aid. As a prewriting aid, it becomes a strategic way to organize ideas for writing.

The activity shown in Figure 14–7, "Understanding Conflicting Perspectives," is similar to the activity in Figure 14–6. It requires students to use both comparative and causal reading skills to answer the second focus question in the unit: Can the use of violence be justified? However, the primary difference between the two is that the activity in Figure 14–7 takes a more in-depth approach to reading the text. It presents four major events that led up to the Civil War and asks students to gather information that can be used to analyze the two conflicting perspectives. Not only must students identify reasons for these events, but they must also link them to democratic values and beliefs that underlie each region's position. Students must then determine the long- and short-term impact of these perspectives on the coming war. They use this information to determine answers to a series of questions that are linked to the second focus question.

Again, the activity provides a model for answering complex questions. It does this by providing students with a guide for analyzing conflicting perspectives. This process requires students to formulate new thoughts about those events. This is perhaps one of the hardest parts to reading social studies material more critically because it requires students to anticipate counter arguments, to weigh alternative explanations, and to explain why one interpretation is preferable to another one.

In summary, these two guides foster reading skill development in two ways. First, they help students form meaningful clusters of information that allow them to make connections between major historical events. Second, they help them construct an argument from materials they read. Students need guidance in how to make connections among important events, connections that go beyond superficial understandings to connections that require higher-order thinking. Specifically, these activities make complex ideas in text more visible to the reader.

Using Reading Skills and Strategies to Build Authentic Knowledge

Authentic knowledge develops when skills and strategies connect information from the text to the larger social context in which students live. Connections are sought between students' lives and the content of the unit. Therefore, the authentic application of skills can

Event	North			South			Consequence	
	Position			Position			Immediate impact	
Dred Scott Case	Reason for position			Reason for position			Long-term impact	
	Values, beliefs underlying position			Values, beliefs underlying position				
	Position			Position			Immediate impact	
Firing on Fort Sumter	Reason for position			Reason for position			Long-term impact	
	Values, beliefs underlying position			Values, beliefs underlying position				

FIGURE 14–7 **Understanding Conflicting Perspectives**

Event	North	South	Consequence
Uncle Tom's Cabin	Position Reason for position Values, beliefs underlying position	Position Reason for position Values, beliefs underlying position	Immediate impact Long-term impact
Kansas–Nebraska Act	Position Reason for position Values, beliefs underlying position	Position Reason for position Values, beliefs underlying position	Immediate impact Long-term impact

What were the different regional perspectives underlying the four conflicting events?

What democratic values were in conflict?

Was violence a response to the resolution of these events?

Focus Question: Can the use of violence be justified?

FIGURE 14-7 *Continued.*

best be measured by determining the extent to which they have value and meaning beyond the instructional context. The purpose of authentic reading activities is to engage students in reflective inquiry, critical thinking, problem solving, or decision making.

To use knowledge in authentic ways, students must be able to apply a number of complex reading skills, such as understanding causal relationships, linking reasons and results with solutions, comparing conflicting points of view, drawing a lesson from the conflict and applying it to a contemporary event. The purpose of the reading guides in this section is to provide opportunities for students to apply their existing knowledge to questions about new content, to learn new content with understanding, to synthesize and communicate what they have learned, and to generate new knowledge or creative applications.

Reading Activities for Authentic Knowledge

The activity shown in Figure 14–8, "Resolving Conflicts," is designed to help students apply what they have learned about a specific problem during the Civil War period to a contemporary event. In this activity students are given a problem that is related to both focus questions. The problem is: Did economic differences between the North and South lead to conflict over the expansion of slavery? The purpose of the first part of the reading guide is to examine reasons, results, and solutions to the problem from different perspectives, the North and the South. Once students have placed this problem and its solutions into a historical context, they are asked for their own solutions. Students are expected to provide a thoughtful response, one that draws on the information in the first part of the activity. Next, it asks for students to identify the lessons that can be drawn from these events. Finally, students are asked to apply their lessons to a contemporary event of their choice. Students are required to research the contemporary event and discuss how the lessons from the past apply to it.

The importance of this activity is that it helps students do more than merely list ideas; it requires them to perform detailed analyses of the events. This means that students must acquire an appropriate depth of understanding to support the lessons they have drawn. Students who have difficulty pulling information from the text and organizing it in a manner that will permit them to craft a response to the focus question need this type of support.

The activity shown in Figure 14–9, "Reasoning with Democratic Values," centers on democratic principles and values, because they provide the basis for considering the ethical dimensions embedded in the unit. It asks students to respond to the focus question: Should individuals use violence to prevent the enforcement of laws they reject? To help students locate information in their materials that addresses the issue, a number of additional questions are offered as guides. Each question allows students to locate important points that are needed in formulating their responses. Ethical issues such as the one in this activity provide an arena for the reflective development and application of prosocial values—liberty, justice, equality, and diversity.

The purpose of the activities shown in Figures 14–8 and 14–9 was to get students to confront a problem in the context of a real situation and reach some resolution to it. Like most authentic situations that call for problem solving and careful thought, these activities contained an element of conflict that centered on an unresolved question about public affairs. This helped engage students by appealing to their interests and experiences through

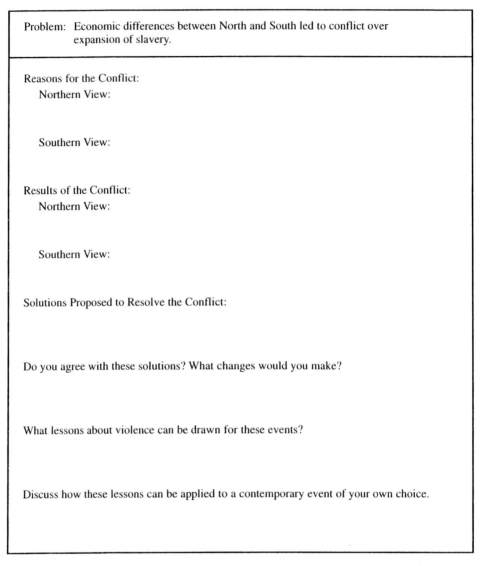

Problem: Economic differences between North and South led to conflict over expansion of slavery.

Reasons for the Conflict:
    Northern View:

    Southern View:

Results of the Conflict:
    Northern View:

    Southern View:

Solutions Proposed to Resolve the Conflict:

Do you agree with these solutions? What changes would you make?

What lessons about violence can be drawn for these events?

Discuss how these lessons can be applied to a contemporary event of your own choice.

FIGURE 14–8 Resolving Conflicts

hands-on as well as minds-on activities. These activities called for students not just to reproduce what they had learned but to use what was learned for some authentic purpose.

The activity shown in Figure 14–10, "Metacognitive Reflections: Judging the Usefulness of the Reading Guide," focuses on the metacognitive knowledge students need to become strategic readers. Because one of the main features of this chapter has been the use of reading guides to improve reading performance, it is important for students to evaluate their utility. As was mentioned previously, guides are not meant to be mindless fill-in-the-

Focus Question: Should individuals use violence to prevent the enforcement of laws they reject?

What democratic values were in conflict during the Civil War?			
Define the democratic values in the context of the Civil War.			
Which democratic values are primary?			
Give an example from current issues in the news that is similar.			

FIGURE 14-9 Reasoning with Democratic Values

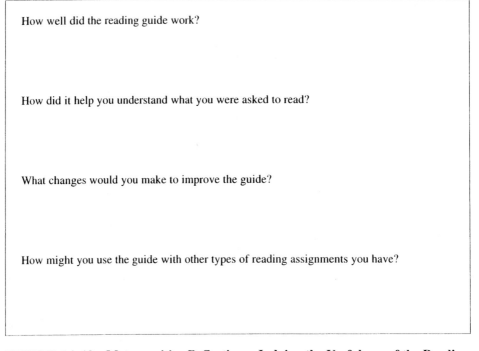

How well did the reading guide work?

How did it help you understand what you were asked to read?

What changes would you make to improve the guide?

How might you use the guide with other types of reading assignments you have?

FIGURE 14–10   Metacognitive Reflections: Judging the Usefulness of the Reading Guide

blank operations, but rather, models of how expert readers of social studies materials might reason their way through complex tasks.

The purpose of this reading guide is for students to evaluate the overall effective of a particular guide. The goal of the activity is to get students to see the guides as tools that help them complete a particular assignment. If they don't work, it is important for students to not only understand their inadequacies but also offer specific recommendations for how they can improve their overall effectiveness. This particular trait is a characteristic of strategic learners; they know when a problem exists and how to correct it. A critical principle underlying the use of guides is for students to recognize *when* and *where* they would be appropriate. Again, this gets at strategic usage and not mechanistic compliance.

Conclusion

The goal of this chapter was to raise questions about the need to more clearly identify the type of content reading activities used to model important skills and strategies in social studies. When students learn to use skills and strategies that are connected with unproductive content, learning is unproductive. The bottom line is that activities must promote powerful ideas that lead to thoughtful learning. If not, classroom instruction becomes a series of decontextualized activities that promote disconnected and fragmented learning. The criteria for social studies reading activities focus on activities that are based on powerful ideas and content, activites that have a significant social education goal as a primary focus, and activities that promote the authentic application of skills. A number of reading-related strategies were described in the context of a unit on the Civil War.

Think after Reading Activity

Peters states that using reading skills and activities will help develop several kinds of knowledge: foundational, generative, and authentic. See if completing the chart below helps you summarize the chapter. This is the "Understanding Powerful Concepts" chart.

Concepts	Characteristics of the Concepts	Examples of the Concepts	Connections between Concepts
Foundational Knowledge			
Generative Knowledge			
Authentic Knowledge			

List three ways this assisted you in summarizing the chapter.

1. _____

2. _____

3. _____

Activity 14–4

Chapter 15

Understanding Literature

Reading in the English or Language Arts Classroom

NANCY FARNAN   ALICIA ROMERO

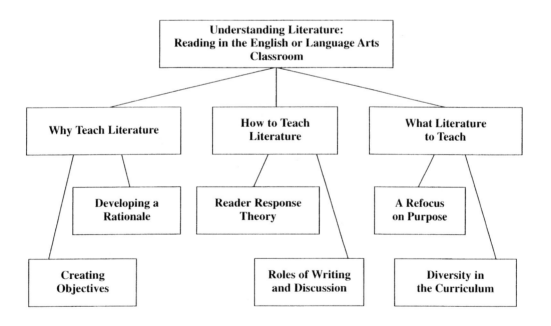

Think before Reading Activity

Think of a book you have read that you particularly enjoyed. Why did you select the book in the first place, and why do you think this book was particularly meaningful to you? Share your ideas with a partner.

_____

_____

_____

_____

_____

_____

_____

_____

_____

_____

_____

_____

Activity 15–1

The authors of this chapter ask and attempt to answer several philosophical and practical questions about the use of literature in classrooms. Among those questions are: Why teach literature? What should we teach? How should we teach it? Is it even possible to teach literature? Using examples based on specific works of literature and excerpts from students' writing, the authors use principles of reader response theory to explore the role of literature in the classroom and ways to support students' understandings.

In her poem titled "After English Class," Jean Little (1990, p. 28) captures the sound of a student voice, a narrator who shares the magic he or she experienced when reading Frost's "Stopping by Woods on a Snowy Evening." The narrator recalls the delight of envisioning "the gentle drift of snow." However, the joy is short-lived because, as the student voice explains, "Today, the teacher told us what everything stood for." The narrator reflects:

It's grown so complicated now that,
Next time I drive by,
I don't think I'll bother to stop.

The poem is funny. At least it seems so, because teachers usually laugh when they hear it. However, the humor is dark; it's not a belly laugh, but rather a nervous giggle accompanied by an affirmative shaking of heads. They recognize something in the poem.

They recognize that while it is not wrong to ruminate about what the woods, the snow, and the darkness mean, there is something inherently wrong in being told what they mean. Teachers recognize that in the telling something is lost. The connection between the narrator and the text in Little's poem is compromised, an occurrence which is sad rather than funny, for reading is about the connection.

This chapter discusses reading in the English or language arts classroom, reading which is both similar and different from reading in other disciplines. The field of English education is broad. English teachers work within their discipline and, increasingly, in interdisciplinary ways. The curriculum includes reading, writing, vocabulary development, oral language development, drama, fiction, nonfiction, and more. Each of these curricular elements represents a large body of knowledge and, as such, is worthy of separate consideration, yet all are interrelated. Obviously, we cannot address them all in one chapter.

The purpose of this chapter is to explore the area of reading, and in that context the authors do not hide our bias toward the importance of the connections readers must make with literature, or any text for that matter, if they are to fully comprehend what they read. A position we take, along with many of our colleagues in the field of reading, is that reading *is* comprehension. Reading is not word-calling (simply decoding words); reading is not eyes simply tracking across pages of print in order to get from one page to another; reading is understanding or, if you will, comprehending. The International Reading Association (IRA) supports this perspective in its 1988 definition of reading, which states, "Comprehension is (1) an active, constructive process; (2) a thinking process before, during, and after reading; (3) an interaction of the reader, the text, and the context" (p. 2). Put another way: "The essential nature of reading is inferring meaning from text" (Norris & Phillips, 1994, p. 394). These authors suggest that at the heart of reading is "the universal human activity of meaning construction" (Norris & Phillips, 1994, p. 394).

There are many ways to support student's reading (i.e., meaning construction) in an English or language arts classroom. First of all, teachers must ensure that students are prepared to read. Many authors in this book discuss the importance of using students' prior knowledge and experience in preparation for reading a text, as a way to promote students' connections with it. For that reason, this chapter does not focus on the multiple issues related to prior knowledge.

However, we believe it is important to emphasize the importance of effectively introducing a piece of literature in such a way that students will not only be ready, but also eager to read. A cold oral reading by students is hardly, if ever, appropriate. Instead, a teacher can set the stage for a work of literature in many ways. One is by reading (with flair and drama) the first couple of paragraphs, pages, or chapter of a particularly compelling text, stopping at a point which leaves students anxious for more, which they then read. In addition, teachers can help students make initial connections to a book by posing a question about which they reflect. write, and discuss. For example, before beginning Harper Lee's *To Kill a Mockingbird,* the teacher can ask students to write about a past incident or period of time and their new insights about what occurred, or a time when they either experienced or saw prejudice at work.

Getting into a piece of literature is critical, and our focus here is on how to support students' understandings as they read, for it is here that readers make inferences, construct meaning, and monitor their understandings. Included in this chapter are emphases on thinking, writing, and discussing as they relate to students' developing understandings of text. As we explore the area of reading in English or language arts, we discuss three questions: Why teach literature? How can it be taught? How do teachers decide which works of literature to teach?

Why Teach Literature?

Perhaps confusion and uncertainty about teaching literature exist, but not because answers are unavailable. Perhaps it is because there are so many different ways of thinking about the role of literature in the classroom. Between 1990 and 1994, ERIC reports the publication of over 8,400 articles and writings related to teaching literature. At the secondary level, the teaching of literature has been influenced by diverse perspectives which set at odds such issues as student-centered vs. teacher-centered instruction; an analytical perspective (associated with intellectual rigor and objectivity) vs. subjectivity and personal growth; and use of classical works vs. contemporary, young adult literature. Hawisher (1990) comments on the pervasive nature of the confusion that surrounds the teaching of literature: "At the heart of the debate in literature teaching seems to be what should be taught, how this particular content should be taught, and finally, why it should be taught" (p. 4).

Remaining for a moment with the latter idea, of why teach literature, several studies provide insights (Farnan, Lapp, Flood, & Tregor, 1991). These studies, conducted with teachers of middle school students, used interview and survey data. The research was descriptive in nature and was conducted in order to discern teacher's beliefs and perceptions concerning the teaching of literature. One of the points addressed in these studies was the straightforward question: Why teach literature? Teachers' responses were sophisticated and wide ranging. They named the following as objectives for teaching literature: (1) to help students better understand the nature of human relationships, (2) to foster universal values, (3) to promote self-understanding, (4) to promote a better understanding of diverse cultures, (5) to expose students to traditional, classic works, (6) to relate literature to history and to support learning across content areas, (7) to foster love of reading, (8) to promote writing development, and (9) to encourage critical thinking.

Obviously, reasons for using literature in the classroom are numerous, and perhaps all are valid, depending on a teacher's objectives. We would argue that teachers must begin with clear goals and objectives to guide their decisions about curriculum and instruction. For example, a preservice teacher, Sara Worthen, who worked with the authors of this chapter, designed a unit centered on Rudolfo Anaya's *Bless Me, Ultima.* Her broad goal, borrowing from Cullinan's (1989) metaphor of literature, was to promote understanding (i.e., comprehension) of the novel by helping students see it as a mirror of some of their own experiences and values, as well as a window into another culture. Given this broad goal, she developed several objectives, one of which was for her students to understand and appreciate Mexican-American culture. Given this objective, she was then able to design her instruction around activities such as the following: (1) students writing about Antonio's struggles in entering school and facing a new language and culture, (2) students posing questions about culture in their reading logs and seeking answers through discussion and research, and (3) promoting understanding of the Spanish language and culture by having Mexican-American classmates explain Spanish words and customs embedded in the novel.

We can best help students make connections to a work of literature by first clarifying our goals and objectives relative to the literature. Why do we select a particular text? Should students select their own readings? How do we want students to experience the literature? How can classrooms be designed to support the goals?

Literature Instruction

Just as there are many possible reasons or objectives for teaching literature, there are many different ways to teach it. Particularly at middle and secondary levels, educators often teach literature as if their main objective were for students to learn about and extract information from it, and certainly there is much information available to extract—about the genre, writer, writing style, historical context, characters, themes, symbolism, and so forth.

This information-based approach to literature, which Rosenblatt (1991) refers to as the efferent stance, is not bad. However, it ignores a critical element of the literary experience. Rosenblatt defines literature as an esthetic experience, which involves "reading with attention, of course, to what the words refer to, but mainly to what we are experiencing, thinking, and feeling during the reading" (1991, p. 444). According to Rosenblatt, readers have two primary purposes for reading, one being esthetic, captured in her description above, where reading is an esthetic experience, and the other being efferent, in which the primary purpose for reading is to glean information. Although Rosenblatt describes literature as an esthetic experience, when teachers emphasize interpretation of symbolic meanings, finding figures of speech, reciting events in sequence, and describing settings and characteristics of main characters, they are treating it otherwise, as an efferent rather than esthetic experience.

The problem is that too often students' readings of literature result in responses that are only at surface, informational levels; it has been documented that the instruction itself determines whether children experience literature from an efferent or esthetic stance (Farnan, 1988; Kelly & Farnan, 1991; Many and Wiseman, 1992). In addition, it has been well documented that traditional instruction, unfortunately, has tended to involve students with literature primarily at literal, concrete levels indicative of an efferent stance (Durkin, 1984; Petrosky, 1980; U.S. Department of Education, 1986).

Teachers ask questions such as "Where does the story take place?" "Who is the main character?" or "What happened to Hamlet's father?" Again, we want to emphasize that these are not bad questions. Insights concerning plot elements, historical contexts, and so forth can enrich a reader's understandings. Rosenblatt (1991) talks about the efferent and esthetic stance not as mutually exclusive, but as two end points on a continuum. A natural reading will include elements of both. A predominately esthetic response does not preclude the garnering of information from a reading, and vice versa. The point is, based on what is known about reading as a relationship between a reader and a text, it is important to encourage students' experience with literature, to emphasize an esthetic stance that lets students delve into poems, stories, and novels as texts full of sensations, images, and feelings, as well as collections of ideas and information.

Rosenblatt's definition of literature highlights the idea of literature as experience and, thus, emphasizes what we know about reading. That is, reading involves a transaction between a reader and a text. As Rosenblatt (1982, p. 269) described it, reading and understanding literature involve a "two-way process, involving a reader and a text at a particular time under particular circumstances." The issue, then, is to design instructional processes that support the transaction between reader and text. Reader response theory offers a way to think about meeting this objective. Reader response theory focuses on the importance of the relationship between reader and text. According to Mailloux (1982, p. 85), "Perception is . . . interpretive; reading is not the discovery of meaning but the creation of it."

The point is, readers and texts are both critical to a reading. Meaning is not contained in a work of literature, and development of literary understandings involves much more than merely collecting bits and pieces of information. In order to understand fully the rich and complex layers of meaning found in quality works of literature, readers must do much more than become acquainted with ideas, feelings, and sensations set forth by other people, in this case a writer. Readers must be able to relate those ideas and feelings to what they think and do themselves. According to Probst (1990, p. 105), "If we are to have literate people, rather than people who appear literate, we must get students to do more than receive the literature of the culture. We must get them to participate in the culture, to join the conversation."

A reader's transaction with text can be thought of as a feedback loop, in which readers begin the process of reading and understanding as they bring all of their knowledge, experiences, and beliefs to the text and interpret what is written in light of what they know. This loop is sustained in accordance with the way psychologists indicate that meaning is perceived—actively and constructively. Thus, the text and the reader's prior knowledge and feelings never operate independently of one another.

Bleich (1978) offers a paradigm for describing readers' active participation in the construction of meaning. This paradigm consists of three components: perception, affect, and association. These components, or elements of response, are critical to a reader's personal response to literature. Perception refers to what a reader notices (perhaps as interesting, important, confusing, and so forth) in a work of literature; affect refers to a reader's feelings and attitudes about a reading; and association speaks to connection readers make between their life experiences and a work of literature.

If we translate these three elements into ways of thinking about literature, they center on questions such as the following:

1. What did you (the student) notice in the story (perception)? This includes students thinking about what they find to be important, interesting, surprising, or even confusing.
2. What does this remind you of in your own life (association)? This involves students thinking about their personal experiences and the experiences of people around them, as they relate to the literature.
3. How does the story (or book or poem or chapter) make you feel (affect)? This includes ideas about not only how the story makes the reader feel, but also why?

As readers approach a work of literature, it is virtually impossible not to mobilize these three elements. It is virtually impossible to read (given that reading means comprehending) without perceiving what's in a text, without having some kind of affective reaction to it, and without associating it in some way to our own lives and the world as we know it. Therefore, because readers are active participants as they comprehend text, objectivity and reading comprehension are mutually exclusive. Objectivity assumes that a static truth exists in the observed, which is independent of the observer. This is the opposite of what actually occurs when individuals read and respond to text; readers can only interpret and, thus, comprehend what they read in light of existing thoughts, feelings, and experiences. Put another way, words printed on a page are comprehended as a literary work only after they have been symbolized and resymbolized by a reader with his or her own background of knowledge and experience.

Discussion and Response

Teachers can support students' interactions with text through the talk that goes on in classrooms, where the objective is to help students become part of a lived-through experience with literature, emphasizing an esthetic rather than an efferent stance. Students can make connections with what they read through their perceptions, affect, and associations. For example, students' discussions can center on questions such as the following (Farnan & Fearn, 1991; Farnan & Kelly, 1988; Kelly & Farnan, 1991), all of which relate in some way to Bleich's elements of response:

1. What did you notice in the book?
2. How does the story make you feel?
3. What does the story remind you of in your own life?
4. If you were going to tell someone about the book, what three things would be important for you to share? Tell why they are important.
5. Did your feelings about what you read change as you were reading? If so, explain.
6. If the author were here, what would you like to say to him or her?
7. What do you think is the most important or most interesting part of this story? Why do you say this?
8. Who do you think was the most important character in the story? Why do you say this?
9. What was your favorite part of the book? Tell what it was and why you liked it.
10. If a friend asked you whether he or she should read this book, what would you say and why?

We can see evidence of students' connections with literature in the following reflections on what they read. In a middle school classroom of twelve- and thirteen-year-olds, students were discussing Langston Hughes's poem, "April Rainsong." The teacher directed members of the class to form small groups of three to four students and discuss the question "What does this poem remind you of?" The following is an excerpt from their tape-recorded conversations (Farnan and Kelly, (1993):

Student 1: This poem reminded me of today because it's slightly raining. I agree with the author because I love rain too. Rain reminds me of my life because it's like many teardrops, and my life is kind of sad. But it also makes me feel good and puts me to sleep. I like to go home and take a shower and lay down and listen to the rain. I know, I'm kind of weird, aren't I? (Laughter in the group)

Student 2: The poem makes me feel happy too. It reminds me of warm rain and flowers sparkling with water in the morning. It makes me feel kind of sad too because I know the rain doesn't come often here in California and I miss it. It used to rain so much in the place I used to live. I love being inside with my family and having hot chocolate and snuggling down in front of the television watching cartoons. Somehow the rain brings me and my family closer together, but I don't know why. This poem makes me think of all these good things.

Notice that students elaborated on their feelings and observations. They made explicit connections between what they read and their own lives. As they reflected on what they perceived in the poem, students applied their understanding of it to what they knew and to their life's experiences. Interestingly, McGee (1992) found that student-centered literature discussions, conducted as open forums for conversation and not prompted by a specific question, promoted connections between literature and text among children as young as grade 1. Their discussions contained evaluations of a work, direct application of personal reactions

---

Think while Reading Activity

Choose a book you have enjoyed, one you think a class of grade 11 students (or pick a grade between 6 and 12) might appreciate, one you would like to sell them on. Using this book and the criteria presented in this chapter, outline book talk for them.

Book Talk Criteria:

_____

_____

_____

_____

_____

Book Talk Outline:

_____

_____

_____

_____

_____

Activity 15–2

to support their understanding of a story, and inferences, generalizations, and interpretations that led the adults in the room to admit that at times "they (the adults) had not thought of a particular interpretation before it emerged" (p. 186).

Scott (1994) describes literature circles in which her middle school students participate on a weekly basis. They form groups of six to eight in which they all read the same book. Students then meet to discuss their reading, setting their pace for reading from one literature circle meeting to the next. She uses a variety of techniques to support discussion, such as providing a reflective question or prompt to get them started and asking students to bring an index card with three issues they would like to raise related to the book (and page numbers).

Book talks, designed for a student to sell others in the class on what he or she read, is one way to support productive sharing; they function, in a way, as movie previews do, to entice audiences to see an upcoming film. (Some teachers call them "book commercials.") Librarians can come into a class and present book talks with the intent of bringing students into the library in search of their next "good read," and students can present tantalizing excerpts, share elements of a plot, and offer their personal reactions. They can only effectively champion a book if they have fully consumed and understood it, and one of our primary goals is that students become active consumers of literature.

Writing and Literature

Research of the past fifteen years in reading and writing suggests that instructional integration of reading and writing can increase students' reading, writing, and thinking skills (Stotsky, 1983) and that reading and writing, although not identical language processes, are similar language skills (Applebee, 1977; Baghban, 1984; Squire, 1983). Both are active processes through which readers and writers transact with print to construct meaning.

Writing allows students to engage in thoughtful reflection of ideas and feelings. In their in-depth study of the relationship between writing and thinking, Langer and Applebee (1987) concluded that "writing seems to be at least one very useful way that teachers can orchestrate the kinds of cognitive engagement that leads to academic learning" (p. 131) and, in addition, that writing can help students focus on concepts and relationships among ideas.

Writing is a natural extension of students' engagement. The genre of the personal response essay tends, according to Beach and Hynds, "to be significantly higher in level of interpretations than students writing in the formal mode" (1991, p. 476). If students have been experiencing texts in terms of their perceptions, feelings, and associations, then the writing they are asked to do should be exploratory as well. In his monograph on writing, Newkirk (1989, p. viii) argues that all essays should be explorations. He explains that

> a good essay opens up the possibility for new conversations rather than closes down such opportunities. . . . The word "essay" to most of us signals a logically developed and very tight treatise on a fairly limited topic. To think of the essay as a vehicle for beginning new conversation is liberating. It suggests that the function of writing is inquiry, critical thinking, and learning.

It is this view of the essay which we offer in this chapter. Asking students to write personal response essays gives them a chance not only to display their understandings of a reading, but also to make connections between the work of literature and their own lives. Students are respected for what they bring to the text. When they are allowed (and encouraged) to engage in talk about what they read, they form a community of readers. Then, through their writing, they create worlds about what they read.

What does it look like to apply reader response theory in the context of reading and writing in a literature-based curriculum? (Some of the following student samples, along with others, can be found in Flood et al., 1995.) What follows is an account of what students can accomplish in a reader response atmosphere.

In a classroom in San Diego, California, grade 12 students read such books as Toni Morrison's *Beloved,* Al Santoli's *Everything We Had,* and Amy Tan's *The Joy Luck Club.* It is important to say that the teacher, who happens to be one of the authors of this chapter (Romero), is also an avid reader. Therefore, she is an enthusiastic advocate of reading, and the books her students read are ones she believes will interest them. Routinely, students in this classroom are asked to read sections of a book, then come to class with questions, interesting insights, and whatever they think will contribute to the class' talk about the reading. The teacher's role is to provide an atmosphere that supports freedom to express feelings and perceptions. For the most part, these are the students' discussions, and the teacher's voice is only one of the many heard in the room. Her role is not as authority of the text, but rather as a contributor, who also orchestrates different modes of discourse over the course of a reading.

For example, after reading, writing about, and discussing *Beloved* over a period of several weeks, her students decided to put the main character on trial. They designed a courtroom in the classroom. An attorney was invited in as a guest speaker, who instructed students on processes of questioning witnesses. Every student participated and every student wrote a piece describing his or her role in the case. The classroom courtroom activities held all of the emotion and tension seen in actual courtroom dramas.

For those who have not read *Beloved,* it is important to realize that there is no trial in the book. In those days, slaves did not have a right to trial. The following is an excerpt from the closing statement, written and delivered, by the student who was the prosecuting attorney:

> Most honorable judge, ladies and gentlemen of the jury, you have spent the last several days listening to both sides of this most saddening case. You have heard both sides argue their points thoroughly and professionally. Defense, however, has one glaring flaw in its argument that this murder is justified. That flaw, ladies and gentlemen, is that there can be no justification for the gruesome, horrid death of Beloved, an innocent two-year-old child.

The student continues, making an eloquent plea for the defendant's guilt, ending her statement with the following:

> Please, ladies and gentlemen of the jury, don't let this great crime go unpunished. A life is gone, the fire of the human spirit, Beloved's spirit, extinguished before she

could ever begin to experience what she could do with life. And Sethe Suggs is the cause. She cannot go unpunished. And I have faith in each and every one of you to come to a verdict of guilty—for Beloved's sake.

This statement is an example of how students can create worlds in their writing. This student created the voice of an attorney prosecuting a woman accused of committing a crime. The writer is aware of her audience, the jury. Her tone is consistent throughout and her purpose for writing is clear. This student participated in a close study of the novel *Beloved* by reading it, discussing it, and writing about it before performing this text.

The following excerpt comes from a senior high school student who wrote after the class read Santoli's book of testimonies of American soldiers in Vietnam. During their reading, students talked together in small groups about their impressions and personal knowledge of the war itself. In the class were students whose fathers had gone to Vietnam and students whose ethnic heritage was Vietnamese, some of whom lived there during the war and others who had never seen their homeland. Students spoke candidly to each other about what they read. This is what a Vietnamese-American student wrote in his personal response essay:

In my opinion, Al Santoli made a very wise choice in using the oral tradition to portray the Americans' experience in Vietnam. *Everything We Had* does an exceptionally thorough job in illustrating the realities of what these men and women went through. But in my opinion, there is a flaw within this book, and that is we, the readers, hear nothing from the ARVN, the Viet Cong, or the Vietnamese civilian. How can we get a clear picture of the true horror of wars if all we're offered is such a limited viewpoint.

The American soldiers in this oral history did a fabulous job in depicting the war from their standpoint, but in order to obtain and understand the full picture of such a controversial war requires views from all sides of the war. To be offered a single perspective of the war and to be expected to understand the true horror of the war would be like trying to understand the beauty of the Mona Lisa painting without viewing her smile. The American soldiers did indeed provide a very vivid picture of the horror and beauty of the war through their eyes and their experiences. But like any individual, they are limited to a very small perspective.

Therefore, all the horrors and beauties of war cannot be delivered through one group. In order to find the "missing link" which will reveal "the side of Vietnam we never knew," the lost commandos, the Amerasian children, the Agent Orange orphans, and many other Vietnamese veterans and citizens must be heard. To refuse these people the right to reveal their side of the story is to refuse the public the right to learn the true reality of war.

This student chose to write about his objections to the book. He offered a reasoned and critical evaluation, which emerged from his opportunities to experience the book through his own reading and the classroom conversations. The student felt free to express his personal opinion. His argument is a passionate one, growing from a learning process that honored a reader response perspective.

Amy Tan's *Joy Luck Club* was another book read by this class. After reading and much talking and writing about the *Joy Luck Club,* students wrote their response essays. Because students were used to thinking about literature in terms of their perceptions, feelings, and associations, they were comfortable with this kind of writing. The following excerpts from student essays illustrate their understandings about the book, as well as the connections they made between the work of literature and their own lives.

While reading the novel, the first thing I encountered was my ignorance of the entire Chinese culture. I found myself thinking that because of the language barrier I shied away from people who could not speak English clearly. After reading this novel, I took a long look at myself and came to the conclusion that I'm not nearly as open-minded as I thought I was. I do not consider myself a racist or someone who stereotypes. On the other hand, why was I so surprised to read that the mothers and daughters of *The Joy Luck Club* were people a lot like me?

I could especially relate to Jing Mei Woo. Her mother wanted her to be a genius or great at something. But Jing Mei did not seem to be especially talented in the things her mother wanted her to be good at. In short, she felt like a failure, especially when her mother compared her to Waverly, who was a class genius. Having brothers and a sister, I feel I have also been a victim of comparison. My sister is great at every sport she tries. However, I choose to work instead of play sports, but it still makes me envious when she brings home trophies. . . . Jing Mei eventually grew up and realized that she has many talents that Waverly doesn't have. As I grew older, I realized that there are many things that I'm good at and my self-confidence has grown.

I think that moving to America was a positive experience for these women. I realize that the first generation struggled with the language and the culture, but, they succeeded in teaching their children good values in any culture. The arguing between the mothers and daughters represents the contrasting cultures. Tan shows how the mothers do not want to let go of their Chinese culture and want to raise their children with respect to the Chinese ancestry. But these second-generation Chinese children only see themselves as American.

In the above excerpt, Shannon reflects on new understandings about the Chinese culture and her own prejudices and feelings about it. Part of her understandings concern a newly developed sense of the similarities, as well as differences, among cultures, and she explores the similarities between Chinese and Americans by comparing relationships within her own family to the relationships among characters in Tan's book.

In the next excerpt, Phung, a student whose family emigrated from Vietnam, delves into meanings she sees in the novel and how she relates to them.

Living in the United States gave me a different mentality than that of what I would have had if I had continued to live in Vietnam. Being raised in San Diego practically all my life gave me the opportunity to see a different perspective than the traditional Asian viewpoint. The two cultures viewed life completely differently; however, I believe I was able to combine the two to define my own individuality. Being Asian-American did not necessarily mean that I sacrificed my Asian culture to interact with that of the American traditions. I did not lose myself, but actually found strength within me to examine the two cultures. In my own quest to find myself, my journey did not take me away from, but took me deeper and deeper into the Vietnamese language, customs, and values.

Amy Tan's novel depicted the mother-daughter bond to the core. She clearly expressed the different relationships shared between each family; however, in many ways, they were similar. Tan showed how each daughter lost a sense of her culture, but in the end found that her mother was always right in explaining that one day the Chinese blood within them would flow out. And it did. The daughters' attempts to find themselves and return to their culture completely identified with me.

Finally, Norma writes about her understandings of the novel and how she generalizes from it to her world.

After having read *The Joy Luck Club,* I can agree with the critics' comments. This book goes beyond a set of four Chinese women's stories. The book portrays the lives of all immigrants to America.

Relating to the book was, for me, not very hard. My ancestors from Mexico also had unusual customs, as did the Chinese. Their morals have always been strict. If a child does something wrong, he is considered dishonored by his family. Being dishonored by your family is as if your life is no longer worth a penny. We see this in An-Mei Hsu's mother's story. She was "banned" from her home because she married Wu Tsing, a man who had three wives already. She, being a widow, could no longer marry another man. This is, of course, something everybody does here in America and it is not considered a sin. . . .

Amy Tan, I believe, is taking her own personal life and converting it into the four young girls. She conflicted with her mother as a child. Now, as a woman, she sees everything that her mother taught her more clearly. I, too, am an Amy Tan. When my mother taught me about our culture, I saw my culture like something meaningless. Now, as I become a woman, I see that culture is not only my ancestors, but also myself. If I deny my roots, I am also denying myself.

As did the other students, Norma illustrated not only her understanding of the novel itself, but she also brought the book into her own life and described insights about her own culture. Each of these excerpts shows the power of the esthetic response, through which students are encouraged to construct their own meanings and make personal connections to works of literature.

As students read and write about literature, portfolios become a powerful tool for the collection of ideas. Portfolios, which are discussed in greater detail in other chapters of this book, are an integral part of the English or language arts classroom and serve a variety of critical functions in student writing as well as reading (Farnan & Kelly, 1991).

What to Teach

When deciding what to teach, it is important to go back to teachers' purposes for teaching literature. Cullinan (1989) uses the metaphors of the window and the mirror when she describes the value of literature in the classroom. According to Cullinan, literature opens a window onto new worlds and new understandings, while also offering a mirror through which readers' reflections of themselves emerge.

In the context of these metaphors, the English or language arts curriculum needs to include a variety of works, from those which represent the classic canon of works traditionally taught to those which represent diverse, multicultural perspectives. Here we would like to make what we believe is an important point. English departments are sometimes ambivalent about adding other works to the traditional canon. We would argue that criteria for literature selection should be inclusive rather than exclusive, where decisions about what is taught should center on issues of quality. Of course, "quality" can be a rather subjective criterion, but it can be judged, among other issues, on whether the literature encourages an esthetic stance, through which students actively transact with the text, and whether the literature offers students both a mirror and a window into experience.

Students at the middle school level might read such works as Orwell's *Animal Farm,* Soto's *Baseball in April,* Forbes's *Johnny Tremain,* Paulsen's *Woodsong,* the Houstons' *Farewell to Manzanar,* and folk tales from many lands. At the high school level, they might read Shakespeare's *Hamlet,* Sophocles' *Oedipus the King,* and James Joyce's *Portrait of the Artist as a Young Man,* as well as Toni Morrison's *Beloved,* Amy Tan's *The Joy Luck Club,* Niehardt's *Black Elk Speaks,* and Sandra Cisneros's *The House on Mango Street.*

Use of a variety of quality works of literature provides a diverse yet cohesive English or language arts curriculum. Figure 15–1 shows how students in one senior English class began to create links between diverse works of literature. In this activity, students were given a chart with only a few spaces filled in. In groups, students completed the links. Figure 15–2 shows one group's completed chart, an activity which required that students create their own themes which linked the books.

It is important that teachers choose books that will be rich, interesting, and appropriate for their students. We would also argue that, ideally, teachers must be voracious readers. They must be knowledgeable about the works available and be able to introduce students to a variety of quality pieces of literature. In addition, teachers must be confident enough to take unexpected student reactions seriously. Students may or may not, for reasons of their own, like a particular literature selection. It is important to allow that dialogue in the classroom, without the teacher's opinion being held up as the only correct one. Here, a teacher's theoretical perspective is critical. From the perspective of response theory, the last thing the teacher will want to do is deny a reader's (student's) thoughtful point of view or experience with the literature. An interpretation should take into account textual information and be coherent (Norris & Phillips, 1994), but it is natural that diverse individuals will have diverse experiences with a particular text. This is to be cultivated and can become thoughtful discussion as students and the teacher explore the conditions that bring about the various points of view.

Making Meaning	*Oedipus the King*	*Things Fall Apart*	*Hamlet*	*Color Purple*	*Bless Me, Ultima*
Heroic qualities of the main character					

FIGURE 15–1 Linking Books, Linking Cultures

Making Meaning	*Oedipus the King*	*Things Fall Apart*	*Hamlet*	*Color Purple*	*Bless Me, Ultima*
Heroic qualities of the main character	Brave Courageous Prominent	Fearless Stands up for beliefs Hard worker	Vengeful Witty	Heart powered by die hard. A survivor. Later a fighter.	Good hearted Endured Blends in with white world
Problems that the main characters face	Plague Prophecy Who done it?	White suprema-cy Superiority Technology Son's beliefs Violent temper	His father's murder. His uncle's men. His mother's adultery.	Marriage Father's abuse Lost children Sister	Going to a white school Growing up Religion
Does the main character accomplish goals?	Oedipus—self punish-ment	Got message across, but lost battle.	He did it all except for his mother—to change her ways.	Got her kids back, divorced and was happy.	Tony makes his own dream.
What I learned from the book	Honorable to keep your word	Stand up for what you believe.	What comes around goes around. Can't play with fire.	Love comes in many forms. God delivers to faithful. Good to those who wait.	Mexicans a blend of Indian and Spanish culture. Catholic and Indian religions. Magic spells.

FIGURE 15–2   Linking Books, Linking Cultures

Think after Reading Activity

Complete the chart below for a book you might teach to your students. (You decide the grade level—middle to senior high.) Decide on an overall goal for teaching this book. Then list two or three objectives, with at least one instructional idea for each.

Title:

_____

Goal:

_____

_____

_____

Objective and Instructional Ideas:

_____

_____

_____

_____

_____

_____

Activity 15–3

Conclusion

It is important for teachers to have a sense of why they teach literature, how it can best be taught, and what works are important to use in classrooms. In this chapter we have discussed each of these questions and tried to offer clear instructional implications. It is obvious to us that we have omitted as much as we have included. We have dealt with reading, discussion, and writing in the context of literature, and a fairly narrow range of literature at that, as we have not explicitly discussed poetry, nonfiction, and the diversity of genres. Neither have we explicitly addressed myriad additional issues related to the teaching of writing. However, within the confines of this chapter, we have attempted to focus on some critical issues related to reading in English or language arts classrooms.

To highlight our focus, we quote Gary Paulsen, a writer of books for early adolescents, who emphasizes the importance of literature in the classroom and the importance of providing a classroom context where students make personal connections with what they read. In his introduction to *The Winter Room* (1989), he speaks to these ideas when he states,

If books could have more, give more, be more, show more, they would still need readers, who bring to them sound and smell and light and all the rest that can't be in books. The book needs you.

C h a p t e r *16*

The Role of Reading and Writing Instruction in Mathematics

JOAN F. CURRY

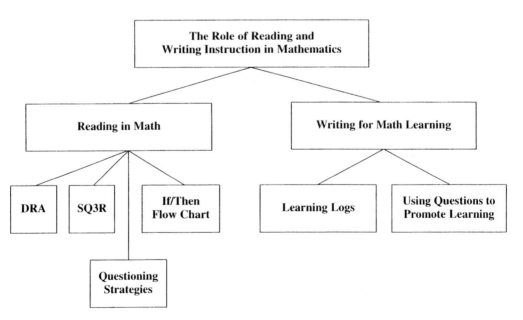

Think before Reading Activity

As you've realized from reading this text, writing is an important part of every curriculum area. Can this be true for math? What might writing look like in math? Is it more than numbers? Jot down your ideas and then add to them as you read this chapter.

_____

_____

_____

_____

_____

_____

_____

_____

_____

_____

_____

Activity 16–1

This chapter carefully delineates the use of the directed reading activity (DRA) as an instructional strategy to teach a mathematics lesson. In addition, the chapter discusses the relationship between learning mathematics and writing, explores further the role of writing in understanding mathematics through the use of a learning log and describes the use of a flow chart to support mathematical thinking.

Constructing meaning is the core of a mathematics curriculum. As students begin to construct meaning in mathematics, they use processes which are not unlike those used in writing where meaning construction lies at the center of the process. In mathematics, identifying the problem and thinking about how to solve the problem occur simultaneously. Whether in writing or mathematics, processes interact to help the writer or mathematician solve problems, that is, to construct a composition or a mathematical solution.

Writing also involves an interaction between drafting and revision, elements which interact as writers write, reflect, rethink, and revise as part of drafting. Similarly in mathematics, students think through various possibilities as they work toward problem solution, all the while making adjustments when needed as the process moves forward. Finally, in writing, reflection and sharing provide feedback for a writer concerning whether a piece of writing works (Farnan & Fearn, 1993). Certainly, the same is true in mathematics, when issues such as the following are dealt with: Is the solution the most efficient one? Does it represent a coherent representation of meaning in terms of the topic (or problem) posed?

Reading in Mathematics

As mathematics teachers know, reading mathematics is vastly different from reading other subjects. When reading a mathematics book, the student is actually reading several kinds of language: (1) the language that appears in a mathematics lesson and rarely elsewhere, such as the vocabulary words "rhombus" and "equation"; (2) words that have multiple meanings with very specific meanings in mathematics, such as "prime" and "set"; and (3) the language of symbols and numbers.

There are strong links between reading skills, knowledge of mathematics vocabulary, and problem-solving ability. These are reflected in the specific skills needed to read mathematics, which fall into the following five categories (Ciani, 1981; Pachtman & Riley, 1978):

1. The ability to recognize and pronounce symbols.
2. The ability to attach literal meaning to mathematics concepts.
3. The ability to interpret literal meanings in terms of mathematical symbols (i.e., understand supporting details, interpret graphs and charts, interpret equations and formulas).
4. The ability to apply interpretations and solve the word problems using such skills as analyzing the information and moving back and forth between general language, mathematical terms, and numerical symbols.
5. The ability to use specialized study skills, such as rate adjustment, locational skills, following directions, and test taking.

The Critical Role of the Teacher

The range of reading ability in a mathematics classroom can span a ten-year period, ranging from a reading level of grade 3 to a reading level commensurate with that of a second-year college student. Yet, in many classrooms, all students must use the same mathematics text regardless of the discrepancy between their reading abilities and the difficulty of the text. This discrepancy can be bridged, however, through teacher guidance and effective instruction. Through skillful application of these two variables, all students can learn to comprehend the mathematics text.

Because effective instruction is so crucial to students' abilities to comprehend from texts, let's look at some instructional strategies that may be used to teach mathematics lessons.

Directed Reading Activity

Perhaps one of the most powerful strategies to teach a lesson may be found in the use of the directed reading activity (DRA). The DRA systematizes the way in which students approach a text. The teacher takes an active role as she or he leads students through the text and teaches them how to read and use the information in the text. The steps in the DRA include:

1. **Readiness:** Involves motivation and exploration of students' prior knowledge relative to the task. The new assignment should be discussed with regard to past work in order to develop a frame of reference for students.
2. **Vocabulary development:** It is crucial that vocabulary be taught prior to reading the text.
3. **Instruction in reading skill or skills needed to comprehend the assignment:** Some possibilities may be cause and effect, finding the main idea, summarizing, sequencing, interpreting graphic aids.
4. **Springboard questions:** Set the purpose for reading by asking questions that will direct students' thinking prior to reading.
5. **Reading the assignment:** Students silently read the assignment, keeping in mind the springboard questions. Specify follow-up assignment, if required.
6. **Review and follow-up activities:** Review may begin with answering the springboard questions. Further questioning evolves; students are asked to prove their answers by reading aloud from the text those sections that support their responses. Skills may be reviewed. Further reading or projects related to the text material may be undertaken.

DRA in the Mathematics Classroom

Now that we have reviewed the major parts of a DRA, let us see how the teacher of mathematics can adapt this activity for use in her or his classroom.

Readiness

This component makes use of students' prior knowledge. Identify the skill, concept, or principle that is to be presented in the lesson to the class. Tie the new lesson to what has been previously learned. Sometimes a preassessment activity can be completed to determine students' preparation to learn the new material and their general comprehension of the text material.

Vocabulary Development

Instruction in mathematics vocabulary must be an intrinsic part of a mathematics lesson so that it will more likely be applied in problem solving. Mathematics has a technical vocabulary unique to the discipline, but it also has vocabulary that, while used in a special way in math, also has a general meaning. To help students learn the vocabulary of mathematics, the use of structural analysis can be very effective.

By using structural analysis (prefixes, roots, and suffixes), students can dissect a word to see if there are any recognizable parts that will give clues to its meaning.

The teacher may prepare a worksheet, similar to that in Figure 16–1, which students may keep in their notebooks and which may be added to throughout the semester as new morphemes, smallest meaningful units, are introduced to students. Words having specific math meanings and also general meanings may be taught using the instructional design delineated in Figure 16–2. The teacher may list the word and teach the mathematical

Morpheme	Math Usage	General Usage
bi (two)	biangular bilinear bimodal binomial bisect	bicycle biplane bicuspid bifocals
cent (hundred)	centimeter percent centigram	century centipede centigrade
circum- (around)	circumference circumradius circumcenter	circumnavigate circumstance circumspect

FIGURE 16–1   Morpheme Worksheet

Word	Math Meaning	General Meaning
base	The number that indicates the grouping used in a numeration system (e.g., base 2, base 10)	The bottom of something considered as its support; a main ingredient
power	The number of times (as indicated by the exponent) a number is to be multiplied by itself $4^2 = 4 \times 4$ $5^3 = 5 \times 5 \times 5$	Possession of control, authority, or influence over another; physical might
product	The number resulting from multiplying together two or more numbers or expressions $2 \times 4 = 8$ 8 is the product	Something produced or made

FIGURE 16–2   Word Worksheet

Directions: Match the symbols in column A with their meanings in column B by placing the correct letter from column B in front of the number that it defines in column A.

Column A	Column B
_____1. =	a. therefore
_____2. <	b. number
_____3. %	c. is equal to
_____4. >	d. is less than
_____5. +	e. minus or negative
_____6. -	f. percent
_____7. #	g. is greater than
_____8. ∴	h. plus or positive

FIGURE 16–3   Match-Up Sheet

meaning for the word through contextual clues, through examples, or through the dictionary. Students should generate their own general meanings for the words and write them under the column entitled "General Meaning." After students have completed their general meanings for words, a few minutes could be spent sharing their meanings with their classmates.

To comprehend math and be able to compute accurately, it is essential that students be able to identify math symbols on sight. After teaching the symbols needed, it might be useful to have students match the symbols to their meanings, as is done in Figure 16–3.

Setting the Purpose and Objective of the Lesson

Start with a particular example of a skill or principle, rather than a general or symbolic representation. For example:

Goal: To learn that solving a linear equation in one variable with integer coefficients can be summarized in the following manner:

The solution to a linear equation of the form

$$a \cdot x + b = c \text{ is } x = \frac{c - b}{a}$$

This general representation is too difficult for beginning students. Instead, start with a particular example so that students can more readily understand and apply the skill.

Example

$$6x + 8 = 4$$
$$6x + 8 - 8 = 4 - 8$$
$$\frac{6x}{6} = \frac{-4}{6}$$
$$x = \frac{-4}{6}$$

Proof

$$6x + 8 = 4$$
$$6\left(\frac{-4}{6}\right) + 8 = 4$$
$$-4 + 8 = 4$$

Discuss the steps with the class as you move from the simple to the general and explain each step as it is completed.

Example: $6x + 8 = 4$
Question: What can we do to both sides of the equation?
Response: We can add a –8 to both sides of the equation.
Question: What will adding a –8 to both sides of the equation do?

Using students' prior knowledge, elicit from them the fact that when a –8 is added to each side of the equation, the equation is still balanced and adding a –8 to the left side of the equation negates the +8, leaving the left side of the equation reading 6x.

Question: What will happen when we add a –8 to the right side of the equation?
Response: Adding a –8 to the right side of the equation adds a negative number to a positive number, in which case the numbers are subtracted and the answer to the problem takes on the sign of the larger number.

$$+4 + (-8) = \begin{array}{r} -8 \\ +4 \\ \hline -4 \end{array}$$

The above response would also depend on students having the prerequisite skills, which would no doubt have been taught during previous lessons.

The equation would now look like this:

$$6x = -4$$

Question: If we want to solve for the variable x, what can be done?
Response: Both sides of the equation may be divided by the number 6.
Question: If we divide 6x by 6, 6x/6, what happens to 6?
Response: 6 divided by 6 is equal to 1, so the left side of the equation reads simply 1x or x.
Question: If we divide –4 by 6, –4/6, what happens?
Response: The answer is –4/6, and the right side of the equation will read –4/6.

Question: What is the solution to the example?

Response: x = –4/6

Question: Suppose we wanted to prove our answer. How could it be done?

Response: The equation can be solved, substituting the answer –4/6 for the variable x.

Question: The equation is 6x + 8 = 4. Let's substitute –4/6 for x and prove our answer. How would the equation look with the substitution?

Response: 6(–4/6) + 8 = 4 or another way 6/1 × –4/6 + 8 = 4

Cross multiply: –4/1 = –4; 6 cancels out: –4 + 8 = 4

Add +8 and –4, subtract 4 from 8, and the answer takes the sign of the larger integer. Again, students call on prior knowledge.

Ample practice must be given in order for the students to internalize the learning. Moving too quickly from one example to another without allowing the necessary time for students to see the application of the skill in various situations can be detrimental to learning.

Reading and Practice

During the reading of an assignment, students must have a systematic way in which to approach the reading of mathematics problems, a system that is general enough to fit almost all the kinds of problems to which students would be exposed. Such a technique is SQ3R. The purpose of the SQ3R method (survey, question, read, recite, review) is to sys-

---

Think while Reading Activity

The author is going to describe several strategies—SQRQCQ, RQ4S2T, and the If/Then Flow Chart—which help students construct meaning in mathematics. As you read, make some notes that help you to remember these strategies.

Name of Strategy	SQRQCQ	RQ4S2T	IF/THEN
Definition of Strategy			
Features of Strategy			
Implementation			

Activity 16–2

---

tematically lead students through a textbook assignment by using reading techniques that will help them reach the goal of comprehending the text (Robinson, 1946).

For the mathematics teacher, two adaptations of SQ3R can be useful. The first variation is the SQRQCQ technique by Fay (1965). This technique is as follows:

Survey: Read the problem quickly to determine the purpose.
Question: What is the problem?
Read: Look for details and interrelationships.
Question: What processes should be used in the problem?
Compute: Do the computation.
Question: Does the answer make sense? Check it against the facts in the problem.

Singer and Donlan (1980) suggest another alternative to SQ3R. Their technique is called RQ4S2T.

R Read the problem carefully.
Q1 Question: What facts are given?
Q2 Question: What do I have to find out?
Q3 Question: What shall I let x equal?
Q4 Question: How shall I represent other information given in the problem?
S1 Set up equations by translating words of problems using answers to Q1, 2, 3, and 4 for left and right members of the equation.
S2 Solve the equation.
T Test answers of solutions in the equation by substituting the answer in the equation.

These techniques can be useful in helping students comprehend mathematics text. Students need strategies because they must generate the information needed in solving the problems.

Should you not wish to use specific formulas to help your students learn from their texts, you might consider teaching them the following simple process.

The students ask themselves: What am I looking for? What am I trying to find out? They read the problem twice.

What facts do I need to solve the problem? Is the information in the problem? If the information is not in the problem, where can I find it?

What should I do? Guess and check? Draw a picture? Make graphs? Charts? Try to solve the problem using simpler numbers? Can I solve it in my head? Can I find a pattern?

What tools should I use to solve the problem?

Using my selected tools, have I found the correct answer? Is the answer I have found sensible? Does it fit the facts of the problem? Does my answer match my estimate?

Teachers can aid students by establishing a pattern with them that will facilitate their ability to comprehend the text and also their problem-solving behavior. Prior to solving the problem, the teacher may ask questions to ascertain whether they understand the problem and then discuss possible solutions and strategies. While students are working, the teacher may observe them and give them hints as needed. The teacher should require that the students check back and reread the problem, substituting their answers in the problem. If the teacher uses a consistent method of solving problems, students will internalize the process and be better able to solve problems on their own.

Reading and Practice Prior to Computation

Another method of attack to reading word problems that may be utilized at the beginning of the lesson involves the following steps:

1. Students must read the assignment once at a moderate speed to get the general idea of the word problem.
2. Major ideas of the problem are discussed. (The teacher should discourage too much detail.)
3. A student reads aloud the different parts of the problem.
4. During the above recitation, the teacher interrupts at crucial points, for example, when the student should draw a figure, do some calculating, or seek some additional information.
5. During the reading aloud of the problem, all students and the teacher may interrupt and ask the reader or each other any questions.
6. All books are closed after the first five steps.
7. Students then take a quiz on the content of the word problem.
8. The teacher reveals the answers immediately.

This strategy can be effective because it models for students the kinds of questions they should apply to the text in an effort to comprehend effectively; it also helps them find the core of the verbal statement by focusing on the selection of the main idea and how it relates to the rest of the problem.

Another technique to convert elements of a word problem into a workable equation is the "If/Then" flow chart (Clarke, 1991). With this strategy, it is important that the students first determine the purpose of the problem.

Steps in an If/Then Flow Chart

1. Read the problem first.
2. Determine what *kind* of a problem it is.
   Is it a distance problem?
   Is it a interest problem?
3. *If* it is an interest problem, find a formula to solve it.

4. Using the formula, create an equation.
5. *Then,* solve the equation.
6. *Then,* check the answer.

Classroom Questioning Strategies

The use of skillful questioning techniques is often seen as a mark of a successful teacher. Skillful teachers match their questions to the ability levels of their students. Generally, students encountering difficulties in mathematics should be asked questions requiring knowledge of facts and skills before they are asked higher-level questions relating to concepts and principles. Less competent students may need a series of questions to arrive at a correct answer. Let's look at an example. Solve the following quadratic equation:

$$6x^2 + 5x - 30 = 0$$

A student less competent in mathematics could be asked the following question to help him or her develop a system to solve the problem: What are the possible factors of 30 and 6? By asking that question, the teacher allows the student to participate in the classroom discussion and also invests the student in the problem, making it more likely that he or she will heed the discussion and learn from it.

When a question is posed by the teacher and a student does not answer it correctly, the teacher must ask herself or himself some questions. For example, if the student is unable to solve the following equation,

$$\frac{4x}{6} - (4 - 6x) = 30$$

the teacher may well ask herself or himself the following:

Is the student unable to work with fractions in equations?

Does the student not know the rules guiding operations with integers?

Is the student unable to apply the basic laws of equalities to the writing of equivalent operations?

In this manner, questioning can be diagnostic and evaluative.

Cooperative Learning in the Mathematics Classroom

Some of the purposes of cooperative strategies are to help students accomplish tasks and to use social skills necessary for success. Successful cooperative experiences are based on the ideas that all students are capable of understanding and learning, that positive interdependence is promoted through common subject matter tasks, and that students, by solving

---

Think while Reading Activity

Using the Learning Log activity format, jot down your responses to the teacher-generated questions listed in that section of the chapter. Use the information in this chapter for the content of your Learning Log entries.

_____

_____

_____

_____

_____

_____

_____

_____

Activity 16–3

---

their own problems, become more autonomous and self-sufficient. Over time students who use cooperative learning strategies attain higher achievement, use diverse learning strategies, experience greater learning retention, and learn to appreciate the differences of others. (O'Leary & Dishon, 1985).

The mathematics classroom is an especially appropriate place for cooperative learning experiences to occur. You, the teacher, organize the classroom in groups which you consider to be the optimal size for the assigned task. (Many teachers choose five as the ideal number in a cooperative group.) You monitor student behavior and take notes to be used later in giving feedback to students. You may also provide assistance by responding to group questions.

The students learn to recognize and value interdependence. They learn to distribute leadership throughout the group. They acquire skills and learn how to effectively collaborate.

The Learning Log

The learning log or journal can be a tremendous asset to mathematics students because it enables them to "write to learn." For the learning log to be effective, it must be used regularly. Each student must have a notebook in which to keep an ongoing record of his or her own learning as it happens. Logs are not necessarily meant to be shared with other students, but with the teacher.

The end of the mathematics period is a productive time for students to write in their learning logs. A five-minute period of time is adequate for the process. At the onset of this activity, it might be useful for students to respond to such teacher-generated questions as:

What did I understand about today's lesson?

What did I not understand?

Where did I get confused?

What could help me?

What questions do I have that were not answered in today's lesson?

Do I feel free to ask questions in class about things I do not understand?

Remember, this type of writing is personal and active. At first, students may experience difficulty in writing. They may feel unsure of how much to say about what they learned or did not learn during a class period. To ensure that students will be honest in their writings, teachers must be accepting and nonjudgmental about the students' revelations. Also, because the major purpose of the learning log is to communicate content ideas or problems, little emphasis should be placed on spelling errors, punctuation, or the like. As students begin to use their logs, and get input from you the teacher, they will begin to appreciate them as valuable communication tools.

The following are samples of students' writings in their logs from the very beginning of the semester. Some suggestions are included which may be useful as you begin using the logs in your classroom.

What did I understand about today's lesson?

I learned that when the problem says $6x = 24$, you can divide each side by the number 6 to find the answer. I also learned that "x" can be any number.

What did I not understand?

I did not understand why adding a negative number to a positive number makes me subtract. Why can't I add?
I did not understand why I had to use the sign of the larger number when I subtracted positive and negative numbers.

The first teacher-generated questions should be very direct and very simple. In this way, students gain confidence as they respond in their logs. They get experience responding in writing about concepts which are fairly easy. Because of the simplicity of their first writing experience in the mathematics learning log, they see the writing as not something to be feared, but rather as another method to clarify and improve their understanding of math concepts.

When you read the learning logs, you can easily discover which students need further work on a concept and which students understood the lesson. The log can be a tremendous asset in planning lessons.

As students begin to feel more comfortable writing in their logs, further teacher-directed questions can be added.

Where did I get confused? What could help me?

I got confused when you started to add a –8 to both sides of the equation. Going over things more slowly would help me. I don't want to ask questions in class. Others think I'm stupid if I do.

You did not give enough time to practice what you taught. I need time to think over what you said.

When students work together in small groups, their talking bothers me. I can't concentrate.

To determine your students' thinking abilities relative to tying past knowledge to a new situation, ask students to solve a new problem which would demonstrate such an ability. As they work to solve the problem, ask them to write their thinking in their logs, step by step.

Pose the following problem:

If one side of a square is increased by 8 feet and an adjacent side decreased by 2 feet, a rectangle is formed whose perimeter is 40 feet. Find the length of a side of the square.

Directions to the students:

You are to find the core of the above statement. You are to mark out any word that you think is unnecessary. You are not to distort the meaning of the problem. You must defend your reason for dropping a word in writing in your log.

Samples of student responses:

The word "if" can be dropped. It does not add anything to the problem.
I can restate the problem in my own words without changing the meaning of the problem. Read my deletions.

As students begin to solve the problem, the following are samples of their responses in their logs.

Student A

All the sides of the square can be called "x." If I add 8 to one side, I get x + 8. So one side is x + 8. The other side is x – 2. I have a rectangle, so I have to have 4 sides. The two opposite sides are equal. I have to have 4 numbered sides, so I need 2(x + 8)s and 2 (x –2)s. The perimeter, or distance around the rectangle, is 40. I have to add all four sides.

$$(x + 8) + (x + 8) + (x - 2) + (x - 2) = 40$$

$$x + x = 2x$$

$$8 + 8 = 16$$

So, I have $2x + 16$

Now I add $x + x = 2x$

$-2 + -2 = -4$ Negative numbers give negative numbers.

I now have

$2x + 2x = 4x$

$16 + (-4) = 12$ Positive numbers combined with negative numbers mean that you must subtract the numbers and give the answer the sign of the highest number.

Now I have

$4x + 12 = 40$ I can subtract 12 from each side without changing the value of the equation.

$$4x + 12 = 40$$
$$\underline{- 12 \quad -12}$$
$$\frac{4x}{4} = \frac{28}{4}$$
$$x = 7$$

I now have $4x = 28$. I can divide each side of the equation by 4 because in an equation what I do to one side I can do exactly the same to the other.

To check my answer I can put the number in the equation.

$$(x + 8) + (x + 8) + (x - 2) + (x - 2) = 40$$
$$(7 + 8) + (7 + 8) + (7 - 2) + (7 - 2) = 40$$
$$15 + 15 + 5 + 5 = 40$$

I am right!

Student B

In the beginning, I had a square. All the x's are equal because it is a square.
I will add a +8 or a –2 to two sides. I can now put the sides together.
I will put parentheses around the sides and multiply each side by 2, because I have to have a 4 sided figure since I started with a square. I know that if I add the sum of the sides together, it should equal 40, so that is what I did.

$2(x+8) + 2(x-2) = 40$

When I multiply (x+8) by 2, I say 2 times x is 2x and 2 times a +8 equals +16.
When I multiply (x–2) by 2, I say 2 times x is 2x and 2 times –2 equals –4. Then I can put all the figures back into the sentence or the equation

$2x + 16 + 2x - 4 + 40$

I add 2x plus 2x and it equals 4x.
+16 and –4 equals +12. (when you add numbers with unlike signs, you really subtract and give the answer the sign of the higher number)

Now I have 4x + 12 = 40
I can take –12 from each side of the equation since it will not change the answer
if you do the same thing to both sides of the equation. +12 and –12 equals zero
40 – 12 equals 28

$$4x + 12 = 40$$
$$-12\quad -12$$

$$\frac{4x}{4} = \frac{28}{4}$$

$$x = 7$$

I can divide each side by 4 (I am
treating each side of the equation
the same as I have to.

The answer is 7.

I can check my answer by putting the number 7 into the equation.

$$2\,(7+8)\ +2\,(7{-}2)\ =\ 40$$

$$2\,(15)\ +2\,(5)\ =\ 40$$

$$30\ +\ 10\ +\ 40$$

The answer checks out.

You will notice that Student A and Student B write their thinking processes quite differently. Student A is much more terse.

As you look at Student C's log you will notice that she clusters work immediately and seems to be able to see relationships without writing it all out. She opts to do the problem by using the adjacent sides of the rectangle.

Student C

$$(x + 8)\ +\ (x{-}2)\ +\ (x + 8)\ +\ (x{-}2)\ =\ 40$$
$$2x\ +\ 6\ +2x\ +\ 6\ =\ 40$$

$$4x\ +\ 12\ =\ 40$$
$$-\ 12\quad -12$$

$$4x\ =\ 28$$
$$x\ =\ 7$$

I used adjacent sides of the
rectangle, then I added the 2x's to get 4x,
added the +'s and the –2's and got the 12.

I took the –12 from each side to get 28 and
then divided each side by the 4. When you
check it out, it works.

As a teacher looking as the learning logs, one thing is quite evident: students understand that the object must be four sided, a square or a rectangle. This learning was based on an earlier lesson.

As you can readily see, writing in the learning log has many advantages. As the term progresses, the writing can involve itself with subjects other than how one goes about solving a problem, but starting with such a structure helps students get used to the idea of writing in their logs and helps them have something to write about in the very beginning. As the term progresses, the writing may become more personal, but this may not happen with all your students.

Teachers who have 150 students daily could not possibly read each learning log every day. However, it would be possible to read one class's learning log per day. An alternative would be to read the logs of the classes in which new lessons have been presented. Whatever decision you make relative to the frequency of reading the learning logs should be made very clear to students. In this way, no problems will arise relative to student expectancy of teacher response to their logs.

Conclusion

Written mathematics contains more ideas per line and per page than most other disciplines. Words and symbols are continuously combined and students' comprehension depends on their ability to discern the relationship between the words and the symbols. Using some of the techniques presented in this chapter may help students build the necessary bridges to achieve the end result—that of developing the requisite skills necessary to learn from their mathematics texts.

Think after Reading Activity

The author discussed many meaningful strategies to help students learn math. Choose one of these strategies, create a math problem, and then use the strategy to write an imaginary dialogue a teacher might conduct with a class to help solve the math problem.

Strategy:
_____

Teacher:
_____
_____
_____

Student:
_____
_____
_____

Teacher:
_____
_____
_____

Student:
_____
_____
_____

Activity 16–4

Chapter 17

Reading and Writing in Sports and Physical and Health Education

LANCE M. GENTILE   MERNA M. MCMILLAN

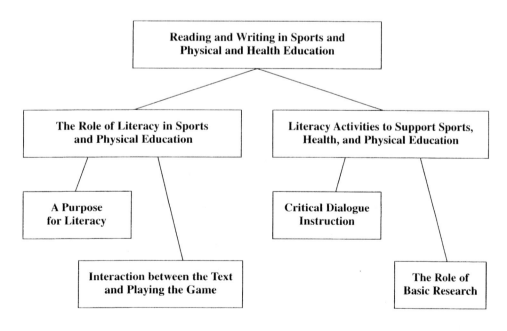

Think before Reading Activity

As schools take on a growing number of roles in the lives of students, all academic disciplines are affected. What do you think would be three important goals for coaches or teachers to address in sports or physical and health education classes? List those goals below:

1. _____

2. _____

3. _____

Now, star the goals that may in some way involve players' and students' development of literacy, including their capacity to listen, speak, read, write, view, or observe. Be prepared to share your list. As you read this chapter, think about your goals in relation to the ones the authors discuss.

Activity 17–1

Coaches and physical or health educators can play a significant role in the school-wide goal of developing players' and students' literacy. This chapter presents important information to achieve this aim.

Educators have long recognized the crucial relationship between physical activity, good health, and learning. Plato placed gymnastics at the highest level for training his philosopher-king. Spinoza claimed, "Teach the body to do many things: this will help you perfect the mind and come to the intellectual level of thought."

Sports and physical or health education are uniquely suited to teaching content literacy strategies because of many players' and students' background knowledge, experiences, and interest in the following:

1. The international focus on sports and physical and mental health.
2. The expanded interest in proper nutrition, diet, and weight control.
3. Media coverage of sports and fitness figures who act as models and ambassadors for literacy by encouraging youth to stay in school, develop a life of the mind, read to deepen and broaden one's knowledge of the world.

Content area literacy instruction in these fields is supplemental and is not intended to supercede or detract from play, performance, or exercise. It is focused on teaching strategies for getting meaning from reading and writing by showing players and students how to "play the game" through thoughtful, independent interaction with textual materials.

Your role as a coach or physical or health educator can support content area literacy instruction in three ways. First, you can show players and students how to become strategic readers and writers by capitalizing on their background knowledge, interest, and motivation in athletics, fitness, and wellness to locate specific information, identify unfamiliar vocabulary, analyze ideas or make interpretations, make inferences or draw conclusions, identify fact and opinion, cross check information or knowledge, and construct their own meanings (Tharp & Gallimore, 1976).

Second, you can model your own thinking to show players and students how to employ higher-order thinking to critically evaluate what they read, write, listen to, or view in your content areas and how these strategies may transfer across other curricula (Vygotsky, 1962).

Third, you can show players and students how to apply these strategies in meaningful literacy learning experiences to augment play or performance and strengthen fitness or health management (Palinscar & Brown, 1984).

This chapter describes several activities for content literacy instruction to strengthen the teaching of your subjects and to develop players' and students' reading and writing strategies for effective, independent learning. These are suggestive rather than prescriptive; they help guide rather than dictate an approach.

Critical Dialogue Instruction (CDI)

A critical dialogue is a structured conversation between you and your players or students (Gentile & McMillan, 1992, 1994). CDI makes use of excerpts drawn from paper or hardback literary books, magazines and newspapers, audio and video cassettes, and other sources. The conversation focuses on ideas, issues, problems, and ethical dilemmas that arise in sports and physical or health education depicted in a particular excerpt. CDI involves players or students in listening, speaking, reading, writing, and viewing or observation.

It is important not to rush CDI. All players or students should be included in the conversation and instructional activities. Two or three different class periods may be required to complete the full range of critical dialogue instruction.

Your role in CDI is twofold; you are a facilitator and a model (Palinscar, 1986):

Facilitator

- Identify and present written and audio-visual material related to sports and physical and health education in ways that access and develop players' or students' background knowledge, experiences, and interests.
- Establish clear, meaningful purposes for literacy learning that encourage players or students to think about, discuss, and begin questioning what they hear, see, read, and write.
- Solicit and respect all players' or students' attempts to respond during CDI.

Model

- Demonstrate specific examples of applying strategies using excerpts from written or audio-visual materials related to sports and physical and health education that transfer to literacy assignments across the school-wide curriculum.
- Demonstrate to players or students the importance of listening to each other as well as to you and to the information presented in audio-visual materials.

- Demonstrate higher-order thinking skills to show them how to solve problems and analyze or make meaningful connections and applications between what they hear, see, read, or write and what they have experienced in their own lives.

Purpose

Many players and students read sports biographies, novels, articles in magazines, and the sports section of a newspaper. They have seen films and videos related to sports and sports figures. They follow sports on television and are familiar with and interested in players, coaches, games, fitness programs, statistics, and specific contests or events. Using excerpts from these materials and resources you can facilitate listening, speaking, reading, writing, and viewing or observation through CDI to teach:

vocabulary and figurative or technical language

higher-order thinking

creative writing.

Objectives

1. Players or students will work with the coach or physical or health educator to establish the rules for conducting a critical dialogue.
2. Players or students will identify new or unfamiliar vocabulary and figurative or technical language contained in excerpts from sports and physical or health literature, related audio or video cassettes, and expository textual materials.
3. Players or students will apply what they learn in CDI to a creative writing activity focused on a specific problem or situation in their own lives.

Material

Besides paper and pencils you will need an excerpt from a sports novel or biography or newspaper or magazine article. For example, the following excerpt is from an article by Alexander Woolf that appeared in *Sports Illustrated* on March 16, 1992. It is entitled, "Blue Angel: Duke's Divine Spirit and Working Class Ethics Forge an Exemplary Program."

> At West Point, Krzyzewski constantly wanted to quit. The entire U.S. Military Academy seemed to be set up so he would fail. On an overnight trip his freshman year, Krzyzewski pitched a tent for the first time. The other cadets dug ditches around their tents, the way they learned in Boy Scouts, but Krzyzewski nearly floated away that night when it rained. He also flunked phys. ed. as a plebe. ("People think it's black kids who can't swim," Krzyzewski says, "but it's city kids who can't swim.") Yet by the end of his first year he wasn't merely swimming, he was leaping blindfolded into a pool from a 20-foot-high tower while wearing fatigues and boots and carrying a rifle. "At West Point," he says, "I learned how to grow from having my ego hurt." (p. 67)

Think while Reading Activity

CDI is a literacy activity that can be used in physical education. Define CDI:

_____

_____

Now imagine that you are a high school principal conducting your yearly observation of a PE coach. You expect to see the students and coach out on the field. Instead the coach is conducting a terrific CDI lesson. What would your comments be after observing this lesson?

_____

_____

_____

_____

_____

_____

_____

_____

_____

_____

Activity 17–2

Organizing a Critical Dialogue: Facilitating Instruction

Step 1

Introduce the activity and work with players or students to establish the ground rules for conducting a critical dialogue. Some may not understand or value the function and purpose of seminar instruction and see these open learning experiences as opportunities to act out. You and your players or students should agree on the rules for conducting CDI.

It is important to create opportunities for all of them to participate in CDI. But, it is not uncommon for some to dominate a classroom conversation while others remain silent and successfully avoid having to contribute to a group discussion. Others who have tried in the past to contribute to these conversations are overshadowed by those who are more assertive or verbal or by those who are perceived as being more intelligent. Their efforts may be met with ridicule, causing embarrassment and discouraging them from further participation. You can help reluctant players or students assert themselves appropriately in these situations by providing a safe, open, and structured classroom environment.

One way to encourage all players or students to take part in a critical dialogue is to give each one three to five "chits" or slips of paper. Each time someone contributes to the conversation they remove one slip from their hand and place it on the desktop. When all of that person's slips lie on top of the desk he or she must remain silent until everyone else has used up the remaining slips in their hand.

Step 2

Give a copy of a literary or expository textual excerpt to every member of the group. Introduce the material and access and develop players' or students' background knowledge about the person, issue, or topic (Langer, 1984; Ogle, 1986;). It helps to write this information on the chalk board as "What we know about . . ." (List #1). Ask one player or student to write the information down on a separate sheet of paper. Next, ask the group what more they would like to know about the person, issue, or topic. Record this information on the board as "What further questions do we have about . . ." (List #2). Ask another player or student to write this information down as well.

People can only think about a topic, idea, or issue to the extent they have information about it. When their fund of background knowledge or experience is deficient, they are unable to make higher-level connections or form broader and deeper connections so they can learn more. Showing players and students how to access and apply this knowledge and experience to learn more about sports or physical and health education is a primary strategy for effective reading, writing, and studying in any content area.

Step 3

Identify a few key vocabulary, technical, or figurative expressions in the excerpt that you think students are unfamiliar with. For example, introduce the excerpt by saying: "This article is about Mike Krzyzewski, the well-known Duke University basketball coach. Read the title of the article from which this passage is taken. What does the word 'exemplary' mean? What are 'working class ethics'?" Or you can quote from the author that Krzyewski "flunked phys. ed. as a plebe." Then ask, "What is a plebe?" Give players or students ample opportunity to make interpretations; compare and contrast their responses.

Many players and students lack the vocabulary and language facility to participate fully in and to enjoy literacy. Helping them acquire a broader vocabulary in sports and physical or health education can teach them the value of developing their power of clear and precise self-expression in other content areas.

Guiding Critical Dialogue Instruction: Modeling Strategies and Higher-Order Thinking

Step 1

Work with players or students to identify meaningful purposes for reading the excerpt (Blanton, Black, & Moorman, 1990). For example, ask students to read the first sentence of the excerpt ("At West Point, Krzyzewski constantly wanted to quit."). Now say, "From our list of 'What more do we want to know about' and after reading this first sentence, what purposes can you identify for continuing to read this excerpt? I am going to write a few of your suggestions on the board. We will discuss these and choose one of them as our main purpose for completing the reading. Afterwards I will ask you to respond to this purpose and we will see if we are able to answer any of our previously recorded questions from the 'What more do we want to know' list as well."

Players and students should complete reading the excerpt for the established purposes and questions. After they have finished, survey their responses. Learning to establish meaningful questions and purposes in content reading using sports or physical and health educational material and reading to fulfill these purposes is an important strategy that transfers to school-wide reading assignments.

Step 2

Now ask, "What are the facts contained in this excerpt? What do we know for sure?" If they have difficulty establishing this information, help them by modeling a few examples: Krzyzewski attended West Point. That is a fact. Krzyzewski was never a Boy Scout. That is a fact. What other facts can you locate?"

Modeling strategies for identifing, condensing, and synthesizing the facts in content reading helps students locate specific information that is important to understanding literary and expository material (Duffy, Roehler, & Hermann, 1988). Getting the facts straight helps students make more critical analyses and form better arguments or interpretations using not just sports or physical and health related materials, but across school-wide required textbook reading assignments.

Step 3

Next ask, "What were you thinking as you read this passage?" Their responses might begin with such phrases as, "I was thinking that . . ., I was wondering about . . ., I didn't know that . . ., When I read this one line, I said to myself . . ., I thought . . ., etc." If they have difficulty explaining what they were thinking or if you wish to help them expand their thoughts, model some of your thinking. For example, you might say: "We've talked some about Mr. Krzyzewski's fears and the way he learned to overcome them. When I was reading this excerpt I was thinking about my own fear of failure and what I try to do to cope with it. Sometimes I am more successful than others, but I have to constantly talk forcefully and encouragingly to myself in threatening situations and then do the best I can to confront the source of my fear."

Learning to express thoughts from reading sports and physical or health related materials focused on players' and students' background knowledge, experiences, and internally motivated interests is another important strategy for developing higher-order thinking: making assumptions, inferences, generalizations, predictions, and forming hypotheses and conclusions. Players and students gain valuable practice in literacy listening to the teacher model his or her own thinking using literary and expository textual materials.

Step 4

Now ask, "What were you feeling as you read this excerpt? Their responses might contain such phrases as: "I felt sorry for Krzyzewski because . . ." "I laughed when I read . . ." "I was surprised that . . ." "I've been afraid of the water and I know how he felt . . ." etc. If students have trouble expressing their feelings about this excerpt, or if you wish to offer them a personal response, model some of your feelings. For example, you might say: "While I was reading this passage I was feeling there is a lot we lose and miss when we let our fears control us. Look what Krzyzewski would have missed had he never been able to cope with and overcome his fear of the water."

Players' and students' ability to express feelings in relation to persons, ideas, or issues in sports and physical or health education is important to their developing a personal sense of values, ethics, and principles or codes of conduct. Through the filter of their own emotions they can relate to and better understand the human condition and spirit, not just in ways that apply to performance in these content areas, but to what is learned across the school-wide curriculum.

Step 5

Use multimedia or supplementary literature or text to link characters, ideas, issues, or problems to a broader range of experiences.

For example, use an excerpt from the videocassette, *Hoosiers.* In this segment Gene Hackman, who plays a high school coach, and his rural team arrive in Indianapolis for the finals of the Indiana State Basketball Tournament. His undersized team is overwhelmed by the prospect of meeting larger, and supposedly more sophisticated, big-city players and playing in front of a huge coliseum crowd. Ask players or students to watch this segment for the purpose of describing how they would feel in the situation these players find themselves. Give them ample opportunity to discuss their feelings. Then continue showing the video.

Think while Reading Activity

To close Critical Dialogue Instruction, one of the question probes is: "What is the most important thing you learned from reading the passage?" Answer this question in reference to the information you have read so far in this chapter. Has it changed your thinking about the role of literacy in sports and physical education? Include this in your answer.

_____

_____

_____

_____

_____

_____

_____

_____

_____

_____

_____

_____

_____

Activity 17–3

After being in the coliseum a short time Hackman senses his team's anxiety. He walks them out onto the arena floor and involves them in measuring the height of the basket and various other dimensions of the playing surface. When each measurement is complete, he reminds the players that these are the same as those of any other gym in which they have played. He tells them that in order to overcome fear in any situation the first step is to size up the threat accurately.

Now ask one or more follow-up questions: What comparisons can you make between Krzyzewski and Gene Hackman? What differences do you see between Duke's team and the *Hoosier* team? What do you think are the problems that both coaches and teams might have to face; how are they alike? How are they different? How do you feel each coach or team attempts to cope with their problems?

Helping players and students identify similarities, differences, or polarities and describe the ethical dilemmas or questions as they apply to sports and physical or health education can stimulate higher-order thinking skills and strategies that transfer to the development of literacy across all content curricula.

Closing Critical Dialogue Instruction

Step 1

Ask, "What is the most important question you have at this point related to what we have read, discussed, and watched?" Provide players or students ample opportunities to present their questions. If they have difficulty identifying questions or you have a poignant question, model it for them. For example: "One of the questions that has occurred to me throughout our reading, conversation, and after watching portions of the *Hoosiers* video is: How can someone 'learn to grow from having the ego hurt'? It would seem that only a special kind of person, someone very secure and with a strong ego, can learn to grow after having it wounded. What do you think about this? How does someone develop a strong ego? What is the difference between a strong and a big ego?"

Step 2

Now ask, "What is the most important thing you learned from reading the passage, the conversation, and watching the excerpts from *Hoosiers?*" If they have difficulty doing this or if you have learned something important, model it for them. For example, you might say: "I think the most important thing I learned from all of our work together is that everyone at sometime or another is afraid of something. It seems all of us are vulnerable and are challenged by many different circumstances.

Learning to identify main ideas and significant details and processing this information in ways that make it personally important is a vital strategy in literacy that also transfers across the school-wide curriculum.

Step 3

This is the point at which you involve players or students in a creative writing activity. You can elicit written responses that require them to apply what they have learned during CDI to a significant problem or situation in their own lives (Graves, 1983; Tompkins, 1994).

For example, they should first work in small groups to:

- Decide what they wish to write. This can be a letter, telegram, brief essay, poem or short story, newspaper or magazine article or editorial, an advertisement, or a script for a play or news/sports broadcast.
- Decide on a topic or idea and identify the audience for their writing.
- Decide who is responsible for writing specific portions of the project and how the final draft will be composed.
- Write a first draft.
- Work with the teacher and together to edit and revise the material and write a final draft.

Some of the ideas or issues they might consider are:

- What difference can the ideas presented in the *Sports Illustrated* excerpt, our dialogue, or the *Hoosiers* video make in your life?
- What alternatives do you see for solving a personal challenge that is similar to the one that confronted Krzyzewski, Gene Hackman, or his team?

You can also introduce a related quotation from another author and ask students to write to compare or contrast the ideas in the quoted material with those in the *Sports Illustrated* excerpt or the *Hoosiers* video.

For example, you might say: "This is a quotation from the science fiction writer, Ray Bradbury. I'd like you to think about it in relation to what we read about, and describe how the ideas presented in both are alike or different." Then you could read or distribute a copy of the following quotation from Bradbury:

> If we relied on our intellect, we would never have a friendship: we would never have a love affair: we would never open a business, because we'd be cynical. That's ridiculous. We must be jumping off of cliffs all the time and building our wings on the way down.

Using this approach helps players and students make reading and writing connections and applications not only in the content areas of sports and physical or health education but across the curriculum.

Basic Research in Physical and Health Education

Purpose

An abundance of evidence suggests that people who perform regular aerobic exercise, requiring the heart and lungs to work, suffer less cardiovascular disease than those who lead sedentary, inactive lives. Students can use literacy to conduct basic research and improve cardiovascular performance in physical and health education: reading to understand physiological effects of aerobic exercise; writing in a journal to clarify thoughts and feelings related to aerobic or nonaerobic exercise.

Objectives

1. Players and students will identify vocabulary and technical language related to cardiovascular functions.
2. Players and students will identify basic research techniques in physical and health education.

Procedure

Watches with sweep second hands or stop watches will be needed, as well as pencils and paper. After setting purposes for conducting basic research in physical or health education, discuss some of the following vocabulary and technical language:

Aerobics	*Research*
aerobic exercise	random sample
anaerobic exercise	experimental group
pulmonary artery	control group
recovery time	data
cardiovascular performance	pre- and post-test

Step 1

Divide players or students in pairs. Each pair forms a research team. Make sure each team has one watch, a pencil, and paper. Demonstrate the proper method for measuring a pulse rate using the sweep hand of a watch. Press your middle finger to the jugular vein and count the number of beats per minute. Now ask one player or student in each team to locate and measure his or her partner's pulse. When the first team member has done this successfully, the other student does the same for him or her. When they have done this accurately for each other, each player or student measures and records in their journal the other's pulse using three criteria:

- Pulse rate at rest.
- Pulse rate after two minutes of running in place.
- Pulse two minutes after the student stops running in place, to determine the recovery rate, or the rate at which the heart returns to its normal beat.

Step 2

Once both players or students in each team have located, measured, and recorded these data for each other, give each student a slip of paper and ask each one to write his or her name on this slip. Count the total number and place all of them in a hat. Withdraw half of this number of slips, read each name aloud, and record it on a separate sheet of paper or on the board. This group will be the "experimental" group. The players or students whose names appear on the other half of the slips in the hat will be the "control" group.

Step 3
Players or students in the experimental group will be asked, depending on their level of fitness, to walk or jog at least two miles each day for a period of one month. Those in the control group will do no cardiovascular activity for the same period.

Step 4
During this month players or students should write each day in their journals, recording their thoughts, feelings, and experiences, and noting any changes in weight, appetite, mood, or energy level.

Step 5
At the end of the month, ask each one to remeasure his or her partner's pulse rates using the same three criteria from the first measurement. They should record these figures in their journals and compare pre- and post-test results, identifying and describing any differences in these data. They will also interview one another to identify their thoughts, feelings, questions, or concerns and note changes in weight, appetite, mood, or energy level. They should discuss this information and record in their journals any conclusions or insights they gain after comparing the data and interviewing each other.

		Experimental Group	**Control Group**
		Bobby Long	*Richard Smith*
Pulse at rest	pre-test	92	80
	post-test	85	81
2 minute run	pre-test	145	150
	post-test	135	150
2-minute recovery	pre-test	115	125
	post-test	100	126

Step 6
When all players or students have recorded the significant information in their journals, facilitate a conversation with the whole class focused on their conclusions from this study. It may be helpful for you to invoke pertinent information from texts related to the topic to expand or deepen your discussion. Excerpts from these texts may be applied using the structure for Critical Dialogue Instruction (CDI) presented earlier.

Reading and Writing about Health Topics

What follows is a description of one possible project, reading and writing about early suicide.

Purpose

In health education classes students study cases of preadolescent or adolescent suicide. Students read to examine myths and facts related to early suicide and write in response to Critical Dialogue Instruction (CDI).

Objectives

1. Students will identify specific myths and facts related to early suicide.
2. Students will identify the danger signs of early suicide.

Procedure

The materials used include an anonymous poem written by a fifteen-year-old boy two years before he committed suicide, as well as paper and pencils.

Step 1
Access and develop students' background knowledge related to early suicide by facilitating a discussion concerning the following myths. Students may answer true or false and support their beliefs based on what they think they know to be true.

- Talking about suicidal feelings will cause a person to commit suicide.
- All suicidal people want to die and nothing can be done about it.
- People who talk about suicide never do it.

Step 2
After this initial discussion, present the following facts to students and compare these with some of the true or false responses they have made to the three aforementioned statements.

- Talking about suicidal feelings can help relieve a person's suicidal pain.
- Most suicidal people are ambivalent and frequently call for help after an attempt.
- Threatening suicide is a warning that should never be ignored.

Step 3
Discuss the five warning signs of early suicide (Ross & Lee, 1983):

- Suicide threats.
- Statements revealing a desire to die.
- Previous suicide attempts.
- Sudden changes in behavior (withdrawal, apathy, severe mood swings).
- Final arrangements (giving away prized personal possessions).

Step 4
Encourage students to locate more information regarding early suicide in newspaper or magazine articles or pamphlets published by local suicide and crisis centers or community

mental health agencies. Ask them to bring these to class and use excerpts from them with the whole class to broaden and deepen the conversation.

Step 5
Afterwards, give students a copy of the following poem and ask them to read it to compare the author's statements to any of the warning signs of early suicide.

To Santa Claus and Little Sisters

Once . . . he wrote a poem.
And called it "Chops."
Because that was the name of
his dog, and that's what it was
all about.
And the teacher gave him an A.
And a gold star.
And his mother hung it on the
kitchen door, and read it to
all his aunts . . .
Once he wrote another poem.
And he called it "Question
Marked Innocence."
Because that was the name of
his grief and that's what it
was all about.
And the professor gave him
an A.
And a strange and steady look.
And his mother never hung it
On the kitchen door, because
he never let her see it.
Once, at 3 a.m. . . . he tried
another poem . . .
And he called it absolutely
nothing, because that's what
it was all about.
And he gave himself an A.
And a slash on each wrist.
And hung it on the bathroom
door because he couldn't reach
the kitchen.

Step 6
When students complete reading the poem, facilitate CDI with them by asking the following questions:

What do you know for sure about the author?

What were you thinking while reading this poem?

What were you feeling while reading the poem?

What is the most important question you have after reading the poem?

What is the most important thing you learn from this poem?

Step 7

Now ask students to move into groups of three or four. Explain to them that they are going to do some writing related to the class discussion of early suicide and the poem they have read. Their written responses should focus on what they think is important to know about early suicide and how this can apply to their own lives or the lives of their friends. When they are in their groups they should decide:

- what they are going to write (This can be a newspaper or magazine commentary or editorial, poem, essay, or short story, a reflective statement on some of the feelings they may share with the author of this poem, or a letter to the author, or his parents or friends.)
- whom they will write to.
- how the writing responsibilities will be divided among the group members.
- how they will organize each person's contribution to create the first draft of their writing.

Step 8

When these decisions are made they are ready to begin writing and developing the first draft. When this is completed the teacher should work with each group to help them edit and revise their writing to form a final, polished draft of their work.

Coaches and Physical and Health Educators as Literacy Models

Many players and students look up to coaches and physical or health educators. You can influence them in positive ways because they see you as role models. They can learn from you:

- the importance of literacy in developing athletic performance and principles, and a greater knowledge of sports and physical and health education.
- more effective means of weight control and nutrition.
- better mental or emotional adjustment.
- better ways to spend leisure time.

Using the ideas presented in this chapter, you can model for them (Joyce & Clift, 1984):

1. Real purposes and strategies for becoming literate.
2. Literacy learning experiences that identify important biographical information, and ideas or issues in your content areas using textual and related audio-visual material.

3. Listening and viewing strategies as well as the power of developing vocabulary and figurative or technical language.

3. Higher-order thinking required for critically analyzing related audio and video cassettes, discussing and writing about what they read, view, or listen to in ways that support the development of literacy across the school-wide curriculum.

4. Basic methods for identifying and investigating problems in sports and physical or health education, collecting and organizing data, evaluating information related to and derived from these studies, and making interpretations or drawing conclusions based on the results.

5. Ways to motivate themselves to develop and use literacy in the areas of sports and physical and health education to become active, lifelong learners.

Think after Reading Activity

There is a common misconception that athletes are not strong in academics. At the same time, many universities and colleges are working to increase the academic requirements for their athletes. Assume that you are a coach at a small college. Write a short memo to the Dean of Academic Affairs suggesting ways in which the entire academic staff can become literacy models for the athletes.

To: Dean of Academic Affairs

From: Head Coach

After reading an article about sports and literacy, I suggest that the entire faculty at River View College discuss their roles as literacy models for the college's growing athletic student body. The following suggestions are some of the main points from the recent article I read and found valuable:

1. _____

2. _____

3. _____

4. _____

5. _____

Activity 17–4

C h a p t e r *18*

Vocabulary Instruction in Content Areas

MICHAEL F. GRAVES   WAYNE H. SLATER

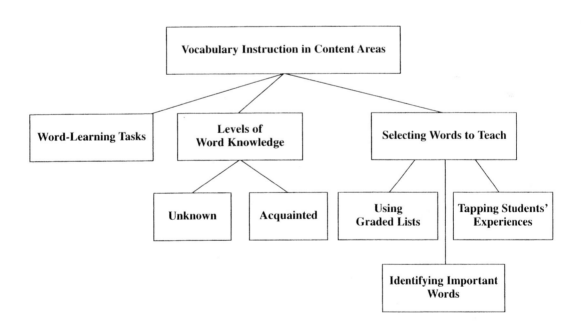

Think before Reading Activity

What do you do when you encounter a word that you are unfamiliar with? You may actually have more than one strategy, depending on the situation. Briefly describe two or three strategies you have used.

_____

_____

_____

_____

_____

_____

_____

_____

_____

_____

_____

Activity 18–1

This chapter presents a plan for content area vocabulary instruction. A major thesis of the chapter is that there are different word-learning tasks and that these different tasks require different sorts of instruction. The chapter is divided into four major sections. In the first section, we discuss six word-learning tasks. In the second section, we discuss different levels of word knowledge that students may attain. In the third section, we discuss ways of selecting words to teach. Finally, in the fourth and longest section of the chapter, we discuss teaching procedures appropriate for each of the different word-learning tasks students face.

The importance of vocabulary is daily demonstrated in schools and out. In the classroom, the achieving students possess the most adequate vocabularies. Because of the verbal nature of most classroom activities, knowledge of words and ability to use language are essential to success in these activities. After schooling has ended, adequacy of vocabulary is almost equally essential for achievement in vocations and in society. (Petty, Harold, & Stoll, 1968, p. 7)

Appearing in a review of research on vocabulary instruction completed over two decades ago, this particular statement represents an almost universal attitude toward vocabulary held both by educators and those outside the field. Additionally, a number of theorists and researchers have made much more specific claims for the importance of words. Among them are that the language one speaks, including the lexicon of the language, actually constrains thought (Sapir, 1921; Whorf, 1956/1940) or at least channels it (Carroll, 1956), that vocabulary knowledge is one of the best predictors of verbal ability (Jensen, 1980; Terman, 1918), that vocabulary difficulty strongly influences the readability of texts (Klare, 1984), and that teaching the vocabulary of a selection can improve students' comprehension of the selection (Beck & McKeown, 1983).

The number of words appearing in material used by children up through grade 12 is probably in the neighborhood of 100,000. Although no one student will encounter all of these words, and although students do not need to learn all of these words (Beck, McKeown, & Omanson, 1987), they do need to learn a substantial number of them. Of course, not all of these words could be directly taught. Students acquire many of the words that they know from wide reading (Anderson & Nagy, 1993; Fielding, Wilson, & Anderson, 1986), and encouraging students to read widely should promote vocabulary growth as well as accomplish many other important objectives. Additionally, instruction which attempts to teach students to better use context cues and word parts to learn new words seems very likely to promote word learning (Buikema & Graves, 1993; White, Sowell, & Yanagihara, 1989).

However, we believe that beyond the vocabulary learning that comes from wide reading and the vocabulary learning that can be promoted by teaching students to better use context clues and word parts to unlock word meanings, students' success in content classes can be promoted by direct instruction in vocabulary. In fact, we believe that vocabulary is a crucial part of instruction in content areas. Such instruction should focus on the words necessary to understand the content being presented. It should also be appropriate for the students being taught and the words being presented and should foster appropriate depth of word knowledge. In our judgment, word learning should not be considered a single task. Rather, it should be considered a series of quite different tasks that vary considerably depending on learners' knowledge of the words and concepts to be taught, the depth and precision of meaning to be taught, and the extent to which learners are expected to incorporate the taught words into their productive vocabularies.

In the remainder of this chapter, we will describe six word-learning tasks, briefly discuss levels of word knowledge, describe teaching procedures appropriate for each of the six different word-learning tasks in some detail, make some suggestions for selecting content vocabulary to teach, and make a few concluding remarks about vocabulary instruction.

Word-Learning Tasks

Here, we describe six word-learning tasks, each of which makes different demands on the learner and on the teacher. The tasks are learning to read known words, learning new meanings for known words, learning new words representing known concepts, learning new words representing new concepts, clarifying and enriching the meanings of known words, and moving words into students' productive vocabularies (for other discussions of these tasks, see Graves, 1985, 1987; Graves, Watts, & Graves, 1994; Ryder & Graves, 1994).

Learning to Read Known Words

Learning to read known words, words that are already in their oral vocabularies, is the task of beginning readers. Such words as *surprise, stretch,* and *amaze* are ones that students might be taught to read during their first three years of school. By the end of the primary grades, good readers will have learned to read nearly all the words in their oral vocabularies. However, the task of learning to read all of the words in their oral vocabularies remains for many less able readers in the middle and secondary grades, and thus it is something that content teachers who have at least some less able readers in their classes need to be concerned with.

Learning New Meanings for Known Words

Learning new meanings for words that students already know with one meaning is a task presented to all students, not just less able ones, because all students come across words that are used with new meanings as they read. Teaching such words occupies a special place in content areas because words often have different and important meanings in particular content areas. The meaning of *product* in mathematics classes, that of *legend* in geography or history classes, and that of *force* in physics classes are three examples of such words.

Learning New Words Representing Known Concepts

Another word-learning task students face is learning to read words which are in neither their oral nor their reading vocabularies but for which they have an available concept. For example, the word *indigenous* would be unknown to the majority of students, but many would have the concept "native born" readily available. All students continue to learn words of this sort throughout their years in school, and we believe that the largest number of words students learn in the middle and secondary grades will be this sort.

Learning New Words Representing New Concepts

A very demanding word-learning task is learning to read words which are in neither the students' oral nor reading vocabularies and for which they do not have an available concept. Learning the full meanings of such words as *fulcrum, mores,* and *temerity* is likely to require most students to develop new concepts. All students continue to learn words of this sort throughout their years in school.

Clarifying and Enriching the Meanings of Known Words

Still another word-learning task is that of clarifying and enriching the meanings of already known words. The meanings students originally attach to words are often imprecise and only become fully specified over time (Anglin, 1977). Students might not initially, for example, recognize any difference between *brief* and *concise,* or they might not realize what distinguishes a *cabin* from a *shed,* or not realize that the term *virtuoso* is usually applied to those who play musical instruments. Students will expand and enrich the meanings of the words they know as they repeatedly meet them in new and slightly different contexts, but because the accretion of meaning from context is a slow and by no means sure process for many students, some more direct approaches to the matter seem warranted.

Moving Words into Students' Productive Vocabularies

The last word-learning task we will mention here is that of moving words from students' receptive vocabularies to their productive vocabularies, that is, moving words from students' listening and reading vocabularies to their speaking and writing vocabularies. Older students, for example, might have a fairly thorough understanding of the word *dogmatic* when they hear it or read it, yet never use the word themselves. Direct methods of getting students to use the words they do know in their daily language are called for, and these methods may well include helping students more thoroughly learn the words' meanings.

Think while Reading Activity

The section "Levels of Word Knowledge" describes three levels: unknown, acquainted, and established. When you read a chapter in your own content area, what was your level of word knowledge? How did it vary when you read a chapter that wasn't your area of expertise? Compare this experience with how you imagine a junior high or high school student might feel in a similar situation.

Activity 18–2

Levels of Word Knowledge

In addition to there being different word-learning tasks, there are different levels of word knowledge. Beck, McKeown, McCaslin, and Burkes (1979), for example, distinguish three levels: *unknown, acquainted,* and *established.* A word at the *unknown* level is just that, unknown. A word at the *acquainted* level is one whose meaning is recognized but only with some deliberate attention, and a word at the *established* level is one whose meaning is easily, rapidly, and perhaps automatically recognized.

Obviously, we want any vocabulary instruction to move students' knowledge of the words beyond the first level. However, we know that learning a word thoroughly requires a number of exposures in a variety of contexts (Beck & McKeown, 1983), and that thoroughly knowing a word involves a number of skills, including, perhaps, associating it with a range of experiences, readily accessing it, being able to articulate one's understanding of it, flexibly using it, and recognizing synonyms, metaphors, and analogies that employ the word (Calfee & Drum, 1986). Certainly, no single encounter with a word is likely to achieve all of these goals. On the other hand, no single encounter with a word need accomplish all of these goals. Instead, any particular instructional encounter with a word can be considered as only one in a series of encounters that will eventually lead students to mastery of the word. In many instances, the first instructional encounter with a word will get

---

Think while Reading Activity

As you read "Methods of Teaching Words," think how these suggestions will help you when you are teaching in the classroom. Write down some of the ideas you want to remember.

_____

_____

_____

_____

_____

_____

_____

_____

_____

_____

_____

_____

_____

Activity 18–3

students only to the *acquainted* level. However, we know that even a brief encounter with a word will leave some trace of its meaning and make students more likely to fully grasp its meaning when they again come across it in context (Jenkins, Stein, & Wysocki, 1984). Moreover, brief instruction, provided immediately before students read a selection containing the word, may be sufficient to prevent their stumbling over it as they read.

Thus, we—along with McKeown and Beck (in press)—believe that there is a place for relatively brief vocabulary instruction methods that serve primarily to start students on the long road to full mastery of words and that prevent them from stumbling over unknown words when reading, as well as a place for much more extensive and ambitious instruction that enables students to develop thorough understanding of words and perhaps use the words in their speech and writing.

Methods of Teaching Words

Here we describe teaching procedures appropriate for each of the six word-learning tasks we have listed. Instruction appropriate for some of these tasks will promote deeper levels of word knowledge than others. Also, for some of the tasks, we describe several teaching procedures which differ in the depth of word knowledge they promote. At the end of this section, we discuss the importance of enriching students' oral vocabularies, particularly those of students who are acquiring English as a second language.

Learning to Read Known Words

In learning to read known words, the basic task for the student is to associate what is unknown, the written word, with what is already known, the spoken word. To establish this association, the student needs to see the word at the same time that it is pronounced, and once the association is established, it needs to be rehearsed and strengthened so that the relationship becomes automatic. We have listed these steps below to emphasize just how straightforward the process is.

See the word.

Hear the word as it is seen.

Rehearse that association a myriad of times.

Because the words' meanings are not what is being taught, it is not mandatory that they are initially presented in context. However, students do need to encounter the words in context very soon after initial instruction, and wide reading in materials containing numerous repetitions of such words is by far the best form of rehearsal for these words and an essential part of students' mastering them.

One of the most important points to remember when teaching these words is that there is no need to teach their meanings. These are words students already know and understand when they hear them; they simply cannot read them.

Learning New Meanings for Known Words

If the new meanings do not represent new and difficult concepts, the procedure for teaching new meanings for known words is fairly simple and straightforward. The approach shown below is one appropriate method.

Product

Acknowledge the known meaning. something made by a company
Give the new meaning. the number made by multiplying other numbers
Note the similarities between the The similarity is that in both instances some-
meanings (If any). thing is produced or made by some process.

If the new meanings to be learned represent new and difficult concepts, then the procedure we suggest in the section on teaching new concepts is more appropriate.

Learning New Words Representing Known Concepts

Listed below are three approaches to teaching new words representing known concepts. These require differing amounts of teacher time, differing amounts of class time, and differing amounts of students' time and effort, and they are likely to yield different results.

1. Ask students to look up the word in the dictionary and give them the word in context.
2. Give a synonym or definition of the word and a brief context (either in writing or orally).
3. Give a definition of the word and a rich context (either in writing or orally).

An additional procedure which has proven successful in teaching new words representing known concepts is one called the context/relationship procedure (see Ryder & Graves, 1994). The heart of the procedure is a brief paragraph which uses the target word three or four times. The paragraph is followed by a multiple-choice item which checks students' understanding of the word. A sample paragraph and multiple-choice item and the steps for presenting each word are shown below.

Conveying

The luncheon speaker was successful in *conveying* his main ideas to the audience. They all understood what he said, and most agreed with him. *Conveying* has a more specific meaning than *talking*. *Conveying* indicates that a person is getting his or her ideas across accurately.

Conveying means
___ **A.** putting parts together.
___ **B.** communicating a message.
___ **C.** hiding important information.

1. Explain the purpose of the procedure.
2. Pronounce the word to be taught.

3. Read the paragraph in which the word appears.
4. Read the possible definitions, and ask students to choose the best one.
5. Pause to give students time to check a definition, give them the correct answer, and answer any questions students have.
6. Read the word and its definition a final time.

Presenting words in this way takes about a minute per word, and results have repeatedly indicated that students remember quite rich meanings for words taught in this fashion.

Learning New Words Representing New Concepts

Because two of the methods we describe in the next section can also be used to teach new concepts, here we consider only one method, generally referred to as the Frayer model (see Frayer, Frederick, & Klausmeier, 1969). The major steps of our version of the method, which is slightly different from the original, are shown below.

1. Define the new concept, giving its necessary attributes.

   Temerity is a characteristic of a person. A person demonstrates *temerity* when he or she exercises reckless boldness, ignoring serious dangers.

2. Distinguish between the new concept and similar but different concepts with which it might be mistaken. In doing so it may be appropriate to identify some accidental attributes that might falsely be considered to be necessary attributes of the new concept.

   Temerity differs from *foolishness* in that *temerity* necessarily involves some element of danger.

3. Give examples of the concept, and explain why they are examples.

   The cliff divers of Acapulco demonstrate *temerity* because doing so is definitely dangerous and the divers are admired by many for their bravery.

4. Give non-examples of the concept, and explain why they are non-examples.

   Someone who drives after drinking too much is not demonstrating *temerity* because there is nothing admirable here.

5. Present students with examples and non-examples, ask them to identify which are and are not instances of the concept and to state why, and give them feedback.

   Crossing the Pacific in a one-person sailboat (example)
   Eating a whole watermelon (non-example)

6. Have students present their own examples and non-examples of the concept, have them discuss why they are examples or non-examples, and give them feedback.

Although using the Frayer method takes time and effort from both students and teachers, the fruits of the labor are well worth the effort, for with this method students can gain a new understanding of a part of the world.

Clarifying and Enriching the Meanings of Known Words

Here we present three methods of clarifying and enriching the meanings of known words. Importantly, the first two of these methods are also particularly useful in preteaching vocabulary to improve comprehension of a selection. They serve this purpose because they focus not just on the word or words being taught but also on related words and on the part the words play in the selection.

In the first method recommended, the teacher begins by choosing six to eight words from an upcoming selection that might cause difficulty for students. In content texts these should represent key concepts and related words. Next, the teacher selects an additional four to six words that are likely to be familiar to students. These familiar words are used to help students generate sentences.

Once the ten to twelve words are selected, they are put on the board. If some students in the class know the definitions, they can define them. If not, the teacher should provide short definitions. Following this, students are given the topic of the selection and asked to create sentences which use at least two of the words and which are *possible sentences* in the selection they are about to read. The sentences students create are then put on the board, and students are instructed to read the selection.

Following the reading of the selection, the teacher returns to the sentences on the board, and the class discusses whether each of them could be or could not be true given the content of the reading selection. Having students provide rationales for either decision furthers their understanding of central concepts of the selection. Sentences that could be true are left as they are. Sentences that could not be true are discussed by the class and modified so that they could be true.

Shown below are some of the words Stahl and Kapinus (1991) selected form some science texts they worked with, as well as some possible sentences students might generate with the words.

> Potentially Difficult Words: *front, barometer, humidity, air mass, air pressure,* and *meteorology*
>
> Familiar Words: *clouds, rain,* and *predict*
>
> When a *front* approaches it is quite likely to *rain.* (could be true)
>
> When a *front* approaches, it is very unlikely to *rain.* (could not be true)

The second method of clarifying and extending the meanings of known words, and of introducing vocabulary in a way that is likely to improve comprehension of a selection, was suggested by Johnson and Pearson (1984) and is called semantic mapping. This procedure can also be useful for teaching new concepts. With this method, the teacher puts a word representing a central concept—usually from an upcoming reading selection—on the chalk board, asks students to work in groups listing as many words related to the central concept as they can, writes students' words on the chalk board grouped in broad categories, has students name the categories and perhaps suggest additional ones, and discusses with students the central concept, the other words, the categories, and their interrelationships. (See Figure 18–1.)

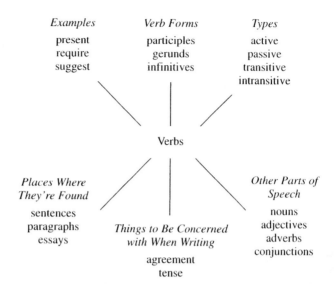

FIGURE 18–1 A Semantic Map

The third method of helping students clarify and enrich the meanings of words is a form of intensive instruction developed by Beck and her colleagues (see Beck & McKeown, 1983). As is the case with semantic mapping, this method can also be appropriate for teaching new concepts. Below are some features of intensive instruction.

1. Words are presented in semantically related sets of ten or so words presented over a five-day period. One set of words Beck has used—a set semantically related in they they all referred to *people*—includes rival, hermit, novice, virtuoso, accomplice, miser, tyrant, and philanthropist.
2. Students work extensively with the words, spending about half an hour a day on the ten words during the week they are taught and doing ten to fifteen activities with each word.
3. Instruction is deliberately varied, and the various activities are designed to accomplish various purposes. Students define words, use them in sentences, do speeded trials with them, make affective responses to them, compare them to each other and to other concepts, keep a written record of their work with them, and are encouraged to use them outside of class.

> Examples of the varied tasks Beck has used include the following: Students are asked to respond to words such as *virtuoso* and *miser* with thumbs up or thumbs down to signify approval or disapproval of the concept and to explain their responses. They are asked which of three actions an *accomplice* would be most likely to engage in—robbing a bank by himself, stealing some candy, or driving a getaway car. They are asked such questions as Could a *virtuoso* be a *rival?* Could a *virtuoso* be a *novice?* Could a *philanthropist* be a *miser?*

Results of several studies have indicated that students working with intensive instruction gain deep understanding and mastery of the words and that this in-depth knowledge enables them to better comprehend materials containing the words.

Moving Words into Students' Expressive Vocabularies

Students can be encouraged to move words into their expressive vocabularies by your providing a model of precise word use, your encouraging students to employ precise and mature words in their speech and writing and recognizing appropriate diction when they display it, and your providing time and encouragement for various sorts of word play that prompts students to work with words they might otherwise not speak or write.

A more direct approach to fostering expressive vocabulary has been developed by Duin and Graves (1988). The major features of this instruction, which is a modification of Beck's, are shown below.

1. Words are taught in groups of ten to fifteen related words presented over three to six days. The words are not necessarily semantically related, but they do lend themselves to writing on a particular topic.
2. Students spend about half an hour a day with the ten to fifteen words taught during the three to six days of instruction, doing ten to fifteen activities with each word.
3. Instruction is deliberately varied, and the activities are designed to accomplish various purposes. Students define words, use them in sentences, do speeded trials with them, make affective responses to them, compare them to each other and to other concepts, keep a written record of their work with them, are encouraged to use them outside of class, and do several short writing assignments with them. Each word is taught in terms of the concept it represents, the relationships it shares with other words, and the subject domain within which it can be used in writing.

> Students discussed how *feasible* space travel might soon be for each of them. They were asked if they thought their school could find a way to better *accommodate* handicapped students. They distinguished between new words such as *retrieve* and related words such as *return* by filling in sentence frames with the more appropriate of the two words. They wrote brief essays called "Space Shorts" employing the words in dealing with such topics as the foods that would be available in space and judged each others' use of the words.

Studies have indicated that students working with this sort of instruction use a substantial proportion of the taught words in essays targeted to their use, and that the essays of students who have received the instruction are judged markedly superior to those of students who have not received it. Equally importantly, these studies have shown that students thoroughly enjoy learning and using words in this way.

Enriching Students' Oral Vocabularies

Many of the words that students eventually incorporate into their reading vocabularies, they first learn orally. Thus, the development of oral vocabulary is crucial and helps to build reading vocabulary. One place that working with oral vocabulary is important is in content areas such as science, math, and social studies. It is often a good idea to work with new content words orally as well as in reading.

The development of oral vocabulary is particularly important for students for whom English is a second language. Some of these students come to secondary schools with relatively small oral vocabularies in English, and these students need as many opportunities as possible to build their oral vocabularies. We suggest two approaches here.

First, be aware of the fact that students, particularly some ESL students, need to build their oral vocabularies. Try to create a classroom atmosphere in which articulate speech and appropriate diction are recognized and valued. Be aware of your own diction. Choose the precise word for what you want to say and use it, and from time to time mention to students that you are using a particular word for a particular purpose. Be aware of when a word you are using may be new to some students, and highlight and briefly teach such words. Also, be aware of the diction of your students. Encourage adroit word usage and reward it—that is, recognize it publicly. Also, point out skillful word usage in the speech and writing of others. All in all, do everything possible to make your classroom a word-rich environment.

Second, give ESL students numerous opportunities for discussion with students whose first language is English. Small-group work, cooperative learning, and various projects can provide such opportunities. Remember, some ESL students use little or no English in their homes, so if they are going to hear and speak much English, they will have to do so in school.

Selecting Vocabulary to Teach

Once you have considered the sorts of words that need to be taught, the level of word knowledge that you want your students to achieve, and the instructional procedures you can use, you still have the task of selecting specific words to teach. Two steps are useful here. The first is getting some idea of just which words students are likely to know, and the second is setting up criteria for selecting the words.

One way of getting an idea of which words students are likely to know is to consult Dale and O'Rourke's *The Living Word Vocabulary* (1981). This book is a word list which presents the results of vocabulary tests administered to students in grades 4, 6, 8, 10, 12, 13, and 16. In all, the tests included about 43,000 items testing about 30,000 words, with several meanings of many of the words being tested. *The Living Word Vocabulary* answers the question, "What percent of my students are likely to know this word with this meaning?"

Another source of information about what words students know is the students themselves. You can identify the words in upcoming selections that you think will be difficult and build multiple-choice or matching tests to find out whether or not the words are difficult. Constructing such tests is time consuming and certainly not something to be done for every selection. Several experiences of identifying words and then checking students' performance to see just what was difficult will sharpen your general perceptions of which words are and are not likely to cause students problems.

In addition to testing students on potentially difficult words using these traditional types of tests, you can take the opportunity to ask students which words they know. Research (White, Slater, & Graves, 1989) has suggested that students can be quite accurate in checking words on a list that they do and do not know. Presenting students with such a list is certainly much quicker than constructing, administering, and scoring a multiple-choice or matching test. At the same time, some students seem to have little knowledge of what words they know, and asking students to identify words they do and don't know ought to be part of a broader program through which you seek to become increasingly adept at determining students' vocabulary strengths and weaknesses.

Once potentially difficult vocabulary is identified, criteria for identifying the most important words to teach need to be established. The answers to four questions should be helpful in establishing these criteria. The first question is, "Is understanding the word important to understanding the selection in which it appears?" If the answer is "No," then other words would usually take precedence for teaching.

The second question is, "Are students likely to be able to assign the word a meaning using their context or structural analysis skills?" If the answer is "Yes," then they probably ought be allowed to do so. Having students use their word identification skills when they can will help them consolidate these skills and reduce the number or words that need to be directly taught.

Another question to ask is, "Can this word be used to further students' context, structural analysis, or dictionary skills?" In other words, "Can this word be used to help students develop a skill they can later use independently?" If the answer is "Yes," then dealing with the word can serve two purposes. It can aid students in learning the word, and it can help them acquire a generative skill. Thus, for example, one might deliberately teach the word *regenerate* because some students still need to master the prefix *re-*.

The final question we would suggest asking is, "How useful is this particular word outside of the selection being currently taught?" By and large, the answer to this question will depend on the word's frequency. The more frequent a word is in the material students will be dealing with in the future, the more useful it is the them to know it. Moreover, the more frequent a word, the greater the chances that students will retain the word once it is taught. *The American Heritage Word Frequency Book* (Carroll, Davies, & Richman, 1971) lists the frequency of some 86,000 words found in materials written for school-age children. It is, therefore, a very useful resource for identifying more and less frequent words.

As a final note regarding these four questions, we should add that they are not independent. In fact, the answer to one question may suggest that a word should be taught, while the answer to another suggests that it should not. Just what to do in such cases is a matter of teacher judgment, but the answers to the questions can inform that judgment.

Conclusion

In this chapter on vocabulary instruction in content areas, we have described six word-learning tasks, discussed several levels of word knowledge, described teaching procedures which are appropriate for each of the six word-learning tasks and which foster different levels of word knowledge, and made some suggestions for selecting content vocabulary to teach.

Summed up in this way, the task of teaching content area vocabulary appears to be complex, and in fact the task is more complex than we would like it to be. Teaching is a complex business, and teaching vocabulary is a part of that complex business. At the same time, no one teacher is expected to accomplish all of the various tasks of vocabulary instruction. You can choose which word-learning task is most important at a particular point in your class, which level of word knowledge you expect students to achieve with particular words, what teaching procedure or procedures will be most appropriate for the words in a particular selection your students are reading, and of course what specific words you wish to teach. We are hopeful that the discussion and teaching procedures presented here will inform the choices you make and by doing so improve your students' learning of the vocabulary of your subject and their learning of the subject itself.

Think after Reading Activity

The authors describe six word-learning tasks and teaching procedures appropriate for each of the six different tasks. Using the left-hand side of the chart below, take about one minute and write down as many of the six as you can remember. Do you think they are in your receptive vocabulary yet? Then look back in the chapter to fill in any remaining word-level tasks. Add the name of a teaching procedure for each one.

Word-Learning Task	Teaching Procedure
1. _____	_____
2. _____	_____
3. _____	_____
4. _____	_____
5. _____	_____
6. _____	_____

Activity 18–4

Chapter **19**

Study Techniques That Ensure Content Area Reading Success

DONNA M. OGLE

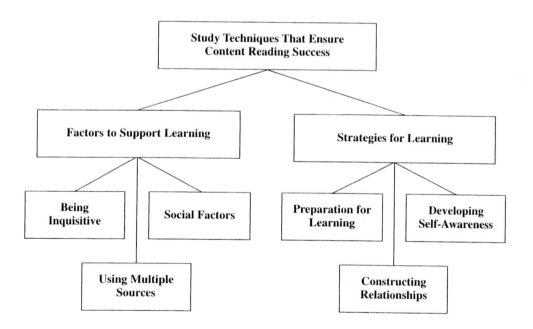

Think before Reading Activity

In order to reach this level of education you've leaped across many educational hurdles. How do you rate yourself as a learner? Do you think of yourself as an inquisitive learner? Think back for a moment about the events and people who helped you become successful. Briefly write your reflections here.

_____

_____

_____

_____

_____

_____

Keep your own experiences in mind as you read this chapter.

Activity 19–1

This chapter focuses on how teachers can help students develop both the desire to study and learn and the expertise needed to succeed. Five components of learning supported by current research are presented, and their instructional applications are developed with specific suggestions for transfer to independent student use. These factors are (1) initiating learning with inquisitiveness and questions, (2) utilizing the social factors that can facilitate learning, (3) using multiple sources of information when learning, (4) adjusting learning strategies to fit the goals and materials used, and (5) becoming self-aware and self-monitoring of one's own learning. The chapter concludes with a reminder that improving students' study behaviors is the responsibility of the total school faculty.

Students need to be able to use a variety of strategies if they are to be successful and confident learners in middle and secondary schools. These important strategies for studying and learning do not develop automatically; most students need instruction in strategies specifically designed for expository, conceptually dense content learning. Bragstad (1982) reported on an informal experiment with three classes of bright freshmen. The teacher gave the direction, "I would like to see how you use this complex instrument, your brain, in reading a chapter. Please open your book to page 49. Just begin reading the chapter. I'll stop you when I have finished my observation" (page 75). At the end of three minutes she asked them to write the title of the chapter and three major concepts presented. Not one student had even looked at the title. For concepts they selected details from the first few paragraphs of the text. Bragstad summarized, "They did not have an organized method of attack for studying a chapter in a textbook. Without instruction and supervised practice, students usually do not use the brain efficiently in reading to learn" (page 75).

A second concern is the lack of students' general interest in learning. Not only do students not know how to learn, many students currently in our schools seem uninterested in investing much of their energy in learning. A national conference on student motivation (Tomlinson, 1992) examined this problem and suggested that "one of the biggest disincentives to academic effort can be school-wide peer pressure. For many children, school's chief virtue is the opportunity it presents to make and be with friends. By the time most children reach adolescence, their need to belong to a crowd with similar interests and values is paramount" (p. 11). They go on to say that "research shows that student crowds may take harsh measures to set limits on academic achievement" (p. 11).

This chapter will examine what teachers can do to provide instruction that can effectively help students learn how to learn. The ideas are addressed to all content teachers; the development of active learners is not the responsibility of just one department. In addition, it is not the intention of this chapter to overlook the basic skills of studying. However, several sources exist that provide guidelines for teaching ways to organize study time, make notes, organize information, and prepare for tests. This chapter is intended to enhance that teaching.

Think while Reading Activity

List a few strategies you know that help spark student interest before, during, and after a reading assignment.

Before

_____

_____

_____

During

_____

_____

_____

After

_____

_____

_____

In the next four sections of this chapter (Inquisitiveness, Social Factors in Learning, Using Multiple Sources of Information, Developing a Repertoire of Strategies) you'll read about many more strategies that develop student inquisitiveness. As you read, add to the list you began above.

Did note taking help you develop a greater repertoire of learning strategies? If so, how?

_____

_____

_____

Activity 19–2

Specific instructional applications of current research in learning will be discussed in the sections that follow. These include (1) initiating learning with inquisitiveness and questions, (2) utilizing social factors that can facilitate learning, (3) using multiple sources of information when learning, (4) adjusting learning strategies to fit the goals and materials used, and (5) becoming self-aware and self-monitoring of one's own learning.

Inquisitiveness

The one characteristic that differentiated "A" high school students from others in research by Estes and Richards (1985) on study habits and test performance was their inquisitiveness, their active involvement in learning. These achieving students asked questions of the material they were reading, tried to put ideas into their own words, were aware of their level of understanding, and reread to make sense.

In my own work with both remedial and regular students, inquisitiveness continually appears as a critical variable in learning. When students perceive content to be learned as something that is personal and meaningful, they put much more energy (both cognitive and emotional) into the experience. However, clinical experience has provided us with many examples of students who are accustomed to not thinking of text material as having any relationship to their own interests. They have learned a passive waiting game in school; they assume that before long the teacher will leave them alone and others in the class will take over.

How can teachers help students become more inquisitive? Two suggestions are easily implemented: (1) help students relate the learning to their own lives and what they know; (2) help them formulate questions they want to have answered in their studying. Both of these suggestions assume that teachers are interested in what their students think and are willing to respect their ideas.

Teachers can model these important interactive components of learning through group instructional strategies like KWL (Ogle, 1986), KWL Plus (Carr & Ogle, 1987), PReP (Langer, 1981), and anticipation guides (Readance, Bean, & Baldwin, 1981). In these strategies teachers elicit from students what they know about a topic and establish with the group a sense of uncertainty about some of their content knowledge that can be turned into questions appropriate to the learning task.

In KWL the teacher engages students in a brainstorming session about the key concepts of a topic to be studied or a chapter to be read. As students share their ideas, usually some disagreements ensue and they begin to question what they "know." From this dialog the teacher can help students frame questions at points of ambiguity. The teacher records the process by writing on the board or overhead information and ideas students contribute and their questions. This provides a stimulus for students to write on their own worksheets what particular items they know and want to learn. (See Figure 19–1.) The teacher next elicits what categories of information the students anticipate the article should contain. The teacher might ask, "What key categories of information would you expect a political scientist to include in a chapter on governments in Western Europe?" Their initial brainstormed lists of ides can be used to help students begin to see potential categories within the context of their prior knowledge. Again, what students generate as key categories is listed on their worksheets for reference later.

Name: _____

KWL Strategy Sheet

What We Know	What We Want to Find Out	What We Learned and Still Need to Learn

Categories of Information We Expect to Use	How to Find Information
A.	A.
B.	B.
C.	C.
D.	D.
E.	E.
F.	F.
G.	G.

FIGURE 19–1   Strategy Sheet
Source: Ogle (1986).

After this preparation, students read the material and jot down information they learn. When the reading is completed, the class discusses what has been learned, what questions have been answered, and what new questions have emerged. In this straightforward way the teacher models an interactive study approach for students, an approach they can use in their independent study.

If the material needs to be rehearsed to be retained in long-term memory, the additional postreading steps of constructing a semantic map from the material and then turning that into a summary are important follow-ups. In our work with social studies (Carr & Ogle, 1987) we found that students needed to manipulate new material and reorganize it to make it meaningful to themselves. The addition of mapping and summary writing significantly increased both short- and long-term learning.

Teachers can help students develop an active and personal approach to learning through a variety of other strategies. Students can be given warm-up material, like an article from a magazine or newspaper, to help them think about a topic and discuss their ideas. A list of vocabulary words can be put on the board, and students can be asked to be detectives, finding out why those words will be important in their learning. (Vocabulary Scavenger, Estes & Vaughan, 1986). Anticipation-Reaction Guides (see Readance, Bean, & Baldwin, 1989) also serve nicely to create cognitive disequilibrium and curiosity about topics of study. All the teacher needs to do is write a series of three to ten statements on key concepts (some true, some partially true, and others false) and ask students individually or in small groups to indicate if these statements are true or false. As students debate which statements are accurate and which are not, they develop more active, personal reasons for reading. They can return to these same statements at the end of their unit of study and compare their responses, thus clearly seeing their own changes in thinking. These and similar activities help students begin to think about the content, what they know, and what they might learn prior to initiating their own reading. They stimulate curiosity and create motivation for learning.

Students who have learned to begin new units with an inventory of their own knowledge and assumptions can use this same entry point for independent study. They jot down ideas they expect to find in reading; they preview questions at the end of chapter sections; they skim over the context and study graphic aids to mentally check their state of knowledge. This process of conducting an inventory also helps learners develop a focus around aspects of the topic that are unclear.

Asking questions prior to reading is the second way teachers can help students become more involved with their own learning. I have already suggested that students generate their own questions about a topic prior to reading. As they study materials it is also important to focus on the content of a particular author. A good strategy to use during reading is the SQ3R. This approach (Robinson, 1970) suggests that students Survey a text, turn each subheading in a textbook into a Question, and then Read to find the answer to the question. Reciting the answer to the question, reading on with other questions and then Reviewing at the end provides an ongoing active stance for readers. Anderson and Armbruster (1984) have developed a strategy for study in which the reader/learner writes a main idea question prior to reading a selection of text and then reads for the answer. Both of these strategies focus on the reader framing questions and reading to locate answers.

These self-questioning techniques are most effective when they are framed in the larger context of students' interests and their need to know. By beginning with their own knowledge, students can formulate meaningful personal questions for inquiry. Current interpretations of strategies like SQ3R try to do just that. Devine (1981) suggests that students should ask their own questions. "Jot down the questions that you, personally, want answered. What might the author be able to tell you about the topic that you don't already know? What are you curious about here? Sometimes turning the heading and subheading into questions helps" (p.45). Students become more involved in studying and learning new information when they link the content to what they already know and generate questions that can guide their learning.

Recently more attention has been given to fostering students' inquisitiveness and putting them at the center of learning. Beane (1990) has written strongly about the need for middle grade students to shape their own curriculum. He suggests that students and teachers brainstorm together what they want to learn and how they will go about learning. In whole language classrooms, teachers and students together establish both content and activities for learning.

Social Factors in Learning

Learning is not just an individual endeavor but is affected by the larger social context. Both Piaget (1970) and Vygotsky (1978) as theorists have long stressed the social nature of learning. When teachers and students are connected, they create a community of learners in which everyone, including the teacher, learns.

Teachers can do a great deal to create a community of learners. Yet, the larger socio-cultural settings of the home and out-of-school communities are also strong influences on students' willingness to engage in school learning. Students whose friends discourage study and performance find it hard to work at school priorities. With the increasing influx of families from all over the world in our schools it becomes even more important for us as teachers to develop sensitivities to cultural differences. We need to be aware of the cultural norms and the values of our students and we need to help them become part of our school culture.

A key to creating more real communities in our classrooms is the use of cooperative group activities and paired learning. Larson and Dansereau (1986) have developed a simple form of paired learning to help students. In the process Dansereau originally developed, students each silently read a designated portion of text. After reading, one student acts as "recaller" and the other as "listener." The recaller orally retells to the partner what has been read without looking back at the text. The listener only interrupts for clarification. When the recaller is finished, the listener has two tasks: (1) to point out and correct any ideas that were summarized incorrectly and (2) to add any ideas not included in the retelling. During this elaboration time, both partners can work together to reconstruct their understanding of the text. For the next portion of the text, the partners change roles and proceed in the same manner. After several experiments using paired reading, Dansereau concluded that "cooperating pairs, using the dyadic strategy, outperformed individuals both during cooperative learning and during transfer; and that active listening is more effective than passive listening" (p. 518).

Learning can be made more interactive and social in a variety of other ways. Using older, successful students as models provides verification from "socially acceptable others." This approach was successfully used by the University of Minnesota Technical College Reading Center (Starks, 1980) to increase students' receptivity to study strategies the faculty were trying to teach. Students in the program surveyed others to determine the best places on campus to study. Later they developed interviews to determine how their successful peers studied: how many hours a week, where they studied, and what worked best for them. These were shared within the class and led to a slide program on good study locations and habits and later development of a study file, with information contributed by students about what kind of strategies were most successful for different courses. Peers became the bridge for freshmen needing help learning how to study.

After reading the Minnesota study, teacher Jane Hunt tried the same process with grade 7 and 8 students who were not convinced that they needed to learn ways of studying. Hunt had her class develop questions and then interview successful high school and college students. When class members made reports on their individual interviews, they became much more convinced of the need to think about learning and to develop approaches to study that would fit different situations. The older, respected peers were able to teach what the teacher could not.

Teachers who are aware of the social context for learning can adjust their teaching to maximize whatever factors are possible for positive experiences in learning. Peers, older students, community members, and teachers all can help students develop reasons for studying and valuing learning. Social interaction can generate energy that often is lacking in the isolating and competitive orientation that tends to permeate secondary schools. The attention to cooperative learning in classrooms around the country is preparing students to work together in ways that certainly can foster community and enhance learning.

Using Multiple Sources of Information

Teachers need to guide students beyond dependence on a single text for at least four important reasons: (1) some textbooks are poorly written; (2) many are not conceptually appropriate for all students; (3) given the range of reading abilities in any classroom, one text can hardly be adequate; and (4) recent curriculum integration efforts have highlighted the importance of multiple perspectives in building meaning.

What can teachers and students do? One important step is to broaden the range of materials used in teaching any one course. Many teachers who use the KWL/Plus framework have added an additional section—How we will learn. They do this because they have learned that whenever students start identifying what they want to know, a single textbook is inadequate. Students brainstorm the variety of possible sources of information available. For example, a group that was studying spiders listed twelve different sources of information—a list that included magazines, newspapers, the local pest-control service, the zoo, and an online encyclopedia. It is not difficult to bring in additional sources of information. Films, videos, corollary readings, magazines, newspapers, and computer programs all can help students elaborate on and clarify what they are learning.

Beginning a new topic with a more simple text or a piece of literature can help make the content clearer to students. Part of our job as teachers is to help students not only use multiple sources of information, but know how to select appropriate ones for their own learning needs. At times simple materials are needed. For example, when I am confronted with a new content to teach, I often turn to children's books to learn the basic concepts. Children's authors often do an excellent job of presenting central concepts in easy, clear language with multiple illustrations and examples.

Another resource often overlooked in initial learning is other people close at hand, other students, family members, and teachers. Good students often spend hours talking together, checking out course content and clarifying what is expected of them. Less secure students often have not thought to ask someone else or are afraid to expose their ignorance. Experts seldom learn alone, but regularly test their ideas with colleagues both orally and in writing. Novice learners need to learn that such social interaction is valid and often very useful.

As we develop a fuller understanding of how readers use multiple sources of information to construct meaning, teachers need to provide rich opportunities for students to become facile in constructing meaning from many types of resources. Students coming from whole language and integrated curriculum experiences will have had both the opportunities and the expectation that they use multiple sources of information. This can be a real asset to our attempts to create more critical thinkers and will help us guide students in recognizing alternative points of view.

Developing a Repertoire of Strategies

Teachers need to introduce students to a variety of strategies they can use when reading to learn from text materials. In planning how to help *prepare* students for studying, teachers and students can use the guide in Figure 19–2. This guide, based on the reading model developed by Palinscar, Ogle, Jones, & Carr (1986), focuses on the three recursive phases of the reading process. Together teacher and students can assess their strategies. Do they have ways to prepare for learning. Do they anticipate the content they will study by survey materials? The KWL process, group brainstorming, categorizing important vocabulary, and anticipation/reaction guides establish the importance of beginning with what students think they know.

These models can then be transferred into students' independent work. KWL worksheets provide a vehicle for transfer of that strategy. Brainstorming can transfer into the construction of a quick list of what a student thinks prior to reading. Working through the questions and activities at the end of chapters before reading is similar to completing anticipation guides. Relating course content to other experiences can be done as students discuss their learning and consciously try to make connections. When teachers consciously model activities and then help students transfer the basic cognitive and affective components to independent studying, students can become active learners.

Teachers can help students develop a variety of ways of *building and refining meaning* as they read and study. Writing and drawing help many students construct ideas and relationships. One strategy that works well is for students to develop semantic maps of the text (see Chapter 20). Another way to visualize ideas is to draw key ideas or images associated with content.

All students should know good note-making strategies. Both Cornell note taking (Pauk, 1989) and two-column notes (see Chapter 13) stress the importance of not only writing ideas from the speaker or written material, but secondly of adding one's own elaborations and structure to what is read. In both systems the right side of the page is used to take notes from the author or speaker. The left is reserved for the learner's own summary, categories or questions that trigger the key points the author made. Later the learner can cover the right part of the notes and review with the questions and category labels on the left.

LEARNING PROCESS	TEACHING ACTIVITIES	INDEPENDENT STUDENT APPLICATION
Anticipation		
Preview text	Survey with students Identify organizational structure Study graphics, pose questions	Survey before reading Use graphic aids
Activate knowledge	Anticipation guide Group brainstorming KWL process Vocabulary categorization Question generation	Answer questions in text Reflect on ideas Brainstorm
Focus interest and set purpose	Generate questions KWL	Generate questions and focus Connect to other experiences and reading
Building Knowledge		
Clarify and construct meaning	Make notes (Cornell or BAM) Create group semantic maps Paired reading Reading study guides Journals	Make notes Create semantic maps or graphic organizers Rehearse orally Visualize ideas, think of analogies Monitor confusion, mark questions SQ3R
Consolidating Learning		
Construct	Write group summaries Create map of text Discuss key ideas and perspectives	Write personal summary Rehearse and reconstruct orally Identify author's perspectives and point of view
Consolidate	Dialogue journals Compare to other texts Debate issues	Create mnemonics Review notes Ask and answer questions Connect to other texts and experiences
Assess achievement	Discuss outcomes, value of study Identify unanswered questions Evaluate process and outcome	Evaluate ideas and outcome Compare entry knowledge to that gained

FIGURE 19–2 Learning Process Sheet

Written review is good for many students, but some do better with oral rehearsal. Paired reading, mentioned earlier, provides a model for students to transfer to their independent study with a read/recite process. As students review work, they may note questions or spots in their reading that create confusion. These can be discussed later in a group.

Students also need ways of *consolidating* their learning, rehearsing new content, and finding applications. Teachers who have identified the learning outcomes they expect at the beginning of a unit can help students plan their approaches to consolidating their learning. If students have written down their own entry knowledge and ideas, they can return to those (KWL/Plus, anticipation/reaction guides, and journals) to identify areas that need more study and attention. In our early research with KWL we found that simply reading and studying material was not sufficient to retain new content. Students need several opportunities to explore and utilize the ideas. Therefore, we added two additional steps. After reading, students create a semantic map that blends together both prior knowledge and the new information, using categories appropriate for this consolidation. Finally, students write a summary, with each branch of the map easily turned into a paragraph.

Knowing how to write summaries of what is being studied is a basic tool for all students. Another good way to help students learn to write summaries has been developed by Hayes (1989). With GRASP, teachers model summary writing with students and provide practice in short encyclopedia-type articles. After reading the content, students jot down all the ideas they remember. Then they identify key topics, which are used as categories under which these ideas are organized. As they begin to write summaries of this information, the teacher guides students to leave out unnecessary details, combine information when possible, and add ideas to make the summary coherent. The teacher models turning the first category into a sentence and then has students do the rest with suggestions from the group.

Teachers can help students also by guiding them in how to use different memory strategies that are appropriate for a range of learning needs. Teaching students to use mnemonic devices can be very useful if the learning task requires memorization of discrete information or basic frameworks that lack other cognitive connections. For example, to use the Linnean classification system in biology one needs to remember the order: kingdom, phylum, class, order, family, genus, and species. A mnemonic device works perfectly for such basic learning. When I was faced with the task of remembering this system, I devised the mnemonic of K. P. Cofgs, and have associated that name with the system ever since.

Such mnemonics are not useful when learning more abstract concepts, however, like how business and other interests influenced the outbreak of the Civil War. Cause and effect relations need to be established in this kind of learning with such devices as concept maps. Helping students put new ideas into their own words is central to consolidating information. Many excellent ideas for writing have recently made their way across the content areas. One of the most used and easiest to implement is the learning log or content journal in which students regularly write in their own words what they are learning and how it relates to their own experiences and interests. Writing provides an invaluable tool to help students in all content areas put content and concepts into their own language.

Different kinds of learning require different learning strategies. Teaching students to summarize what has been learned in written form, to tell major ideas to someone else, to ask and answer questions, and to find ways to apply knowledge to the solution of new problems are all strategies that can help students incorporate new ideas and material into their own knowledge systems. Their use depends on the particular context and the learning goals.

Just as different learning tasks require different approaches to study, so, too, students vary in their ways of learning. Some students have distinct preferences. For example, some approach learning in a linear way; they want to know exactly what is expected and study very systematically, often preferring a traditional outlining approach for taking notes. Other students need to see things more visually and holistically; they often respond well to semantic mapping and like the recursive reading and writing that goes with it. Part of the task for students and teachers is to learn and try a variety of approaches to study learning to find those that are best suited to students, to content, and to course or personal objectives.

Developing Self-Awareness

Students need to develop both a variety of ways of learning new content and an awareness of their own learning and achievement of their objectives. What can teachers do to help students monitor their learning? They can work with students in three areas of monitoring: awareness of one's knowledge, awareness of task demands, and awareness of appropriate learning strategies.

Awareness of One's Own Knowledge

A beginning point is ensuring that students know ways to assess their own comprehension. The strategy worksheet of the KWL, which is basically used as a group instructional tool, can be transferred to independent use. By learning to make a list of what they think they know and raising questions, students become more aware of their own knowledge. Then, as they read actively, they can make notes. Students who read the questions at the end of the chapter first and try to answer them are engaging in self-assessment. As students are reading or taking notes, they also need to be monitoring what they are taking in and holding themselves accountable to make sense of the content. Anderson (1980) has provided students an easy distinction to help in self-monitoring. He suggests students ask themselves if a passage "clicks or clunks." If it "clunks," then some alternative fix-up strategy is needed to make sense of the ideas.

As students interact with course content, they must continually blend old with new knowledge; sometimes that means altering prior assumptions and ideas. Some of the best research in this area comes from the "misconception" research in science that has demonstrated how difficult it is for instruction to alter students' ideas (see Anderson & Smith, 1984; Roth, 1986). If students are to deal with their misconceptions, teachers need to help them identify those misconceptions, contrasting prior assumptions with the course content. If students jot down their own ideas prior to studying or discuss them with others, they may be able to learn to alter firmly established ideas. On the KWL worksheet, for example, teachers can have students continually revise the ideas they listed in the Know column

---

Think while Reading Activity

Monitoring your own learning is another way of saying that you are aware of what you need to study and learn. But young students usually don't know how to do this or that it even exists. Complete this KWL Guide as you read the next part of this chapter.

KWL Guide for Monitoring Your Own Learning

What I Know	What I Want to Know	What I Learned and Still Need to Learn

Activity 19–3

---

as they read and learn. In this way, the need for accommodation of existing knowledge can become concrete to students.

Awareness of Task Demands

In addition to knowing what one knows and understands, students also need to be aware of the task demands. In school learning this means, for example, distinguishing between preparing for essay exams and multiple-choice tests. Paris and Jacobs (1984) use the analogy of planning a trip to help students think about how to prepare for learning; when we have a sense of where we are going, we can plan our course of action (or determine how to reach our destination). This kind of analogy can help students think about monitoring their learning in relation to the outcomes they want to achieve. Teachers can be direct about their own objectives and ask students to be clear about what they perceive to be their responsibilities.

Awareness of Appropriate Learning Strategies

Students who are aware of their own knowledge levels and the demands of the task need also to be able to select appropriate strategies to accomplish their goals. This means first understanding that learning is a process that takes time and conscious effort before, during, and after engagements with particular class experiences or materials. For many students, planning a course of interactive, sequential activities is a new concept. However, teachers can help them become more "planful" of their learning until it does become automatic. Knowing what to do and when is the goal. Using charts like the ones in Figures 19–1 and 19–2 can be helpful. Students can define their own knowledge, the goals or outcomes desired, and the activities that will help them get there.

Working Together in Learning

The teaching of study strategies is a joint venture of all teachers and students. From teachers' introduction of strategies and modeling of their uses in school learning, students can begin to learn how to learn. Then they need support to become self-confident and active in their own studying. This often depends on the encouragement and involvement of peers and mentors, not just teachers. The goal is that students become aware of the factors involved in successful learning—inquisitiveness, social support, using multiple sources of information, adapting strategies for learning to the situation, and self-monitoring—and independently apply that knowledge in and out of school.

Think after Reading Activity

At the beginning of the chapter in the Think before Reading Activity you rated yourself as a successful student. Think of all the new ways you have learned about studying and learning as you've read this chapter. Turn back to the Think before Reading Activity and in the space below reevaluate your answer.

_____

_____

_____

_____

_____

_____

_____

_____

_____

_____

Activity 19–4

Chapter **20**

Using Concept Mapping as an Effective Strategy in Content Area Instruction

DIANE LAPP   JAMES FLOOD
ROBERT P. HOFFMAN

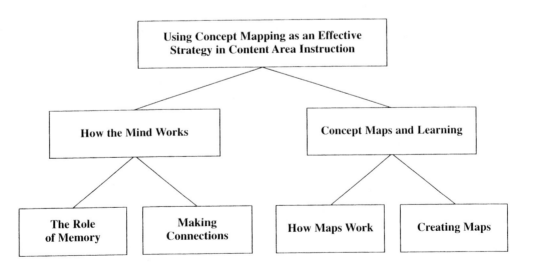

Think before Reading Activity

Before you begin reading this chapter, take two minutes (time yourself!) to jot down all the things that come to mind associated with the Declaration of Independence.

_____

_____

_____

_____

_____

As you read this chapter, think about how you knew these things, where this knowledge came from, when you learned it.

Activity 20–1

This chapter describes concept mapping, a powerful instructional strategy designed to help students be successful learners. Its purpose is to help them organize prior knowledge and construct new understandings. The strategy can effectively be used before, during, and after the study of a particular topic or concept. The authors provide examples of using this strategy to expand thinking and learning.

The Declaration of Independence. Take a moment to jot down the first things that come to mind when you read those words.

Did your list include things like: thirteen colonies, Patrick Henry, American Revolution, George Washington, Philadelphia, John Hancock, parchment, Benjamin Franklin, Thomas Jefferson, King George III, England, Boston Tea Party, 1776, Independence Day? Perhaps some equally relevant thoughts, such as "birth of the United States," also came to mind.

Why were the items you thought of on your list? How were they "attached" in your mind to the idea of the *Declaration of Independence?* Some of the ideas may have popped into your mind at once, while others required a bit more effort to bring to the surface. Some may have been inferred from others. For example, if the *Declaration of Independence* was signed in Philadelphia, and Benjamin Franklin was a leading citizen of that city, then he must have signed it. (He did.) And since Patrick Henry was a fiery revolutionary statesman, he too must have signed it. (He didn't.)

The things that we "know" do not appear to be stored as discrete items that we call up one at a time from separate pigeonholes in our minds. Instead, information and ideas seem to be connected with each other, even interdependent, in a web or network arrangement. When we recall one thing, several associated ideas always seem to come to mind along with it. As teachers, we need to understand how learners obtain, store, and process knowledge, including skills. This chapter will review some of what we understand about how our minds work, specifically how we add new knowledge to our long-term memory, or how we "learn." Then we'll take a look at a specific strategy for helping students better accomplish the learning we ask of them in school.

How Do Our Minds Work?

Cognitive psychology is the study of how the mind does what it does. One of the central processes cognitive psychologists study is how we obtain new information from the environment, how we store it in our memory for short or long periods of time, and how we retrieve it when we need it.

Think of all the different kinds of information you obtain in a typical day. The alarm clock in your ears signals that it's time to get up. When you first open your eyes, familiar sights confirm that you are in your bedroom at home. Your skin feels the air temperature. Your nose tells you someone is making breakfast. Your taste buds tell you the banana you're eating is a bit unripe, as you visually scan rows and columns of language symbols and pictures in your morning newspaper. Most or all of the new information we receive in a day comes to us through our senses.

But while our senses are almost continually receiving new information, they do not register everything. We've all had the experience of looking at something without seeing it. Until I asked you this question, were you aware of whether a heater or air conditioner fan is blowing right now? Close your eyes and try to list all the colors in the cover of this book. We don't pay attention to most of what is in our perceptual field either because it

---

Think while Reading Activity

Did this ever happen to you? Suddenly, you've got a great idea! Then before you know it, it's gone, or maybe you're lucky and shared it with a friend. Perhaps you even wrote it down. Then later you wondered where that great idea came from in the first place? The next part of this chapter will give you some information about how our minds work and just where our great ideas come from. Jot down some notes before you read this section about how you think minds work. Add to your list as you read.

_____

_____

_____

_____

_____

_____

_____

_____

Activity 20–2

seems unimportant or because we have become habituated to it. We've seen something so often we no longer notice it. We seem to register things that are changing the perceptual field or are of high value to us within that field.

Even when our senses do register some new information, little of it ever makes it into our long-term memory. Most is discarded moments after it is perceived. A telephone number you looked up yesterday for the first time is more than likely not available to you today without looking it up again. Can you remember what color shirt or blouse you wore last Thursday? Things we paid attention to only briefly or without making an effort to remember seem simply to have been erased from memory once we were through with them. This erasable memory is called short-term or working memory. Research has shown that most people can retain and work with about seven chunks or separate bits of information at any given time in working memory. We must let go of a seven-digit telephone number to make room for other, new information.

Sometimes, however, we can retrieve information we encountered days, weeks, years, even decades ago from what we call our long-term memory. Most of the items associated with the *Declaration of Independence* were probably acquired years ago, perhaps in elementary school. If you're a teacher, you may have recently worked with some of these ideas with your students, but even so it might easily have been many months or years since you last thought of them. Why can you retrieve this information taken in so long ago when you cannot remember the colors on this book jacket or yesterday's telephone number?

To answer this question, let's go back to our idea at the beginning of the chapter that our mind resembles a web or network rather than a collection of separate slots or pigeonholes. We began building this mental web before we were born, and we've been working on it ever since. We've been adding new bits of information to it. We've been strengthening the connections among some of those bits of information, and we've been constructing new links among the bits of information already there. The key here is that we can't add new information to our web unless it can be linked with some information already in the web. This already existing information structure is called our prior knowledge.

Prior knowledge plays an important role both in perception and in long-term memory. When new information comes to our senses, we may not perceive it at all if it doesn't seem to fit into our network of prior knowledge. Look at a window in your classroom, office, or study for a moment, then look back down at this book. Try to visualize or describe the details of the window design. Did you notice things like the number of panes of glass, or whether the window frame was made of metal or wood? You probably have enough previous experience with windows to have been able to "see" those things. But your past experience with windows might not have been extensive enough to enable you to notice whether the mullions are fluted or plain. You may not have noticed whether or not there *were* mullions. You may not have been aware there is anything *called* a mullion (the dividing bars that separate individual window panes). Sherlock Holmes and his successors have made their reputations by seeing things that others overlooked. They noticed them not because they had keener senses, but because they knew what to pay attention to based on their prior experience or knowledge of criminal acts. Prior knowledge helps us pay attention to things and perceive them.

Once we've succeeded in registering some new item of information in short-term memory, prior knowledge again plays a role in determining whether that information is quickly erased or whether it is eventually integrated into long-term memory. If I tell you that George Mason drafted the *Virginia Declaration of Rights,* the chances of you remembering that tomorrow are pretty slim. But if you also discover that some of the ideas expressed in the *Virginia Declaration of Rights* made their way into the *Declaration of Independence,* now you have some prior knowledge (all the things you know about the *Declaration of Independence*) with which you can link this new bit of information. By discovering some additional things about the *Virginia Declaration of Rights* (that it was adopted on June 12, 1776, just weeks before the *Declaration of Independence;* that it became a model for the *Bill of Rights;* that it contained the phrase "all men are by nature equally free and independent and have certain inherent rights," and these rights include "life and liberty, with the means of acquiring and possessing property, and pursuing and obtaining happiness and safety"), the chances of your recalling it next time you think of the *Declaration of Independence* increase. Existing information serves as hooks on which to hang or associate new information. Prior knowledge provides a structure into which we can link new information.

Once new information has become part of our long-term memory we may retrieve it by activating a linked idea. Mentioning George Washington may bring Valley Forge to mind, and vice versa. The strength and number of links determine the relative ease and speed of recall.

How Do We Learn?

As noted above, our cognitive network changes constantly. Links are weakened through disuse, or strengthened by repeated use. We integrate new information into the network by linking it with existing or prior knowledge.

Look in any dictionary and you'll discover that definitions mainly describe relations among categories, parts, and characteristics that the reader might already know. We might describe an automobile, for example, as a type of transportation device. Its important parts include wheels, axles, a motor, and seats. The defining characteristics of an automobile might include that it is self-propelled and can be steered.

Other links involve principles, procedures, or rules for predicting what will happen under certain circumstances, or how things work. The relationship among pressure, temperature, and volume of a gas is a principle of science. Knowing this relationship allows one to predict how raising the temperature, for example, will affect the volume or pressure. Learning is the process of constructing any of these types of links or relationships in our long-term memory and being able to retrieve and use them in appropriate contexts.

Prior knowledge is most useful when it is familiar, that is, frequently used and personally significant. Suppose you're learning how the heart works. Seeing a diagram of a heart with the parts labeled or reading a description of what it does may mean very little until you come across the bit of information that the heart is a type of pump. You know something about pumps. Perhaps you've used one to fill your bicycle tires with air. This association with pumps gives you a place to locate the new information about hearts in your cognitive network. Because of the link, you may be able to retrieve them together from your long-term memory.

Any given individual's prior knowledge is not necessarily complete, correct, or consistent with other individuals' prior knowledge, even within a limited subject area. Naive conceptions, alternative conceptions, or misconceptions may abound. A popular example among science teachers is students' naive idea that the urinary tract is somehow part of, or directly connected with, the digestive tract. The urinary tract is a separate system connected with the digestive tract only by way of the circulatory system.

Different strategies for forging or strengthening mental links are appropriate under different conditions. Where there is little prior knowledge, such as when we're learning multiplication tables, rote learning may be useful. Rote learning often requires repetition or rehearsal to create an enduring link. Do you repeat a person's name to yourself when first introduced? You're mentally rehearsing the link between the person's form and name. Mnemonic devices can also be used to help remember new bits of information. If you have taken music instruction, you may have learned the names of the spaces of the treble clef by linking them with the word "FACE."

In situations where more prior knowledge exists, new ideas are more likely to endure if we link them in our cognitive network with important and frequently used ideas. However, since this type of learning relies to a greater extent on prior knowledge, it has some limitations. If a learner's prior knowledge is incomplete or inaccurate (like some students' naive conception of the urinary tract), new information may fit poorly or not at all, or compound already existing errors.

Both these learning strategies are designed to help us construct new links in our cognitive network. Cognitive science tells us that this is a highly individual process, depending on the extent and accuracy of each learner's prior knowledge, on learning styles, and on personal interests. As teachers, we no longer see ourselves as transferring our expert knowledge to our students. Instead, we find ourselves in the role of coach as learners construct their own cognitive networks. The teacher's role is to assist learners by providing strategies they can use to carry out the knowledge construction process themselves. One strategy that has proved very useful is the concept map.

How Do Concept Maps Aid Learning?

A concept map is a spatial representation of a selected portion of a person's actual or desired cognitive network. The representation is always a crude approximation of the mental structure, and may be more or less detailed as needed for a particular learning task. Figure 20–1 is an example of a concept map representing the concept "blizzard."

The concept map in Figure 20–1 might be interpreted as follows: "There are several types of violent storms, and one of them is called a blizzard. Blizzards are distinguished from other storms because they have very cold winds and powdery, driving snow." It represents someone's mental model to the extent that the idea of a "blizzard" conjures up thoughts of violent storms with very cold winds driving powdery snow. It is a crude representation in the sense that it does not show *all* the links this person probably has with the word "blizzard."

Notice the spatial organization of the concept map in Figure 20–1. In this case, "blizzard" is in the middle of the map. "Violent storm" is shown above "blizzard." Characteris-

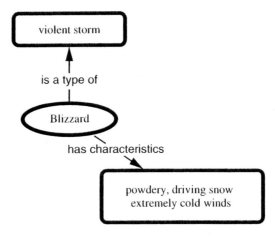

FIGURE 20–1   Concept Map of "Blizzard"

tics of blizzards are shown below. This vertical arrangement maps onto our idea of hierarchical relationships. Super-ordinate or broader categories may be placed higher in the representation, with subordinate elements lower. But concept maps are not confined to hierarchical links. In Figure 20–2 we've added some principles, or rules, about the cause of blizzards.

Ordering ideas sequentially or causally rather than by grade or rank is "other than" hierarchical; these are heterarchical links. Concept maps can represent both hierarchical and heterarchical relations.

The different parts of concept maps are also evident in Figures 20–1 and 20–2. Concept maps consist of concepts linked by labeled relations. Concepts are usually nouns; relations typically contain verbs. For example, the noun "blizzard" is linked to the noun

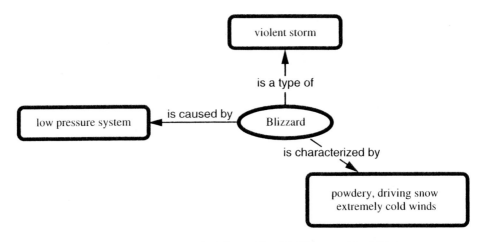

FIGURE 20–2   Concept Map of "Blizzard" with Heterarchical Link

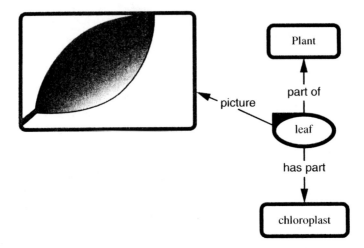

FIGURE 20–3   Concept Map of "Leaf" with Picture

phrase "low pressure system" by the verbal phrase "is caused by." We can represent concepts with pictures as well as text. Figure 20–3 shows a concept map that uses a picture to help represent a concept.

Concept maps can represent knowledge at any level. Let's suppose that you're teaching a unit on photosynthesis. You've determined that your students need to know a certain amount of detail about the substances and events involved in photosynthesis, and they also need to see how these details fit into the big picture. We could use the map in Figure 20–4 as an overview of the concept of photosynthesis.

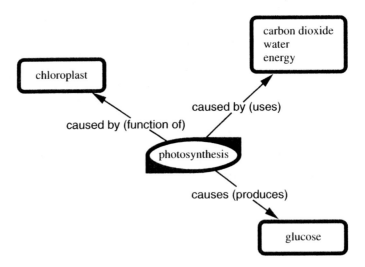

FIGURE 20–4   Overview Map of "Photosynthesis"

Figure 20–5 zooms in on one concept, "carbon dioxide," to show greater detail. Of course, an expert's overview might be a neophyte's detail map, and one can almost always go deeper into a concept that one has done in the past. We can adapt concept maps to the level of detail needed by a particular user.

Teachers and students can use concept maps and concept mapping in a number of ways. One of the most effective methods is for learners to collaborate on the construction of a concept map representing the theme or topic under discussion in a classroom. A class studying the structure of the U.S. Government, for instance, might create an overview map showing the relationships among the executive, legislative, and judicial branches. Later they might elaborate their maps to show specific interactions, such as those between the various levels of the judicial system, the relationship of lobbyists to Congress, or the relationship of the executive branch to specific departments.

Teachers may use concept maps to diagnose student understanding. Having students construct maps at the beginning of a unit can help the teacher see what they already know, what gaps exist, and what alternative conceptions may be obscuring deeper understanding.

Sometimes just being able to browse an expert's map is useful for learners who have some fragments of knowledge but are struggling to see how they all fit together. Students might also construct their own map with the opportunity to compare it with the expert map at various stages.

Student or expert maps may be handy to guide a systematic review of a unit in preparation for an exam. We can ask students who are accustomed to constructing concept maps to interpret or build them as part of a unit assessment.

Each of these strategies can help learners make explicit the links they perceive among concepts, thus creating and strengthening the relationships in their own mental maps. As one's personal understanding increases, one's concept map representations will also grow in clarity and sophistication.

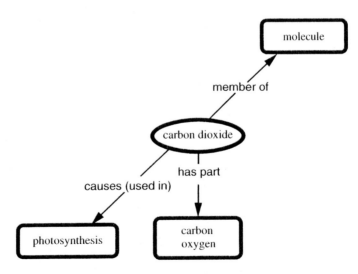

FIGURE 20–5   Detail Map of the Concept "carbon dioxide"

Think while Reading Activity

Think of a specific situation in which a concept map would help you in your studies. Below, briefly describe the situation and what the concept map might look like.

_____

_____

_____

_____

_____

As you read the following section, think about your future classroom and consider how your students will benefit from knowing how to create a concept map. Take down some notes in the form of a concept map as you read.

Activity 20–3

How Can Students Learn to Create Concept Maps?

Several strategies can help students use mapping most effectively. Students may need time and quite a bit of practice to produce good concept maps, but getting to that stage is just as useful as accomplishing the result. Teachers can aid their students' efforts in several ways.

One important issue has to do with the links or relations between concepts. It may be useful to note that most relations fall into a few broad categories. Some teachers like to introduce students to just one or two categories at a time and have them practice using them before adding others. Here is a list of some frequently used categories of relations, along with some appropriate labels for concept map links:

set/subset	has example/is an example of
whole/part	has part/is a part of
characteristics	has characteristic/is a characteristic of
causal	causes/is caused by
spatial/temporal	occurred at/location or time of

Your students may need to add some labels to this list, depending on the specific subject they are studying. For example, if they are mapping a food web, they might wish to use an "eats/is eaten by" label. Keeping the number of labels to a minimum helps make building and comparing nets easier.

Notice that most relational labels need a reciprocal label. That is, if squirrels "eat" nuts, from a nut's point of view, it "is eaten by" squirrels. This may be difficult for students to grasp at first, but some practice swapping subjects and objects and thinking about ideas from both viewpoints is usually effective.

Another strategy for helping students learn to label relational links appropriately is to use a set of questions. The entire class might work together to generate an appropriate set of questions for the subject area or topic within an area you're planning to teach. Begin by asking "What is it important to know about the concept?" If the concept is a "thing," students might suggest that it is important to ask: "What is it used for?" "What are some examples of it?" What are its' parts?" "What are its characteristics?" If you are studying an event, they might ask "What causes it?" "What happens after it?" "Does it have stages?" and so on. As students study a text or perform an experiment or accomplish a task, they can ask appropriate questions of each new idea they encounter. They can associate each question with a specific label that they can use to map the idea. Again, starting students off with just one or two questions and then gradually building their repertoire can be an effective strategy.

Almost anything can be the subject of a concept map: a passage from a text or piece of literature, a science experiment, a family tree, a field trip, a conversation or discussion, a description. One of the most useful ways of using concept maps in the classroom is in the context of cooperative learning. The whole class can construct overview maps in a summary discussion or gradually over the course of an entire unit. Detail maps can be the task of small groups, who may then share their maps with the whole class as part of presentations or peer coaching.

You and your students don't need any special materials to begin using concept maps. Paper and pencil will get most individual activities started. Use butcher paper or chalk boards for whole-class or small-group activities. We generated the examples in this article using SemNet® (Faletti, Fisher, Lipson, Patterson, & Thornton, 1986), a Macintosh computer concept mapping program for schools.

SemNet® allows a great deal of flexibility for students creating and editing concept maps. For example, students can quickly and easily merge their individual concept maps into a group map on, say, marine mammals. Individuals or small groups could build maps around particular relations such as "has characteristic/are characteristic of" or "eats/eaten by," or around categories of marine mammals such as "whales" or "dolphins." They can then merge these maps to create a large map for use as a marine mammal database to inform student writing, review, or problem solving. Students can use the map as a reference for playing a classroom game in which they identify marine mammals from a limited number of clues. They can temporarily hide selected concepts to test their own understanding.

SemNet® also allows the user to copy and paste pictures into their concept maps (see Figure 20–3), and to export lists of linked concepts to text files. We developed this chapter by first mapping all the ideas we wanted to include (Figure 20–6 shows the screen for

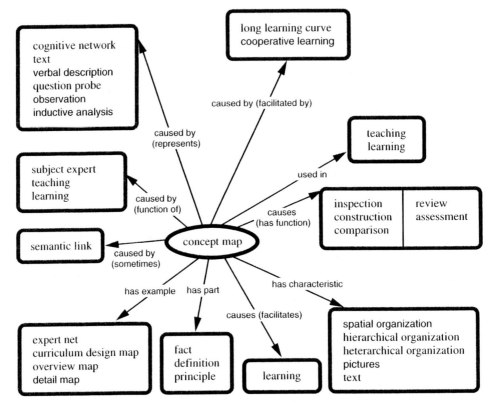

FIGURE 20-6   Map of the Concept "Concept Map"

the concept "concept mapping"). Then we exported the list of these ideas into Microsoft Word where we further organized and sequenced them. A small portion of the list looked like this:

45: information—has example/example of→ new information
43: new information—has example/example of→ sensory input
48: new information—has example/example of→ discarded information
46: information—has example/example of→ prior knowledge
33: discarded information—has example/example of→ busy street
39: sensory input—has characteristic/characteristic of→ short duration
51: sensory input—has example/example of→ sight
52: cognitive process—has part/part of→ information

Finally, we transformed this organized list of ideas into conventional prose. The Sem-Net® concept map served as an outline for the chapter.

The critical feature of teaching concept mapping is not the medium used, whether pencil and paper or a computer program, but rather, it is helping students learn to ask appropriate questions about the subject matter and answer them by representing them in a spatial format.

How Can Students Use Concept Mapping?

Concept mapping is a powerful learning tool because it helps students make their implicit mental constructions explicit and build new mental links modeled on their own or others' representations. Here are two portions of lesson plans for teaching concept mapping. The first is an exercise that helps students learn the use of a specific relationship or link (adapted from a lesson plan by Fisher & Faletti, 1993).

Lesson Plan 1

1. Ask students to look through magazines, and find and cut out a picture of an animal that lives in the Brazilian rain forest.
2. Paste the picture in the middle of a sheet of construction paper and label it with its name.
3. Ask the class to brainstorm about questions they might ask about their chosen animal. List the questions on the board. Someone will suggest that it is important to know what they eat.
4. Guide students to use the magazine article and library resources to answer the question "What does this animal eat?" by making a list of the plants and animals that form its diet.
5. Paste the list on the bottom right corner of the construction paper, and draw a line linking the list and the picture of the animal. Label the line "eats."
6. When everyone has completed their animal, put all the pictures on the wall. Have each individual or small group connect items on the food lists of their animal with the picture of the same animal on someone else's construction paper using a piece of brightly colored yarn. For example, if some particular snake eats a particular frog, connect the frog on the snake's "eats" list with the picture of the frog. If the frog eats an insect, connect the insect on the frog's "eats" list with the picture of the insect. In short order your class will have collaboratively constructed a food web, and a concept map based on the "eats" relationship.
7. Students might follow this exercise by exploring each of their questions (from step 3 above) one at a time. For example, students might rearrange the concept map to show order and genus relationships among the plants and animals, using the relationship "has member/member of."

The following exercise uses students' understanding of concept mapping to help them construct new knowledge.

Lesson Plan 2

1. Use small groups or a whole class activity to list all the characters in a work of literature you are studying.

2. Brainstorm and list on the board all of the questions you might ask about the characters. For example, "What do they look like?" "What is their occupation?" "What mannerisms do they have?"

3. If useful, have small groups of students categorize the questions. In the example above, the first and third questions might both be categorized as "characteristic" questions. The second also might be a "characteristic" question or it could be thought of as "causal," depending on the nature of the story. Let students discover which it should be as the activity develops.

4. Now distributively assign characters to small groups of students and ask them to answer as many questions as they can about each one, using quotations from the piece of literature.

5. Have the groups put each character's name in the middle of a piece of paper and connect the list of answers to each question with a line labeled with the question. For example, the main character and narrator of Mark Twain's *The Adventures of Huckleberry Finn* might be given the characteristic "energetic" or "action-loving" based on the passage in which he confesses, "Then for an hour it was deadly dull, and I was fidgety." Thus, the character "Huck" would be connected with a line labeled "has characteristic" to a list of characteristics including "energetic."

6. Once all the questions about each character have been explored in this way, students might use the resulting concept maps to write their own descriptions of the character, or perhaps draw a picture of the character to add to the concept map.

7. The class might construct a larger map from their individual character maps by representing the relationships between characters. Are they blood relations, friends, enemies, partners, lovers, coworkers?

Think after Reading Activity

Imagine that you and your students are developing a concept map on the chalk board as your principal walks into the room. After class she asks you why you were doing that (concept mapping). You respond by saying you want to help students be more effective learners. "Good," she responds, "but why are your using that particular strategy?" Write your answer to her question.

_____

_____

_____

_____

_____

_____

_____

_____

Activity 20–4

Since most of what we know seems to be stored in long-term memory in some sort of network arrangement, almost any topic lends itself to some form of concept mapping. Introduce concept mapping in small, easy stages and give students plenty of time to refine their ability to ask appropriate questions about different topics. The payoff can be thinking habits that will serve students in all areas of study for the rest of their lives.

Chapter *21*

Using Questioning Strategies to Promote Students' Active Comprehension of Content Area Material

HELENE M. ANTHONY   *TAFFY E. RAPHAEL*

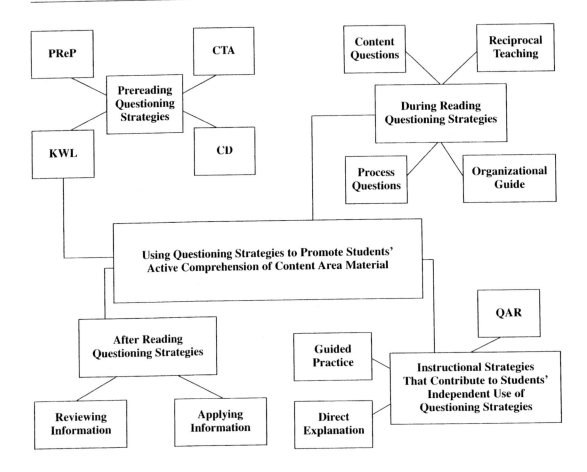

This chapter describes the importance of prereading, during-reading, and postreading questioning activities for improving students' comprehension of content area material. First the authors describe a number of questioning strategies that have been effective with expository text. Then they describe instructional strategies that contribute to students' independent reading of content area material. A sample lesson with teacher-student dialogue is included.

Why Is Content Area Reading a Concern?

"Seven of the students in my third-period English literature class have been identified as having a reading disability. Their reading scores suggest they are two or three years below grade level. Will they be lost in my class?"

"I require students in my U.S. history class to read historical fiction, oral histories, and magazines in addition to the textbook. They seem to have difficulty knowing how to approach these different materials."

Think before Reading Activity

Think of a subject, sport activity, or place you'd like to find out more about (e.g., learning to play the drums, hang gliding, Tahiti). Assume that you've just returned home from the library with a nice stack of books about your subject. They're full of great pictures and you're looking forward to a cozy afternoon poring over them. As you begin to thumb through the books, what kind of questions do you think you would ask yourself? Complete the information below:

My book is about:

_____

_____

_____

Things I want to know:

_____

_____

_____

Questions:

_____

_____

_____

_____

_____

_____

_____

_____

_____

Activity 21–1

"Several of us in the building have students with limited English proficiency. They're having a great deal of trouble reading their science and social studies books. Are there specific things we could be doing to help them understand more?"

These comments and questions illustrate the concerns expressed by both beginning and experienced teachers regarding content area instruction. As we move toward full inclusion of students with special learning needs, serve increasing numbers of students with limited English proficiency, and incorporate a diversity of materials into content area teaching, the important role of reading in content area learning and the important role of the content area teacher in facilitating reading comprehension become ever more evident (Gaskins, Benedict, & Elliot, 1991). Recent findings (e.g., Alvermann & Hayes, 1989; Armbruster et al., 1991; Ciaerdello, 1986) indicate that content area teachers do not explicitly address read-

Think while Reading Activity

The following sections elaborate on a variety of prereading, during-reading, and after-reading questioning strategies. As you read this part of the chapter, take some notes about these strategies.

Prereading Strategies

PReP   KWL

_____   _____
_____   _____
_____   _____

CTA   Concept of Definition

_____   _____
_____   _____
_____   _____

During-Reading Strategies

Content Questions   Organizational Questions

_____   _____
_____   _____
_____   _____

Process Questions   Reciprocal Teaching

_____   _____
_____   _____
_____   _____

After-Reading Strategies

Reviewing Information   Applying Information

_____   _____
_____   _____
_____   _____

Which one of these do you think you are most likely to use in your class? Very briefly describe why you think this is an important activity.

_____
_____
_____
_____

Activity 21–2

ing processes and that they do, indeed, focus on factual information. These same studies also reveal that content area teachers spend significant amounts of instructional time asking questions. Therefore, in this chapter, we will examine how teachers' questioning behaviors have the potential to improve students' comprehension of content area material and promote more meaningful understanding of content area information (Davey, 1989; Harms, Woolever, & Brice, 1989; Ryder, 1991; Wedman & Moutray, 1991).

What Questioning Strategies Have Been Effective in Developing Students' Comprehension of Expository Text?

Substantial research (e.g., see Chapters 6, 14, 22) has documented that background knowledge, knowledge of text structure, and text processing strategies, for example, comprehension monitoring strategies, contribute significantly to a reader's comprehension of content area material. Content area teachers can plan lessons with questioning practices and strategies that increase students' conceptual knowledge, develop knowledge of text structures, and enhance use of text-processing strategies. Most lessons involve preparing students for the content to be read, directing students to read a specific portion of the text, and then discussing with the students what they have read (Davey, 1989; Ryder, 1991). Mason and Au (1986) identify these three phases as prereading, guided reading, and postreading. In the following sections, we present, compare, and discuss questioning practices for use during these three phases of instruction.

Prereading Questioning Strategies

Learning new information requires prior knowledge of some related information. This does not mean that students must know the content before it is taught. Langer (1982) states, "It is this writer's contention that almost everyone knows something (however remote) about almost everything" (p. 150). Accessing that knowledge (however remote) is the objective of prereading activities (see Chapter 22).

Activities related to building background knowledge serve several purposes, including (1) developing background knowledge when students have little or none available, (2) helping students access appropriate background knowledge they already have but may not recognize as relevant, and (3) exposing background knowledge that is inaccurate and incompatible with the text. Prereading questions share the fundamental assumption that through appropriate questioning by the teacher or self-questioning by the student, relevant background knowledge can be made available.

Prereading Plan (PReP)

In Langer's prereading plan (Langer, 1982, 1984), questions are used to prompt students to activate background knowledge relevant to a central concept from a text. PReP has three phases designed to bring students' background knowledge to a conscious level in preparation for reading. The first phase, *initial associations with the concept,* requires that teachers review the section of text to be read by students, decide on a key concept, and select a word, phrase, or picture that can be presented to the group to start a discussion on the topic. For example, when introducing a text on the reasons underlying a "civil war," the discussion could begin with a question by the teacher such as, "What do you think of when you hear the words civil wars?" During this phase, the goal is to have students brainstorm as many free associations with the chosen concept as possible.

During the second phase, *reflections on initial associations,* students are asked to explain their free associations. Teachers ask questions such as, "Where did that idea come from?" and "Why does the term 'civil wars' make you think of the North and South fighting battles?" Langer considers the social aspects of PReP important. By listening to the associations and explanations of others, students are extending their background knowledge. This sharing may also help to correct accessing of potentially misleading background knowledge (e.g., responding with "fighting over slaves"), providing students an opportunity to correct misconceptions (e.g., generalizing from one issue over which the American Civil War was fought to all civil wars). Finally, this phase provides the basis for students' understanding of how text and background knowledge interrelate.

In the final phase of PReP, *reformulation of knowledge,* students again make free associations with the original concept, prompted by the question, "Do you have any new ideas about civil wars?" Often, student responses in this phase reflect a higher level of understanding than responses in the first phase, that is, the use of superordinate concepts, analogies, and characteristics versus remotely related firsthand experiences or phonetic word associations. Langer notes that the phases of PReP can provide diagnostic information for the teacher, as well as enhance students' comprehension. In examining students' responses, the teacher can determine if the level of prior knowledge that students demonstrate is sufficient for their understanding of the reading selection to come.

PReP provides teachers with an opportunity to model prereading questioning strategies. Through these questions (i.e., "What do you know about . . .?" "How do you know that?" and "Do you have any new ideas about . . .?") and group discussions, the teacher is demonstrating for students the need to consider information they already have, collaborate with peers to enhance their knowledge base, and reflect on new information.

For students to become fully aware of the value of such activities and to recognize the points for invoking them, a component beyond modeling is critical. Studies by Roehler and Duffy (1991), focusing on teacher explanations of reading comprehension processes, suggest that giving students reasons for why a particular strategy is being used (i.e., how the strategy can help a reader understand the text) is the kind of information that lays the foundation for students' eventual independent question asking.

Concept-Text-Application (CTA)

Another technique that helps teachers model prereading question asking for students is concept-text-application (Wong & Au, 1985). Like PReP, CTA uses guided discussion to enhance background knowledge before reading. Although designed for use with elementary students, this technique can easily be adapted for older students in content area classes. During the concept phase, or C-phase, the goal is to find out what students already know and determine what they need to know.

As in PReP, the teacher previews the reading and selects a main idea or key concept for the prereading discussion. This prereading phase is followed by students' reading of the text and a group discussion (text application). Both of these phases will be discussed later in the chapter.

Inference Training

Inference training (Hansen & Hubbard, 1984) is a third method designed to activate background knowledge. The technique is described to students as comparing "your own life" to situations in a text. After reviewing the selection, the teacher identifies several key ideas and generates two questions for each. The first question asks students to think of a personal experience related to one of the key ideas. The second question gives students some specific information about the situation in the text and asks them to hypothesize what might happen. As in the other methods, ideas are shared in a group discussion and students are therefore exposed to a variety of experiences that helps to extend their background knowledge for interacting with the text.

What I Know/What I Want to Learn/What I Learned (KWL)

A questioning strategy that logically extends the approaches described above is Ogle's KWL (see Chapter 19). Her work extends the previous methods, with its focus on transferring the control of prereading question asking from the teacher to the students themselves. The KWL method moves beyond teacher modeling by having students take responsibility for the questioning prior, during, and after reading.

Concept of Definition (CD)

A frequent prereading activity in content area lessons is the introduction of new vocabulary words. Schwartz recommends introducing students to a strategy for determining word meanings from their subsequent reading. Concept of definition (CD) instruction teaches students to organize conceptual information, through the use of self-questioning prompts, into categories (What is it?), properties (What is it like?), illustrations (What are some examples?), and comparisons (What other concept fits under this category?). Students are encouraged to place information regarding a specific term on the Basic CD Map, a graphic organizational pattern that can be internalized and applied to new vocabulary in numerous texts and subject areas.

Summary

We know that what readers bring to a text determines to a large degree what they comprehend from that text. Thus, prereading questions are intended to activate, review, and develop background knowledge, preview key concepts, and set purposes for the reading to follow. The importance of preparing students for reading through prereading questioning cannot be overstated, particularly for students with limited English proficiency whose decoding and comprehension abilities can be greatly enhanced when appropriate background knowledge is activated (Langer, 1982). Teachers' questioning strategies are the result of their advance reading of the material and their identification of the key concepts and principles presented in the text. Furthermore, when teachers ask prereading questions, they serve an important role in modeling for students appropriate activities for their eventual independent question asking prior to reading.

During-Reading Questioning Strategies

Whereas prereading questions are designed to build or activate background knowledge, question asking during reading serves an important role in what is referred to as comprehension monitoring (Paris & Winograd, 1990). Readers who formulate questions while reading anticipate what is to come in the text and look for information that can confirm or disconfirm their predictions. Because these readers have questions, they can more easily check if the message they are constructing makes sense and if the ideas are interrelated. Good comprehenders, therefore, know what ideas to attend to, how to group these ideas together, and when a comprehension failure has occurred (Garner, 1988). Passive readers, in contrast, read line by line and do not spontaneously connect ideas and determine their relationships. The task is similar to memorizing a list of unrelated details (Taylor & Samuels, 1983). During-reading activities, therefore, should help students become aware of their comprehension failures and prompt the use of appropriate strategies to guide and improve comprehension. According to Niles (1985), during-reading questions should (1) check the meaning that students create from the text (content questions) and (2) focus on the strategies used to arrive at such meaning (process questions).

Content Questions

One example of guided discussion or during-reading questioning that extends a prereading strategy and models the asking of content questions is found in the text-application phase of Wong and Au's CTA (1985). Following the prereading discussion, students read a short section of text silently and then are asked questions related to the purpose for reading that has been established in the concept phase, or C-phase. This is followed by a discussion of other information in the text. Preparation for the text phase, or T-phase, requires teachers to develop "cueing" questions that focus the students' attention on a text's major points.

Continued guided discussion about the concepts in the text uncovers failures in comprehension. For example, Wong and Au (1985) cite a text about the Loch Ness monster that describes an echo sounder, a concept that did not arise in the prereading activity focusing on whether or not monsters were real. The teacher, modeling for students appropriate question asking, asked a series of content questions (e.g., "How does the echo sounder work?" and "What do the sounds tell you?"). The students' answers to these questions (e.g., "It picks up sound," and "It tells you where there are lots of fish") indicated that they did not understand the concept of echo sounder. Using questioning, the teacher was able to make students aware of the comprehension failure and the need to take action to restore understanding; in this case, information from outside the text was required.

Process Questions

In addition to focusing on content, during-reading instruction should also focus students' attention on the process. Niles (1985) suggests that to develop independent, strategic readers, it is necessary to make the process visible through teachers' asking of questions about the reading process. She describes the role of "intervening questions." For example, assume as a teacher you have asked students to read silently a section in a social studies text about the pioneers' westward movement and the dangers of crossing the Mississippi

River. A content question guides students to identify information from their text (e.g., "What were two dangers the pioneers faced in crossing the river?").

Process questions focus on strategies used in their reading and question answering. Thus, a process question for this selection might be, "We've seen a great deal of information in the news about the Mississippi River flooding. How can that information help us think about the pioneers?"

Process questions focus on a variety of elements, including making predictions, confirming or disconfirming those predictions, or noting characteristics of the text that cue important ideas such as paragraphing, underlining, or use of italics. In short, these are the types of questions readers ask when monitoring their comprehension.

One possible guide for developing such questions is knowledge of the organization of ideas in a text or the text structure. This knowledge can provide the teacher with information for deciding both when and what to ask students. For example, assume students read a selection that describes the problem some plants in swampy areas have making food. The plants solve the problem by eating flies. The structure of this text is problem/solution. A content question would refer to the type of problem (getting food) and its solution (eating flies). A process question could ask students about the problem/solution text structure and how it helps readers to identify important information.

Organization Guides

A number of researchers have examined the structures or patterns of texts, and many names have been used to describe these: story maps, story grammars, idea maps, pattern or organization guides. The essential feature of these is that they reveal the predictable relationships of ideas for a given text.

The narrative structure is the most familiar to middle school students because it is the organization used for a large majority of reading selections in basal readers. Content area texts represent a challenge in that the selections use unfamiliar structures. To compound the problem, many content area texts tend to be "inconsiderate," that is, not well structured (Armbruster, 1984). Therefore, text structure instruction can serve two functions: (1) helping students comprehend material that is organized in a different way from their reading instruction selections, and (2) giving them a guide for organizing poorly structured texts.

Raphael and Kirschner (1985) instructed middle school students in comprehending social studies material written in a compare/contrast text structure. They provided students with a list of four questions specific to this particular text structure: (1) What is being compared or contrasted? (2) On what are they being compared or contrasted? (3) How are they alike? and (4) How are they different? Initially, students were presented with brief, clearly written paragraphs of comparison and contrast found in social studies texts (e.g., colonists' and Native Americans' view of land; early and late immigrants). Students used the guiding questions to identify important information and supporting details and also were taught how to use key words and phrases to locate relevant information.

This instructional program was extended by Raphael, Kirschner, and Englert (1988) to aid in both composing and comprehending the additional text structures of problem/solution and explanation. The results of this study and other studies (e.g., Flood, Lapp, and Farnan, 1986; McGee and Richgels, 1985) suggested that having students become authors of expository text was one vehicle for internalizing the question guides. Students who were writers themselves learned the importance of text structure questions and the key words and phrases used to signal to readers the organization of their text (Englert & Raphael, 1990; Raphael, Englert, & Kirschner, 1989).

Reciprocal Teaching

An example of how teachers can model the application of the preceding concepts to reading expository or content area text is found in Palincsar and Brown's (1986) reciprocal teaching procedure. This method is a good example of a technique that is actually a synthesis of several strategies. Palincsar and Brown used reciprocal questioning training to teach students to ask both process and content questions after reading segments of informational text. This instruction took place gradually over several weeks, focusing on four components: (1) summarizing in a simple sentence the paragraph or selection read, (2) generating a question related to the selection read to ask a peer, (3) demanding clarity or asking for resolution of anything from the selection that was not clear or did not make sense, and (4) predicting or generating a question for the next section to be read. Initially, teachers modeled each component for the students; then gradually teacher and students shared responsibility or took turns generating each component, until finally the students assumed complete control (Palincsar, 1986).

Summary

During-reading questioning, whether teacher- or student-generated, should promote student understanding of content, as well as the processes of reading that lead to understanding. Questioning activities that help students "see" a text's organization and use that organization to select important ideas, group ideas together, and anticipate information based on what questions should be answered can promote these text-processing and comprehension-monitoring goals.

After-Reading Questioning Strategies

In content area reading, it is important for students to *remember,* as well as *comprehend,* what they have read. After-reading activities should provide students with additional opportunities to practice or rehearse what has been learned from the text, as well as to increase the associations that can be made between the textual information and their own background knowledge. Postreading questioning is perhaps the most familiar component of reading instruction.

Reviewing Information

One purpose of postreading questioning to increase comprehension of expository text is to ask students to review the information before summarizing. There are several ways to accomplish this. One way is to have students review the text in terms of the question that was posed during the prereading discussion. In Wong and Au's (1985) CTA procedure, teachers repeat the main idea question in the application phase. Students summarize all the information about this question that has been discussed with each section of text. In Ogle's (1986) KWL technique, students write down what they learned from their reading either while they are reading or immediately after reading. This information is then compared with the questions that were generated and written down by students in the "What I want to learn" phase. A discussion follows in which students summarize what questions were answered and what questions remain unanswered. In this way, attention is focused on reading to answer student-generated questions.

Another way to assist students with the summarization task makes use of the text's structure. Raphael and Kirschner (1985) found that using the comparison/contrast text structure question guide aided students in selecting and organizing relevant information when summarizing across two passages. Jones, Pierce, and Hunter (1988–1989) advocate teaching students to create their own graphic outlines for summarizing text information. Teachers can facilitate student construction of graphic representations by asking students "What are the main concepts described in this selection? How are they related to one another and to other knowledge that you have on this topic? Why did you choose this graphic form over another to represent this selection?" Note that, during the reviewing information phase, both content and process questions should be asked. In this way, students review both the subject matter of what they have read, and they are directed to attend to how they decided on the information to include in their summary or graphic organizer.

Applying Information

Another purpose of postreading questioning is to help students integrate the information into their personal experience. Hansen and Hubbard (1984) recommend that teachers model the asking of inferential rather than literal questions so that students will interpret text in terms of their background knowledge; that is, teachers should ask questions that promote reader/text interactions that facilitate comprehension and learning from text (Wixson, 1983). As in the summarization task, the idea is to avoid memorizing facts unconnected to what is already known.

Finally, there are extension activities whose primary purpose is to transfer the control of the processes modeled to encourage students to use what they have learned indepen-

---

Think while Reading Activity

Teacher-generated questioning strategies are only part of the equation for student success. Another part of the equation is instructional strategies that contribute to students' independent reading of content area material. As you read the next section, jot down some strategies that help students become successful and independent content area readers and learners.

_____

_____

_____

_____

_____

_____

Activity 21–3

dently. One activity suggested by Wong and Au (1985) is to have students write a "parallel report." When writing a parallel report, students use the previously read selection as a guide, answering the same questions for a related but different topic; for example, Wong and Au mention writing about Big Foot or the Cyclops after reading about the Loch Ness monster.

What Instructional Methods Contribute to Students' Independent Use of Questioning Strategies?

In this chapter we have examined the types of knowledge students need to comprehend expository text. We also have demonstrated the potential utility of using questioning strategies before, during, and after reading text in order to develop students' knowledge about text content, text structure, and text-processing strategies. Now we focus on a third issue of interest to content area teachers: What instructional methods facilitate students' use of questioning strategies while reading expository text independently? How can questioning techniques best be presented by teachers and used by students to encourage self-questioning in our middle school and high school readers?

Direct Explanation and Modeling

In this first phase of the instructional sequence, the *teacher* has the responsibility for explaining the questioning strategy under study. First, the teacher provides students with a direct explanation of the strategy including (1) a definition of *what* the strategy is, (2) a reason *why* they are learning the strategy (i.e., how it will help them in their content area reading), (3) the steps in *how* to use the strategy, (4) the appropriate times *when* the skill is useful, and (5) ways to decide *how well* they used the strategy and its effectiveness in enhancing their comprehension (Roehler & Duffy, 1991; Winograd & Hare, 1988). A sample of such explanation and modeling can be seen later in the dialogues for introducing question/answer relationships.

The second component of this phase of instruction is teacher modeling. Having given students a direct explanation, the teacher then performs the task while thinking aloud, thereby making the mental processes visible to the students. This might include asking and answering questions like the following: "What do I know in my head about this question from my personal experiences and things I've read before or seen on television?" "What does the text tell me about this question?" and "What ideas do I get when I put together what's in my head and what's in the text?"

Guided Practice

During direct explanation, the teacher performs all the steps in using the strategy. In contrast, when conducting a guided practice, the teacher asks students to take responsibility for more of the steps until they are in control of the entire procedure. During this time, teachers provide students with some type of support or instructional scaffolding (Applebee

& Langer, 1983). The metaphor of a scaffold is used to illustrate the idea that the support provided by the teacher during guided practice is *temporary* and *adjustable*. This scaffolding (e.g., a list of questions on the board, an acronym such as KWL, or a question guide sheet for text structure) helps students follow the steps in the strategy even though they could not perform the task independently (Rosenshine & Meister, 1992).

Guided practice also provides opportunities for students to receive corrective feedback to improve their use of a strategy. Palincsar and Brown's (1986) reciprocal teaching is a vivid example of instructional scaffolding as the students prepare to take over the role of the teacher.

Therefore, students' independent use of a strategy is the result of sufficient guided practice. Once control of the strategy has shifted from teacher to student, it becomes important for teachers to *monitor* students' performance. Any scaffolding that has been provided can be adjusted or removed (and then replaced) according to students' needs.

Transferring Control to the Learner: Question/Answer Relationships (QARs)

One illustration of a strategy designed to bridge the gap from teacher to student control of the questioning process is question/answer relationships (Raphael, 1982, 1986). QAR is a program designed to demystify the questioning process, providing teachers and students with a common vocabulary to discuss different types of questions and sources of information for answering these questions, both of which are fundamental to students' eventual generation of questions. Four QARs have been proposed based on the Pearson and Johnson (1978) taxonomy of questions, distinguishing between questions that invite answer information right from the text and questions most appropriately answered with information from the reader's knowledge base.

Text-based QARs are classified as Right There (i.e., words used to make up the question and words used to answer the question are "right there" in the same sentence of the text) and Think and Search (i.e., information to answer the question is in the text, but one must "think" about how the information relates and "search" across the text for relevant information). *Knowledge-based* QARs are classified as Author and You (i.e., information to answer the question is not available in the text, but you must have read the text to understand what the question is asking) and On My Own (i.e., the answer can be provided from the reader's own background knowledge, without even reading to text). Teaching students about QARs is most beneficial after students have had modeled for them appropriate prereading questions, guided reading questions, and postreading discussion questions (e.g., using CTA, inference training, and others discussed in the previous sections).

After modeling, a period of explicit instruction in the elements of QAR is important. These elements include (1) the text being read and questioned, (2) the questions generated to promote comprehension, (3) the answers to the questions, (4) the question/answer relationship, and (5) the justification or explanation for selecting a given QAR. Initially, the teacher provides all five elements: asking students to read the text, asking the questions, providing an appropriate answer, identifying the QAR, and explaining why. Such modeling may proceed as follows:

T: (following an assigned reading of a text on the pioneer movement from the Mississippi across the Great Plains) You have just completed reading about some pioneers and will be answering some questions about the text. One useful strategy is to think about different sources for finding the answer information. Let's look at some examples together. The first question asks, What are some of the provisions the early settlers brought with them on their journey? Look back in your book to pages 85, 87, and 88. Notice on each page there is a description of different kinds of provisions. When we put all this information together, we can answer the question. The answer is clothing and personal goods, equipment for beginning to farm, building supplies, medical equipment. We had to "think and search" across the text; thus this is a Think and Search QAR.

Notice that the teacher provided all the information, with little input from the students. As transfer of control occurs, there is a shared responsibility between teachers and learners in which the teacher leads the learner to select and implement appropriate strategies. With QAR instruction a second step is for the teacher to provide text, question, answer, and QAR, but have the students explain why the question and answer represent a given QAR. If students appear to understand the reasons underlying a selection of a QAR, the next step is for the student to provide the QAR and the reason why. Third, teachers may progress to providing only the text and question, with students' providing the answer, QAR, and reason why, as follows:

T: You have just finished reading the selection on pioneer movement west from Mississippi and are to answer some comprehension questions about what you've read. This is a good opportunity to use your knowledge of QARs to help you. Let's look at the first question, What are some of the provisions the early settlers brought with them on their journey? What do you think the answer could be?

S: Medical supplies.

T: Where did you find that information?

S: On page 87 it discusses the lack of medicines available once they left the cities.

T: Good, what else?

S2: Clothing, because they couldn't buy cloth and things out west, and also farm equipment to set up plowing and stuff because they needed to get food started right away.

T: Good! And how did you know that?

S2: It was on page 85 and also a little at the end of the chapter.

T: Who can summarize the information so far?

S3: They brought clothing, farm equipment, medicine.

T: What kind of QAR does this represent?

S4: A Think and Search.

T: Why?

S4: The answer is in more than one place.

S3: Each part of the answer was in more than one place, but it was all in the text somewhere.

Notice the increased dialogue as students share in the responsibility of strategy selection and location of answer information, while the teacher maintains control of the selection of text and the questions asked. Eventually, the teacher may wish to have students not only answer questions, but generate them as well, such as in a reciprocal teaching activity (Palincsar & Brown, 1986). At the extreme, students could generate their own text in writing expository reports related to the content area reading, providing questions to their readers, thus demonstrating total control over the elements in QAR instruction.

Moving through a procedure such as the one described provides students with the understanding of *what* QAR is and *how* QAR can be used to locate information. A further step to transfer control is to help students understand *when* and *why* they should draw on their knowledge of QAR.

The following dialogue provides an example of initial attention to the "when" and "why":

T: You are all becoming very skilled at knowing the four QARs and how they can be used to locate information. Does anyone have any idea about *when* to use QARs?

S1: Well, if we're asking each other questions and you say you want us to ask better questions, we can ask whether you mean Think and Search or Author and You.

T: That's certainly one time to use what you know about QARs. Can anyone think of a time you could use QARs when I'm not around?

S2: Maybe if we've been answering questions after a chapter and can't find the answer we could try to use Author and You or On My Own.

S3: Or maybe we could ask a friend what kind of QAR it is if we're stuck.

T: Great! You've thought of good examples of when and why QARs are useful. Sometimes, when we are asking each other questions or answering questions in our social studies or science books or even if we get stuck and ask a friend for help, knowing about QARs comes in handy.

The teacher would eventually help students to determine how well the strategy worked by checking if their answers make sense or checking their answer with their peers.

Conclusion

The quantity of research that has focused on questions underscores how pervasive questioning activities are in today's classrooms. Yet pervasiveness alone does not promise that questions are effective tools to aid comprehension of text. It is our hope that the information provided in this chapter extends understanding of the important role that questions play during comprehension instruction, provides some specific guidelines for teachers in their questioning practices, and suggests strategies for using questioning as a vehicle for enhancing all students' independence by becoming thoughtful and strategic readers.

Think after Reading Activity

Explain the difference between content and process questions and when you would use each type.

_____

_____

_____

Briefly describe a lesson in your content area that you might teach or that you have observed being taught. Then, write two content and two process questions you might use in conjunction with this lesson. Explain why and how you would incorporate each into the lesson.

Lesson:
_____

_____

_____

Content Questions:
_____

_____

_____

_____

Process Questions:
_____

_____

_____

_____

Activity 21–4

Chapter *22*

The Significance of Prior Knowledge in the Learning of New Content-Specific Ideas

PATRICIA L. ANDERS   *CAROL V. LLOYD*

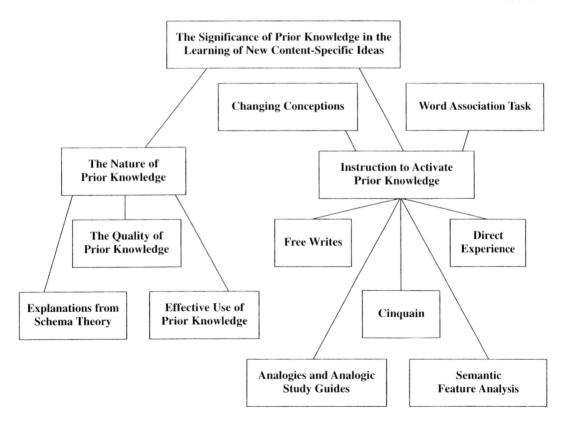

Think before Reading Activity

Before you started to read this textbook, how much did you know about content area instruction? How important do you think it is to have some knowledge about a course or a new project before you start? How does prior knowledge affect learning?

_____

_____

_____

_____

_____

_____

_____

_____

_____

Activity 22–1

The purpose of this chapter is to synthesize what is believed about the nature of prior knowledge and to suggest reading and writing activities that teachers can use to help students build, select, and activate prior knowledge. Doing so will increase the potential that successful learning occurs in subject area classes.

One of the most powerful and important assumptions undergirding theory, research, and instruction in content area literacy is that prior knowledge, what a learner knows when encountering new information, affects understanding and learning. Well-developed prior knowledge is so powerful that it affects comprehension more than reading ability (Townsend & Clarihew, 1989). To demonstrate the power of prior knowledge on comprehending or composing text, read the following paragraph and then write down what you remember:

> Rocky slowly got up from the mat, planning his escape. He hesitated a moment and thought. Things were not going well. What bothered him most was being held, especially since the charge against him had been weak. He considered his present situation. The lock that held him was strong but he thought he could break it. He knew, however, that his timing would have to be perfect. Rocky was aware that it was because of his early roughness that he had been penalized so severely—much too severely from his point of view. The situation was becoming frustrating; the pressure had been grinding on him for too long. He was being ridden unmercifully. Rocky was getting angry now. He felt he was ready to make his move. He knew that his success or failure would depend on what he did in the next few seconds (Anderson, Reynolds, Schallert, & Goetz, 1977, p. 372).

This is an example of ambiguous text: that is, the author intended for the interpretation of the text to be open-ended. The researchers who administered this passage to college students, majoring in either music or physical education, discovered that most students had one of two interpretations. Most of the music majors interpreted this passage to be about a prison break and the physical education majors interpreted the passage to be about wrestling.

The Nature of Prior Knowledge

The notion that prior knowledge is important for new learning is deceptively simple because there are many kinds of prior knowledge. Cognitive psychologists point out that learners possess prior knowledge about the structure of text; reading, writing, and studying processes; and the nature of ideas or concepts about which they are learning. Prior knowledge about ideas, the nature of those ideas, and how to help students learn about ideas is the focus of this chapter.

Cognitive psychologists attempt to explain how knowledge is represented, learned, and stored in the mind. One cognitive theory, schema theory, offers a compelling explanation. According to this theory, what one knows is organized in hierarchies. In other words, ideas are categorized: some ideas, supraordinate ideas, are general and abstract and incorporate other second-order, or coordinate ideas, which link specific, concrete, subordinate ideas (Klausmeier, 1980). For example, let's say that "learning in the content areas" is a supraordinate concept. One coordinate idea (a category that fits in the bigger idea) might be "prior knowledge." Another coordinate idea might be the "nature of text" and another

---

Think while Reading Activity

Imagine that you are a teacher and next week is parent-teacher night at your school. You would like to discuss the significance of prior knowledge with the parents because you are convinced that it is critical to student success. How are you going to explain what prior knowledge is and its importance? Use the information in the next section to prepare some comments.

_____

_____

_____

_____

_____

_____

_____

_____

Activity 22–2

might be "teachers' goals." Each of these categories of information about learning in the content areas have details linked to them. Hence, the category of "prior knowledge" would include subordinate ideas such as "characteristics of prior knowledge," "historical background," "conditions for learning," and "classroom activities." In this example, each of those subordinate details could also be divided into further details. This collection of related, hierarchically arranged ideas is a schema. (See Figure 22–1.)

A second characteristic of a schema is that some or all of its component concepts may be related to concepts in other schemata. Thus, when a concept is triggered in one's mind, networks of related ideas may also be triggered (Rumelhart, 1981). For example, extending the above example, the category of prior knowledge might cause readers of this chapter to think about their own schooling experiences, especially related to a teacher successfully providing experiences that built on prior knowledge. Or alternatively, a reader might be reminded of circumstances when prior knowledge had not been taken into account. Learning occurs when new information relates to an existing schema. Hence, learners are continually organizing and reorganizing old and new information to creative varying structures of knowledge (Pearson, Roehler, Dole, & Duffy, 1992). This process is identified by psychologists variously as synthesis, consolidation, and integration.

Schema Theory and Content Area Literacy Instruction

Content area teachers who are convinced that schema theory is helpful for explaining how students learn and thus choose to teach with a schema theory perspective need to consider three conditions that affect learning: (1) background knowledge must be appropriate and accurate, (2) background knowledge must be sufficient, and (3) background knowledge must be activated. If the theory is right and if these conditions are met, the potential is greatly increased that students will integrate prior knowledge with new information and will create new schemata or elaborate ones they already have—i.e., learn.

Background Knowledge Must Be Appropriate and Accurate
If background knowledge is to serve as a bridge to new learning, then it must be appropriate to the topic of the lesson and must be accurate. Following are examples that illustrate how these two characteristics of a schema can affect learning.

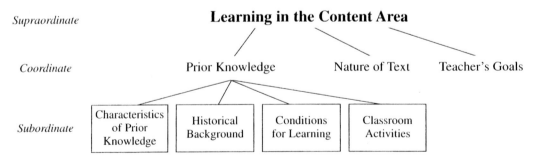

FIGURE 22–1   Schema of Hierarchically Arranged Ideas

Inappropriately Used Background.   Sometimes students come to class with background knowledge that interferes with new learning, even if that background is, in another context, appropriate and accurate. For example, when new concepts are represented by vocabulary that also exist as part of students' everyday language, there is a strong likelihood that the common, everyday meaning will prevail and learning a new meaning will be difficult. Imagine the consequences of interpreting in everyday language a word that is being presented in a new, specialized way. An example is the word root. Consider the respective meanings of this word in the context of biology (the classification of plants with certain kinds of roots), math (find the square root), social studies (finding our roots), home economics (the nutritional qualities of root vegetables), English (read a description of pig behavior in *A Day No Pigs Would Die*), or on a hallway bulletin board (Come root for the volleyball team!).

Nicholson (1984) found that students' prior knowledge of particular vocabulary words and their related ideas often interfered with their understanding of classroom materials. He asked junior high students in English, math, social studies, and science classes about their lessons as they were doing them. In a social studies class, students were interpreting a summary diagram about industrial development in China. The diagram showed four factors affecting the location of factory industries, one of which was the availability of markets. When asked about the diagram, one student interpreted markets to mean places where workers get food; another student thought they meant open-air stalls. Although both students had schemata about markets, theirs were not about markets as used in the context of the lesson.

Analogies.   Related prior knowledge can be used to the learner's advantage. Since a schema is organized hierarchically and because nodes of a schema may be linked with nodes of other schemata, it is possible to use analogous information to understand new information. To demonstrate this, Hayes and Tierney (1982) investigated the effects of readers' background knowledge regarding baseball on the comprehension of a passage about the game of cricket. Many similarities exist between the two games; thus, it seemed reasonable that knowledge of baseball would serve as an analog to the game of cricket. When grade 11 and 12 students with varying amounts of background knowledge about baseball were asked to read a newspaper article about cricket, prior knowledge was a major factor influencing comprehension: those readers with more prior knowledge about baseball comprehended more than those students with less prior knowledge about baseball.

Another question asked in this study evaluated the consequences of activating students' prior knowledge of the related topic, baseball, and reading a text that made explicit analogies between baseball and cricket. Here is an example of a text embedded with analogies:

> The center of activity is an area in the middle of the field called the pitch, *which corresponds to the infield in baseball* (p. 264).

The italicized portion of text presents the analogy, or comparison, between the two games. Hayes and Tierney found that students who first read about baseball, thus activating prior knowledge, and then read a text that made explicit analogies between baseball and cricket, received some of the highest scores on various measures of reading comprehension.

Alternative Conceptions.   What happens to the learning process when students have prior knowledge about a topic but that knowledge is contradictory to the ideas presented in a lesson? Inaccurate prior knowledge is called variously a misconception, preconception, naive conception, or alternative conception. Research results demonstrate that alternative conceptions have profound effects on learning (Smith, Blakeslee, & Anderson, 1993). In a study investigating the role of activated prior knowledge, researchers found that when students read a text with ideas that conflicted with their prior knowledge, the students' prior knowledge affected their understanding more than the conflicting text (Alvermann, Smith, & Readence, 1985). Other studies indicate that students with *very little* background knowledge perform better on measures of reading comprehension than those students who have *inaccurate* background information (Holmes, 1983; Lipson, 1982).

Prerequisite Prior Knowledge Can Be Identified.   Both theory and research support the impact of prior knowledge on learning; however, few guidelines exist for the classroom teacher to answer such questions as (1) how should a teacher determine *what* background is important for particular concepts and (2) how should that background be developed (Tierney & Cunningham, 1984)?

Once key prerequisite concepts are determined and selected, teachers can design lessons to evaluate whether or not students have the necessary prerequisite prior knowledge. The Word Association Task (Zakaluk, Samuels, & Taylor, 1986) described later in this chapter would be an appropriate activity to inform teachers of students' prior knowledge. If students lack this essential or prerequisite prior knowledge, then the focus of the prereading lesson should be to teach these missing concepts.

It is important that teachers be aware of the influence prior knowledge has on learning, but it is also important to have some means of assessing what students already know about a topic and to determine what background will facilitate new understandings. By this time, we hope you are convinced that prior knowledge affects comprehension and learning.

Background Knowledge Must Be Sufficient

It is not only the quality but also the quantity of one's background knowledge that affects comprehension (Chi, Hutchinson, & Robin, 1989). Intuitively we would predict that a larger or more extensive schema about the topic being studied would facilitate learning better than a smaller or less developed schema. Results of studies that have compared readers with these two contrasting quantities of prior knowledge of specific topics have supported the theory; readers with high prior knowledge perform better on measures of comprehension than similar students with low prior knowledge. To demonstrate the powerful effects of the quantity of prior knowledge on comprehension, Spilich and others (1979) compared adults with either high or low knowledge of baseball on measures of comprehension. The subjects listened to a half-inning account of a fictitious baseball game, wrote down everything they could remember, and answered a completion test. Those who had the greater amount of prior knowledge performed better on both measures of comprehension. The high prior knowledge subjects also demonstrated a higher quality of comprehension; they have more information about the events of the half inning, elaborated details to the greater extent, and were more likely to recall the events in the correct order.

Background Knowledge Must Be Activated

Subjects were asked to interpret the following paragraph in a study conducted by Bransford and Johnson (1972). Using your prior knowledge, determine the meaning of the paragraph before you continue reading.

> The procedure is actually quite simple. First you arrange things into different groups. Of course, one pile may be sufficient depending on how much there is to do. If you have to go somewhere else due to lack of facilities, that is the next step; otherwise you are pretty well set. It is important not to overdo things. That is, it is better to do too few things at once than too many. In the short run this may not seem important but complications can easily arise. A mistake can be expensive as well. At first the whole procedure will seem complicated. Soon, however, it will become just another facet of life. It is difficult to foresee any end to the necessity for this task in the immediate future, but then one can never tell. After the procedure is completed one arranges the materials into different groups again. Then they can be put into their appropriate places. Eventually they will be used once more and the whole cycle will then have to be repeated. However, that is part of life (p. 400).

What do you think is the topic of this paragraph? Some of the subjects in Bransford and Johnson's study were asked to read the paragraph just as you did, without any clues regarding the topic, to rate it according to how understandable it was, and to recall it. The subjects rated it low in comprehensibility and were not able to recall much of the text. Another group, however, was given the title *before* reading. The title was "Washing Clothes." Did you guess the topic? To the group apprised of the title, the paragraph was understandable and they recalled much of the text. Bransford and Johnson interpreted

---

Think while Reading Activity

While you are reading about prior knowledge-related activities, decide which one you would like to use when you are teaching. Copy the activity below but include facts that are specific to your content area. Be prepared to explain your decision-making process to a partner in class.

_____

_____

_____

_____

_____

_____

_____

_____

_____

Activity 22–3

these results to indicate that having prior knowledge is not a sufficient condition; rather, "previous knowledge must be *activated* in order to facilitate one's current abilities to understand and learn" (Bransford, 1979, p. 135). Thus, content area teachers should use methods that help students activate their prior knowledge.

This chapter has emphasized the influence prior knowledge has on students' potential to learn ideas. Students benefit from teacher-provided activities that are designed to activate, organize, and make sufficient their prior knowledge, thereby increasing the possibility that new or altered schemata (student learning) will result. Thus, the activities we suggest below are designed to support the student in the *process* of constructing schemata in the content area.

Prior Knowledge-Related Activities

We have selected a few reading and writing activities that relate specifically to prior knowledge.

Word Association Task

The first activity, the word association task (Zakaluk, Samuels, & Taylor, 1986), is useful because it is designed to determine what prior knowledge students bring to a new topic. First, select a key word or phrase that represents the main idea of the new topic and is likely to stimulate students' background knowledge. If the topic is the relationship between the economy of the southern states and slavery, the stimulus term might be "southern plantations needed slaves." Have the students write the stimulus term on each line of a piece of notebook paper. (This helps them remember to respond to this term and not to others they think of.) Direct students to write down as many words or phrases they can think of in three minutes that are related to the stimulus term. Though Zakaluk describes a scoring procedure, you may choose to read through your students' responses to determine the amount and depth of their background knowledge. You can then use this information to plan your lessons, and to help students make connections between their prior knowledge and new concepts.

Free Write

An alternative to the word association task, the free write (Macrorie, 1988) asks students to write everything they know about a topic for a specific length of time. Students should not concern themselves with grammar, punctuation, or spelling; rather, they should get everything they can think of that might be related to the topic down on paper. Keeping the free writes provides both students and the teacher opportunities to monitor learning.

Changing Alternative Conceptions

When students hold alternative, naive conceptions about ideas, it is essential that instruction is designed to help them confront those conceptions (Posner, Strike, Hewson, & Gertzog, 1982). Simply reading the "correct" information does not help students exchange their existing conceptions for new ideas (Guzzetti, Snyder, & Glass, 1992). What has helped students "change their minds" are instructional practices that encourage them to examine their current understandings, read the "correct" information, and then contrast their prior knowledge with the new ideas. In the next section we present some ideas for helping students replace naive conceptions with accurate ones. First, ask students to identify their current understanding about an idea. This could be accomplished by asking them to draw a picture, to make a prediction about a demonstration they are about to watch, or to answer a question about a common misconception. Next, have students read the part of the text that addresses the concept. Last, have students look back at their original understandings and reconsider them. This last part should be conducted within a small-group or whole-class discussion so that students can focus on their reasoning.

A modification of the *discussion web* developed by Alvermann (1991) could also be used to help students confront their alternative conceptions and change them. First, you must be aware of your students' typical naive understandings. Looking at their responses from the word association task or free write will inform you of some of these. Next, write a question that addresses the alternative conceptions that may interfere with your students' learning. Create a graphic aid like the one in Figure 22–2. In pairs, have students list the

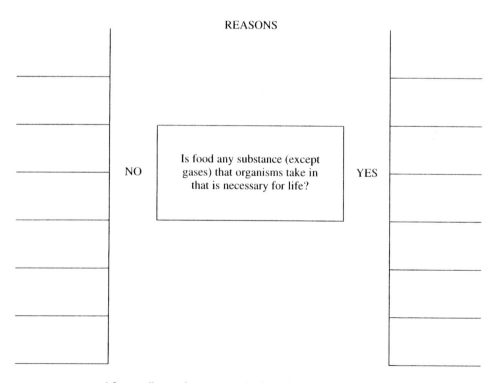

REASONS

NO   Is food any substance (except gases) that organisms take in that is necessary for life?   YES

After reading, write your conclusions about the question here:

FIGURE 22–2   Discussion Web

reasons they believe that the answer to the question is "yes" or "no." Next, have students read materials on the topic and with their partner re-evaluate their original understandings. At the bottom of the graphic aid, have students write a brief paragraph that contrasts their prior knowledge about the question with their new understandings.

Semantic Feature Analysis

A fourth activity is the semantic feature analysis (SFA) and an adaption called semantic/syntactic feature analysis (SSFA). Whereas the word association task and free write are appropriate for the beginning of a unit of study, the SFA and SSFA are more likely to be used to activate prior knowledge before reading a particular content area reading assignment. Both the SFA and the SSFA are conducted first in a group, then individually as each student reads, and finally, as a group when students and their teacher again discuss the activity. Thus, students share prior knowledge and help each other recall experiences and information that might have bearing on the topic being studied. Further, the activity facilitates students' thinking about relationships between and among the supraordinate concept and coordinate and subordinate concepts, thus laying the groundwork for the construction and elaboration of schemata.

The first step in developing the SFA or the SSFA is to select the supraordinate concept to be studied, the connecting or coordinate concepts, and the related details or subordinate concepts. This can be done by reading the assignment and listing words or phrases that represent ideas within the text. Table 22–1 lists the conceptual vocabulary chosen from a

TABLE 22–1   Important Ideas and Related Vocabulary

The Fourth Amendment

*citizen's right to privacy
*law and order
 search and seizure
 unreasonable
*search with search warrant
 probable cause
 property
 possession
*search without search warrant
 absolute privacy
 consent
 hot pursuit
 moving vehicle
 stop-and-frisk
 plain view
 during an arrest
*evidence allowed in court
 exclusionary rule
 evidence

*coordinate concepts

reading assignment related to the Fourth Amendment. The phrase Fourth Amendment represents the supraordinate concept. The words with asterisks represent the coordinate concepts, and the remaining words and phrases represent subordinate ideas.

Next, organize the words and phrases into a relationship chart as shown in Table 22–2. Notice that the supraordinate concept is the title of the relationship chart, the coordinate concepts are the column headings across the top of the chart, and the subordinate concepts are represented by words and phrases listed down the side of the chart.

Before students read the assignment, give each a copy of the relationship chart and make one into an overhead for use at the front of the room. Display the overhead and briefly introduce the topic of the assignment and ask students to say anything they know about the topic. Point to each coordinate word or phrase and ask students to tell what they think the term might mean. Participate in this discussion, including your knowledge about the terms. Accept what students say, and when a naive conception or disagreement occurs point out that "we seem to be uncertain about this. We will have to read to find out. Let's remember to come back and check on that point after we've finished our reading." This sort of language honors students' prior knowledge and helps to set purposes for reading the assignment.

TABLE 22–2 Semantic Feature Analysis Relationship Chart

Important Ideas

Important Vocabulary	Citizen's right to privacy	versus Society needs to keep law and order	Police search with a search warrant	Police search without a search warrant	Evidence allowed in court
search and seizure	+		+	?	
unreasonable search and seizure			0	+	
probable cause to search				?	+
your property and possessions	+				
absolute privacy					
you give consent					
hot pursuit					
moving vehicle					
stop-and-frisk					
plain view					
during an arrest					
evidence					
exclusionary rule					

Following the defining of the coordinate concepts, each subordinate concept is discussed. This discussion begins with the teacher explaining the meaning of the term in the context of the lesson. Students are then asked to predict the relationship between each subordinate term or phrase and each coordinate term or phrase. The following symbols are used to signify each relationship: a plus sign (+) represents a positive relationship between the two terms, a zero (0) represents no relationship, and a question mark (?) represents that no consensus can be reached without further information. The teacher and the class complete the relationship chart by discussing and attempting to reach consensus on the relationship between and among each of the coordinate terms and the subordinate terms.

Student involvement during the discussion is critical to the success of both SFA and SSFA. One key to a successful discussion is to ask students why they predict a certain relationship rating, thus encouraging students to use their prior knowledge regarding the topic. In turn, this type of discussion appears to invite other students to activate what they already know about the topic, often recalling information that they couldn't remember when the topic was first introduced.

After completing the relationship chart, students read to confirm their predictions and determine the relationship between the terms for which no agreement could be reached. After completing the reading, the relationship chart should be reviewed and any of the predicted relationships changed based on evidence from the reading.

The SSFA adds one more step. In addition to preparing the chart, prepare sentences with a blank for a coordinate idea and one or two subordinate ideas. Following the reading and before the postreading discussion, have the students use the chart to fill in the blanks based on their understanding of the terms. The sentences can also be discussed in class to resolve differences in answers. A sentence that might have been created for the "Fourth Amendment" relationship chart is the following:

The constitution of the United States seeks to protect a *(citizen's right to privacy)*, meaning that police need a *(probable cause to search)* and, except under special circumstances, *(you give consent)* for the search.

Direct Experience

Another activity consistent with schema theory is direct experience or hands-on learning. The purpose of this type of activity is to build on students' background knowledge through first-hand experiences with the concepts and vocabulary important to the lesson.

The following procedure and example is based on an activity successfully used in science classrooms (Lloyd & Contreras, 1985). As with the SFA and SSFA, the first step is to identify major concepts that form the framework for a lesson. Next, identify the vocabulary that names those concepts. For example, the words selected for a grade 4 lesson on the water cycle included clouds, evaporation, water vapor, and condensation. Although students could most likely decode or identify some of those words without difficulty, it was unlikely that they had an accurate or complete scientific understanding of some words.

The next step is to prepare a lesson requiring students to directly participate in an activity that develops the concepts and uses the vocabulary. In the water cycle lesson, students were provided a cup filled with ice water on a humid day. As water formed on the outside of the cups, they were asked to describe their observations and make predictions about the source of the water. Through careful questioning, the teacher helped students develop a concept of condensation. When students reached the conclusion that the water originated from the air and condensed on the cup because of the low temperature of the cup, the teacher named the concept: "We need a name for this. It is called condensation."

Analogies

As explained earlier in this chapter, analogies can be used to show relationships between new ideas and familiar information.

Peabody (1984) developed a powerful lesson to teach the abstract concepts of chemical bonding through the use of concrete examples. To develop the concept of covalent bonding in which electrons are equally shared by two identical atoms, Peabody used the analogy of twins, Nella and Nellie, who were identical in every possible way. When they receive a bicycle from their parents, she lead the students to agree Nella and Nellie would share the bicycle equally. To demonstrate unequal electron sharing, she introduced Nancy and Nick. Though they, too, will share a bicycle, Nick is older and stronger and will get the bicycle more often. To develop the concept of electron transfer, or no sharing at all, Peabody described Mertle, "a sweet little girl" and her big brother Nerd, "a big meany." When they receive a bicycle, Nerd keeps it all to himself. All three bicycle analogies are diagrammed on the board during the discussion, followed by diagrams that illustrate how electrons are shared or transferred in chemical bonding.

Analogical Study Guides

Another activity that may also take advantage of analogical thinking for linking prior knowledge with new information being read is the use of analogical study guides. Bean, Singer, and Cowen (1985) developed this sort of a guide to help high school biology students learn the functions of cells by comparing them to functions in a factory. The guide was composed of three columns: the left side listed the cell structures, the middle contained the functions of each structure, and the right column had the analogy (see Table 22–3).

TABLE 22–3   Analogical Study Guide

CELLS		
STRUCTURE (parts)	MAIN FUNCTIONS (jobs)	ANALOGY (comparing cell to a factory)
Cell wall	Support, protection	Factory walls
Cell membrane	Boundary, gatekeeper	Security guards
Cytoplasm	Site of most metabolism	Work area
Vacuoles	Store food, water, minerals	Warehouse

Adapted from Bean, Singer, and Cowen (1985) and Bean, Singer, Cowen, and Searles (1987).

Cinquain

Our final recommended activity is the cinquain (Allen & Allen, 1982). This simple and elegant activity is recommended because it (1) helps students develop the prior knowledge they need for subsequent lessons and (2) provides an opportunity to consolidate, integrate, and synthesize the new information that has been connected with prior knowledge.

The cinquain is a five-line poem that reflects both affective and cognitive responses to a concept. Guidelines for writing a cinquain are:

Line 1 is a one word title.

Line 2 is two words that describe the title.

Line 3 is three words expressing an action.

Line 4 is four words expressing a feeling.

Line 5 is another word for the title.

An example of a cinquain that represents the ideas presented in this chapter is:

Background
Necessarily varied
Activating, selecting, relating
Making connections: exciting learning
Schema

Conclusion

The ideas presented in this chapter help to explain why learning is not a simple matter of "covering material" or "cramming for the test." Most of us have many courses on our college transcripts, the content of which we cannot recall because we "covered" the material,

---

Think after Reading Activity

Look back to the thoughts you listed in the Think before Reading Activity in this chapter. How has your knowledge of the significance of prior knowledge expanded after reading this chapter?

Activity 22–4

but we did not learn it. As educators, we cannot afford the luxury of teaching courses that have little or no effect on students' lives, let alone on their schema. What we do is important, and we must take advantage of all we know about learning and teaching to do as well as we must. The described effects of prior knowledge on learning and the suggested activities are representative of what research and theory predict should work; you and your students will make these activities come alive in the context of the classroom as you grapple together with the compelling questions of your content.

Moving beyond Reading and Writing in the Content Areas to Discipline-Based Inquiry

JOHN F. O'FLAHAVAN   *ROBERT J. TIERNEY*

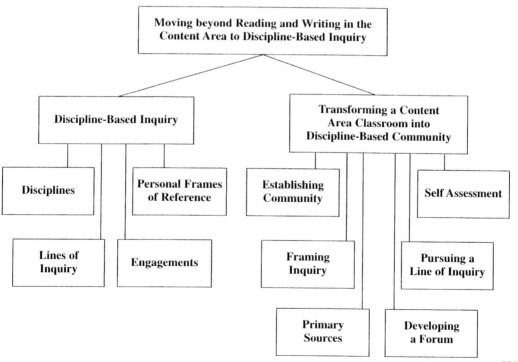

Think before Reading Activity

What were the elements of an instructional experience in which you really learned?

_____

_____

_____

_____

_____

How is your knowledge in a particular content area different from the knowledge of a professional who works in this field?

_____

_____

_____

_____

_____

How is it similar?

_____

_____

_____

_____

_____

Keep these ideas in mind as you read this chapter.

Activity 23–1

This chapter explores the idea of replacing the term "content area learning" with "discipline-based inquiry." Our thesis centers on creating a classroom-based disciplinary community grounded in inquiry. In such a community students are immersed in ideas that shape a particular discipline and use the tools of inquiry to construct ideas in the discipline. We discuss how to create a sense of community within a classroom and how, within the community, to socialize students into the ways of thinking, interacting, and knowing that characterize various disciplines, using literacy as a tool for learning.

Fifteen years ago, few content area teachers at the secondary level taught reading or writing in any systematic fashion. Since then, scores of "reading in the content area" (e.g., Vacca & Vacca, 1986) and "writing across the curriculum" texts (e.g., Fulwiler, 1987) have been published and read widely. As a result, more teachers today are inclined to incorporate reading and writing activities, alone or in combination, in their content lessons and to provide supplemental reading and writing strategy instruction, such as how to read a science text effectively or how to compose a research report from a variety of information sources.

Despite this progress, we suggest that the assumptions underlying content area learning channel undue emphasis on learning from textbooks at the expense of other sources of information, remembering text-based information rather than using that information for generating and confirming or disconfirming hypotheses, and using reading and writing for the purpose of enhancing reading comprehension rather than as tools for forging connections between texts, observations, conversations, and the like. Thus, the reading and writing activities found in most content area classrooms do not serve the same cumulative and generative functions found in many real-world, discipline-based inquiries. (For a comparison of the two views, see Table 23–1.)

In this chapter, we propose a next step in the ongoing reformation of content area instruction. We suggest that the prevalent term *content area learning* be replaced with *discipline-based inquiry.* A major concern underlying our approach is that content area learning has focused on the learning of content isolated from the ways in which inquiry is conducted within specific fields of study. For example, we have taught students historical content but not the inquiry processes valued by historians, thus separating the learning of history from the processes involved in becoming a historian. History should not be isolated from doing history, science should not be isolated from doing science, problems should not be isolated from problem solving.

Our thesis, therefore, is that if you wish to cultivate in your students the ways of thinking appropriate to your discipline, immerse your students in the ideas that shape your discipline and help your students adopt the tools of inquiry that helped construct those ideas. Then create a classroom-based disciplinary community grounded in inquiry from the very beginning. For example, if you teach art and wish to cultivate artists, then invite your students to participate in school as practicing artists participate in the world outside of school. Create the conditions in which students can study the techniques and products of practiced and emergent artists as they produce art. Engage students in reading, writing, and talk as a means of understanding and responding to the art that is produced around them.

TABLE 23–1   Reading and Writing in the Content Areas versus Reading and Writing for Discipline-Based Inquiry

Reading/Writing in the Content Areas	Reading/Writing in Discipline-Based Inquiry
One line of study	Multiple lines of inquiry
Information gathering purposes	Ongoing inquiry, driven by interest
Recognition and recall	Data gathering, hypothesis-testing analysis
Product oriented	Process and product oriented
Restricted forms and products	Multiple forms and modes of presentation
Class-wide activity	Decentralized activity in an emerging community
Students as respondents and recipients	Students as inquirers and apprentices
Focus on single, secondary source text	Focus on diverse primary source materials

---

Think while Reading Activity

The following are four key facets of conducting inquiry in discipline-based classrooms. Use the space to take notes about each idea as you read this section.

Disciplines

_____

_____

_____

Personal Frames of Reference

_____

_____

_____

Lines of Inquiry

_____

_____

_____

Engagements

_____

_____

_____

Activity 23–2

This chapter is organized in two parts. The first section outlines the general principles underlying our orientation in the context of several examples, including an in-depth discussion of the relationship between four key facets of conducting inquiry in disciplinary communities: disciplines, personal frames of reference, lines of inquiry, and engagements. The second section illustrates how content area teachers might establish and sustain discipline-based inquiry in their classrooms.

Discipline-Based Inquiry

Every discipline (from anatomy to zoology) depends on reading, writing, and talk in some form to construct its knowledge base. Books, phone conversations, archival journals, conference presentations, and letters are just some of the ways that members of a discipline engage in reading and writing to construct knowledge. These literate and oral engagements do not occur in a conceptual vacuum; they emanate from personal frames of reference in a given topic, which lead to purposeful and meaningful lines of inquiry.

A line of inquiry can be driven by an issue, a problem to be solved, a question, or a hypothesis. Once established, it helps the inquirer determine the engagements which follow—what to do next, with whom, and why. Although not all of these engagements involve literacy *per se,* the processes and byproducts of literacy provide continuity across time.

As an example, imagine a modest high school in a small town where three teachers have been developing ways to link their courses for three classes of twenty-five grade 10 students. The result is an interdisciplinary curriculum incorporating history, English and language arts, and government. Students taking these classes complete common assignments, one of which is a current events project of their choice and design. These collaborative or independent projects must focus on a meaningful current event rooted in historical and governmental issues and result in a text-based product that will contribute to the learning of others, such as a presentation, publication, multimedia exhibit, or debate.

Each classroom is organized in a way that invites students to give and receive assistance in every phase of their projects. For example, students hone their products during English and language arts, which is organized as a reading and writing workshop (e.g., Atwell, 1987). The history teacher helps students develop an historical perspective on their topics in a number of ways, such as providing related primary sources, teaching reading and writing strategies relevant to historical texts, and scheduling guest speakers. The government teacher's contribution is to raise students' awareness to the role of local, state, and national governments in the context of their topics through such methods as holding town meetings in class to discuss current events and teaching students how to access and comprehend related reference materials. In every class, reading, writing, and talk figure prominently as tools for searching for and constructing information in each discipline. Each class has a multimedia station, including several computers, a phone line, audio tape players, a videotape player, and a small reference library.

One day, a grade 10 student reads in the local paper that a developer proposes to raze a vacant rooming house in an historic section of the community and construct in its place a strip shopping mall. A zoning hearing is set; it is one month away. The public is invited to address the city council. While sharing this news during a town meeting in her government class, she learns from another student that the site may have some historical significance. She decides to look into the matter. Where does she begin? How will she proceed? How will she depend on literate activity to deepen her understanding of the issue?

Figure 23–1 depicts the possible "literate footprints" of her inquiry. She begins by calling the local historical society. They suggest that she check *The National Register of Historic Places.* With the help of her history teacher, she learns how to search for information in this reference. This turns up a few leads. She visits the office of the county clerk and begins the process of looking through old real estate deeds and transfers, which leads her to the local library to pore over microfiche of old newspaper editions. All the while, she jots notes of important dates and names as well as questions that need answers, such as "What if I find that this place is important? What then?" She brings this information to her language arts class and shares her progress with a small group of students and the teacher. This conference helps her divide her inquiry into two lines: a search for the site's history and the best way to construct an argument for preserving historic sites.

The initial line of inquiry eventually bears fruit. After many calls to local officials and community members who share a passion for history, and visits to the library and town hall, she finds that the site was once a vital link in the Underground Railroad. At the time,

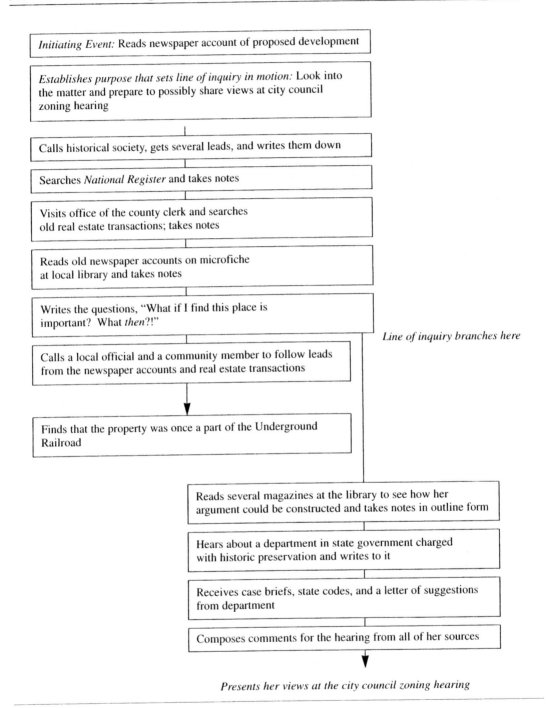

Initiating Event: Reads newspaper account of proposed development

Establishes purpose that sets line of inquiry in motion: Look into the matter and prepare to possibly share views at city council zoning hearing

Calls historical society, gets several leads, and writes them down

Searches *National Register* and takes notes

Visits office of the county clerk and searches old real estate transactions; takes notes

Reads old newspaper accounts on microfiche at local library and takes notes

Writes the questions, "What if I find this place is important? What *then*?!"

Line of inquiry branches here

Calls a local official and a community member to follow leads from the newspaper accounts and real estate transactions

Finds that the property was once a part of the Underground Railroad

Reads several magazines at the library to see how her argument could be constructed and takes notes in outline form

Hears about a department in state government charged with historic preservation and writes to it

Receives case briefs, state codes, and a letter of suggestions from department

Composes comments for the hearing from all of her sources

Presents her views at the city council zoning hearing

FIGURE 23–1   Literate Footprints from a Line of Inquiry

it was owned by a wealthy merchant whose wife was active in antislavery activities. The original dwelling burned to the ground in the early 1900s, was rebuilt according to original specification, and sold many times since. Technically, therefore, only the stone foundation and basement are original.

The student's second line of inquiry is thus shaped by the findings from the first. With the help of her government teacher and a small group of peers, she proceeds to investigate what laws are in place for protecting dwellings that are no longer original but are of some historical significance. A student in history class suggests that she look for similar cases, and her history teacher points her to two periodicals, *Historic Preservation* and the *National Register Bulletin*. While searching these references, she jots notes and begins to shape an outline of her presentation to the city council. Later, in government class, she learns of a department in state government that is charged with historic preservation and writes to it in language arts class. They send state codes, recent case briefs that argued for preserving similar sites, and a cover letter suggesting options in her situation. Finally, with all of her notes, telephone correspondence, photocopied articles, and primary documents, she drafts her presentation in language arts class. In so doing, she considers audience (local politicians), purpose (offer a compromise to save the dwelling and convert it to urban park space), and forum (an oral presentation). She practices delivering it to a mock city council in government class. In the end, all of the presentations at the hearing convince the city council to gather more information and postpone the vote. She leaves the hearing wondering what she should and could do next.

What can content area teachers at the secondary level learn from this scenario? An underlying goal for instruction in all content areas is that students begin talking, thinking, interpreting, reading, writing, and acting as if they were a part of the broader disciplinary community. Rather than simply transmitting discipline-based information to students, content area teachers should consider how to create the conditions in the classroom that compel the kinds of engagements exhibited by the student in the example above. To this end, students will need to develop expertise in identifying a problem of personal or social interest, initiating a line of inquiry, and deploying the appropriate tools and resources needed to sustain the inquiry. Several characteristics of these lines of inquiry are instructive.

First, *to become an inquirer requires having a frame of reference for each inquiry.* Having a frame of reference involves more than just being told the topic for an inquiry or simply choosing one unreflectively. Having a frame of reference involves cultivating a personal perspective and coming to terms with other perspectives on issues, concepts, phenomena, and events.

Students need to be given the opportunity to establish a frame of reference before they are invited to pursue a line of inquiry. Their frames of reference need to be sufficiently robust so that students can begin to generate their own ideas and develop a variety of interests which could then fuel inquiry. In fact, when students begin to ask questions, make predictions, and offer their own opinions, a teacher can feel confident that students have begun to stake a claim to the inquiry.

Second, *lines of inquiry arise from personalized frames of reference and serve social or personal functions.* Moving from the relative comfort of a frame of reference to the dissonant state of needing to know more will often lead to a line of inquiry. The purposes, or functions, served by the line of inquiry can be socially or personally relevant, and may surface as a result of individual choice, assignment, or both. In our historic preservation scenario, the line of inquiry was sparked by social concern and personal interest. In every situation, the functional qualities of the inquiry are defined from the outset by the person or persons engaging in the inquiry.

Students will learn to initiate and sustain productive lines of inquiry if immersed in a general field of study long enough to develop meaningful frames of reference. Teachers can launch diverse activities, such as dramatizations of key events, direct observation of phenomena, and discussions of primary documents, that will germinate students' interests while at the same time helping students construct initial impressions of topics within the field of study. Helping students gain perspective on a range of related topics using reading, writing, and talk as tools for gaining perspective is key to choosing a purposeful and meaningful line of inquiry.

Third, *moving from one engagement to the next is an intentional process, driven by self-determination, and influenced by the nature of the inquiry and the ideas being pursued.* The reading, writing, and talk engagements that shape an inquiry and the inquiries that shape disciplinary thinking evolve not as individual pursuits, but as socially constituted and negotiated activities. Individuals are never insulated from the influences of the social world—authors, peers, experts, novices, texts, and the like contribute to lines of inquiry.

Like the line of inquiry itself, each engagement is driven by a perceived function and is therefore highly situated in each line of inquiry. The byproducts of one engagement— listing what you know and don't know about how hydroelectric dams produce energy— leads naturally to the next engagement—a trip to the library to find a book or article that explains it in language you can understand—which may lead to another—calling an engineer at the local power company to see if he knows of a resource.

While the decision of what to do next and how to do it may require the help of others (e.g., teacher, friend, or mentor), the ultimate choice is left to the individual. The learner in our historic preservation example exhibited tremendous self-determination throughout the course of her investigation. When one engagement turned up a lead or raised new questions, she fashioned subsequent engagements accordingly. In this sense, she rarely worked "independently"; many people contributed to her inquiry in important ways and at critical times.

Students will exhibit self-determination if they are given the same level of social support and are asked to reflect on the process of inquiry itself. This is why building a disciplinary community in the classroom is crucial to promoting highly literate behavior. Ongoing reflection and self-assessment ensures that students understand their own and other's inquiry processes. Such a focus stretches the capabilities of each individual by providing access to models of how one might inquire within a given discipline. Students should be compelled to reflect on the ways that their thinking has changed, the strategies they deploy, the literate forms they enlist when, and the modes of inquiry they choose.

Fourth, *negotiating a line of inquiry in a given discipline requires knowledge of the tools, resources, and products of previous and ongoing lines of inquiry commonplace to that disciplinary community.* The tools, human resources, and products from previous and ongoing inquiries can serve as invitations to an individual to establish personalized frames of reference, which can then lead to meaningful lines of inquiry. You must first establish a

Think while Reading Activity

As you read about developing disciplinary-based inquiry in the content area classroom, fill in each part of the chart. It will help you learn how to create a discipline-based inquiry classroom. Use your own content area for your ideas.

My content area is:

How I will establish community:

How I will frame the inquiry:

How I will pursue a line of inquiry:

How I plan to gather primary sources:

How I plan to develop a forum for the inquiry:

My plan for student self-assessment:

My thoughts regarding the effectiveness of this process:

Activity 23–3

frame of reference to initiate a line of inquiry, but sustaining the inquiry requires knowing where and to whom to turn to get what you want when you need it most. In our historic preservation example, the student's purposes shifted with each engagement. As a result, she turned to a variety of inquiry modes (e.g., reading, writing, and talk) and literate forms (e.g., *The National Register of Historic Places* and a script for her presentation), invoked an array of strategies during each engagement (e.g., document search strategies and writing strategies), and called on people who were more knowledgeable than she when her inquiry stalled.

We suggest that a student's ability to negotiate the tools, resources, and knowledge base of a particular discipline is directly related to the degree to which the student participates in constructing the tools, resources, and knowledge base of the disciplinary community. With the help of a teacher, students can learn from or contribute to the knowledge base in a discipline in the following ways: (1) by deploying the tools of a discipline, such as a computer application, centrifuge, or lab book; (2) by constructing new tools when needed; (3) by using or producing pertinent material resources, such as reference books and videotaped documentaries, when these resources are most useful in the course of an inquiry; and (4) engaging human resources, such as experts or peers. Like the learner in the historic preservation example, the student need not sustain a line of inquiry alone; the disciplinary community offers many and varied types of support within and between engagements.

Lastly, *diversity in lines of inquiry within a disciplinary community breeds diversity of perspective and process, which contributes to a community of inquirers who are, on average, more knowledgeable, strategic, and socially interactive.* A body of knowledge accumulates best from many and varied lines of inquiry, not from a group of individuals participating in the same engagements at the same time. Imagine a variation on our historic preservation example, in which two people investigated solutions to the issue in their own ways, though they conferred with each other periodically. A number of possibilities may have unfolded. First, each inquirer would have achieved a perspective on his or her own perspective as a result of sharing information, resources, and possible solutions. Second, each would have been exposed to the other's inquiry processes, increasingly the likelihood that hybrid processes would evolve. Third, a potentially more comprehensive solution to the problem would emerge.

Transforming the Content Area Classroom into a Disciplinary Community

Content area teachers can invite their students to establish meaningful lines of inquiry by transforming their classrooms into disciplinary communities characterized by inquiry. Coupled with opportunistic and informed teacher facilitation and social interaction, students will construct a shared knowledge base representative of the discipline under study. In so doing, students will inform each other's evolving inquiry processes, ways of thinking, and perspectives on topics.

The following example, "The Pursuit of Freedom," is one illustration of how discipline-based inquiry might evolve. The setting is a middle school in a midwestern city, located in a state which was a free state that bordered a slave state during the Civil War.

The twenty-six students in this social studies class are of diverse ethnic heritage and exhibit a range of cognitive and social capabilities. The students have conducted inquiries before, including the use of primary source research and maintaining portfolios and journals. Our discussion of this example is laid out in terms of establishing a disciplinary community, framing the inquiry, pursuing a line of inquiry, gathering primary sources, developing a forum for the inquiry, and self-assessment.

Establishing Community

How does a teacher create a sense of community in the classroom? The first step is to remember that a community and everyone in it is always under construction, and that everyone in the community must feel that she or he plays an important part in the act of construction. In this sense, students must feel a sense of ownership in how their classroom activities evolve, how the physical space is organized, how time is used, and what learning products are developed when, by whom, and for whom. They must feel involved in their own learning and the learning of others. They need to see the relevance and significance of the content they are studying. They need to feel as if they share in the decisions that impact their learning environment. In most cases, teachers can show that they are willing to share in these decisions by allowing students to take some time to personalize their frames of reference with a focal topic (e.g., Civil War), by asking students to involve themselves in each other's thinking (e.g., frequent writing conferences and peer discussions about readings), by soliciting from students advice about what to teach next (e.g., "What is it about the Civil War that really interests you, confuses you? What do you want to know more about"), by providing responsive instruction within the context of students' lines of inquiry (e.g., a mini-lesson on how to synthesize information from primary sources), and by documenting and making public knowledge as it is constructed by students (e.g., a time line that depicts the key events of the Civil War).

Framing the Inquiry

Framing the inquiry requires that students forge personal connections with the topic at hand. Guided by this, the teacher and students in our middle school illustration engage in reading a number of stories and diary entries that give firsthand accounts of slavery in the South during the mid-1800s. In an attempt to build a frame of reference, the class develops a series of dramatizations of life in different parts of the United States during that time. One dramatization deals with life on a number of different plantations; another dramatizes life in a small town in the Northeast. Each of the dramatizations involves the teacher guiding student improvisations and having the characters discuss their views of the freedoms that they have and what they would like to have. Selected film excerpts that depict the life and attitudes of African Americans regarding slavery and the pursuit of freedom are also viewed.

Pursuing a Line of Inquiry

Moving from collective to more focused pursuits is driven by the desire to help students find inquiries that befit their interests, background, ongoing questions, and preferred modes of inquiry. For example, as students discuss their interests and questions during the dramatizations mentioned above, they evolve individual interests and begin to identify distinct lines of inquiry. Some students wish to pursue more details of the day-to-day lives of African Americans in different parts of the United States at that time; some want to pursue the topic of the Underground Railway; others want to investigate post–Civil War life for African Americans. These quests lead to more focused lines of inquiry for individual students and small groups.

Gathering Primary Sources

Once students establish the purposes for their inquires, the teacher, students, school media personnel, community librarian, and any other knowledgeable resource cooperate to gather primary sources relevant to the lines of inquiry. The goal is to afford students access to primary source materials and to consider how these materials might be examined. For example, the group pursuing the Underground Railway obtains a map of the Railway sites in Ohio and letters from people detailing their history from the local historical society. The group (or media personnel) arranges to visit several sites and interview those living there, create a photo album for each site, and document how each site operated. They read the law that pertained to persons caught operating a site and discuss court cases addressing them. At the same time as they engage in these transactions, they make decisions about how to collect their data and communicate their information to others. Eventually, they decide to co-author an article for the school magazine.

Developing a Forum for the Inquiry

Setting one's sights on an expressive experience, such as writing an article for the school magazine, adds some momentum to the engagements that are part of the line of inquiry. However, this is not the only valued outcome. It is also important that inquiry sustain an individual's or a group's personal interest in a topic; in this sense, inquiry has no culmination. We suggest that the end goal of any inquiry is pursuit for deeper understanding not simply the presentation of facts or an exhibit of knowledge gained over the course of the inquiry.

Self-Assessment

If students are to develop fully as inquirers, they need to study their own and other's evolving inquiries. One way that teachers can facilitate such reflection is by encouraging students to keep tabs of how their inquiries are progressing. This may involve the equivalent of maintaining a search log within their portfolio from which one can trace and revisit the journey, including their process, strategies, breakthroughs, successes, frustrations, and ongoing pursuits.

In our middle school example, students kept a portfolio of their activities and products into which they placed key materials, such as details of plans, a record of primary source materials, and ongoing data collection records. As they concluded their inquiries, they reviewed these materials with peers and wrote an analysis of changes, shifts, developments, struggles, procedures, and ongoing goals. These evaluations served as the basis for teacher-student conferences as well as future learning goals negotiated between the teacher and individual students.

Conclusion

Such movements as "reading in the content areas" and "writing across the curriculum" have played a major role in helping content area teachers in the secondary school find better ways to interlace reading and writing activities into the flow of content area teaching. However, we believe that it is time to explore the next step in the reformation of content area teaching. The next step that we propose in this chapter is to create disciplinary communities grounded in student-initiated and student-sustained inquiry as the chief approach to instruction, and that traditional techniques, such as advance organizers, lecture, and teacher-led discussion of textbook passages support rather than lead inquiry.

Think after Reading Activity

Imagine you are the parent of a high school student who is in a discipline-based inquiry class. He has told you how much he enjoys the class every night for two weeks. Your curiosity is kindled, so last week you took an afternoon off from work and visited your son's class. Now you want to share what you experienced with as many people as possible. You've decided to write a letter to the editor of the local paper.

Use the information in Table 23–1 which compares content area classes and discipline-based inquiry classes to write your letter to the editor. If your last name begins with A to L write a pro discipline-based inquiry letter, but if your last name begins with M to Z write a letter opposed to discipline-based inquiry.

Letter to the Editor of the Lake View Town News

Last week I visited my son's high school class at _____
High School. It was not like anything I had ever seen before in a class. Certainly was nothing like my days in school! When I first arrived in the room_____

_____

_____

_____

_____

_____

_____

_____

Sincerely,

_____

Activity 23–4

Model Programs

Creating Response-Centered Learning Environments

Using Authentic Texts to Extend and Enrich the Curriculum

RICHARD T. VACCA   JOANNE L. VACCA
NANCY PROSENJAK   LINDA BURKEY

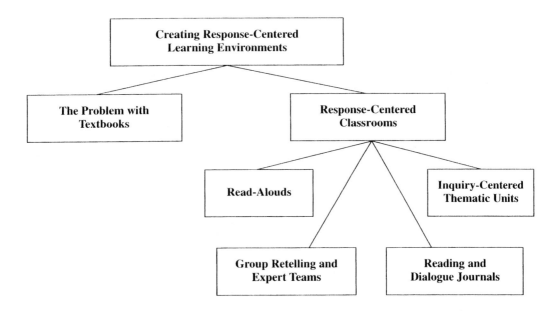

Think before Reading Activity

Many resources besides a textbook can be used for learning in a classroom. Think about this statement for a few minutes, then write a list of some of these other sources on the cluster below. Be prepared to pair and share your list with a classmate. As you read this chapter, add to your list.

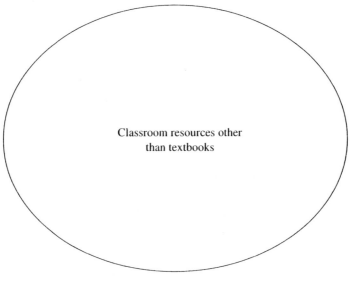

Classroom resources other
than textbooks

Activity 24–1

Textbooks often fail to arouse students' curiosity and interest in a subject or to provide them with intense involvement in and interactions with ideas. More and more content area teachers are turning to authentic, real-world texts, including literature, to extend and enrich the curriculum. Learning environments that are response-centered helps readers to explore texts, construct meaning, and make personal connections. In this chapter, the emphasis is on how teachers plan and organize authentic reading experiences within the framework of lessons and larger units of study. Several instructional options, which will ensure students' success with authentic texts, are explored.

How teachers think about and use texts is an important part of their jobs. Although the decisions made about texts vary from classroom to classroom, three kinds of practice are evident. The first involves the use of one type of text—the textbook—in content areas, often at the exclusion of other types of texts. Some teachers, for example, rely almost exclusively on the textbook as students' primary source of information. The second type of practice involves text avoidance. For one reason or another, some teachers circumvent reading as a tool for learning by focusing instruction on lecturing and other forms of classroom activity. The third kind of practice is what this chapter is all about. Some teachers view the textbook as a source of learning, albeit not the only source. They recognize the powerful role that authentic texts, commonly found in the world outside of classrooms, play in extending and enriching students' understanding of subject matter. These real-world texts include narrative and informational trade books, newspapers, magazines, pamphlets, reference resources, and any other type of print medium that has purpose and relevance in the real world.

Textbooks and Real-World Texts

In most classrooms, textbook assignments are the rule rather than the exception. A textbook, which is designed to convey a body of knowledge, has come to symbolize a graded and fragmented curriculum. For example, a biology textbook is what most students might use to study science in the grade 10. As a result, the textbook *is* the curriculum for some teachers. It serves as a compendium of facts and generalizations which allows a learner—in principle at least—to have easy access to events, ideas, people, and processes to be covered in a subject. Therein lies a major problem with the use of textbooks in content area classrooms. When teachers rely heavily on textbooks, they tend to emphasize content over process in an attempt to cover the curriculum. When textbooks become the single source of information, the curriculum concern for a U.S. history teacher is, more than likely, "How can I cover the Civil War in four weeks?" rather than, "How do I involve students intellectually and emotionally in the people, places, events, issues, ideas, and consequences associated with the Civil War?"

Time constraints in a fractured curriculum are real. Teachers feel an enormous pressure to cover X amount of content before students move on to the next unit in the course or the next course in the prescribed curriculum. Textbooks, as a result, are viewed as efficient informational resources that support what students are learning about in a particular subject area at a particular time. When textbooks are used to cover the content, the downside becomes all too evident: students dismiss the power of text as a tool for learning. Those who do use textbooks are primarily concerned with covering the material and transferring large chunks of information from textbook to test paper.

No wonder some teachers, perplexed that students just don't read textbook assignments anymore, give up on reading as a viable means of learning. From the students' perspective, however, it isn't too difficult to understand why they might choose not to use textbooks that seem bland, lifeless, and even intimidating. Textbooks are tomes whose very size and appearance may discourage some students, especially those who struggle with reading, from attempting to use them in a purposeful manner. Yet we suspect that other students eschew textbook reading because they recognize that they don't have to read in order to be successful in their classrooms. Although teachers tell students that reading is important, the emphasis placed on lecturing and other nonprint means of information-giving unwittingly signals another message: it is okay not to read textbook material to do well.

Think while Reading Activity

You have had a great deal of experience working with textbooks as a student. In the near future you'll also use them as a teacher. The previous section suggested why textbooks alone do not offer sufficient resources for learning in content area classrooms. List three of these reasons below.

1. _____

2. _____

3. _____

What is your response?

_____

_____

_____

_____

_____

_____

_____

Activity 24–2

Too few content area teachers view other kinds of text as viable alternatives to supplant or supplement textbook study. Authentic, real-world texts are print alternatives to the textbook. Readers interact with people, places, and ideas through real-world text experiences that are not possible in textbooks. A textbook, in its attempt to be comprehensive, will contain the minimal essentials necessary to convey information about a topic. However, the use of narrative and informational literature in content area learning situations serves as a magnifying glass that enlarges and enhances the reader's interaction with a subject (Vacca & Vacca, 1993).

The use of authentic texts depends in large measure on a teachers's understanding of open, response-centered learning environments. A response-centered classroom is one that engages students in a process of making connections between what they read and their own prior knowledge and experiences (see Chapter 22). These meaning-making connections allow students to explore what they know already, to rediscover what they know that they don't think they know, and to discover what they truly need to know to extend and elaborate their understandings.

Response-Centered Classrooms

Learning within the context of the classroom depends on the strong interactions and transactions among teachers, students, and texts. When students have the opportunity to actively respond to a wide array of texts in a variety of ways, they are involved in constructive learning processes. They begin to see a text as only one source of knowledge and as a result engage in collaborative efforts to explore additional sources, pool knowledge, and negotiate meaning. The teacher's goal is to plan a variety of classroom experiences that will bring learners and texts together. The sections that follow describe several of the possible activities teachers can employ to create a response-centered learning environment incorporating authentic texts.

Read-Alouds

An often neglected classroom experience in the content areas involves situations in which teachers share texts with students, or students share texts with other students. These shared reading experiences serve useful purposes in a response-centered classroom. First of all, texts that are shared with students are schema builders in that they have the potential to generate background knowledge and activate what students already know about a subject to be explored. When a middle school science teacher, for example, reads a powerful section from Laurence Pringle's *Water: The Next Great Resource Battle,* students quickly become involved in exploring the conditions underlying the water crisis that affects the globe. Not only does the read-aloud support active involvement in the subject of the text, but it also draws students into the material as they generate background knowledge and experience.

Teachers often lead read-aloud sessions. In these situations, they serve as models as they illustrate that the main objective for oral reading in content area classrooms is to communicate ideas to others by interpreting what an author says and feels. Students may read aloud to other students, but they must be familiar with the material and rehearse their parts in advance.

Shared reading should not be confused with round robin reading, in which students usually use the "paragraph principle" to determine in advance which part of the text they will be responsible for when their turn comes to read. In classroom routines that support round robin reading, few students listen to the reader because they are too busy rehearsing their own parts. Hardly anyone pays attention to the message of the text.

Shared reading, on the other hand, has the potential of strengthening the reading process for students. Reading about a subject (or listening to the text being read) has been shown to improve comprehension of conceptually related readings on the same topic (Crafton, 1983). An additional benefit of shared reading, especially of a narrative nature, is that it often draws students into the literary experience, creates interest, and arouses curiosity in areas such as science, health, social studies, and history. A high school history teacher reads Jane Yolen's powerful *The Devil's Arithmetic* to give students a sense of what it must have been like to be an adolescent in a Nazi concentration camp in 1942.

As part of a unit on the Vietnam War, Christa Chaney introduces grade 8 students to Eve Bunting's *The Wall,* a powerful picture book that richly illustrates the story of a young boy who visits the Vietnam War Memorial with his grandfather to locate the name of the boy's father. Chaney shares the story in a read-aloud for several reasons: First, the story is a dramatic narrative that's well worth sharing with students of all ages. The visual appeal of the scenes during the visit to the Wall can be related to on a variety of levels. Second, the text captures the emotional and psychological impact of the Vietnam War Memorial and evokes a strong response from the students. Third, because the story invites reader response, Chaney uses the shared reading experience to engage students in conversation about the Vietnam War and, in the process of class discussion, she elicits what students know already and the questions they have about war. What they want to find out about the Vietnam War becomes a central topic of discussion.

Some teachers are skeptical about using picture books with older learners. Yet Neal and Moore (1991) maintain that picture books are appropriate texts for use with middle and secondary students. They contend that picture books cover a wide range of subject matter and their themes often have universal value and appeal. Because of the short format of picture books, they can be used effectively as read-alouds within the framework of larger lessons. Math teachers have used Mitsumasa Anno's *Anno's Counting House* and *Anno's Math Games II* with older students to clarify and extend mathematical concepts.

Poems, news and popular magazine articles, and selections from biography and informational books also lend themselves to shared reading activities. A high school history teacher shared a magazine article from *Newsweek* on the controversy surrounding holocaust studies in the social studies curriculum. She could have easily provided students with copies of the article to read on their own. However, given the brevity of the article, she felt that her "expert" reading would help students focus more intently on the subject matter. The read-aloud resulted in a lively discussion around the questions, "Do you think it is important to talk about what happened in the concentration camps during World War II? Why is it important to know more about what happened?" Often a timely read-aloud will help students to identify issues and problems that need further exploration and study.

Read-alouds can be used at different points in a lesson. At the beginning of class, use read-alouds to introduce a topic, build and activate schema, raise questions, and provide a frame of reference for concepts under study. The read-aloud has a feed forward effect. It serves as a prereading strategy to arouse curiosity, create surprise, disrupt students' preconceived expectations, cause conceptual conflict, or identify issues and problems to be explored and resolved. A book that can be easily used for these purposes in math, science, or art classes is Molly Bang's *Picture This,* in which she explains how an artist's mind works while composing an illustration.

Read-alouds can be used during a lesson to help students respond to ideas or clarify meaning. When used in concert with a reading journal, students have an opportunity to respond personally to the text. Various kinds of response heuristics—prompts that promote discovery and personal connections through writing—may be used to trigger students' thinking: What feelings did you have as you listened to the text? What did the text make you think of? What experiences have you had that might relate to the text? (See Chapter 15.)

When a text is shared toward the end of the class, teachers use it to help students summarize or synthesize what they have learned or to make projections about the subject. Whatever the case may be, the key to an effective read-aloud is to do it well. Here are some guidelines for preparing a shared reading:

1. Keep the read-aloud short. Five or ten minutes of reading will sustain students' attention better than an extended reading time.

2. Plan the read-aloud in advance. Will the read-aloud serve as a schema builder; to introduce a subject; to clarify, reflect on, or synthesize meaning? Should there be response at the end of the reading or at intermittent points during the reading? Decide how to introduce the reading selection, how to arouse curiosity, how to connect what students know and feel to the text, how to elicit response (through writing or discussion?).
3. Know when to stop reading, especially if the read-aloud will occur over several days. Stopping points should invite prediction and anticipation.
4. Know the text well enough in advance to allow the drama or profundity of the text to be felt by its listeners. A successful read-aloud is one that has been rehearsed.

Group Retellings and Expert Teams

A variation on the read-aloud is to involve students in a process of sharing what they are reading with one another. Collaborative team learning, with texts as the focal point, presents opportunities to bring learners and texts together in response-centered classrooms. Group retellings, for example, underscore the value of having students read authentic texts which are conceptually related to one another (Wood, 1987).

The strategy is simple to enact. Students of varying ability work in groups of three or more. Each group member reads a different text on the same topic. One student may

---

Think while Reading Activity

Select an article from a current newspaper or magazine in the same field as your content area. Using this article, develop a short classroom activity that incorporates the concepts of response-centered classrooms and the ideas about read-alouds and group retellings. Bring your article to class with you.

_____

_____

_____

_____

_____

_____

_____

_____

_____

_____

_____

_____

Activity 24–3

choose to read a brochure; another, a news or magazine article; another, a chapter from an informational book. When the readers get together in teams to respond to what they are reading, each member shares what his or her text was about while the others in the group listen and at any point share additional information and insights into the topic based on their reading.

Wood (1987) uses an example of group retellings in a health class, where students engaged in the study of safety in the home. A group retelling team might include a student who reads a magazine article describing an eyewitness account of a home fire resulting from an electrical overload; a student who reads a brochure from the local fire department that outlines the precautions to take to avoid safety mishaps; a student who reads a newspaper editorial that warns parents against leaving their children unattended and unfamiliar with safety hazards in the home. As Wood explains, group retellings capitalize on the pleasure derived from sharing newly learned information with friends.

A variation on group retellings is to organize cooperative "expert" groups. These expert teams are responsible for inquiring into and developing expertise in a particular aspect of the subject under study. With the help of the librarian, the teacher puts together an array of informational texts to help students become experts on their topics. The expert teams decide how to investigate the topic and which texts and tasks each member is responsible for. The groups meet regularly to share what they are reading and to synthesize their findings into a group presentation.

Reading and Dialogue Journals

Guiding reader response through writing helps students to think broadly and deeply about a subject, personalizing the concepts through vibrant interactions with text. Readers need immediate opportunities to respond to a text, whether it is a selection from the textbook or related pieces of literature. Content area reading journals permit students to record personal reactions and opinions as they read or participate in class activities. The reading journal becomes the student's record of what he or she is feeling and thinking in response to the text, or aspects of the text. A variety of heuristic prompts may be initiated to help students speculate, make connections and discoveries, question, and reflect.

After reading a selection from Toni Morrison's novel, *Beloved,* and a selection from Julius Lester's nonfiction book, *To Be a Slave,* grade 8 students were invited to use their reading journal to record personal reactions to the institution of slavery as depicted in these books. Study the following entry from a student's learning log:

> The facts really don't tell the whole story. Until I read Sethe's rememory of the times at Sweet Home, I didn't believe things could have been that bad. The idea that mothers were afraid to love their children because they thought they might be taken away any day is painful. The slave narratives told the facts about buying and selling slaves, but the idea didn't seem real to me until Sethe tells her story.
>
> Reading about these torn apart families made me think a lot about how lucky my own family is to be together. Even though we fight sometimes, at least we know we'll be there, together, tomorrow.

Personal reactions such as this may be further molded by requiring students to cite an event or action that was "telling" to the reader, one that indicated a major change in plot or ideas, or an exact quote that helped the reader's understanding of the passage. In addition, reactions to the text might be further focused by asking students to draw parallels between the institution of slavery and historical events of the period. Each of these tasks needs to be accomplished during or immediately after reading. If comments and reactions are not immediately recorded, the immediacy of the reaction is lost by the time classroom discussion begins. By requiring immediate response, students are better prepared to enter a classroom discussion.

A variation on the reading journal is to use it as a source of dialogue about texts that students are reading. Personal reactions, questions, or opinions are recorded in a dialogue journal, which is then exchanged with another class member who reads the initial entry and then responds accordingly. When dialogue journals become a regular feature in a response-centered classroom, the journal becomes a true exchange of ideas between reading partners; the partners become aware of one another as readers, and fashion their journal entries for one another. The partner becomes an important part of the meaning-making process because the author of the journal entry is guaranteed to have an audience for her or his ideas. By this dialogue with a steady partner, students become aware of the opinions and reactions of another and are able to compare and contrast them with their own. The dialogue often lifts thought to a high level and causes students to delve more deeply into the text to validate an opinion or prove a point to the partner.

Reading and dialogue journals can be incorporated with the framework of thematic units of study. Thematic units provide a structure for bringing students and authentic texts together. Some teachers organize units within the framework of individual and group inquiry, which is another important feature in a response-centered learning environment.

Inquiry-Centered Thematic Units

Thematic units organize instruction around concepts to be studied, multiple sources of information, and authentic texts within the context of meaningful and relevant instructional activity. In middle and secondary grades, the unit theme usually has a strong topical focus. Used as a planning tool, the thematic unit includes a title reflecting the theme or topic; the concepts to be explored; the texts and information sources to be studied; instructional activities; and provisions for the evaluation of students' knowledge and understanding as a result of participating in the unit. Vacca and Vacca (1993) and Estes and Vaughan (1985) provide several examples of thematic units in different subject areas.

Although there is no one way to plan a thematic unit, an essential aspect of its organization is that both teacher and students have roles. Table 24–1 contrasts the role of the teacher and the role of students along several organizational dimensions of unit.

Inquiry is the backbone of a thematic unit. Individual or group investigation allows students to explore a variety of information sources and texts within the framework of the unit's objectives. Planning inquiry-centered learning experiences requires a certain kind of mind set and commitment on the part of the teacher. When students engage in inquiry, their final products may not conform to the teacher's expectations. They may be pleasant sur-

TABLE 24–1   Planning a Student-Centered Thematic Unit

	Role of the Teacher	Role of the Students
Organizing Content	Select thematic unit Identify key concepts Access students' prior knowledge	Share background knowledge and interests Develop awareness of the purpose and integrated nature of the thematic unit
Organizing Texts	Selection of texts and resources Provide multiple information sources Integrate a variety of literary genres	Share experiences from multiple information sources Articulate needs and interests Take ownership of unit
Organizing Activities	Select activities which support major concepts of thematic unit Give students an active role or voice	Critically read and respond to texts Engage in inquiry Construct personal meaning Become an active learner
Organizing Groups	Provide opportunities for individual, small and large group activities Model collaborative learning strategies	Develop independent learning strategies Collaborate for successful group experiences Become a viable part of a community of learners
Organizing an Evaluation Plan	Use alternative modes of assessment Model strategies and provide evaluation Encourage self-evaluation	Compile thematic unit portfolio for evaluation Conduct peer assessment Become self-evaluators

prises that uncover information and insights that are new even to the teacher. They also may be disappointing, dealing with questions that the teacher finds uninteresting. If, however, the goal of the unit is genuine inquiry, the teacher will judge that students have been successful as long as they have:

1. Made a thoughtful effort to identify and consider questions about the content area that are personally meaningful.
2. Explored a variety of information sources and chosen those that are appropriate to their purposes and abilities.
3. Interacted actively and effectively with print.
4. Selected, synthesized, and organized information that is relevant to their research questions.
5. Communicated information to their peers in ways that reflect care and enthusiasm for the material.

Although inquiry units place great emphasis on students making decisions about *what* and *how* they will learn, teachers cannot simply identify a broad area of study and turn students loose without guidance. Too little direction can be as detrimental to inquiry as too much because it leaves them floundering for a way to begin. Vacca and Vacca (1993) offer the following procedures for guiding inquiry:

I. Raise Questions, Identify Interests, Organize Information.
  A. Discuss interest areas related to the unit of study.
  B. Engage in goal setting.
    1. Arouse curiosities.
    2. Create awareness of present level of knowledge.
  C. Pose questions relating to each area and subarea.
    1. "What do you want to find out?"
    2. "What do you want to know about _____?"
    3. Record the questions or topics.
    4. "What do you already about _____?"
  D. Organize information; have students make predictions about likely answers to gaps in knowledge
    1. Accept all predictions as possible answers.
    2. Encourage thoughtful speculations in a nonthreatening way.
II. Select Materials.
  A. Use visual materials.
    1. Books and encyclopedias
    2. Magazines, catalogs, directories
    3. Newspapers and comics
    4. Indexes, atlases, almanacs, dictionaries, readers' guides, card catalog
    5. Films, filmstrips, slides
    6. Videotapes, television programs
  B. Use nonvisual materials.
    1. Audiotapes
    2. Records
    3. Radio programs
  C. Use human resources.
    1. Interviews
    2. Letters
    3. On-site visitations
  D. Encourage self-selection of materials.
    1. "What can I understand?"
    2. "What gives me the best answers?"
III. Guide the Information Search.
  A. Encourage active research through:
    1. Reading
    2. Listening
    3. Observing
    4. Talking
    5. Writing

    B. Facilitate with questions.
      1. "How are you doing?"
      2. "Can I help you?"
      3. "Do you have all the materials you need?"
      4. "Can I help you with ideas you don't understand?"
IV. Have Students Keep Records.
    A. Keep a learning log which includes plans, procedures, notes, rough drafts, etc.
    B. Keep book-record cards.
    C. Keep a record of conferences with the teacher.
V. Consider Different Forms of Writing.
    A. Initiate a discussion of sharing techniques.
    B. Encourage a variety of writing forms:
      1. An essay or paper
      2. A lecture to a specific audience
      3. A case study
      4. Story, adventure, science fiction, etc.
      5. Dialogue, conversation, interview
      6. Dramatization through scripts
      7. Commentary or editorial
      8. Thumbnail sketch
VI. Guide the Writing Process.
    A. Help students organize information.
    B. Guide first-draft writing.
    C. Encourage responding, revising, and rewriting.
    D. "Publish" finished products.
      1. Individual presentations
      2. Classroom arrangement
      3. Allow for class interaction

Inquiry can be carried out on an individual basis with students choosing their own topics and collecting information independently, or it can be done by small groups. Either way, it seems advisable to provide opportunities for students interactions. When students pursue questions that they themselves have selected, make decisions about the sources of information they will use, and choose the content and form they will use for making their findings public, they have a much greater personal stake in their learning. When students feel such ownership in a unit, they read with a sense of purpose and involvement that is a powerful aid to comprehension.

Conclusion

Teachers can greatly influence learning by the way in which they orchestrate response in the classroom. Access to a variety of authentic texts is an important characteristic of a response-centered learning environment. When teachers extend and enrich the curriculum with narrative and informational books, newspaper and magazine articles having to do with recent developments in their fields, and other real-world texts, they are demonstrating to students that reading is useful and valuable.

Think after Reading Activity

In your content area, choose a concept or idea you will be teaching. Think of various print resources you would use besides your textbook. List two below.

1. _____

2. _____

Using the same idea as above, find one work of children's literature that would complement your study. List the title and author and explain how you would use it in your class.

Book:
_____

Author:
_____

How Used:
_____
_____
_____
_____
_____
_____
_____
_____

Activity 24–4

A Cooperative Learning Approach to Content Area Teaching

ROBERT E. SLAVIN

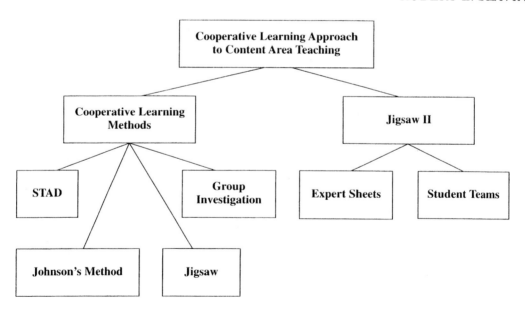

Think before Reading Activity

Think of a situation in which you were given a rigorous assignment. How would you feel if the instructor told you the work had to be completed on your own? Compare those feelings with the ones you might have if you were encouraged to work with a cooperative learning group? Use the Venn diagram below for your answer.

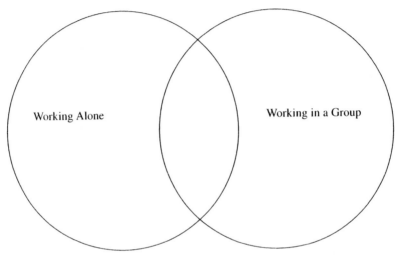

Working Alone

Working in a Group

Activity 25–1

This chapter presents a brief rationale and detailed description of a cooperative learning program called Jigsaw II, an adaptation of Elliot Aronson's Jigsaw model. In Jigsaw II students are assigned to four-member, mixed-ability learning teams. Each team member is given a topic on which to become an "expert." Students read text materials (for example, chapters in social studies texts) looking for information on their topic. They then discuss their topics with members of other teams who have the same topic (the "expert group") and then return to their teams to teach their teammates about their topics. Finally, all students are individually quizzed on material relative to all topics. Team scores are computed on the basis of members' quiz averages, and teams that meet certain preset criteria can earn certificates or other recognition. In addition to Jigsaw II, several Jigsaw variations are described.

Did you ever study with a friend and find that both of you learned better than when you studied alone? Did you ever explain or teach something to someone and then realize that you understood it better yourself? Did you ever find that another student could reexplain what your teacher had taught in a simpler, more comprehensive language? If you have had any of these experiences, then you already know the power of peer interaction to enhance learning. The principle that students' understanding can be increased by discussion among themselves has long been known, but how can this principle be applied in the classroom?

Over the past fifteen years, several researchers have developed and researched specific classroom methods based on the idea that students can be valuable learning resources for one another. These are generally called cooperative learning methods. In them, students work in small, mixed-ability learning groups to learn academic material. These methods can be used at all grade levels and exist in many forms. At the secondary level, some of the most widely used cooperative learning methods are as follows:

Student Teams-Achievement Divisions (STAD). In STAD (Slavin, 1994), the teacher presents a lesson on some topic, and then students work in four-member learning teams to master the material, usually by discussing concepts, drilling one another on worksheet items, or working problems separately, comparing answers, and discussing discrepancies. Following the team study time, students take individual quizzes, and teams may earn certificates based on the average of all team members' scores.

Johnsons' Methods. In cooperative learning methods developed by Johnson and Johnson (1994), students work together in small groups to come to consensus on group worksheets. Students' grades may depend in part on their groups' average scores on individual quizzes. Johnson and Johnson also describe methods for "cooperative controversy," in which students discuss controversial issues by arguing one side, then arguing the opposite side, and finally coming to a group consensus.

Group Investigation. This is a form of cooperative learning based on Dewey's project method in group investigation (Sharan & Sharan, 1992), a method in which students within groups of four to six members each take specific roles in learning about a topic of their choice, preparing a group report, and presenting the report to their classmates. A similar method, which emphasizes cooperation within as well as between small groups, is called Co-op–Co-op (Kagan, 1992).

Jigsaw. The cooperative learning method that is most appropriate for situations in which students must extract information from text is called jigsaw teaching, a program that was initially developed by Aronson and his colleagues (Aronson et al., 1978). The basic idea of jigsaw teaching is that each member of a mixed-ability learning group becomes an expert on one aspect of a topic the class is studying. The experts read information on their topics and then meet others who were assigned to the same topic. Then the experts return to their teams to take their turns teaching their teammates about their topics. An appealing feature of Jigsaw is that by giving each team member a unique area of expertise, students feel that they are making a valuable contribution to their teams, which is a way to enhance students' self-esteem.

Several forms of jigsaw teaching exist. One of the most practical and widely used forms is called Jigsaw II (Slavin, 1994). The principal advantage of Jigsaw II is that, whereas Aronson's original jigsaw teaching model requires extensive materials development, Jigsaw II uses existing textbooks and only requires creation of four topics and a brief quiz for each unit. Because of its practicality and applicability to reading in secondary content areas, Jigsaw II is described in this chapter in detail. However, the chapter also gives information on variations in the basic Jigsaw model.

The following material describing Jigsaw II and other forms of jigsaw teaching is adapted from Slavin (1994).

Jigsaw II Overview

Jigsaw II can be used whenever the material to be studied is in written narrative form. It is most appropriate in such subjects as social studies, literature, some parts of science, and related areas in which concepts rather than skills are the learning goals. The instructional raw material for Jigsaw II should usually be a chapter, story, biography, or similar narrative or descriptive material.

In Jigsaw II, students work in heterogeneous teams. The students are assigned chapters or other units to read, and are given *expert sheets,* which contain different topics for each team member to focus on when reading. When everyone has finished reading, students from different teams with the same topic meet in an *expert group* to discuss their topic for about thirty minutes. The experts then return to their teams and take turns teaching their teammates about their topics. Finally, students take quizzes that cover all the topics, and the quiz scores become team scores. (Figures 25–1 and 25–2 show an expert sheet on U.S. history and questions from a related quiz.) Students on high-scoring teams may receive certificates or be recognized in a newsletter or on a bulletin board. Thus, students are motivated to study the material well and to work hard in their expert groups so that they can help their teams do well. The key to Jigsaw is interdependence—every student depends on his or her teammates to provide the information he or she needs to do well on the quizzes.

**STUDENT TEAM LEARNING
SUBJECT: UNITED STATES HISTORY**

EXPERT SHEET 18: THE UNITED STATES BECOMES AN URBAN NATION

1. Why did immigrants come to America, what type of life did they face when they arrived, and how did they contribute, along with other factors, to the rapid growth of cities?
2. What were the advantages and disadvantages of boss rule in American cities?
3. Describe the life of a city dweller.
4. Discuss a typical strike, why it was started, what were its consequences, and how it was settled.

For Discussion: Many people now are calling for restrictions on immigration. What reasons do they give for such a step? How do they compare with the arguments made in favor of similar measures in the late-nineteenth and early-twentieth centuries? Imagine restrictions had been placed on immigration immediately after the Civil War. How do you think that the future history of the United States would have been different?

FIGURE 25–1 Jigsaw Expert Sheet

Think while Reading Activity

Create an Expert Sheet for "Preparing to Use Jigsaw II."

Expert Sheet for "Preparing to Use Jigsaw II"

To Read:

_____

_____

_____

_____

Topics:

1. _____

2. _____

3. _____

4. _____

Activity 25–2

Selected questions from Quiz 18: The United States Becomes an Urban Nation

1. All the following contributed to the growth of American cities in the late 1800s except
   a. the number of jobs available in the cities.
   b. migration of people from rural areas.
   c. immigration.
   d. the higher living standards enjoyed by most city dwellers.

2. The "new" immigrants came to the United States from
   a. southern and eastern Europe.
   b. China and Japan.
   c. West Africa.
   d. Latin America.

3. Political "bosses" were interested in
   a. reforming city government.
   b. power and money.
   c. running the city properly.
   d. expanding the city's legal powers.

Essay Question: What was life like in the cities of late-nineteenth-century America?

FIGURE 25–2   Jigsaw Quiz Questions

Preparing to Use Jigsaw II

To prepare for Jigsaw II follow the steps described below.

Select the Reading

Select several chapters, stories, or other units, each covering material for a two-to-three-day unit. If students are to read in class, the selections should not require more than a half-hour to complete; if the reading is to be assigned for homework, the selections can be longer.

Prepare Expert Sheets

Make an expert sheet for each unit. This tells students what to concentrate on while they read and which expert group they will work with. It identifies four topics that are central to the unit. For example, an expert sheet for a unit on the Blackfoot Indian tribes might be as follows:

Expert Sheet

The Blackfoot
To read: Pages 3–9 and 11–12
Topics:

1. How were Blackfoot men expected to act?
2. What is a group and what does it do? What are the most important groups for the Blackfoot?
3. What did Blackfoot bands and clubs do?
4. What were the Blackfoot customs and traditions?

As much as possible, the topics should cover themes that appear throughout the chapter instead of issues that appear only once. Give each student a copy of the expert sheet or put it on the chalk board or poster board.

Prepare Quizzes

Make a quiz for each unit. The quiz should consist of at least eight questions, two for each topic. The questions should require considerable understanding, because students will have had ample time to discuss their topics in depth, and easy questions should focus on main concepts, not on small details. In the Blackfoot example, the first two questions might be as follows:

Which of the following was not an expected way of behaving for a Blackfoot man?
a. He was expected to be brave.
b. He was expected to brag about how many of the enemy tribe he had touched.

> **c.** He was expected to clean buffalo meat.
> **d.** He was expected to share buffalo meat.

What are norms of behavior?

> **a.** All the ways of acting that people in a group have
> **b.** The ways people in a group are expected to act
> **c.** Records of great deeds
> **d.** Sharing food with the very old

All students must answer all questions. The quiz should take no more than ten minutes. Teachers may wish to use an activity other than a quiz or in addition to a quiz as an opportunity for team members to show their learning, for example, an oral report, a written report, or a crafts project.

Prepare Discussion Outlines

Discussion outlines are optional. A discussion outline for each topic can help guide the discussions in the expert groups. It should list the points that students should consider in discussing their topics. For example, a discussion outline for a topic relating to the settlement of the English colonies in America might be as follows:

> Topic: What role did religious ideals play in the establishment of settlements in America?

> *Discussion Outline*

> **1.** Puritan beliefs and religious practices
> **2.** Puritan treatment of dissenters
> **3.** Founding of Connecticut and Rhode Island
> **4.** Quakers and the establishment of Pennsylvania
> **5.** Catholics and religious toleration in Maryland

Assigning Students to Teams

A team in Jigsaw II is a group of four or five students who represent a cross section of the class in past performance, race or ethnicity, and sex. Students are assigned to teams by the teacher, rather than by choosing teams themselves, because students tend to choose others like themselves. Follow these steps:

Make Copies of Team Summary Sheets
Before you begin to assign students to teams, you will need to make one copy of a team summary sheet (see Figure 25–3) for every four students in your class.

Rank Students
On a sheet of paper, rank the students in your class from highest to lowest in past performance. Use whatever information you have to do this; test scores are best, grades are good, but your own judgment is fine.

Team Summary Sheet

TEAM NAME _____

Team Members	1	2	3	4	5	6	7	8	9	10	11	12	13	14
Total Team Score														
Team Average														
Team Award														

FIGURE 25–3 Jigsaw Team Summary Sheet

Assign Students to Teams

Each team should have four members if possible. When you are assigning students to teams, balance the teams so that (1) each team is composed of students whose performance levels range from low to average to high and (2) the average performance level of all the teams in the class is about equal. Divide your ranked list into four quarters and assign one student from each quarter to each team, with average-achieving students added as fifth members if necessary (see Slavin, 1994). If the teams you have made based on performance ranking are not evenly divided on both ethnicity and sex (they will hardly ever be balanced on the first try), you should change team assignments by trading students of the same approximate performance level, but of different ethnicity or sex, among teams until a balance is achieved.

Think while Reading Activity

Think of a unit in which you think Jigsaw II would be useful. Prepare a beginning for the Jigsaw II activity by completing the following:

Unit Topic:
_____

Expert Sheet:
_____

To Read:
_____
_____
_____

Topics:

1. _____
_____
_____

2. _____
_____
_____

3. _____
_____
_____

4. _____
_____
_____

Activity 25–3

Fill Out Team Summary Sheets

After you have finished assigning all students to teams, fill in the names of the students on each team on your team summary sheets, but leave the team name blank until the students decide what their team name will be.

Assigning Students to Expert Groups

Whereas team assignments should remain stable for about six weeks, expert group assignments may be changed for every Jigsaw II unit. You may wish to assign students to expert groups randomly, by simply distributing roles at random within each team. Alternatively, you may wish to decide in advance which students will go to each expert group, forming the expert groups to ensure that there are high, average, and low achievers in each. If your class has more than twenty-four students, you should have two expert groups on each topic so that there will not be more then six students in each expert group. The reason for this is that an expert group larger than six can be unwieldy.

Jigsaw II Schedule of Activities

Jigsaw II consists of a regular cycle of instructional activities, as follows:

Reading: Students receive expert topics and read assigned material to locate information.

Expert group discussion: Students with the same expert topics meet to discuss them in expert groups.

Team report: Experts return to their teams to teach their topics to their teammates.

Test: Students take individual quizzes covering all topics.

Team scores and recognition: Team scores are computed, and teams that meet preestablished criteria receive certificates or other recognition.

Reading

Time: One-half to one class period (or assign for homework).

The first activity in Jigsaw II is distribution of texts and expert topics, assignment of topics to individual students, and then reading. Pass out expert sheets, and then assign students to take each topic (go to each team and point out students for each one). If any team has five members, have two students take topic 1 together. Assignments to expert groups may be random or may be prepared in advance. (If they are prepared in advance, try to make sure that each expert group has high, average, and low readers.)

When students have their topics, let them read their materials. Alternatively, the reading may be assigned as homework. Students who finish reading before others can make notes.

Expert Group Discussions

Time: One-half class period.

Have all students with expert topic 1 get together at one table, all students with expert topic 2 at another, and so on. If any expert group has more than six students (that is, if the class has more than twenty-four students), split the expert group into two smaller groups. If students are to use a discussion outline, distribute it to them in each expert group.

Appoint a *discussion leader* for each group. The discussion leader need not be a particularly able student, and all students should have an opportunity to be discussion leader at some time. The leader's job is to moderate the discussion, calling on group members who raise their hands and trying to see that everyone participates.

Give the expert groups about twenty minutes to discuss their topics. Students should try to locate information on their topics in their texts and share the information with the group. Group members should take notes on all points discussed.

While the expert groups are working, the teacher should circulate through the class, spending time with each group in turn. Teachers may wish to answer questions and resolve misunderstandings, but they should not try to take over leadership of the groups; that is the discussion leaders' responsibility. They may need to remind discussion leaders that part of the job is to see that everyone participates.

Team Report

Time: One-half class period.

Experts should return to their teams to teach their topics to their teammates. They should take about five minutes to review everything they have learned about the topics from their reading and their discussions in the expert groups. If two students on any team shared topic 1, they should make a joint presentation.

Emphasize to students that they have a responsibility to their teammates to be good teachers as well as good listeners. You may wish to have experts quiz their teammates after they make their team reports to see that they have learned the material and are ready for the quiz.

Test

Time: One-half class period.

Distribute the quizzes and give students adequate time to finish. Have students exchange quizzes with members of other teams for scoring, or collect the quizzes for teacher scoring. If students do the scoring, have the checkers put their names at the bottom of the quizzes they checked, and spot-check several quizzes after class to be sure that the students did a good job of checking.

Team Scores and Team Recognition

To figure team scores, put each student's quiz scores (percent correct) on the appropriate team summary sheet and divide by the number of team members who were present, rounding off any fractions. (See Figure 25–4.)

Team Summary Sheet

TEAM NAME _Fantastic Four_

Team Members	1	2	3	4	5	6	7	8	9	10	11	12	13	14
Jim	92													
Ilene	83													
Gary	92													
Susan	100													
Total Team Score	367													
Team Average	92													
Team Award	*Jayce F. Logan*													

FIGURE 25–4 Example of Team Scoring

Two levels of awards are given based on average team scores. Teams achieving scores of 80 percent receive a Great Team award, and those scoring 90 percent receive a Super Team award. Note that all teams can achieve the awards; teams are not in competition with one another. If all teams are consistently failing to make Great Team, or if all are consistently making Super Team, you may adjust the suggested criteria.

You should provide some sort of recognition or reward for achieving the Great Team or Super Team level. Attractive certificates to each team member may be used, with a large, fancy certificate for Super Teams and a smaller one for Great Teams. Many teachers make bulletin board displays listing the week's Super Teams and Great Teams or displaying Polaroid pictures of the successful teams. Others prepare one-page newsletters or give students special buttons to wear. Some teachers give Super Teams a homework pass, or include team scores as a small part of students' grades. Use your imagination and creativity, and vary the rewards from time to time; it is more important that *you* are excited about students' accomplishments than that you give large rewards.

Students' grades should be computed primarily based on their individual quiz scores, not on their team scores. However, some secondary teachers will give students up to five bonus points on their grades based on team success. For example, you might give five bonus points (on a hundred point scale) for being on a Super Team, three for being on a Great Team. This way, team scores can increase a student's grade but not decrease it; if you allowed team scores to diminish grades, some students would see this as unfair, because they happened to be on a team with low achievers or unmotivated teammates.

Think after Reading Activity

Imagine that you are ready to leave school for the day and a student's parent walks into your room requesting to talk with you. How would you respond to these comments: "When I was in school I learned on my own, sitting quietly and not working with any other students. It was fine for me. I graduated in the top 10 percent of my class and went to a great college. I have a terrific job. The old way worked for me. It is tried and true. Why are you using this Jigsaw technique?"

_____

_____

_____

_____

_____

_____

_____

_____

_____

_____

Activity 25–4

Other Ways of Using Jigsaw

Jigsaw is one of the most flexible of all cooperative learning methods. Several modifications can be made that keep the basic model but change the details of implementation. Instead of having the topics refer to narrative materials given to students, have students search a set of classroom or library materials to find information on their topics. Have students write essays or give oral reports instead of taking quizzes after completing the experts' reports. Instead of having all teams study the same material, give each team a unique topic to learn together and each team member subtopics. The team could then prepare and make an oral presentation to the entire class. Methods similar to this are described by Kagan (1992) and Sharan and Sharan (1992).

For more on original Jigsaw, see Aronson and others, 1978. For other Jigsaw modifications, see Kagan (1992). For information on other forms of cooperative learning, see Slavin (1994).

Chapter **26**

Assessment in the Content Areas
Solving the Assessment Puzzle

ROGER FARR   ROBERT PRITCHARD

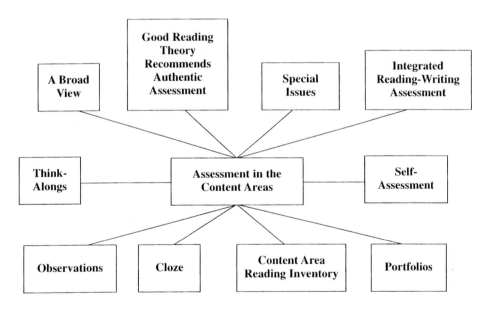

Think before Reading Activity

In high school you took the SAT to get into college. There's the GRE for graduate school, the MCAT for medical school, and the LSAT for law school.

Do you think that standardized tests and chapter and unit tests are the most appropriate ways to assess you as a student? Can other types of assessment give teachers the information needed to assess you? Reflect on this and write your answer below.

_____

_____

_____

_____

_____

_____

_____

Activity 26–1

Reading assessment has become a genuine puzzle in the content areas. Confusion and debate continue regarding the goals for school reading assessment and about the kinds of assessments needed to achieve those goals. The major cause of the confusion is a lack of clarity of the purposes and audiences to be served by assessment. Any consideration of the assessments to be used should focus on the purposes for assessment,—and whether current tests achieve those purposes.

Content area teachers need specific information to plan instruction. Their students need to be involved in self-assessment that helps them understand their own literacy development. Decision makers need information as to whether students can do the kinds of reading, writing and thinking they need to do to cope with the demands of effective citizenship.

The Assessment Puzzle

Reading assessment in the content areas needs to be considered in the context of the total assessment program in a school. Improving assessment in the content areas is dependent on understanding how formal and informal assessment fits together. Those who wish to improve assessment in the content areas must become involved in the planning and focus for the total school assessment program. At the very least, there must be an understanding of the school district assessment program and the different audiences served by that program. Therefore, this chapter will begin with a brief overview of some of the causes of the assessment puzzle now faced by most schools and by content area teachers in those schools.

Criticism of Schools Led to More High-Stakes Assessments

Public disappointment with high school students' reading achievement led to extensive criticism of schools. The conviction that many students were receiving high school diplomas and yet were almost totally illiterate became firmly established in the public's mind (Purves, 1984). The Peter Doe case in California exemplified that concern (Saretsky, 1973). The case concerned a high school student who sued the school district for graduating him without teaching him to read. As a result of this kind of dissatisfaction with educational outcomes, the use of standardized, norm-referenced assessment intensified, and state minimum competency testing programs proliferated (Madaus, 1985; Salmon-Cox, 1981).

The Search for Alternative Assessments Has Lead to More Assessment

Besides dissatisfaction with the schools, there has been a quest for assessments that are closely aligned with more holistic views of language development. Some curriculum theorists concerned with the mismatch between curriculum and assessment have determined that if curriculum is to change, the reading tests must change. This has caused a proliferation of new assessments—both formal and informal (Brown, 1986; Burstall, 1986; Priestley, 1982; Stiggins, Conklin, & Bridgeford, 1986).

Included in this mix have been modifications of conventional tests with new item formats and the addition of the assessment of behaviors not often included on traditional tests. These new variables include assessments of background knowledge, student interests and attitudes, and metacognition. Other assessments in reading have taken an entirely different approach to assessment relying entirely on student work samples collected in portfolios (Jongsma, 1989; Valencia, 1990; Wolf, 1989). Portfolios have themselves taken many different forms. There are show portfolios, which include only a few carefully selected samples, and working portfolios, which include a broad sample of work and which are used to guide and organize daily instruction. In addition, numerous professional publications have published articles calling for the use of a broader range of teacher observations and informal assessment techniques (Cambourne & Turbil, 1990; Goodman, 1991).

Different Audiences Need Different Information

We need to understand that tests have only one general purpose. Tests should be considered as nothing more than attempts to systematically gather information. The information is used to help children learn about their own literacy development and to give teachers and others concerned with students' literacy the information they need for curriculum planning. The outcome in selecting and using any assessment should be whether it helps students. There are, of course, different groups that need this information.

The public. Members of the general public, who make decisions through their elected officials, including school boards, have a vested interest in the future of children and in their effective and cost-efficient instruction. It is recognized as vital to everyone's and the nation's future that schools are producing educated students.

Administrators. Ideally school administrators would rely most heavily on performance assessments that are criterion-referenced. These performance measures should compare student performance with a clearly defined curriculum. However, because we live in a complex world where mobility and diversity are the reality, administrators also need norm-referenced comparisons of their students' performance.

Parents. Although parents share the public's interests, they have a vested interest in their own individual children. To monitor their child's progress and to be active in his or her education, parents want criterion-referenced reports. Additionally, parents are also typically interested in how their children perform on normed tests in comparison to children from across the country.

Teachers. A teacher's primary concern is helping students learn. Although they are necessarily aware of normed assessment's comparative reports as a kind of outcome accountability, they are primarily interested in the kind of information that will support the daily instructional decisions they need to make. This kind of information has been generated by criterion-referenced tests and by other types of assessment that can be used more effectively in the classroom as a part of instruction.

Students. Students need to become good self-assessors if they are to improve their literacy skills. They need to select, review, and think about the reading and writing they are doing. They need to be able to revise their own writing and to revise their comprehension as they read. If students understand their own needs, they will improve. Students should be the primary assessors of their own literacy development.

Good Reading Theory Recommends Authentic Performance Assessment

Most published tests have not adequately responded to emerging reading theory that explains reading comprehension as a meaning-constructing process. Many of these tests are still based on the assumption that they can be used to identify specific subskills. The following alternatives to these tests are more consistent with current reading theory.

Authentic assessment. Relatively wide acceptance of a constructivist, context-specific definition of reading has promoted a careful analysis of current reading and language arts tests. The analysis has been focused on determining if the tests match what is known about reading comprehension. It has led to the conclusion that the reading required on most tests is not much like the reading behavior that our new understanding describes.

Performance assessment. Attention to authenticity has accompanied and helped generate the development and use of performance assessment. A student's language behaviors need to be assessed, it is contended, as they are used in real-life situations. Reading performance assessment must look at the reading act in progress or judge comprehension of a text as it is applied in some realistic way.

Observation. Observation is one way to do this and can lead teachers to meaningful insights about the progress and needs of individual students. Yet teachers need to be trained about what they can look for and what those signs suggest. They need to develop useful ways to make discrete notes about observations and to synthesize what they find. Observation generates many details in relatively random order, and they seldom become clearly useful until they are gathered into patterns that can direct instruction.

Portfolios. Another highly valuable form of performance assessment is the portfolio. For these collections, students and teachers select numerous samples from drafts and final versions of various kinds of a student's writing. The idea is to demonstrate the student's progress and development in the combined process of reading, thinking, and writing.

Integrated assessment. Assessments in which thinking, reading, and writing are integrated have been developed in recent years. Such assessments have been developed by classroom teachers, school districts, and publishers in an attempt to integrate reading and writing and to assess reading and writing with more realistic activities. These vary widely, but for most of them the student is given a writing task related to a text that is supplied. The task has been deemed to be authentic because it is typical of something the student might do in real life, including the kinds of activities often used for learning in the classroom.

For example, one such test asks students to read a nonfiction article that categorically discusses and describes how insect-eating plants lure, capture, and digest their victims. The task is to write a fictional piece telling what a mother bug might say to her children in cautioning them about these plants. Teachers use what the students write to assess students' understanding of the text. They rate other integrated behaviors as well, such as the student's organization and application of the text's content to the task and factors related to writing.

Such reading and writing assessments encourage students to develop a variety of responses based on their interpretation of the reading selection, their background knowledge, and the direction they choose to take in constructing a realistic response. These kinds of performance assessments provide teachers with valuable insights regarding a student's ability to read, write, and construct a meaningful response to an interesting task. Prewriting notes, first drafts, and teacher observation notes all make the assessment a valuable source of information.

In addition, the final drafts can be scored to serve as information that can help determine accountability. The responses can be scored following a rubric, a list of criteria that describes several levels of performance in each of the categories to be analyzed. Samples of actual student papers ("anchors") that represent each score level described by the rubrics can also be used in scoring. Thus these tests are criterion-referenced.

Special Issues in the Content Areas Focus Assessment

The information that content area teachers need to know about students' reading abilities is largely determined by two factors. The first is that students vary greatly in the extent to which they are prepared to read the printed materials encountered in most content area classrooms. The second is that there are characteristics unique to content area materials that require applications of reading skills that make direct instructional assistance necessary.

The most important of the unique characteristics of content area materials is that they are primarily expository rather than narrative. As such, they are written to inform and are mainly concerned with the presentation of factual material. Besides the presence of technical and specialized vocabulary, most contain format and organizational features not found in other materials, particularly those used during developmental reading instruction (Herber, 1978).

From these two factors emerge at least seven areas or categories of information that content area teachers need to know about their students and that they should consider when planning for instruction. These include: (1) students' ability to perform the kinds of integrated reading and writing tasks that make up much of learning in the content areas, (2) students' interests and attitudes, (3) the reading strategies that students employ when they attempt to understand and apply content area reading, (4) students' background knowledge of the subject area, (5) students' instructional reading levels, (6) the extent to which particular materials are appropriate for student use, and (7) students' skill with study techniques.

These seven areas are the ones with which content area teachers need to be most immediately concerned, although the exact informational needs will vary as a function of subject area, grade level, teaching and learning styles, curricula, and the particular printed materials in use. The remainder of this chapter describes informal techniques of gathering this information. Some of the procedures have only recently begun to be used in content area classes. Others have been used for many years. All of them are based on a model of assessment which suggests that a variety of ways of looking at reading achievement is always more valid. Hence, all of these techniques are consistent with the assessment principles discussed above.

Think while Reading Activity

As you read "Integrated Reading and Writing Assessments," select three purposes for assessment in the content area you will teach. List those below and for each one name an assessment you would use to measure student learning and growth.

1. _____

_____

_____

2. _____

_____

_____

3. _____

_____

_____

Activity 26–2

Integrated Reading and Writing Assessments

Most of the important activities that students engage in while working in content areas involve the effective use of reading and writing to accomplish specific tasks. The class-room teacher needs to develop integrated reading and writing activities that determine if students can accomplish these kinds of tasks. The assessments should, in fact, be examples of the kind of instruction that has been carried out. This kind of performance assessment should be based on the following criteria:

1. The activities should ask the students to write to a specific audience and for a specific reason.
2. A variety of text genres should be used (as long as they relate to the focus of the reading activity). Such text genres may include maps, diagrams, fiction, and nonfiction selections.
3. The texts used for the assessment should cut across content areas.
4. The purpose for writing should give the students some direction for the activity, but it should be written in such a way that students will provide their own perspective on the problem.

An example of such an integrated reading and writing assessment follows:

The Task

The students read a problem statement that tells of a situation being faced by the California Water Commision. The Commission has several options they can follow regarding the distribution and conservation of water, but they are not sure what to do. They are asking high school students to suggest solutions to the problem.

The Reading Materials

Students are provided with three reading selections. One is an article from a popular news magazine that discusses the California water problem. It provides some charts and graphs about water use and population growth. Another reading source given to the students is an article from an encyclopedia. The article describes various water problems, solutions to improving water conservation and distribution, and facts about water. Another reading selection is from a scientific journal.

The Activity

The task is explained and discussed with students. They are told that it is a test, and they are also told that this is the kind of real task they will face in a variety of jobs and life. They are told that there is no single solution. They are told they can use the reading selections to help them develop a suggestion that they are to write to the California Water Commission.

The assessment is untimed. Some teachers provide prewriting suggestions to help students get started. Students are encouraged to take notes, develop a first draft, review their draft, revise, and produce a final draft. If collaboration is a goal of instruction, it should be a part of this assessment activity. In a like manner, if students use dictionaries as a normal part of their class writing activities, then dictionary use should be allowed during the test. These kinds of performance tests should model your classroom instruction. They should also provide as realistic an activity as can be provided within a typical classroom.

The integrated reading and writing activities described above are designed to determine:

1. How well students can read and understand the variety of content area text material they will have to read to solve real problems.
2. How well students can organize and focus their writing on a specific purpose.
3. How well students can focus on a specific audience to accomplish a specific purpose.

Scoring the Students' Final Drafts

The performance assessments described above can be evaluated by teachers to determine how well the students read and understand the content area selections; how well they organize and write about the topic; and how well they understand the task and are able to accomplish a specific task. The scoring should follow general criteria such as these:

Reading	The response indicates the student read well because the writing reveals:
	• a reasonable understanding of the writing task and accompanying reading selections
	• the selection and use of relevant reading selection information
	• an appropriate interpretation of the reading selection information
Writing	The response indicates the student wrote effectively because the writing reveals:
	• clear and effective word choice
	• effectual use of a variety of sentence structures
	• few or no mechanical errors that interfered with meaning
Task Accomplishment	The response indicates the student accomplished the task effectively because the writing reveals:
	• an effective organization that demonstrates a clear understanding of the audience and the purpose for writing
	• a paper in which the main points are effectively presented and supporting details are provided

You may want to develop a three or four point scale for each of the three dimensions listed above. You could rate responses as one, two, or three for each dimension (reading, writing, and accomplishment of task). Of course, you may want to modify the criteria for each of these dimensions. However, whatever criteria you develop should reflect what you feel is important and what you are trying to accomplish with your students. In addition, it is important for students to be aware of the criteria by which their responses will be judged.

Although the evaluation of the final drafts is an important and useful aspect of using integrated reading and writing prompts, the activities also have much value when they are added to a portfolio and discussed with students. The students' prewriting notes, first drafts, and final drafts should all be added to their portfolios. These materials will be very helpful when you discuss with the students the various work samples.

Self-Assessment

Asking students direct questions is one of the more valid methods of gathering information about their reading abilities. The most common type of self-assessment technique is the interview, during which teachers engage individuals or small groups of students in discussions carefully crafted to direct conversations toward perceptions of reading strengths, weaknesses, likes and dislikes. Because interview techniques can be time consuming, content area teachers may find it more advantageous to solicit student perceptions of their own reading through some type of written instrument. Most often, instruments of this nature incorporate some form of written record such as a log, journal, or checklist of interests and habits (Wixson, Bosky, Yochum, & Alvermann, 1984).

Self-assessment techniques are primarily used for gathering information about attitudes and interests, but they can be used for other purposes as well. One of the most promising for content area teachers is a method in which students are asked to demonstrate how they might go about course-related tasks or reading assignments. For example, students might be asked to describe the steps they would follow to solve a word problem. This allows the teachers to evaluate the processes students use in comprehending material or the manner in which ideas are organized as assignments are completed.

Think-Alongs

Another technique for gaining insight into student processing behavior is the think-along, an oral or written representation of a reader's process of constructing meaning from, or in relation to, text (Farr, 1990). When used for assessment purposes, think-alongs provide teachers with important information regarding how students think and the strategies they use when they attempt to understand and apply content area reading. By opening a window into processing behavior and enabling teachers to observe the cognitive operations involved in constructing meaning, think-alongs can help teachers find meaningful ways to integrate instruction and assessment.

Think-alongs require students to describe what they are doing and thinking while reading. If the think-along is done orally, students record their thoughts on audiotape. An oral think-along tells the teacher if students are familiar with particular strategies, if they recognize when they are useful, and how well the strategies can be employed; it is usually collected individually and, therefore, may not be a practical alternative in some situations. Written think-alongs provide more flexibility because readers record their thoughts in a prescribed or semiprescribed manner on a teacher-prepared guide sheet. This approach enables the teacher to involve groups of students in the process simultaneously.

In addition to choosing the most appropriate means of collecting the think-along data, teachers must consider other factors as they prepare to use think-alongs in their classes. The reading materials used for think-alongs need to be of sufficient difficulty and length to bring processing behavior to the surface. If the material is not challenging enough, processing of the text occurs at a subconscious level and as a result will not be accessible to the reader. If the material is too short, students will not have the opportunity to get into the text and therefore will have little or no strategic activity to report. In general, reading passages should be at the student's instructional reading level and should be at least 200–250 words in length.

Think-alongs work best when they have first been modeled by the teacher. For example, after first discussing a purpose for reading, the teacher reads a book, article, or other text aloud to the students. As the teacher does this, she or he interjects, in a stream-of-consciousness fashion, thoughts about the text and the task of comprehending it. The running comments might cover predictions about what might happen, portions of the text which are unclear, experiences from the reader's background that the text is triggering, or anything else relevant to the reading that crosses the teacher's mind, with particular emphasis on reading and thinking strategies.

The insights think-alongs provide are crucial at a time when research indicates (Vacca & Vacca, 1989) that too many content area teachers are guilty of assumptive teaching; that is, they tell students what to do without showing them how to do it. This tendency to assume that students already have the skills and know the concepts teachers are supposed to teach leads to frustration and passivity on the part of students. In contrast, think-alongs enable students to become more active and reflective readers and learners while providing teachers with a valid and viable basis for making instructional decisions.

Observations

Observations of student performance are among the most natural, subtle, and least threatening of all informal assessment techniques. Observations allow teachers to monitor either individuals or small groups of students, and virtually all types of classroom activity can be observed, from daily work samples to unique or periodic activities. For instance, as students are working on a task, the teacher can circulate throughout the classroom, unobtrusively noting student performance and trying to detect patterns of behavior which may indicate that a problem exists. If the teacher desires, these findings can be recorded on an observation checklist when collected or in a teacher journal when time permits. In either case, the teacher will have a record which, when used in conjunction with the information yielded by other assessment techniques, can be the basis for sound instructional decision making.

Of the data yielded by this technique, those with the greatest applications to the instructional decisions typical in a content area classroom are (1) determining effective prereading strategies, (2) identifying word-recognition skills students use most or least effectively when they encounter specialized or unfamiliar vocabulary, (3) assessing students' abilities to use locational or reference skills, and (4) observing oral reading (Early & Sawyer, 1984). Thus, observations are useful not only for general screening or the identification of students with gross reading strengths and weaknesses, but they also allow teachers to monitor identified skills and to gather specific information about student performance.

Observation can be a valid assessment technique when the settings in which it occurs simulate as closely as possible authentic situations. Obviously, the classroom provides an authentic setting for the observation of student reading behaviors. Consequently, content area teachers who engage in carefully controlled or structured observations can reduce the likelihood that extraneous factors or behaviors are synthesized into their assessments of student performance.

Informal Reading Inventory

The purpose of an informal reading inventory (IRI) is to estimate students' independent, instructional, and frustration reading levels and to determine if materials are appropriate for student use. An IRI consists of a series of sequential reading selections, graded in difficulty, which students read and about which they answer questions. Traditionally, IRIs are comprised of both oral and silent reading passages, one each at succeeding levels of difficulty. Of greater value to content area teachers, however, would be a modified IRI, in which only silent reading passages are given to students. What content area teachers sacrifice in the more diagnostic oral reading portion of this instrument, they gain in the validity and reliability of a modified IRI and in its appropriateness for making instructional decisions; passages used for silent reading can be selected from the textbooks and other materials used in the content area classroom. Thus, student performance will yield estimates not of general reading ability, but of students' ability to read and understand those materials which will actually be used for instruction.

Generally, modified IRIs contain graded passages between 1,500–3,000 words in length, which have been selected so that complete thought units and paragraphs are retained. If passages are selected from content area textbooks, as is recommended, then the passage should be representative of the textbook. Teachers may find it advantageous to select more than a single passage and to choose one from the beginning, middle, and end of the textbook. If an estimate of instructional reading level is sought as an initial screening device, however, then passages from the beginning of the textbook, or passages which are typical of the total text, should suffice. The following, abbreviated version of an IRI was developed from a science textbook, although the specific questions used would obviously vary from teacher to teacher and subject to subject.

Volcanoes

1. On what page would you find the chapter entitled "Volcanoes"?
   [locate appropriate page in Table of Contents]
2. What part of the book would you use to find pages on which the word "magma" is located?
   [index]
3. Which part of the card catalog would you use to find information about volcanoes?
   [subject index]
4. What does the word "molten" mean?
   [melted]
5. What causes a volcano to erupt?
   [gas pressure building up deep within the earth]

Recommended criteria for interpreting student performance on comprehension questions vary slightly, although a score of approximately 90 percent or better is generally acknowledged to indicate ability to read the material independently; 70–90 percent correct is generally considered to be indicative of an appropriate instructional level; and scores below 69 percent represent the frustration level (Estes & Vaughn, 1985). Thus, for the preceding example, the teacher would check the students' responses, calculate the percentage of correct answers, and determine at which level each student was reading the material tested. This information would provide the teacher with insight into the relative strengths and weaknesses of each student vis-a-vis the textbook from which the passage was selected and as a result could be used as the basis for instructional decisions such as the provision of alternative reading materials.

Cloze Procedure

The purpose of the cloze procedure is to determine the extent to which particular materials are appropriate for student use. The cloze procedure consists of the systematic deletion of words from selected passages of text. Based on the psychological principle of closure, which is the human tendency to complete an unfinished pattern or sequence and recognize it as a meaningful whole, this procedure can assess the ability of students to process the language of a reading selection, construct meaning from that selection, and make connections between ideas encountered in content area materials. Ability to supply a word where one had been deleted is an indication of how familiar the reader is with the language and content of a passage, and is also a measure of how closely the language and background knowledge of the author and reader are synchronized (Taylor, 1953).

Cloze tests typically are constructed using a passage selected from the textbook or other materials students will be expected to read during content area instruction. It is generally recommended that a 250–300 word passage containing complete thought units or paragraphs be selected, and that passages from the front of a textbook be used because later passages are likely to be laden with concepts built on previously read material. In addition, while no absolute guidelines exist, content area teachers usually delete every fifth word when preparing the test. However, the first and last sentences of the selection should be left intact to preserve its coherence. This results in a total of approximately fifty deletions or blank spaces. Finally, no time limit should be imposed upon student completion of the task, and because some students may be unfamiliar with the cloze format, practice should be provided with a sample passage before the procedure is employed as an assessment technique.

The following is a model of a cloze test which content area teachers can use when constructing their assessment instrument.

Poisonous Snakes in the United States

A great many people are afraid of snakes and think that any snake should be killed on sight. Actually most _____ are harmless, and some _____ do a lot of _____ by eating such animals _____ field mice and rats. _____ are, however, some poisonous _____, and some are very _____ indeed. About 10,000 people _____ each year in India _____ from the bites of _____ snakes, and thousands more _____ in other tropical regions.

Students should be required to generate the *exact* word that has been deleted for each blank space encountered in a cloze passage, even though the selection of an appropriate synonym indicates that the student is concentrating on meaning and is using context clues effectively. The rationale for requiring an exact word is threefold. First, the absolute objectivity inherent in using only exact words stabilizes the criterion scores used in interpreting results. In other words, if synonyms were accepted, we would not be able to use the scoring criteria explained below. Second, when the purpose of this procedure is to distinguish those students who can successfully read content area materials from those who cannot, no advantage is gained by accepting synonyms. If we did, everyone would simply have a higher score. Third, synonyms are difficult to evaluate, making the scoring process longer and more tedious.

A number of modifications to the cloze procedure exists. Roe, Stoodt, and Burns (1990) suggest that because of the concept density and technical vocabulary of many content area materials, teachers may at times delete every tenth (rather than every fifth) word. Less frequent deletions provide readers with more context clues, thus simplifying the task. As a vocabulary development technique, Rubin (1992) advocates leaving out specified words, such as key words in a passage, rather than every "nth" word. Richardson and Morgan (1990) argue that accepting synonyms is appropriate if the cloze procedure is being used for instructional rather than readability purposes. Jacobson (1990) suggests allowing students to complete a cloze passage twice, first individually and then in a small group. Cunningham and Cunningham (1978) describe a variation called the "limited cloze procedure", in which students are provided a list of words arranged alphabetically from which they choose the word considered most appropriate for each deleted word in the text.

Guthrie, Seifert, Burham, and Caplan (1974) developed the "maze" procedure, in which students choose from among three alternatives provided for each deleted word. Some of the alternatives are syntactically acceptable and some are not. Whether a content area teacher chooses to use any of these modifications will depend on that teacher's instructional objectives.

Although slight variations exist in the recommended criterion scores for interpreting student performance on cloze measures, most are derived from or closely based on the research of Bormouth (1966; 1968), who advocated that scores of approximately 44–57 percent correct constitute estimates of instructional levels, and that scores of 58 percent or above and 43 percent or below reflect levels of independence and frustration, respectively. It is important to note that Bormouth's recommendations apply only to those cloze tests in which every fifth word has been deleted and only exact replacements have been accepted.

Content Area Reading Inventory

Among the most useful of all assessment instruments is the content area reading inventory (CARI), which enables the teacher to discover the extent to which students have developed the reading ability and study skills necessary to understand and learn successfully from content area materials. Usually teacher constructed and group administered, the CARI generally comprises three sections which assess student ability to (1) utilize parts of textbooks and other supplemental materials such as library resources, (2) recognize and understand specialized and technical vocabulary, and (3) comprehend information read. The following format, developed by Readence, Bean, and Baldwin (1992), illustrates the specific sections of a typical CARI.

Section I: Textual Reading/Study Aids
  A. Internal Aids
    1. Table of Contents
    2. Index
    3. Glossary
    4. Chapter Introduction/Summaries
    5. Pictorial Information
    6. Other Pertinent Aids
  B. External Aids
    1. Card Catalog
    2. Reader's Guide
    3. Encyclopedias
    4. Other Pertinent Aids

Section II: Vocabulary Knowledge
  A. Recall
  B. Contextual Meanings

Section III: Comprehension
      A. Text Explicit Information
      B. Text Implicit Information
      C. Author Organization

A section that addresses prior knowledge and metacognitive awareness may also be included (Conley, 1992).

Although suggested guidelines for the design and construction of a CARI vary somewhat, we recommend that each of the main sections of the inventory contain twenty to twenty-five questions. Not only does this enhance the reliability of the instrument, but it also allows the teacher to assess a broader range of specific reading behaviors. For example, in the study skills section students may be presented with specific tasks to complete, such as using parts of the textbook to locate information, using the card catalog or other library resources to answer questions, or outlining a particular passage from the textbook.

The section that addresses vocabulary may include the presentation, in context, of words contained in the text. Students may indicate the meaning of words through the identification of synonyms or some word-recognition strategy such as phonetic or structural analysis or the use of context clues. Typically included in the comprehension section is a representative passage of approximately three to four pages taken directly from the textbook. Postreading questions are developed which ask students to demonstrate both literal and inferential comprehension of the material read (Vacca & Vacca, 1989; Tonjes, 1991).

The primary advantage associated with the use of the CARI is that it measures student performance on materials actually used in a course or unit of study. Thus, its results provide teachers with information they can directly use to plan instruction while providing students with a rationale for completing it seriously. Additionally, the inventory is flexible enough to be individually or group administered at either one setting or over several class sessions. Depending on design and scoring techniques, it may allow the teacher to determine the manner in which students go about completing tasks. Of major concern to teachers who employ this technique are the criteria used to evaluate student performance. Teachers must establish their own standards and criteria for determining whether students can or cannot successfully complete the reading and study tasks required in a particular course or unit. However, a recommended criterion that still appears to have gained wide acceptance is that proposed by Shepherd (1982), who advocated that student performance of 60–85 percent correct in any particular section or on the whole inventory should be adequate for instructional purposes.

Portfolios in the Content Area Classroom

Portfolios in content area classrooms are collections of samples of students' writing and other materials, reflecting student reading and thinking as much as writing. The varied materials are put into the portfolio by both the student and the teacher. The container or holder of these items can be an expandable folder, a box, or just space on a shelf. It may be a combination of these things. In a classroom in which portfolios play a major role, the folders, boxes, or other containers are easily accessible to the students. It is essential that students' portfolios be out in the classroom where students can get at them whenever they want.

The holders should be large enough to keep the numerous papers, tapes, and other materials that an individual student and the teacher will add to it over a period of time. As the student designs and individualizes the cover or holder for the portfolio, its physical appearance can make a powerful statement, too; and it becomes a part of the collection it holds.

The portfolio becomes a developing repository of the student's thought, ideas, and language-related growth and accomplishment. Above all, it becomes a powerful tool for managing the student's development as a language user and thinker. In a classroom where portfolios are in regular use, their centrality is obvious.

In addition, portfolio assessment can play a role in the formal assessment process. Pointing this out is not to contend that portfolios be used for product assessment and as a replacement of performance or standardized tests. There are several reasons that this is a bad idea. Perhaps the most important of these is that if portfolios are made to fulfill the information needs of standardized tests, structured and narrow specifications will be enforced on portfolios. They will soon contain only certain things and will be evaluated using specific criteria. This will happen in a effort to make portfolio assessment more reliable. Portfolios would lose their informality and their value in promoting student reflection followed by choice. The openness that enables them to reflect the language and thinking processes of the individual students who collect them would be gone, too.

Scoring portfolios as outcome assessments would be very time-consuming. The scoring would, nonetheless, be unreliable unless the structure of the portfolios were so specifically defined that they could no longer serve as effecting instructional management tools. Despite this concern, portfolios can serve as backup assessment when there is concern about the validity of more formal performance assessments or standardized tests. When a teacher feels that a particular student's achievement has been invalidly assessed by such instruments, the portfolio can be used to demonstrate what the student has accomplished throughout the year.

The primary purpose for having portfolios is to use them for developing student self-assessment and for analyzing the development of students as language users by teachers and others. Students take control of their own learning in an effective portfolio program. They think about their goals and review their work with a focus on what they think they need to do to improve. Portfolios provide the opportunity for students to become active learners. This happens because portfolios promote ongoing analysis of the samples and other materials they contain. Just deciding what order to put the material into requires evaluating it in some way and invites rationalizing any decisions made. This is just one way that portfolios promote self-analysis and provide the opportunity for students to take responsibility for their own learning as they reflect about reading and writing.

Planning the Portfolio Program

There are three questions that must be answered before a portfolio program can be established in a content area classroom. Those three questions are (1) What goes in? (2) Who puts it there?, and (3) How is it looked at and why? The answers to those three questions form the planning for a portfolio program.

What Goes in the Portfolios and Who Puts It There?

A key aspect of portfolios that serve assessment effectively is that they are inclusive not exclusive. Students should be encouraged to include almost anything they want, and teachers should add what they think will inform their assessment and promote student assessment. In short, portfolios are apt to contain lots of materials. Although teachers may want to discourage students from packing their portfolios with lots of workbook sheets, they should not set up criteria for inclusion that tends to limit what students can include.

Teachers and students both add materials to the portfolio. The teacher may decide that a particular assignment or project would be a good benchmark for students to keep in their portfolios. Benchmarks are key activities that the teacher has developed to ascertain student development in regard to key course goals. Students should view the portfolios as the place they keep their reading and writing materials for the particular class. The portfolios may include notes and writing ideas, reactions to what has been learned and taught, and all kinds of writing materials.

How Are Portfolios Looked at and Why?

The portfolios are the focus of student/teacher conferences. A minimum of twice a semester, the teacher should schedule individual conferences with each student. During these conferences, the student and teacher should review the materials in the portfolio and discuss the student's progress. The student is encouraged to select and discuss the items in the portfolio that he or she liked best and to comment about what made the activity interesting and worthwhile. The teacher should be a listener and should ask questions that push students to reflect and comment on their progress. Conversations should be more focused on

---

Think while Reading Activity

If the instructor for this class required you to keep a portfolio that described your growth in this class, what would it look like? What samples of your work would you include? What criteria would you use to select your pieces for your portfolio?

_____

_____

_____

_____

_____

_____

_____

_____

Activity 26–3

the content and ideas of what has been read and written than on the strategies and mechanics of reading and writing. Students should come to realize that it is their ideas that are important and not merely the mechanics of reading and writing.

A major goal of the conference is to develop student self-assessment of reading and writing. Therefore, take a listening stance. Begin with open-ended questions. Questions that are open-ended encourage students to share their beliefs and understandings about reading and writing. These questions should be followed by probing questions that help students reflect about the things that have intrigued them as they have worked on specific projects, and how they have clarified their thoughts about issues and topics they have encountered. The questions should help students make connections between content areas—and between reading and writing that they may not have considered previously.

The questions you ask in a portfolio conference should grow out of (1) your analysis of the student's portfolio, (2) what you have learned about the student from other sources, such as your own observation, and (3) what you learn during the conference by listening carefully to the student. The list offered here poses questions you can ask yourself. As a checklist, it enables you to think about aspects of student language use that it is useful to understand and to translate some of the items into questions that fit a particular interview as it develops. The checklist is of perspectives that can be revealed during portfolio conferences, and you may wish to prepare some questions you can use to prime a conference or to keep it moving productively. You may ignore the list altogether in conferences where you engage in a discussion with the student that moves you quite uniquely through considerations of that student's interests, strengths, attitudes, uses of language, and opportunities to improve as a language user.

1. What are the student's most apparent reasons/purposes for reading and writing? Which of them seem the most important to the student? What evidence is there of reading being applied in some way? Why did the student write most of the pieces in the collection?
2. How idea oriented is the student? Does she or he seem to value encountering ideas in reading? How willing and eager is the student to share ideas?
3. How much confidence does the student have as a thinker? Is she or he a risk taker and willing to encounter and experiment with new ideas? How willing and ready does the student appear to be to explore her or his own interests through writing and reading?
4. Where does the student tend to get her or his interests and ideas? Is the content of the portfolio traceable to other writers, to friends, to family, to classroom experience? Is the student's writing style influenced by authors and genres? Is she or he able to draw on such sources? Do preferences for authors, content, etc., relate to the student's background and personal experiences?
4. How aware does the student appear to be of the authors of texts and other sources read? Does the student visualize particular audiences for the things she or he writes?
5. How responsive does the student's use of language appear to be? Are responses to reading aware of author's intent, other readers' responses? Is there evidence that feedback from others has been incorporated into the student's writing and reading selections? Is this student a reviser? If so, what guides the revisions?

6. How expressive is the student's language? What distinguishes or describes the diction and apparent lexicon of this student? How precise is word choice? How fresh? How imaginative?

7. How clearly are ideas presented, summarized, reviewed, applied to individual purposes for reading and writing? How good or controlled a thinker does the student appear to be? Is there evidence of ideas connected logically, of organizational schemes, of use of or grasp of comparison/contrast, cause and effect, time sequence, etc.?

Both the teacher and the student should take notes during (or immediately after) the conference about things that need to be worked on, new projects that are to be developed, and reading and writing strengths. Preferably these notes should be kept on the same sheet of paper. In this way, the teacher's notes help to guide the student to become a self-assessor. The notes then become part of the portfolio.

Here are some basic tips to help develop an effective portfolio program for your content area classroom:

Portfolios belong to students and not to teachers.

Portfolios should be kept out in the classroom where students can have access to them.

Think after Reading Activity

A variety of performance-based assessments are described in this chapter. Choose one of these you would use in your own classroom.

Name of the assessment:

_____

How would you use this assessment strategy in your classroom?

_____
_____
_____
_____
_____
_____

Why do you think it's important?

_____
_____
_____
_____
_____
_____

Activity 26–4

Students are responsible for keeping records (logs) of their reading and writing.

Student/teacher conferences are an essential part of portfolio process.

Portfolios are not replacements for other forms of assessment.

Portfolios are vital to the overall assessment program in every content area classroom.

Conclusion

All content areas require extensive reading, and therefore all content area teachers are obligated to find out the reading strengths and weaknesses of their students. The extent to which teachers need information about students' reading abilities is a function of the degree to which they tailor instruction to the unique reading demands of their subject. The purpose of this chapter is to provide information about the assessment of students' reading abilities so that content area teachers can make more informed decisions about the available alternatives for measuring reading abilities.

This chapter describes in general terms the type of information about students' reading abilities that most content area teachers need to know and also the alternative methods that most teachers can and do employ. Arguments are presented in favor of the appropriateness of informal methods of assessing student reading abilities, with special emphasis on integrated reading and writing assessments and establishing a portfolio program. However, because our theoretical model of reading does not automatically eliminate some approaches to assessment, we have also included more traditional techniques such as the cloze procedure, the informal reading inventory, and the content area reading inventory. This pragmatic approach to assessment, which maintains that one should assess in the manner most likely to yield the information needed, can provide content area teachers with the information they need to make day to day instructional decisions.

Theory Becomes Practice
A Design for Content Area Lesson Planning

JAMES BARTON

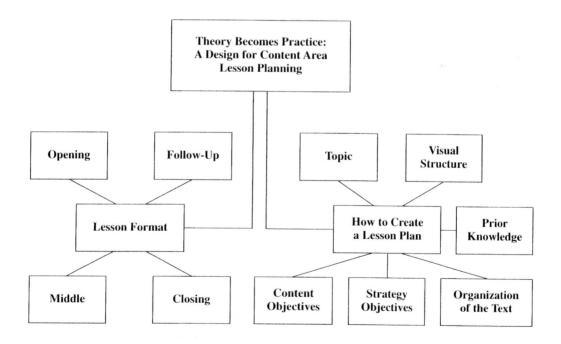

Think before Reading Activity

When you become a teacher, you will be responsible for creating lessons for each of your classes. How do you think you might create a content area lesson that is designed to combat the difficulties of expository text? Reflect on this for a few minutes and then write your answer here. Keep your ideas in mind and compare them to the ideas presented in this chapter.

_____

_____

_____

_____

_____

_____

_____

_____

_____

_____

_____

_____

Activity 27–1

This chapter shares an approach to content area lesson planning designed to combat the difficulties of expository text. The approach makes use of instructional strategies from the field of literacy (such as engaging students in active learning by relating their prior knowledge about a topic to the new material at hand) to help students learn new ways of thinking in a given discipline. The chapter describes each facet of the lesson plan with real classroom examples and offers a step by step description of the process used to develop these lessons.

For many content area teachers, the challenge of working with expository text can be a burdensome enterprise. Exposition, as distinguished from narrative text by its heavy concentration of factual information as well as the absence of a story-like structure, can be daunting for students and teachers alike. In fact, student complaints about expository text sound very similar to the complaints of teachers: expository texts contain too much information to possibly remember or cover, they are written in ways that routinely mask what is important and what is nonessential, they are heavy and difficult to carry around, they contain too many unfamiliar vocabulary words, they are boring and lifeless.

The goal of this chapter is to share a design for content area lesson planning that overcomes (for students and teachers alike) the difficulties inherent in reading and using expository texts.

The Lesson Format

A lesson plan that attempts to cover multiple topics in one class period is frequently a source of confusion to students. Accordingly, this alternative format consists of a four-phase lesson structure designed to help teachers focus on a single, clearly explicated instructional goal. The four parts of the lesson design are an opening, a middle, a closing, and a follow-up (Calfee & Associates, 1981.) During each phase, the teacher is concerned with process (the ways of formally thinking about the content) and structure (the ways the content can be visually organized and reorganized for retention) as well as the lesson's content. The payoff for this allocation of instructional attention is independent thinking. Because the ways of thinking about a lesson's content are made explicit in a highly organized fashion, students gradually learn (with guidance and support) to transfer the thinking processes they have used in one lesson to the next learning opportunity. However, I am not proposing that this lesson design is the only correct way to teach independent thinking— simply that this alternative has the virtue of clarity in its emphasis on the establishment of an explicit instructional purpose and provides a forum for engaging students in active learning.

Opening

In a lesson's opening, the teacher attempts to achieve five related goals. In actual practice these five facets may overlap and occur in different combinations during the course of the opening, but they must be explicitly stated in ways that students will relate to and comprehend. The five goals are:

1. The teacher succinctly previews the new content to be learned (including central vocabulary words) and seeks to discover how much students might already know about this new material.
2. The teacher endeavors to provide a clear rationale for the lesson by establishing the relevance of the material to the students' lives.
3. The teacher attempts to build student interest in the lesson with a motivating activity, engaging anecdote, or compelling analogy.
4. The teacher introduces students to a visual structure (e.g., semantic map, matrix grid, Venn diagram) that will be used to organize the content.
5. The teacher highlights the ways that students will be called on to think about the content (e.g., following a sequence of events, establishing causes and predicting likely effects, developing a personal perspective in response to a particular line of reasoning).

Let's look at a sample opening from a math class for high school sophomores (Tassinari, 1990.) In this particular lesson, the teacher's instructional goal is to introduce her students to the mathematical processes for determining probability. Here is how the opening proceeds:

Goal #1—Today we are going to learn a way of mathematical thinking that you use often in your lives but may not know the technical term for . . . this way of reasoning is called probability. Can anyone offer a working definition for this new term based on your reading of the introduction to Chapter 11 for homework last night? (All student responses are welcomed and considered in turn.)

Goal #2—It is important to understand the way that probability works because, in today's world, we are constantly forced to make decisions based on our guesses about how things are going to turn out. In other words, in situations where we do not have all the information we need to come to a decision, we had better be able to make the best possible guesses we can. Probability means making the best guesses we can possibly make about how events will turn out in the future.

Goal #3—For example, here I have a six sided die in my hands. (Teacher holds up die to show the class the six different faces.) What do you think are the chances of me rolling a five? (Teacher solicits students' responses and writes them on the board.) Now, I'm going to ask six or seven of you to roll the die. Let's see how many times a five comes up. (The die is rolled and the actual tallies are compared with the students' guesses) So, from this activity we can see how well your guesses panned out. Let me introduce you to a formula that is often used to measure probability:

$$\text{Probability} \quad = \quad \frac{\text{possible \# of successful outcomes}}{\text{total \# of "equally likely" outcomes}}$$

This formula will help you to make more educated guesses about the likelihood of a certain outcome occurring. In our experiment with the die, what was the only successful outcome we would consider? That's right, the rolling of a five. How many outcomes were likely to occur? Six? That's correct, a one or two or three or four or five or six could each occur. So, according to our formula, the probability of rolling a five is 1/6. Any questions up to this point?

Goals #4 and #5—In today's lesson we will utilize a matrix grid to compare and contrast our best guesses about the answers to certain problems with the responses we get when we apply our probability formula. Then, we'll add a column to record what happens when we actually try the problems ourselves here in the classroom. We'll add new problems to the chart as we go.

In this opening, the teacher immediately establishes an explicit content goal for the class, along with a real-world rationale for the students' involvement with this material. She attempts to determine if the students grasped the definition offered by their expository text, and quickly moves to a motivational activity designed to capture student attention and provide a further purpose for learning how to use the probability formula. To complete the opening, the teacher introduces the visual structure (the matrix) and shares the thinking processes (comparing and contrasting) students will be using to complete the lesson.

Middle

The lesson middle is a forum for teacher/student and student/student interaction with the content of the lesson. Here the teacher guides the students in using the appropriate thinking strategies to organize the content within the established visual structure. Students may be encouraged to look to their texts for more information during this phase, but a key factor in the success of the middle is the teacher's ability to ask pertinent questions and foster group discussion (rather than function as a dispenser of information.) Experience has convinced me that the most effective lessons encourage students to do more work than the teacher in three key ways:

1. Students should be struggling to understand the relationships among the different pieces of information they are working with.
2. Students should be trying out their ideas verbally.
3. Students should be stretching to respond to the teacher's "why" questions.

Let's see how the approach applies in the middle of our math lesson:

Goal #1—Okay, let's develop our matrix! What did I say would be our first column? What was our first problem with the die? Let me add a few more problems for us to work with. How will I organize the rest of our matrix? What information belongs in each category? Is everybody with me so far? All right, now we have four columns and our visual structure looks like this:

The Problems	Our Class Responses		Formula Responses	Demonstration Responses
Dice What's the probability of rolling a five?	1/2 1/6 1/4	1/3 2/3 1/5	1/6	1/6
Cards What's the probability of picking a king?				
Balls What's the probability of picking a white ball?				

Goals #2 and #3—Let's work together on the next problem. Notice I am now holding a deck of 52 cards. What would you guess is the probability of pulling a king out of this deck? Why did you make this particular guess? (Students make their guesses, which are then recorded on the matrix.) Now, in teams of two, use the probability formula to solve this same problem. (The teacher gives the groups time to work out the formula.) Okay, who has an answer they are willing to share? Did anyone else come up with this same response? How did you derive this particular answer? What did those of you with different answers do differently in applying the formula? Can we all agree on one common answer to enter into our matrix? According to our visual structure, what should we do next? That's right, it's time to demonstrate the problem to see what happens in real life. Cindy, Jerome, and Mitch, please come up to the front of the room and assist me in picking out some kings. (After the students perform this activity, the teacher enters the demonstration response on the matrix, and the class moves on to the next problem for further reinforcement.)

As you can see from this example, the lesson middle hinges on the kinds of opportunities students have to actively construct the visual structure. It would be pointless for the teacher do all the talking during this phase of the lesson, for it is in the verbal interaction that students take ownership of the concepts they are learning. Most of the teacher talk in this example focused on guiding students' thinking with timely questions and helping the class move forward in an organized direction.

Closing

In many ways, the lesson's closing is a mirror of its opening segment. The important content information is reviewed, along with the processes and structures used to illuminate this content. However, unlike the opening, in the closing it is the students who do the review for each other and for their teacher. This student-centered review helps to reinforce what has been learned up to this point and affords the teacher an opportunity to assess students' mastery of the lesson.

Here is the closing of our sample math lesson:

What would you say was the purpose of today's lesson? So, in your own words, what is probability and how does it work? How did we go about organizing our knowledge about probability? How did this organization help us to think about the concept? Why should we bother to learn about this particular topic? Can anyone come up to the board and recreate the probability formula I shared with you at the beginning of today's class? When might this formula be of use to you?

Let's try one more probability experiment. In a moment I'm going to ask you to break up into your cooperative groups—your task will be to come up with a probability "challenge" for the rest of our class. You may use either dice, cards, balls, or some other raw materials to construct a probability problem for the rest of the class to guess at, solve, and demonstrate. Be sure to use the probability formula yourselves on your problem so you can distinguish correct from incorrect responses. Any questions? You have 15 minutes to get into your cooperative groups and create your challenge. (After 15 minutes the teacher facilitates group sharing until each group has tried each new problem.)

In this closing, the teacher's questions focus on what the concept of probability means, how the students went about studying the concept in today's lesson, and why the concept is a relevant one to study. The activity she coordinates gives her students an opportunity to reinforce the probability process for one another. It also gives her a chance to evaluate individual student's abilities to use and articulate what they have learned during the lesson.

Follow-Up

Because student discussion is emphasized throughout the entire lesson, the actual coverage of content may vary considerably from the teacher's initial expectations. The follow-up is designed, therefore, to give students more opportunity to independently practice with the content, extend the concepts they are learning, and personalize the learning experience. A lesson's follow-up can take many forms. In my experience, the most effective follow-up activities tend to be relatively open-ended in nature, stress the development of writing skills, and tie new information into the body of knowledge students are currently exploring. Opportunities for practice are important; time and feedback are required for students to develop a sense of autonomy and competence. As is true throughout the rest of the lesson, explicitness continues to be a key goal during this phase. It is essential that the teacher be clear about what it is the students are expected to do independently and how their efforts will be integrated into upcoming classroom activities.

These elements are present in our math lesson's final segment:

> We're about out of time for today, so I'd like you each to take what you've learned today and apply it for homework tonight. Go back to Chapter 11 and choose any three of the sample problems that appear throughout the chapter. Create your own matrix using the categories we developed today, and reorganize your three problems to show your initial guess about the answer, the solution you get by applying the probability formula, and how the problem plays out in real life. We'll use your matrices tomorrow in class to build a new visual structure to explore a related topic called set theory. Any questions about your assignment for tonight? Good work today class, thanks, and see you tomorrow.

In this example, the teacher prepares her students for independent practice by instructing them to follow the new process they are learning with information from their texts. If all goes well, this activity will reinforce the concept of probability and the new ways of thinking about and organizing the concept. Note also that the teacher is very explicit about the ways the students' independent work will be re-integrated into the next class session. This clarity of purpose helps to insure that a greater percentage of students will actually do the homework they are assigned.

Think while Reading Activity

Figure 27–1 is a chart that helps teachers ask key questions for lesson design. As you read this Chapter, jot down information about these key terms.

Topic:

_____

_____

Content Objectives:

_____

_____

Strategy Objectives:

_____

_____

Organization of the Text:

_____

_____

Visual Structure:

_____

_____

Evaluation:

_____

_____

Activity 27–2

How to Create a Lesson

The central component of this approach to lesson planning is the middle, because this is where the bulk of the action (and interaction) takes place. Accordingly, the middle is where lesson planning begins. Once the lesson's middle is constructed, the opening, closing, and follow-up segments can be developed around it. With the assistance of David Wong at Michigan State University, I have created a series of key questions to assist teachers in designing the middle of their lessons (see Figure 27–1). These questions focus on the content, process, and visual structure of the proposed lesson, as well as student prior knowledge about the content and the organization of the expository text passage. (For more information about the organizational patterns of expository text, see Chambliss & Calfee, 1989. In this article, the authors examine the impact of text structure on the accessibility of the content of science textbooks.) I believe these areas represent the key issues teachers at all grade levels invariably need to consider when constructing lessons based on expository texts. To illustrate this point, let's consider the questions in relation to a segment from a chapter on "Infectious Diseases and the Immune System" in a high school biology book. The topic of this segment is AIDS. This example is intended to reinforce the point that this approach to expository lesson planning places the classroom teacher (not the textbook publisher) in the position of instructional authority. The teacher's decisions about the key questions in Figure 27–1 will help shape not only the middle but the rest of the lesson as well.

The teacher in this example was constructing his lesson on AIDS for high school seniors in an advanced placement biology class (Moscarelli, 1991.) Here is how he answered the key questions I've posed.

Topic: *What is the expository passage about?* The passage is an overview of the immune deficiency disease called AIDS.

Content Objectives: *What do you want the students to learn about this topic?* I want them to explore their current understanding and misconceptions about how AIDS is transmitted and prevented, and I want them to learn accurate information about how the disease acts on the immune system.

TOPIC: What is the expository passage about?	
CONTENT OBJECTIVES: What do you want the students to learn about this topic?	
STRATEGY OBJECTIVES: What kinds of thinking will the students need to do to learn the content?	
ORGANIZATION OF THE TEXT: How is the passage organized, and is this pattern appropriate for this lesson?	
STUDENT PRIOR KNOWLEDGE: What do the students already know about the topic or a related topic?	
VISUAL STRUCTURE: What visual representation might be most appropriate for this lesson?	

FIGURE 27–1   Key Questions for Lesson Design

Strategy Objectives: *What kinds of thinking will the students need to do to learn the content?* They will need to find bits of information in the text and organize this information into coherent chunks, and they will need to compare and contrast their own knowledge with the information in the chapter.

Organization of the Text: *How is the passage organized, and is this pattern appropriate for this lesson?* The passage is descriptive, with headings that indicate the major chapter topics. However, the specific information we will be seeking is somewhat randomly distributed throughout the passage.

Student Prior Knowledge: *What do the students already know about the topic or a related topic?* The students have accumulated a good deal of "popular" knowledge about AIDS, including some misconceptions and inaccurate beliefs.

Visual Structure: *What visual representation might be most appropriate for this lesson?* Since the text is poorly organized and the students will need to group previously unrelated facts into common groups, a semantic map or web may be most appropriate for this material.

The actual web appears in Figure 27–2, and you will note it is constructed according to the specific content objectives this teacher established for his lesson.)

In this instance, the lesson middle will consist of a visual web and a discussion about prior (student generated) knowledge about AIDS and new (text generated) knowledge about this topic. Now that the middle is designed, the rest of the lesson can be put into place.

As difficult as it sometimes is to establish what it is we really want our students to learn, these decisions are absolutely central to the creation an effective lesson. It is likely that no two teachers' lessons will look quite the same using this approach to planning, because variance in your answers to the key questions will lead you to employ different

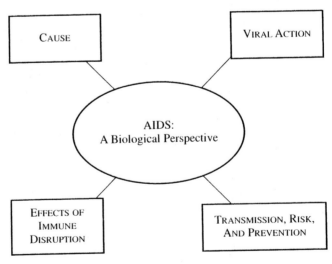

FIGURE 27–2   Visual Structure for Sample Lesson on AIDS

visual structures and methods for student interaction. In this way you can gear your lessons to different instructional goals, different levels of textbook difficulty, and different levels of student achievement.

Conclusion

The purpose of this chapter has been to suggest an approach content area teachers can use to help students develop their abilities to comprehend the information in expository textbooks. This approach to lesson planning allows subject matter specialists to expand their instructional repertories while remaining true to their respective disciplines. Planning a lesson using this design will initially be more time consuming, but the approach quickly becomes internalized and the final product has a number of advantages. First, it promotes explicit language and meaningful interactions between teacher and students. Second, a stress on structure and process helps students to organize new information and learn how to think in a given discipline. Third, the stage is set for purposeful student activities that transfer these ways of thinking from one lesson to the next. A few experiences with a consistent lesson format using this design will lay the foundation for a more coherent curriculum.

Explicitness, student talk, visual organization, and an emphasis on thinking processes—these are the keys to independent thinking and the solutions to expository textbook difficulties.

Think after Reading Activity

The author states in the Summary of this chapter that "This approach to lesson planning allows subject matter specialists to expand their instructional repertories while remaining true to their respective disciplines." How do you think the information in this chapter will help you develop effective lessons?

Activity 27–3

C h a p t e r *28*

Preferred Instructional Practices in the Content Areas

KAREN D. WOOD

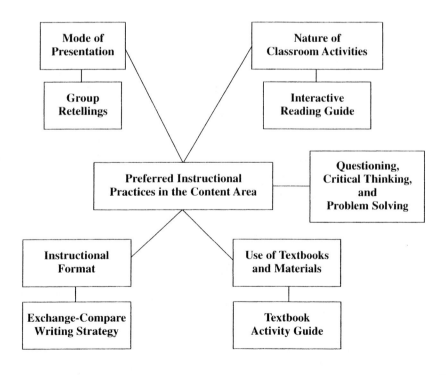

Think before Reading Activity

Pretend you are going to visit your junior high school or high school this afternoon. How do you think you will view the teachers' instructional practices? What strategies are they using to reach their students? Do they use the textbook? If so, how?

Activity 28–1

This chapter presents a research into practice view of content area instruction. Unfortunately, what research exists regarding the prevailing instructional practices in today's middle and secondary schools does not present a flattering portrait. This chapter is in no way intended as an indictment of our schools, but rather is an attempt to determine what needs repair and how we can fix it. As a former middle school teacher, I recall most vividly my desires and the desires of my colleagues for new and better ways of teaching and reaching our adolescents. It is my hope that this chapter will meet at least some of those needs.

Classroom observational research suggests a vast need for improved instruction in our middle and secondary schools (Wood & Muth, 1991). Consequently, the purpose of this chapter is twofold: to describe the specific findings from research, and to offer alternative ways of providing instruction in the content areas. The research will be reviewed and suggestions given in five areas: (1) mode of presentation, (2) instructional format, (3) use of textbooks and materials, (4) nature of classroom activities, and (5) questioning, critical thinking, and problem solving.

Mode of Presentation

Throughout the nation, the primary mode of presenting new content is the lecture approach (Cuban, 1984; Goodlad, 1984). Not surprisingly, the higher the grade level the more frequently the lecture approach is used, with high school and college instructors the main employers. This classroom arrangement in which the teacher dominates class discussion as an information dispenser is still prevalent despite an abundance of research attesting to new and more effective means of conveying information (Readance, Bean, & Baldwin, 1992).

Collaborative learning is receiving increasing attention in the professional literature, at conferences, and in staff development sessions. The practice of having students collaborate with one another has been shown to increase everything from achievement to self-esteem (Glasser quoted in Brandt, 1988; Johnson, Maruyama, Johnson, Nelson, & Skon, 1981; Lehr, 1984; Slavin, 1983). According to Johnson and Johnson (quoted in Brandt, 1987), there is more evidence for the benefits of collaborative learning than any other aspect of education.

A number of excellent grouping alternatives are available in the literature. For example, *group retelling* (Wood, 1987a; 1991) is a strategy in which students work in pairs or groups of three or more. Each member reads the same material or a different type of topically related material. Students in each group read the selection and take turns retelling it, in their own words, to other group members, who may interject with related information from their own readings or past experiences. Group retelling is appropriate in all subject areas. Figure 28–1 shows its application to the teaching and learning of mathematics.

Larson and Dansereau (1986) describe a strategy called *dyadic learning* in which students work in dyads (pairs) to study their subject area assignments. After reading their assigned selection one partner assumes the role of listener/facilitator and corrects errors, adds information, or clarifies concepts. Together they can draw charts, maps, outlines, and the like, to assist their understanding and recall. Eventually the partners switch roles and repeat the exercise.

In addition to the lecture mode of presentation, ineffective teaching also occurs when more telling, mentioning, or assigning replaces actual teaching. In such a situation, the teacher may tell the class to write a paper on a related topic, state the required number of pages and components, and yet never actually show them how to go about the process. In

---

Think while Reading Activity

In the next two sections you'll read about Group Retellings and Exchange-Compare Writing. Use the space below to take some notes as you read.

Group Retellings:

_____

_____

_____

_____

_____

Exchange-Compare Writing:

_____

_____

_____

_____

_____

Activity 28–2

Problem: Multiplying decimals
27.5 x .35 = _____

Student

A   First we need to line up the numbers so we can
     multiply, without getting mixed up.

     27.5
     x .35
     ─────

B   Then we start at the right and multiply like we
     usually would. Don't worry about the decimal
     right now.

C   5 times 5 is 25. The 5 goes under the 5s on the
     right and we carry the 2. Then multiply 5 x 7,
     which is 35, then add 2.

A   That's 37. The 7 goes under the 3 and you carry
     3. Then multiply 5 x 2, which is 10, and add 3.
     That's 13. That's 1375.

B   The next row moves over to the left one space. I
     get 825. How about everybody else?

C   That's it. Now we add. Bring down the 5; 7 plus
     5 is 12, carry the 1; 1 plus 3 plus 2 is 6; 1 plus 8
     is 9. That's 9625.

FIGURE 28–1   Transcript of Group Retelling in Mathematics
Source: Wood (1992).

an authentic teaching situation, the teacher explains the assignment, demonstrates the processes, strategies, or tasks to be undertaken, elicits student input, shows examples, and guides the students throughout the learning.

One effective way of conveying task expectations is to engage in what this author refers to as "finished product instruction." In this case, the teacher first shows an example of the finished product (a research paper, a descriptive paragraph, a related project), and then dissects the product, showing students in step by step format how to reach that end.

Instructional Format

At some time or another in our school careers, we have all experienced the well-meaning "Teacher X" who dutifully wrote the vocabulary words on the board (often thirty or more), and required that we look up their definitions in the dictionary. We memorized the definitions for test time, but afterwards promptly forgot them. Preferred approaches to vocabulary development involve both definition and context, where students use their prior knowledge to engage in deeper processing of the concepts (Beck & McKeown, 1991). One strategy that accomplishes these goals is the preview in context.

In the *preview in context* strategy (Readance, Bean, & Baldwin, 1981), the teacher selects important words from a passage, chapter, or segment of text. The number should be limited to a maximum of five or six key words which reflect the main concepts to be studied. Next, the teacher directs the students' attention to each word as it is used in the context of the selection ("Open your books to page 122, first paragraph, and look for the sentence where the word 'eradicate' appears"). Then, students follow along in their text, reading silently as the sentences are read aloud. A teacher-directed questioning strategy is used to help students use the context to derive meaning. (See Figure 28–2). After students seem to understand the word as used in their textbooks, the teacher relates the word to other words through a discussion of similarities and differences of word parts, antonyms, synonyms, and so forth.

The same well-meaning "Teacher X" also can be observed directing the class to "open your books to page 193 and begin reading about the War of 1812, then answer the questions at the back of the chapter and turn them in at the end of class." Preceding this directive there is no purpose set for reading, preview of what is to follow, or guidance for reading.

Preview in Context Strategy
Subject: Social Studies
Topic: Colonial Times

Text: Citizens of all the colonies were angry about the Stamp Act. In fact, a great deal of colonial *protest* had already occurred before the trouble began in Wilmington.

Step One   —Select significant vocabulary. Example: *protest.*

Step Two   —Read word aloud in context.

Step Three   —Have students read silently.

Step Four   —Specify word meaning through questioning.

  T: What does the sentence tell you about the word protest?
  S: It has something to do with trouble.
  T: What was the trouble about?
  S: The Stamp Act?
  T: How did the colonists feel about the Stamp Act?
  S: They were angry because they were against it.
  T: What do you think *protest* means?
  S: Letting someone know you're against something.

Step Five   —Expand word meanings.

  T: Are there words we could substitute for *protest* in the sentence without changing the meaning?
  S: Dissension, rejection, revolution.
  T: Do you know of other times in our history when a government action has met with protest?
  S: The Vietnam War, nuclear waste disposal.

FIGURE 28–2   Teacher-Directed Questioning Strategy
Source: Wood (1990).

A sound instructional framework includes a prereading or preparation phase, a guided reading phase, and a postreading or follow-up phase (Readence, Bean, & Baldwin, 1992). In this framework, more time is spent on instructional readiness, building background by eliciting students' prior knowledge on the topic, preteaching significant vocabulary terms where necessary, and helping students create visual images of scenes to be encountered in their reading.

Similarly, after reading, the lesson does not end with the completion of the end-of-chapter questions. Instead, a postreading phase is added in which students may engage in a follow-up writing activity, conduct a panel discussion, or get in research or interest groups to explore the topic more thoroughly.

One means for accomplishing the objectives of the prereading phase of the instructional lesson is the *exchange-compare writing strategy* (Wood, 1991). The teacher selects approximately ten to fifteen key concepts from the selection to be read, making certain that the terms reflect the most significant information. The terms are displayed on the board or an overhead transparency. Students are grouped in fours and fives heterogeneously and asked to use the words in a passage, predicting the actual selection. If assistance is needed, the teacher may discuss the unknown word in a meaningful context, requesting input and elaborations from the class. Or, the students may use the dictionary to determine the appropriate definition.

The groups then read their predicted passages to the class, reflecting on the various differences and similarities. Lastly, they open their books to exchange their predicted passage with the actual selection. They can now read the selection to follow with the purpose of focusing on the highlighted vocabulary and concepts along the way. Strategies such as

---

Think while Reading Activity

Textbook Activity Guides and Interactive Reading Guides provide opportunities for students to "foster critical and creative thinking." While you're reading the next two sections, jot down some notes about these activities.

Textbook Activity Guide:

_____

_____

_____

_____

_____

Interactive Reading Guide:

_____

_____

_____

_____

_____

Activity 28–3

exchange-compare writing spark student interest by engaging them in a lively, interactive assignment before reading.

Use of Textbooks and Materials

Research reveals that the textbook is the predominant source of instructional content, and that this dependence on the textbook increases at each grade level (Goodlad, 1984). One way to help students deal with the vast amount of print encountered in their reading assignments is by encouraging the peer reading and retelling described earlier in this chapter. In this way, the text is divided into segments and the content is more readily processed and assimilated.

Another way for students to manage print is by developing questions in the form of study guides, which accompany students while they are reading, like "tutors in print form" (Wood & Mateja, 1983). Wood, Lapp, and Flood (1992) offer a review of study guides to provide teachers with the opportunity to match a type of guide with their instructional goals. One of these guides is the textbook activity guide (TAG). The textbook activity guide, developed by Davey (1988), helps students monitor their learning by indicating which portions of the text need additional clarification. Developing a TAG involves five steps:

1. Begin by clarifying the lesson objectives for the chapter or text segment under study.
2. Then, go through the selection and pick out headings, portions, diagrams that relate to your objectives.
3. Next, select which text features are most important in the study guide and sequence them appropriately.
4. Match the reading/study task to the objective (This is where the strategy code shown in Figure 28–3 is employed). When prior knowledge is required, discuss the selection with a partner. When it would be helpful for students to sequence, organize, or show relationships, have them make a chart or diagram. Choose one task for each text portion on the guide.
5. Create a self-monitoring system. Line markers can be placed beside each numbered task to allow students to note their level of understanding. (See Figure 28–3.)

Nature of Classroom Activities

Much evidence exists attesting to the efficacy of using hands-on, student-centered learning activities as alternatives to drill and practice. Such activities foster critical and creative thinking and result in substantial gains in learning (Anderson, Hiebert, Scott, & Wilkinson, 1985; California, 1987; Carnegie, 1989; Eccles & Midgley, 1989). As mentioned previously, engaging students in cooperative learning activities is one effective way to put the learning in the hands of the students. What frequently is assigned as an individual activity can be recast as a paired learning assignment. In this way, students have the opportunity to share ideas with peers and broaden the scope of their own experiences and thinking.

Textbook Activity Guide
Modern Earth Science
Topic: Fossils

Names _____   Date(s) _____

_____

Strategy Codes:

RR – Read and retell in your own words
DP – Read and discuss with partner
PP – Predict with partner
WR – Write a response on your own
Skim – Read quickly for purpose stated and discuss with partner
MOC – Organize information with a map, chart, or outline

Self-Monitoring Codes:
✓ I understand this information.
? I'm not sure if I understand.
✗ I do not understand and I need to restudy.

1. ___PP   pp. 385–391. Survey the title, picture, charts, and headings.
              What do you expect to learn about this section?
2. ___WR   As you are reading, jot down three or more new words and defini-
              tions for your vocabulary collection.
3. ___RR   pp. 385–386 first three paragraphs.
4. ___DP   pp. 386–387 next three paragraphs.
              a. Describe several reasons, why index or guide fossils are
                 important.
              b. How can finding the right type of fossil help you to identify it?
5. ___MOC   Map pp. 387–389. Make an outline of the information.

1. _____   2. _____   3. _____
   a. _____   a. _____   a. _____
   b. _____   b. _____   b. _____
   c. _____   c. _____   c. _____

6. ___Skim   p. 390 first three paragraphs.
              Purpose: To understand the role of the following in the formation
              of fossils:
              _____a. natural cases
              _____b. trails and burrows
              _____c. gastroliths
7. ___DP   pp. 390–391.
              As an amateur fossil collector describe:
              a. where to find fossils
              b. what to use to find them
              c. how to prepare them for display
8. ___WR   p. 392 next to last paragraph.
              Define pseudofossil. Jot down three other words which contain
              the prefix "pseudo." Use the dictionary if necessary.
9. ___DP   Examine the fossil collection being passed around and list eight
              things you have learned by analyzing it.

FIGURE 28–3   A Study Guide
Source: Wood (1987b).

Physical Science—"Sounds"

Interaction Codes:

◯ = Individual   ◯◯ = Pairs   ⊛ = Group   ◯ = Whole Class

⊛ 1.   In your group, write down everything you can think of relative to the subtopics on "Sound." Your group's associations will be shared with the class.

vibrations ——— Sound ——— Doppler Effect

reflection   decibels   pitch

◯◯ 2.   Read the section on page 364 on "Sounds." Engage in a shared retelling with your partner by putting the information in your own words.

◯ 3.   a. Write down three new things you have learned after reading the following sections:
"Sound Waves Reflect"
"Sound Intensity and Loudness"
"We Can Hear Some Sounds"

⊛   b. Compare your responses with those of your group.

◯ 4.   Read to remember all you can about "The Doppler Effect Changes Pitch" on pages 366-367. The association of the class will then be written on the board for discussion.

◯ 5.   Return to the major topics introduced in the first activity. Skim over your reading guide responses with these topics in mind. Next, be ready to contribute, along with the class, anything you have learned about these topics.

FIGURE 28–4   Excerpt from an Interactive Reading Guide

One activity typically done in isolation as seatwork is the reading of the textbook itself. The interactive reading guide (Wood, Lapp, & Flood, 1992) gives students, especially struggling readers, the opportunity to read and answer questions about the text in segments with a partner, group members, and the class as a whole.

Figure 28–4 shows an interactive guide for a physical science lesson on "Sounds." The interaction codes signal to the students to engage in an activity with their preassigned partners or group members. Much opportunity is allowed for classwide discussion after the peer interaction. Also, the teacher is continually monitoring group progress to assist in clarification.

Questioning, Critical Thinking, and Problem Solving

From grade 7 and above, the majority of questions asked by teachers require literal recall of content (Johnston & Markle, 1986; Stiggins, Griswold, & Wikelund, 1989). Yet our society continues to demand workers who can engage in higher-order thinking processes

(Ryder, 1994). Based on these and similar observations, researchers have concluded that critical thinking is not taught extensively in today's classrooms (Johnston & Markle, 1986; Resnick, 1987).

One way to promote critical thinking is through the use of a *reaction guide* (Bean & Peterson, 1981; Herber, 1970), which is designed to stimulate students' thinking and discussion of topics before, during, and after a lesson. It consists of eight statements that reflect the general concepts or misconceptions about a topic. Students must find evidence to confirm or refute each statement. When used in the prereading phase of a lesson, students are asked to agree or disagree with each statement and must substantiate their responses with personal anecdotes, educated guesswork, or prior knowledge. Then the students read the passage with the statements as their guide. After the reading, they return to the statements reacting to them with their newly acquired knowledge to see if they have changed their mind or broadened their view. Figure 28–5 reveals a reaction guide applied to a social studies lesson on Egypt and the Nile River.

The reaction guide is also useful as a review mechanism (after a lesson or unit) to help solidify students' understanding of important concepts. Figure 28–6 shows the reaction guide used as a review strategy in mathematics. Students may work in pairs or small groups, completing one guide between them. Because this strategy is used as a final synthesizing review of concepts previously discussed and practiced, encountering the common misconception again in written form helps students talk aloud with their peers and find evidence for their responses.

Brozo and Simpson (1991) describe a grade 8 classroom in which students were taught question-answer relationships (QAR) in a cooperative setting. Students developed a

---

Egypt, a Child of the Nile

Part A.   Before reading the chapter see how well you can predict what you are going to learn from the chapter. Take turns reading each statement with your partner. In column A, place a check next to every statement that you predict will be proven true in the chapter. Be sure to substantiate your responses. (Remember you and your partner do not have to agree.)

A   B

_____   _____   1. The Nile is the greatest river in Africa.

_____   _____   2. Cairo, the Capital of Egypt, is the most significant port in the Middle East region.

_____   _____   3. Egypt is surrounded by water on the north and east and by desert on the south and west.

Part B.   After reading, put a check in column B by all of the statements you believe are true. How much did you improve your knowledge from your reading?

Part C.   Rewrite each statement that is not correct in order to make it correct. Use complete sentences. You may use your textbook.

FIGURE 28–5   Reaction Guide

Names of group members:

Ryan

Mandy

The Metric System: Meters and Kilometers

Directions: With your partner, take turns reading and discussing each of the statements below. Put a check if you agree or disagree with each statement. Be sure to support your answer with at least one example. Use your book or any other sources for support.

1. The meter is a unit of length in the metric system.

   I agree ___✓___   I disagree _____   because: *On page 142 in our books it said that the metric system is based on the meter.*

2. The kilometer is used to measure long distances, such as the distance between two cities or how far a person can jog in 30 minutes.

   I agree ___✓___   I disagree _____   because: *A kilometer is like a metric mile and a mile measures roads.*

3. You would want is use the meter to measure the distance from Wadesboro to Charlotte, North Carolina.

   I agree _____   I disagree ___✓___   because: *You should use kilometers to measure miles and distance; the meter is too short* .

4. You would want to use the kilometer to measure how deep a swimming pool is.

   I agree _____   I disagree ___✓___   because: *A swimming pool is not a long distance down. It is not that deep.*

FIGURE 28–6   Reaction Guide in Mathematics
Source: Wood (1992).

deeper understanding of subject area concepts by working in groups, discussing and exchanging ideas, and reinterpreting text information. At the same time, they were learning that knowing the source of the answer to a question can help them understand how to process and assimilate new concepts more effectively.

Conclusion

One purpose of this chapter has been to describe the current research that suggests some prevailing instructional practices in middle and secondary schools. The research was categorized in five areas: mode of presentation, instructional format, use of textbooks and materials, nature of classroom activities, and questioning critical thinking and problem solving. A second purpose was to delineate some preferred instructional practices in each of these five areas. These preferred practices, while by no means exhaustive, have the potential to enliven content area instruction for both teacher and students alike.

Think after Reading Activity

This chapter presented many preferred instructional practices. How do you think these strategies enliven instruction for both the teacher and the student?

_____

_____

_____

_____

_____

_____

_____

_____

Activity 28–4

Chapter **29**

Crossing Boundaries with
Literate Actions

A Look inside Successful Content Area Classrooms

DONNA ALVERMANN

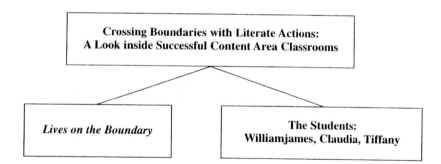

Think before Reading Activity

Life is full of daydreams. As human beings we tend to strive for the best. What do you think one of the best high schools in the United States is like? Write your description here; include your ideas about the students, teachers, their interactions, and the courses offered at this school.

_____

_____

_____

_____

_____

_____

_____

_____

_____

_____

_____

Activity 29–1

This chapter chronicles an imaginary day in the life of three high school students as they move from class to class in the fictitious Nathanielsboro Comprehensive High School in Nathan County, Georgia. Although the school does not exist as such, it is the embodiment of several high schools in which I have conducted observational research over the past seven years. In some instances, the teachers are former students from content reading classes that I taught at the University of Georgia. They graciously allowed me to videotape them using some of the strategies they had learned in class. In other instances, the teachers represent a larger group of professionals who participated in year-long inservice projects aimed at increasing student engagement in content reading. Granted, the brief scenarios presented here paint a picture that is too perfect, but the purpose is to highlight literacy strategies and materials. In all instances, the teachers and students are real persons, but they have been placed in settings different from those in which I originally observed them. This was done out of respect for their privacy and in keeping with institutional review board policies at the university.

Boundaries are usually associated with lines that divide or limit, as in territorial borders or frontiers. History is filled with allusions to boundaries that have marked the extent of one country's territory and the beginning of another's. Take for example the phrase "crossing the Rubicon," a small river separating Gaul from Italy, which marked Caesar's starting point in his conquest of Italy. In his widely acclaimed book, *Lives on the Boundary,* Mike Rose (1989) writes about another kind of boundary, the one we erect as classroom teachers and college instructors when we focus on what our students can't do rather than on what they can do. Rose argues that members of the educational underclass—a term he uses to describe students who struggle daily with classroom reading and writing tasks and who sometimes feel alienated by the process—have literate capacities that are often hidden from view because "they just [aren't] thought to be there" (p. 222). Rose, who himself was once labeled slow, remedial, and underprepared, is convinced that such barriers to student success can be crossed. In fact, he sees hope for such movement if, as educators, we dwell less on labeling students' differences and more on discovering their literate capacities.

In this chapter, I draw upon a fictionalized day in the life of three general-track students—Williamjames, Claudia, and Tiffany—to illustrate how they, aided by teachers knowledgeable in content reading strategies, are able to cross the boundaries Rose (1989) describes. When appropriate, I have tried to show how the strategies and materials the teachers used may have encouraged students to engage in the kinds of literate actions they were capable of undertaking all along.

Monday, 8:35 A.M.

A group of students in Mr. Abner's first-period English class were gathered outside his door, intensely engaged in what appeared to be a game of friendly wager. Hearing the disturbance, Mr. Abner looked up from the stack of papers he was grading. "My road dogs," he mumbled affectionately. It was a nickname that had stuck. Mr. Abner had used the term "road dogs" originally to refer to the students in Nathanielsboro Comprehensive High School who were thought to be "at risk" of dropping out but who managed to stay in school despite the fact they worked part-time jobs and sometimes pushed the limits of the

---

Think while Reading Activity

While reading about Williamjames, Claudia, and Tiffany, note their school experiences.

_____

_____

_____

_____

_____

_____

_____

_____

_____

_____

Activity 29–2

school's rather strict attendance policies. Gradually, the nickname was applied to anyone who worked hard. Students in his classes vied for the honor of being called Mr. Abner's "road dogs."

As Mr. Abner moved toward the door to usher the noisy students inside, he heard Williamjames's voice over the loud ring of the warning bell:

"Naw, he won't ever be able to beat that opener he staged when we started *The Chocolate War.* Remember when . . ."

"The staged boxing match!" interrupted Ramon. "Between Jerry and . . . Yeah, I'm with you. My money says he won't ever be able to top that one—ever!"

"What do you say, gang? Ready to step inside and find out what I have in store for you today?" asked Mr. Abner as he ushered the group into the classroom. He had liked using Robert Cormier's young adult novel as a model for understanding plot and several interrelated subplots. Apparently his students had, too, he mused. It also occurred to him that Cormier's novel had provided insight into social class differences, a fact of life not lost upon his students who came from mostly low-income homes.

Williamjames took a seat next to Claudia as the tardy bell sounded. He felt comfortable around her. She worked weekends at the same convenience food mart where he worked week nights. Both of them hoped to attend a small two-year state college in a neighboring county once they graduated from high school in the spring.

"All right," said Mr. Abner as he visually checked attendance, "we're ready to start a real classic—Steinbeck's *Of Mice and Men.* We'll see the same theme operating here as we did in *The Chocolate War.* We'll see how pain—both emotional and physical—is part and parcel of being accepted by others."

So, thought Williamjames to himself, he was right. No splashy "turn-on" opener today. Actually, he was only half right. Mr. Abner knew that his students would be able to identify quite readily with George's and Lenny's dream of buying their own place. He recalled that one of his "road dogs" had said just the other day that she was going to work hard and graduate so she could buy her dream house.

Mr. Abner chose the Directed Reading-Thinking Activity (DR-TA) as a strategy for introducing Steinbeck's well-known story about two drifters whose friendship and common dream are threatened by circumstances beyond their control. He began the DR-TA (Richek, 1987; Stauffer, 1969) by asking students to predict what a story titled *Of Mice and Men* might be about. Some students took the title literally and responded, "About mice and men?" Others looked for symbolism. Still others, who were familiar with Steinbeck's *Grapes of Wrath,* predicted that the story would be about the Great Depression and how people treated each other. Some discussion about the appropriateness of each prediction followed.

Before directing the students to read the first part of the chapter to check the accuracy of their predictions, Mr. Abner introduced the word *dominate.* He said that students would be able to understand how George was able to *dominate* Lenny if they thought for a minute about last Friday night's football game in which Nathanielsboro had dominated the much stronger, but less skilled opposing team from Ludington. Mr. Abner also reminded students of a strategy for figuring out other unfamiliar words. "Look for clues to the words that are unfamiliar to you," he said. "Sometimes the clue words will be set apart by commas; other times they may be synonyms or antonyms for the unknown word," he added.

Later, after students had completed reading the first section of Chapter 1, Mr. Abner engaged them in a discussion of its contents:

Mr. Abner: Why does George stay with Lenny?

Carmen: When they apply for a job, the foreman often gives it to them because Lenny's strong.

Tamara: Wait, hold it, I thought Williamjames just said that it was because of Lenny that they had *lost* their last job.

Mr. Abner: Okay, right. He killed the mouse. That's foreshadowing, which we talked about yesterday. It's a clue to something that may be important later on. Steinbeck is telling us that for a good reason. But you still haven't told us why George sticks with Lenny.

We leave the discussion now and Mr. Abner's first-period English class, although typically the teacher who uses the DR-TA would lead students into the next set of predictions, and the cycle of predicting, reading, and verifying those predictions would begin again.

Monday, 9:30 A.M.

Claudia finished lacing up her sneaker and gathered with the other students by the chart stand.

"Today," Ms. Dillingworth said, "you'll be learning a new out-of-bounds play called the buttonhole. As you read the diagram, you can see that the play is executed when Player A passes the ball over the defense to Player E, who has moved straight to the basket for a lay-up shot. The other players have also moved to the positions indicated on the diagram. Note that Players B and C are now in position to feed or rebound, while Player D at the top of the key is ready to receive a possible pass." Ms. Dillingworth demonstrated some of the action as she described the play.

Claudia liked Ms. Dillingworth as a teacher because she took the time to make certain that her students had a clear understanding of how the players moved before she removed the chart stand and asked them to carry out the play on the court. Claudia also appreciated the fact that her teacher demonstrated the special meanings attributed to the terms *feed* and *key* as she explained the out-of-bounds play. Claudia had heard and used both of those words many times, but always in a general sense and not, as here, specifically linked to basketball. Like most students, she needed several exposures to new words or meanings before she could call them her own (see Chapter 18).

Monday, 10:25 A.M.

Math lab was the favorite period of the day for Claudia. Each Monday and Wednesday, along with ten other members from her algebra class, she worked independently using commercially prepared computer applications of concepts she had been introduced to in

Ms. Stoll's class. This morning Claudia chose a tutorial on graphing linear inequalities. The demands the tutorial made on her as a reader were considerable, for in addition to comprehending the verbal description of linear inequalities, she also had to work problems that assessed her ability to apply what she had read. Fortunately, Ms. Stoll had prepared her in advance so that she could make the most out of the time she would spend using the computerized tutorial. For example, Ms. Stoll had taught Claudia the value of monitoring (Baker & Brown, 1984) her understanding of the task at hand. To refresh her memory, Claudia pulled her math learning log (see Chapter 16) from her book bag and began to read the notes she had jotted down in class a few days ago.

After completing the tutorial on graphing linear inequalities, Claudia evaluated the learning experience by trying to think of ways the information would be of use to her. She also asked herself whether there were concepts she still did not understand.

Monday, 11:20 A.M.

Williamjames entered the room of his least favorite class—world cultures. He wonders why he ever elected to take the course. "The teacher is okay," he conceded. "It's just the content that is boring!"

Mr. Sutton, who taught the class, was aware of his students' general dislike of the content and worked hard to engage them in a variety of interactive learning strategies. He was particularly drawn to the strategy known as *Group Reading for Different Purposes* (GRDP) (Dolan, 1979), because it enabled students to make use of multiple sources of information (see Chapter 19). He also liked GRDP because it promoted critical reading and encouraged students to elaborate on each other's thinking.

Think while Reading Activity

How do you think your life would have been enhanced if you had attended Nathanielsboro High School?

_____

_____

_____

_____

_____

_____

_____

_____

_____

Activity 29–3

In operation, Group Reading for Different Purposes looked like this: Williamjames, along with his classmates, silently read the first section of the chapter on desert cultures. After completing the reading assignment, he and his three closest neighbors turned in their seats to face one another. Other groups of four were similarly formed around the classroom. Each group had a different task to complete, based on their reading. Group 1, for example, had to list six statements (three factual and three opinion). Later, in large-group discussion, they would ask other classmates to distinguish fact from opinion. Group 2 had to present an alternative explanation to the one given in the text about how deserts shape peoples' lives. Later, in large-group discussion, they would ask the class to choose the stronger of the two explanations.

After the small groups had had an opportunity to complete their tasks, Mr. Sutton reconvened the class for large-group discussion. Each group presented its findings or the product of its work to the whole class.

Monday, 1:10 P.M.

Claudia and her good friend Tiffany usually go early to their ecology class, preferring to spend the last ten minutes or so of their lunch period chatting in the relative quiet of Ms. Rodriguez's room. However, today as they are about to enter the room, Ms. Rodriguez stops them. She explains that something special is going to happen in class today and she needs time to prepare the room. Claudia and Tiffany wait expectantly outside the room speculating about what Ms. Rodriguez has in store for them. They assume it will have something to do with literature because Ms. Rodriguez is fond of integrating literature with her units on the environment. As the first bell rings, students begin filing into Ms. Rodriguez's room. Claudia and Tiffany note instantly that the lights in the room have been turned off and the shades drawn. Ms. Rodriguez begins to pass out individual copies of Scholastic's *Scope Magazine*. She invites the students to turn to a short story by Ray Bradbury titled, "All Summer in a Day." As the students do so, they complain good naturedly about not being able to see well enough to read the selection. Ms. Rodriguez ignores their complaints, saying, " 'What if the environment got so bad that you had to leave the Earth? That's what happened to the children of Venus. Only Margot can remember the Earth— and the sun." With that bit of an introduction taken directly from the text of the story, she asks them to read the selection.

When the students have finished reading, they write about their reactions to the selection in their science journal. Claudia and Tiffany exchange journals and discover that they both chose to write about how Margot must have felt when she was forced to miss the two hours that the sun came out on Venus. They also commented on how she must have felt knowing that it would be another seven years before the sun would break through the constant rain. Tiffany's journal contained a rough chart that compared the sun's presence on Earth with that on Venus. Claudia's journal entry included a poem, written in free verse, which captured her feelings about the warming effect of the sun's rays.

After students have had an opportunity to share their journals with a friend, Ms. Rodriguez invites class members to share orally their responses to the Bradbury piece. A lively large-group discussion ensues. Then, without warning, Ms. Rodriguez flips on the light switch and proceeds to raise the shades. Sunlight fills the room once again, and the class is ready to begin the unit on global warming.

Monday, 2:05 P.M.

During the last period of the day, Claudia, Tiffany, and Williamjames elected to go to the group study area of the media center. There they participated in a study technique known as *Triangular Review* (Herber, 1978). They were studying for a multiple-choice test on Eastern religions in their world cultures class, and Mr. Sutton had suggested that they use Triangular Review because it would provide a means for self-assessing their preparedness. He gave them three separate checklists consisting of key words and phrases that they could expect to see on the exam.

The three students grouped themselves so that two of them were sitting opposite the third member. Each member of the twosome had an identical copy of one of the three

---

Think after Reading Activity

Assume that you are a teacher at Nathanielsboro High School. You have worked in your school for several years, have attended many regional workshops, and have several professional colleagues who teach at schools that follow a traditional educational plan. How would you explain your school's teaching rationale to these friends? Please refer to the following two ideas from Mike Rose's *Lives on the Boundary* in your response:

"students who aren't thought to be there"

"crossing the boundaries"

_____

_____

_____

_____

_____

_____

_____

_____

_____

_____

_____

_____

_____

Activity 29–4

checklists. (The two remaining checklists were set aside for use in the next two rounds of Triangular Review.)

The third member of the review team was in the proverbial hot seat—today, that was Tiffany. It was her job to recall as much information as she could on the topic of Eastern religions. As she began to name off such things as asceticism, Buddha, reincarnation, and the Four Noble Truths, the two reviewers (Claudia and Williamjames) placed a plus sign (+) next to the corresponding terms on their checklists. When Tiffany could no longer think of any new words or phrases, the two reviewers prompted her with clues. An X was placed before items on the checklist that Tiffany recalled with help from the reviewers.

When Tiffany could no longer recall any items, even with the help of the reviewers, the first round of Triangular Review was over. At the end of the first round, Tiffany was given the marked checklists of the two reviewers. The information contained on those checklists was to be used for personal study at home that evening.

Conclusion

While Claudia, Williamjames, and Tiffany were fortunate to have teachers who believed in their potential, regardless of the track in which they were placed, others in their peer group may not have been that lucky. It is for the teachers of those less fortunate students that this chapter and others like it were written. For the ideas expressed here and elsewhere in this volume are the means by which content area learning can come closer to being a reality for all students. Using these ideas to engage students in learning is surely what Mike Rose must have had in mind when he wrote, "If you set up the right conditions, try as best you can to cross class and cultural boundaries, figure out what's needed to encourage performance, . . . there will emerge evidence of ability that escapes those who dwell on differences" (p. 222).

Affiliations

Donna Alvermann is a Research Professor of Reading Education at the University of Georgia and Co-Director of the National Reading Research Center.

Bonnie B. Armbruster is a Professor of Education, University of Illinois, Urbana-Champaign.

Patricia L. Anders is a Professor in the Division of Language, Reading, and Culture at the College of Education at the University of Arizona in Tucson.

Helene M. Anthony is an Assistant Professor of Education at Moorhead State University in Minnesota.

James Barton is an Assistant Professor of Education at the University of Rhode Island.

Thomas W. Bean is a Professor of Reading and Literacy Education at the University of Nevada, Las Vegas.

Linda Burkey is an Assistant Professor at Mount Union College.

Joan F. Curry, a Professor of Teacher Education at San Diego State University, is also the Director of the Program in Reading and Language Arts.

Ernest K. Dishner is a Professor of Education at Penn State University, Harrisburg.

Nancy Farnan is an Associate Professor of Teacher Education at San Diego State University.

Roger Farr is a Chancellor's Professor and Associate Dean for Research and Graduate Development at Indiana University.

Edward Fry is Professor Emeritus at Rutgers University.

James Flood is a Professor of Reading and Language Development at San Diego State University.

Lance M. Gentile is a Professor in the Department of Elementary Education at San Francisco State University.

Michael F. Graves is a Professor in the Department of Curriculum and Instruction at the University of Minnesota.

Shirley Harrison teaches ninth grade earth science at Kalispell Junior High School in Kalispell, Montana.

Lynn Havens is the disseminator for the Content Reading in Secondary Schools (CRISS) Project developed in Kalispell, Montana.

Robert P. Hoffman is an Assistant Professor of Educational Technology at San Diego State University.

Diane Lapp is a Professor of Reading and Language Development at San Diego State University.

Carol V. Lloyd is an Associate Professor at the University of Nebraska at Omaha.

Nancy Marshall is an Associate Professor in the College of Education at Florida International University. Miami.

Merna M. McMillan is Director of Mental Health in Santa Barbara County, California.

Larry Mikulecky is a Professor of Education at Indiana University, Bloomington.

John F. O'Flahavan is an Associate Professor at the University of Maryland, College Park.

Donna M. Ogle, a Professor of Education, chairs the Reading and Language Department of National-Louis University, Evanston, Illinois.

Mary W. Olson is a Professor and Associate Dean of Education at the University of North Carolina at Greensboro.

Charles W. Peters is a secondary language arts consultant for the Oakland Intermediate School District in Pontiac, Michigan.

Robert Pritchard is an Associate Professor of Teacher Education at California State University, Fresno.

Nancy Prosenjak is a doctoral candidate at Kent State University.

Taffy E. Raphael is a Professor in the Departments of Teacher Education and Educational Psychology at Michigan State University.

John E. Readence is a Professor of Education at the University of Nevada, Las Vegas.

Laura R. Roehler is a Professor of Education at Michigan State University and a Senior Researcher in the Institute for Research on Teaching.

Alicia Romero is a lecturer and doctoral student in the Department of English as a Second Language at McGill University.

Nancy Lee Roser is a Professor of Curriculum and Instruction at the University of Texas at Austin.

Martha Rapp Ruddell is a Professor of Education at Sonoma State University, Rohnert Park, California.

Carol Minnick Santa is the Director of Curriculum for Kalispell, Montana, Public Schools.

Diane Lemonnier Schallert is a Professor of Educational Psychology at the University of Texas at Austin.

Stephen Simonsen is a Professor of English at College of the Desert in Palm Desert, California.

Wayne H. Slater is an Associate Professor in the Department of Curriculum and Instruction and the Department of English at the University of Maryland, College Park.

Robert E. Slavin is Co-Director of the Center for Research on Education of Students Placed at Risk, John Hopkins University.

Carl Smith is a Professor of Education at Indiana University and Director of the ERIC Clearinghouse for Reading and Language Arts.

Eleanor W. Thonis is District Psychologist for the Wheatland, California, Schools and a part-time instructor at the University of California, Davis.

Robert J. Tierney is a Professor of Education at Ohio State University.

JoAnne L. Vacca is a Professor and Chairperson of Teacher Development and Curriculum Studies at Kent State University.

Richard T. Vacca is a Professor of Teacher Development and Curriculum Studies at Kent State University.

Karen D. Wood is a Professor of Education at the University of North Carolina at Charlotte.

References

Chapter 1   Mary W. Olson, Ernest K. Dishner

Anderson, R. C., Hilbert, E. H., Scott, A. A., & Wilkinson, I. A. G. (1985). *Becoming a nation of readers: The report of the Commission on Reading.* Urbana, IL: University of Illinois, Center for the Study of Reading.

Anderson, T. H., & Armbruster, B. B. (1984). Studying. In P. D. Pearson (Ed.), *Handbook of reading research* (pp. 657–680). New York: Longman.

Armbruster, B. B., Anderson, T. H., Armstrong, J. O., Wise, M. A., Janisch, C., & Meyer, L. A. (1991). Reading and questioning in content area lessons. *Journal of Reading Behavior, 23,* 35–59.

Austin, M., & Morrison, C. (1963). *The first R: The Harvard report on reading in elementary schools.* New York: Macmillian.

Austin, M., & Morrison, C. (1961). *The torch lighters.* Cambridge, MA: Harvard University Press.

Beck, I. L., Omanson, R. C., & McKeown, M. G. (1982). An instructional redesign of reading lessons: Effects on comprehension. *Reading Research Quarterly, 17,* 462–81.

Bond, G. L., & Bond, E. (1941). *Developmental reading in high school.* New York: Macmillan.

Bretzing, B. B., & Kulhavey, R. II. (1981). Note-taking and passage style. *Journal of Educational Psychology, 73,* 242–250.

Brunner, J. F., & Campbell, J. J. (1978). *Participating in secondary reading: A practical approach.* Englewood Cliffs NJ: Prentice-Hall.

Burton, N. W., & Jones, L. V. (1982). Recent trends in achievement levels of black and white youth. *Educational Researcher, 11* (4), 10–14.

Cattell, J. M. (1886). The time it takes to see and name objects. *Mind, 11,* 63–65.

Center, S. S., & Persons, G. L. (1937). *Teaching high school students to read.* Englewood Cliffs, NJ: Prentice Hall.

Conley, M. W. (1992). *Content reading instruction.* New York: McGraw-Hill.

Crawford, C. C. (1928). *The technique of study.* Boston: Houghton Mifflin.

Day, J. D. (1980). *Training summarization skills: A comparison of teaching methods.* Unpublished doctoral dissertation, University of Illinois.

Durkin, D. (1978 & 1979). What classroom observations reveal about reading comprehension instruction. *Reading Research Quarterly, 14,* 481–533.

Eanet, M. G., & Manzo, A. V. (1976). REAP—A strategy for improving reading skills. *Journal of Reading, 19,* 647–652.

Early, M. J. (1957). What does research reveal about successful reading programs? In M. A. Gunn and others (Eds.), *What we know about high school reading.* Champaign, IL: National Council of Teachers of English.

Farrell, R. J., & Cirrincione, J. M. (1984). State certification requirements in reading for content area teachers. *Journal of Reading, 28,* 152–158.

Fay, L. (1965). Reading study skills: Math and science. In J. A. Figurel (Ed.), *Reading and inquiry.* Newark, DE: International Reading Association.

Flemming, C. M., & Woodring, M. N. (1928). Training high school pupils in study procedures with emphasis upon reading. *Teachers College Record,* December, 589–610.

Gee, T. C., Olson, M. W., & Forester, N. (1989). A survey of content reading program development in U.S. schools. *Reading Research and Instruction, 28* (3), 30–44.

Gray, W. S. (1916). A study of the emphasis on various phases of reading instruction in two cities. *Elementary School Journal, 17,* 178–186.

Gray, W. S. (1919). The relation between studying and reading. In *Addresses and Proceedings of the Fifty-Seventh Annual Meeting of the National Education Association, 57,* 580–586.

Gray, W. S. (1925). Summary of investigations relating to reading. *Supplementary Educational Monographs,* No. 28. Chicago: University of Chicago Press.

Gray, W. S. (1937). The nature and organization of basic instruction in reading. In G. M. Whipple (Ed.), *The teaching of reading: A second report.* Thirty-Sixth Yearbook of the National Society for the Study of Education, Part I (pp. 65–132). Bloomington, IL: Public School Publishing.

Gray, W. S. (Ed.). (1947). Improving reading in content fields. *Supplementary Educational Monograph,* No. 62. Chicago: University of Chicago Press.

Gray, W. S. (Ed.). (1952). Improving reading in all curriculum areas. *Supplementary Educational Monographs,* No. 76. Chicago: University of Chicago Press.

Harris, J. (1990). *Text annotation and underlying as metacognitive strategies to improve comprehension and retention of expository text.* Paper presented at the annual meeting of the National Reading Conference, Miami, FL.

Herber, H. L., & Sanders, P. L. (Eds.). (1969). *Research in reading in the content areas: First report.* Syracuse, NY: Syracuse University Reading and Language Arts Center.

Herber, H. L. (1970, 1978). *Teaching reading in content areas.* Englewood Cliffs, NJ: Prentice-Hall.

Herber, H. L., & Barron, R. F. (Eds.). (1973). *Research in reading in the content areas: Second report.* Syracuse, NY: Syracuse University Reading and Language Arts Center.

Herber, H. L. & Vacca, R. T. (eds.) (1977). *Research in reading in the content areas: Third report.* Syracuse, NY: Syracuse University Reading and Language Arts Center.

Levin, H. M. (1985). *The educationally disadvantaged: A national crisis.* Arlington, VA: ERIC Document Reproduction Service, No. ED 264 313.

Mandler, J. M., & Johnson, M. S. (1977). Remembrance of things passed: Story structure and recall. *Cognitive Psychology, 9,* 111–151.

Mastain, R. K. (Ed.). (1991). *Manual on certification and preparation of educational personnel in the United States—National Association of State Directors of Teacher Education and Certification.* Dubuque, IA: Kendall/Hunt.

McCallister, J. M. (1936). *Remedial and corrective instruction in reading: A program for the upper grades and high school.* Englewood Cliffs, NJ: Prentice-Hall.

McMurry, P. M. (1909). *How to study and teaching how to study.* Boston: Houghton Mifflin.

Moore, D. W., Readence, J. E., & Rickelman, R. J. (1983). An historical exploration of content reading instruction. *Reading Research Quarterly, 18,* 419–438.

Morrison, C., & Austin, M. (1977). *The torch lighters revisited.* Newark, DE: International Reading Association.

Niles, O. S. (1965). Organization perceived. In H. L. Herber (Ed.), *Developing study skills in secondary schools* (pp. 57–76). Newark, DE: International Reading Association.

Nist, S. L., & Kirby, K. (1989). The text marking patterns of college students. *Reading Psychology, 10* (4), 321–338.

Olson, A. V., & Ames, W. S. (1972). *Teaching reading skills in secondary schools.* Scranton, PA: Intext Educational Publishers.

Olson, A. V., & Rosen, C. L. (1967). A study of teacher practices in reading. *Reading Improvement, 4,* 84–87.

Olson, M. W., & Gee, T. C. (1991). Content reading instruction in the primary grades: Perceptions and strategies. *The Reading Teacher, 45* (4), 298–307.

Pauk, W. (1963). On scholarship: Advice to high school students. *The Reading Teacher, 17,* 73–78.

Readence, J. E., Bean, T. W., & Baldwin, R. S. (1992). *Content area reading: An integrated approach* (3rd ed.). Dubuque, IA: Kendall/Hunt.

Robinson, F. P. (1946). *Effective study.* New York: Harper & Row.

Roe, B. D., Stoodt, B. D., & Burns, P. C. (1991). *Secondary school reading instruction: The areas* (4th ed.). Boston, MA: Houghton Mifflin.

Shaw, P. (1958). Rhetorical guides to reading comprehension. *The Reading Teacher, 11,* 239–248.

Singer, H. (1979). Research: Slogans and attitudes. *Journal of Reading, 22,* 756–757.

Singer, H., & Donlan, D. (1988). *Reading and learning from text* (2nd ed.). Hillsdale, NJ: Erlbaum.

Smith, N. B. (1963). *Reading instruction for today's children.* Englewood Cliffs, NJ: Prentice-Hall.

Smith, N. B. (1965). *American reading instruction* (2nd ed.). Newark, DE: International Reading Association.

Stein, N. L. & Glenn, C. G. (1979). An analysis of story comprehension in elementary school children. In R. O. Freedle (Ed.), *New Directions in Discourse Processing.* Norwood, NJ: Ablex.

Stinnett, T. M. (1974). *A manual on standards affecting school personnel in the United States.* Washington, DC: National Education Association.

Strang, R. (1940). *Problems in the improvement of reading in high school and college.* Lancaster, PA: Science Press Printing Company.

Strang, R., McCullough, C., & Traxler, A. (1967). *The improvement of Reading.* New York: McGraw-Hill.

Summers, E. G. (Ed.). (1969). *20-year annotated index to The Reading Teacher.* Newark, DE: International Reading Association.

Uhl, W. L. (1937). The materials of reading. In G. M. Whipple (Ed.), *The teaching of reading: A second report,* Thirty-Sixth Yearbook of the National Society for the Study of Education, Part I (pp. 207–254). Bloomington, IL: Public School Publishing.

U.S. Department of Education, National Center for Education Statistics. (1993). *Issue brief: School enrollment expected to surpass historic all-time high.* Arlington, VA: ERIC Document Reproduction Service, No. ED 360 377.

Vacca, R. T., & Vacca, J. A. (1989). *Content Area Reading* (3rd ed.). Boston: Little, Brown.

Whipple, G. M. (Ed.). (1925). *Report of the national committee on reading,* Twenty-Fourth Yearbook of the National Society for the Study of Education, Part I. Bloomington, IL: Public School Publishing.

Whipple, G. M. (Ed.) (1937). *The teaching of reading: A second report,* Thirty-Sixth Yearbook of the National Society for the Study of Education, Part I. Bloomington, Il: Public School Publishing.

Wrenn, C. G., & Cole, L. (1935). *How to read rapidly and well.* Stanford University, CA: Stanford University Press.

Yoakam, G. A. (1922). *The effects of a single reading: A study of the retention of various types of material in the content subjects of the elementary school after a single silent reading.* University of Iowa Studies in Education, 2, No. 7. Iowa City: University of Iowa.

Yoakam, G. A. (1928). *Reading and study.* New York: Macmillan.

Young, R. N. (1927). *Reading in the junior and senior high school.* Minneapolis, MN: Educational Test Bureau.

Chapter 2   *Thomas W. Bean, John E. Readence*

Bean, T. W., Sorter, J., Singer, H., & Frazee, C. (1986). Teaching students how to make predictions about events in history with a graphic organizer plus options guide. *Journal of Reading, 29,* 739–745.

Bransford, J. D. (1984). Schema activation and schema acquisition: Comments on Richard C. Anderson's remarks. In R. C. Anderson, J. Osborn, & R. J. Tierney (Eds.), *Learning to read in American schools: Basal readers and content texts.* Hillsdale, NJ: Erlbaum.

Carnegie Forum on Education and the Economy. (1986). New York: Carnegie Foundation.

Chall, J. S. (1983). *Stages of reading development.* New York: McGraw-Hill.

Farrell, R. T., & Cirrincione, J. M. (1984). State certification requirements in reading for content area teachers. *Journal of Reading, 28,* 152–158.

Farrell, R. T., & Cirrincione, J. M. (1986). The introductory developmental reading course for content area teachers: A state of the art survey. *Journal of Reading, 29,* 717–723.

Guskey, T. R. (1986). Staff development and the process of teacher change. *Educational Researcher, 15,* 5–12.

Herber, H. L. (1984). Subject matter texts—reading to learn: Response to a paper by Thomas H. Anderson and Bonnie B. Armbruster. In R. C. Anderson,

J. Osborn, & R. J. Tierney (Eds.), *Learning to read in American schools: Basal readers and content texts*. Hillsdale, NJ: Erlbaum.

Hinchman, K. (1992). How teachers use the textbook: Lessons from three secondary school classrooms. In E. K. Dishner, T. W. Bean, J. E. Readence, & D. W. Moore (Eds.), *Reading in the content areas: Improving classroom instruction* (3rd ed., pp. 282–293). Dubuque, IA: Kendall/Hunt.

Lewis, J., Radziemski, C., Blanchard, J. S., & Mason, G. E. (1992). Technology, reading, and content teaching: Into the nineties and toward the 21st century. In E. K. Dishner, T. W. Bean, J. E. Readence, & D. W. Moore (Eds.), *Reading in the content areas: Improving classroom instruction* (3rd ed., pp. 442–452). Dubuque, IA: Kendall/Hunt.

Provenzo, E. F. (1992). Computers in the content areas. In J. E. Readence, T. W. Bean, & R. S. Baldwin (Eds.), *Content area reading: An integrated approach* (4th ed., pp. 335–343). Dubuque, IA: Kendall/Hunt.

Readence, J. E., Bean, T. W., & Baldwin, R. S. (1995). *Content area literacy: An integrated approach* (5th ed.). Dubuque, IA: Kendall/Hunt.

Siedow, M. D., Memory, D. M., & Bristow, P. S. (1985). *Inservice education for content area teachers*. Newark, DE: International Reading Association.

Singer, H. (1992). Friendly texts: Description and criteria. In E. K. Dishner, T. W. Bean, J. E. Readence, & D. W. Moore (Eds.), *Reading in the content areas: Improving classroom instruction* (3rd ed., pp. 155–172). Dubuque, IA: Kendall/Hunt.

Singer, H., & Bean, T. W. (1988). Models for helping teachers to help students learn from text. In S. J. Samuels & P. D. Pearson (Eds.), *Changing school reading programs*. Newark, DE: International Reading Association.

Smith, F. R., & Feathers, K. M. (1983). The role of reading in content classrooms: Assumptions vs. reality. *Journal of Reading, 27,* 262–267.

Chapter 3   Diane Lemonnier Schallert, Nancy Lee Roser

Anderson, T. H., & Armbruster, B. B. (1984). Content area textbooks. In R. C. Anderson, J. Osborn, & R. J. Tierney (Eds.), *Learning to read in American schools: Basal readers and content texts* (pp. 193–226). Hillsdale, NJ: Erlbaum.

Armbruster, B. B. (1984). The problems of "inconsiderate text." In G. G. Duffy, L. R. Roehler, & J. Mason (Eds.), *Comprehension instruction: Perspectives and suggestions* (pp. 202–217). New York: Longman.

Beck, I. L., McKeown, M. G., & Gromoll, E. W. (1989). Learning from social studies texts. *Cognition & Instruction, 6,* 99–158.

Cullinan, B. (1989). *Literature and the child* (2nd ed.). New York: Harcourt Brace Jovanovich.

Fritz, J. (1986). *Make way for Sam Houston*. New York: Putnam.

Fritz, J. (1983). *The double life of Pocahontas*. New York: Putnam.

Garfield, E. (1984). Science books for children. *Current Contents: Life Science,* December 24–31, 3–11.

Garner, R., Gillingham, M. G., & White, C. S. (1989). Effects of "seductive details" and microprocessing in adults and children. *Cognition & Instruction, 6,* 41–57.

Guzzetti, B. J., Kowalinski, B. J. & McGowan, T. (1992). Using a literature-based approach to teaching social studies. *Journal of Reading, 36,* 114–122.

Harms, N. C., & Yager, R. E. (Eds.). (1981). *Volume 3: What research says to the science teacher.* Washington, DC: National Science Teachers Association, Stock No. 471-14776.

Huck, C., Hepler, S., & Hickman, J. (1993). *Children's literature in the elementary school* (5th ed.). New York: Harcourt Brace Jovanovich.

Moss, B. (1991). Children's nonfiction trade books: A complement to content area texts. *The Reading Teacher, 45,* 26–32.

Neal, J. C., & Moore, K. (1992). *The Very Hungry Caterpillar* meets *Beowulf* in secondary classrooms. *Journal of Reading, 35,* 290–296.

Schallert, D. L., Alexander, P. A., & Goetz, E. T. (1985). What do instructors and authors do to influence the textbook-student relationship? In J. Niles & R. Lalik (Eds.), *Issues in literacy: A research perspective* (34th Yearbook of the National Reading Conference) (pp. 110–115). Rochester, NY: National Reading Conference.

Schallert, D. L., Alexander, P. A., & Goetz, E. T. (1987). Implicit instruction of strategies for learning from text. In C. E. Weinstein, E. T. Goetz, & P. A. Alexander (Eds.), *Learning and study strategies: Issues in assessment, instruction, and evaluation.* New York: Academic Press.

Schallert, D. L., & Tierney, R. J. (1982). *Learning from expository text: The interaction of text structure with reader characteristics.* Final report to the National Institute of Education, Grant No. NIE-G-79-0167.

Simon, S. (1992). *Our solar system.* New York: Morrow.

Simon, S. (1989). *Storms.* New York: Mulberry.

Wade, S. E., & Adams, R. B. (1990). Effects of importance and interest on recall of biographical text. *Journal of Reading Behavior, 22,* 331–353.

Wade, S. E., Schraw, G., Buxton, W. M., & Hayes, M. T. (1993). Seduction of the strategic reader: Effects of interest on strategies and recall. *Reading Research Quarterly, 28,* 93–114.

Chapter 4   Edward Fry

Dale, D., & Chall, J. S. (1948). A formula for predicting readability. *Educational Research Bulletin, 27,* 11–20, 37–54.

Fry, E. B. (1977). Fry's readability graph: Clarifications, validity, and extension to level 17. *Journal of Reading, 21,* 242–252.

Klare, D. K. (1984). Readability. In P. D. Pearson, et al. (Eds.), *Handbook of reading research.* New York: Longman.

Spache, G. (1953). A new readability formula for primary-grade reading materials. *Elementary School Journal, 30,* 117–124.

Chapter 5   Bonnie B. Armbruster

Alexander, P. A., Schallert, D. L., & Hare, V. C. (1991). Coming to terms: How researchers in learning and literacy talk about knowledge. *Review of Educational Research, 61,* 315–343.

Anderson, T. H., & Armbruster, B. B. (1984). Content area textbooks. In R. C. Anderson, J. Osborn, & R. J. Tierney (Eds.), *Learning to read in American schools: Basal readers and content texts* (pp. 193–226). Hillsdale, NJ: Erlbaum.

Applebee, A. N., Langer, J. A., & Mullis, I. V. S. (1989). *Crossroads in American education.* Princeton, NJ: Educational Testing Service.

Armbruster, B. B. (1984). The problem of "inconsiderate text." In G. G. Duffy, L. R. Roehler, & J. Mason (Eds.), *Comprehension instruction: Perspectives and suggestions* (pp. 202–217). New York: Longman.

Armbruster, B. B., & Anderson, T. H. (1984). Structures for explanations in history textbooks, or so what if Governor Stanford missed the spike and hit the rail? *Journal of Curriculum Studies, 16,* 181–194.

Bartlett, B. J. (1978). *Top-level structure as an organizational strategy for recall of classroom text.* Unpublished doctoral dissertation, Arizona State University, Tempe.

Baumann, J. (1986). Effects of rewritten content text passages on middle grade students' comprehension of main ideas: Making the inconsiderate considerate. *Journal of Reading Behavior, 18,* 1–22.

Black, J. B., & Bern, H. (1981). Causal coherence and memory for events in narratives. *Journal of Verbal Learning and Verbal Behavior, 20,* 267–275.

Frederiksen, J. R. (1981). Understanding anaphora: Rules used by readers in assigning pronominal referents. *Discourse Processes, 4,* 323–348.

Garner, R., Gillingham, M. G., & White, J. (1989). Effects of "seductive details" on macroprocessing and microprocessing in adults and children. *Cognition and Instruction, 6,* 41–57.

Kintsch, W., & Keenan, J. M. (1973). Reading rate as a function of the number of propositions in the base structure of sentences. *Cognitive Psychology, 5,* 257–274.

Kintsch, W., Kozminsky, E., Streby, W. J., McKoon, G., & Keenan, J. M. (1975). Comprehension and recall of text as a function of content variables. *Journal of Verbal Learning and Verbal Behavior, 14,* 196–214.

Kintsch, W., Mandel, T. S., & Kozminsky, E. (1977). Summarizing scrambled stories. *Memory and Cognition, 5,* 547–552.

Maria, K., & MacGinitie, W. (1987). Learning from texts that refute the reader's prior knowledge. *Reading Research and Instruction, 26,* 222–238.

Marshall, N. (1989). Overcoming problems with incorrect prior knowledge: An instructional study. *Cognitive and social perspectives for literacy and instruction.* Thirty-Eighth yearbook of the National Reading Conference (pp. 323–330). Washington, DC: National Reading Conference.

Marshall, N., & Glock, M. D. (1978–1979). Comprehension of connected discourse: A study into the relationship between the structure of text and information recalled. *Reading Research Quarterly, 16,* 10–56.

McGee, L. M. (1982). Awareness of text structure: Effects on children's recall of expository text. *Reading Research Quarterly, 17,* 581–590.

Meyer, B.J.F., Brandt, D. M., & Bluth, G. J. (1980). Use of top-level structure in text: Key for reading comprehension of ninth-grade students. *Reading Research Quarterly, 16,* 72–103.

Pearson, P. D. (1974–1975). The effects of grammatical complexity on children's comprehension, recall, and conception of certain semantic relations. *Reading Research Quarterly, 10,* 155–192.

Richgels, D. J., McGee, L. M., Lomax, R. G., & Sheard, C. (1987). Awareness of four text structures: Effects on recall of expository text. *Reading Research Quarterly, 22,* 177–196.

Schank, R. C. (1975). The structure of episodes in memory. In D. Bobrow & A. Collins (Eds.), *Representation and understanding: Studies in cognitive science* (pp. 237–272). New York: Academic.

Stein, N. L., & Nezworski, T. (1978). The effects of organization and instructional set on story memory. *Discourse Processes, 1,* 177–193.

Taylor, B. M. (1980). Children's memory for expository text after reading. *Reading Research Quarterly, 15,* 399–411.

Taylor, B. M. (1982). Text structure and children's comprehension and memory for expository material. *Journal of Educational Psychology, 74,* 323–340.

Trabasso, T., Secco, T., & van den Broek, P. (1984). Causal cohesion and story coherence. In H. Mandle, N. L. Stein, & T. Trabasso (Eds.), *Learning and comprehension of text* (pp. 83–111). Hillsdale, NJ: Erlbaum.

Chapter 6   Stephen Simonsen

Anderson, J. R. (1985). *Cognitive psychology and its implications.* New York: W. H. Freeman.

Armbruster, B. (1989). Teaching text structure to improve reading. *The Reading Teacher, 43,* 130–137.

Armbruster, B., Anderson, T., & Meyer, J. (1991). Improving content-area reading using instructional graphics. *Reading Research Quarterly, 24,* 393–416.

Barnett, J. E. (1984). Facilitating retention through instruction about text structure. *Journal of Reading Behavior, 16,* 1–13.

Britton, B. K., Glynn, S. M., Muth, D. K., & Penfield, M. J. (1985). Instructional objectives in text: Managing the reader's attention. *Journal of Reading Behavior, 27,* 101–113.

Chall, J. (1983). *Stages of reading development.* New York: McGraw-Hill.

Chall, J., Jacobs, V., & Baldwin, L. (1990). *The reading crisis: Why poor children fail.* Cambridge, MA: Harvard University Press.

Christensen, F. (1967). *Notes toward a new rhetoric: Six essays for teachers.* New York: Harper Collins.

Clark, C. (1986). Assessing comprehensibility: The PHAN system. In J. W. Irwin (Ed.), *Understanding and assessing cohesion comprehension* (pp. 55–64). Newark, DE: International Reading Association.

Clarke, J. H. (1991). Using visual organizers to focus on thinking. *Journal of Reading, 34,* 526–534.

Clarke, J., Martell, K., & Willey, C. (1994). Sequencing graphic organizers to guide historical research. *The Social Studies, 85,* 70–75.

Conlin, M. L. (1992). *Patterns.* Boston: Houghton Mifflin.

Dahlberg, L. A. (1990). Teaching for the information age. *Journal of Reading, 34,* 12–18.

Day, J. (1980). *Teaching summarization skills: A comparison of training methods.* Unpublished doctoral dissertation, University of Illinois at Urbana–Champaign.

Dunston, P. J. (1992). A critique of graphic organizer research. *Reading Research and Instruction, 31,* 57–65.

d'Ydewalle, G., Swerts, A., & De Corte, E. (1983). Study time and test performance as a function of test expectations. *Contemporary Educational Psychology, 8,* 55–67.

Grant, R., & Davey, B. (1991). How do headings affect text processing? *Reading Research and Instruction, 31,* 12–21.

Henry, L. H. (1993). Clustering, writing, and discussing economic issues. In J. H. Clarke & A. W. Biddle (Eds.), *Teaching critical thinking* (pp. 118–122). Englewood Cliffs, NJ: Prentice Hall.

Joyce, B., & Weil, M. (1986). *Models of teaching.* Englewood Cliffs, NJ: Prentice Hall.

McCombs, M. E., Son, J., & Bang, H-K. (1988, February). *Impact of journalism genres on readership.* Paper presented at the Association for Education in Journalism and Mass Communication, Portland, OR.

Martorella, P. H. (1990). Strategies for aiding students in comprehending social studies matter. *The Social Studies, 81,* 131–134.

Santa, C., Havens, L., & Harrison, S. (1989). Teaching secondary science through reading, writing, studying, and problem solving. (1989). In D. Lapp, J. Flood, & N. Farnan (Eds.), *Content area reading and learning: Instructional strategies* (pp. 137–151). Englwood Cliffs, NJ: Prentice Hall.

Schwalm, D. (1990, November). *Using Christensen's levels of generality to teach reading comprehension.* Paper presented at the Arizona College Learning and Reading Association, Phoenix, AZ.

Simonsen, S. (1992). Postsecondary theories and models of reading and learning from text. *Review of Research in Developmental Education, 11*(4).

Smith, B. D., & Chase, N. D. (1991). The frequency and placement of main idea topic sentences in psychology textbooks. *Journal of College Reading and Learning, 24*(1), 31–41.

Smith, F. R., & Feathers, K. M. (1983). The role of reading in content area classrooms: Assumption vs. reality. *Journal of Reading, 26,* 262–267.

Stewart, R. A. (1989, December). *What color is my chalk? Literacy instruction in a secondary earth science program.* Paper presented at the National Reading Conference, Austin, TX.

Weisberg, R., & Balajthy, E. (1987, December). *Effects of training in constructing graphic organizers on disabled readers' summarization and recognition of expository text structure.* Paper presented at the National Reading Conference, Clearwater, FL.

Chapter 7   Nancy Marshall

Anderson, R. C. (1977). The notion of schemata and the educational enterprise. In R. C. Anderson, R. J. Spiro, & W. E. Montague (Eds.), *Schooling and the acquisition of knowledge* (pp. 415–432). Hillsdale, NY: Erlbaum.

Anderson, R. C. (1982). Allocation of attention during reading. In A. Flammer, and W. Kintsch (eds.), *Discourse processing* (pp. 292–305). Amsterdam: North-Holland.

Anderson, R. C., et al. (1977). Frameworks for understanding discourse. *American Educational Research Journal, 14,* 367–381.

Anderson, T. H., & Armbruster, B. B. (1984). Studying. In P. D. Pearson (Ed.), *Handbook of reading research* (pp. 657–681). New York: Longman.

Armbruster, B. B. (1984). The problem of inconsiderate text. In G. G. Duffy, L. A. Roehler, & J. Mason (Eds.), *Comprehension instruction* (pp. 202–217). New York: Longman.

Kolb, D. A. (1984). *Experiential learning.* Englewood Cliffs, NJ: Prentice-Hall.

LaBerge, D., & Samuels, S. J. (1985). Toward a theory of automatic information processing in reading. In H. Singer & R. Ruddell (Eds.), *Theoretical models and processes of reading* (3rd ed.) (pp. 689–718). Newark, DE: International Reading Association.

Marshall, N. (1981, October). *Active learning from text: teaching students how to read their textbooks.* Paper presented at the annual meeting of the Florida Reading Association conference, Miami Beach, FL.

Marshall, N. (1982, December). *Children's understanding of textbooks as an effect of instruction.* Paper presented at the annual meeting of the National Reading Conference, Clearwater Beach, FL.

Marshall, N. (1986, December). *Prior knowledge: Facilitator or inhibitor of new learning?* Paper presented at the annual meeting of the National Reading Conference, Austin, TX.

McCarthy, B. (1981). *The 4MAT system: Teaching to learning styles with right/left mode techniques.* Barrington, IL: EXCEL Inc.

Palincsar, A. S. (1984). The quest for meaning from expository text: A teacher-guided journey. In G. G. Duffy, L. A. Roehler, & J. Mason (Eds.), *Comprehension instruction* (pp. 251–264). New York: Longman.

Perfetti, C. A. (1985). *Reading ability.* New York: Oxford University Press.

Piaget, J. (1952). *The origins of intelligence in children*. New York: International University Press.

Prichert, J. W., & Anderson, R. C. (1977). Taking different perspectives on a story. *Journal of Educational Psychology, 69,* 309–315.

Roehler, L. R., & Duffy, G. G. (1984). Direct explanation of the comprehension process. In G. G. Duffy, R. R. Roehler, & J. Mason (Eds.), *Comprehension instruction* (pp. 265–280). New York: Longman.

Roth, K. L., Smith, E. L., & Anderson, C. W. (1984). Verbal patterns of teachers: Comprehension instruction in the content areas. In G. G. Duffy, L. A. Roehler, & J. Mason (Eds.), *Comprehension instruction* (pp. 281–295). New York: Longman.

Smith, F. (1981). *Understanding reading: A psycholinguistic analysis of reading and learning to read* (3rd ed.). New York: Holt, Rinehart, & Winston.

Vaughn, J. L., & Estes, T. H. (1986). *Reading and reasoning beyond the primary grades*. Boston: Allyn & Bacon.

Wilson, P. T., & Anderson, R. C. (1985). What they don't know will hurt them: The role of prior knowledge in comprehension. In J. Osborn, P. T. Wilson, & R. C. Anderson (Eds.), *Reading education: Foundations of literate America* (pp. 319–328). Lexington, MA: Lexington Books.

Chapter 8   Martha Rapp Ruddell

Aaronson, E., Stephan, C., Sikes, J., Blaney, N., & Snapp, M. (1978). *The jigsaw classroom*. Beverly Hills: Sage.

Anders, P. L., & Bos, C. S. (1986). Semantic feature analysis: An interactive strategy for vocabulary development and text comprehension. *Journal of Reading, 29,* 610–616.

Anderson, R. C. (1985). Role of the reader's schema in comprehension, learning, and memory. In H. Singer & R. B. Ruddell (Eds.), *Theoretical models and processes of reading* (3rd ed.) (pp. 372–384). Newark, DE: IRA.

Bayer, A. S. (1990). *Collaborative-apprenticeship learning: Language and thinking across the curriculum, K–12*. Mountain View, CA: Mayfield.

Bransford, J. N., & Johnson, M. K. (1972). Contextual prerequisites for understanding: Some investigations of comprehension and recall. *Journal of Verbal Learning and Verbal Behavior, 11,* 717–726.

Carr, E., & Ogle, D. (1987). K-W-L Plus: A strategy for comprehension and summarization. *Journal of Reading, 30,* 626–631.

Covington, M. V., Crutchfield, R. S., Davies, L., & Olton, R. M. (1972). *The productive thinking program*. Columbus, OH: Merrill.

Davidson, J. L. (1982). The group mapping activity for instruction in reading and thinking. *Journal of Reading, 26,* 52–56.

Davis, G. A. (1973). *Psychology of problem solving*. New York: Basic Books.

Dewey, J. (1910). *How we think*. Boston: Heath.

Dyer, P. A. (1985). *A study of the effect of prereading mapping on comprehension and transfer of learning*. Doctoral Dissertation, University of California, Berkeley.

Goodman, K. S. (1985). Unity in reading. In H. Singer & R. B. Ruddell (Eds.), *Theoretical models and processes of reading* (3rd ed.) (pp. 813–840). Newark, DE: International Reading Association.

Guralnik, D. B. (Ed.). (1978). *Webster's new world dictionary of the American language,* 2nd college edition. Cleveland: William Collins.

Haggard, M. R. (1986a). The vocabulary self-collection strategy: Using student interest and world knowledge to enhance vocabulary growth. *Journal of Reading, 29,* 634–642.

Haggard, M. R. (1986b). The vocabulary self-collection strategy: Implications from classroom practice and research. In M. P. Douglass (Ed.), *Reading: The quest for meaning,* Fiftieth Yearbook of the Claremont Reading Conference (pp. 340–351). Claremont, CA: Claremont Reading Conference.

Haggard, M. R. (1985). An interactive strategies approach to content reading. *Journal of Reading, 29,* 204–210.

Haggard, M. R. (1982). The vocabulary self-collection strategy: An active approach to word learning. *Journal of Reading, 26,* 203–207.

Haggard, M. R. (1980). Creative thinking-reading activities: (CT-RA): Bridging the gap between creative thinking and creative reading. *Reading Newsletter No. 10*. Boston: Allyn & Bacon.

Haggard, M. R. (1979). Creative thinking-reading activities (CT-RA): Catalysts for creative reading. *Illinois Reading Journal, 11,* 5–8.

Haggard, M. R. (1978). The effect of creative thinking-reading activities (CT-RA) on reading comprehension. In P. D. Pearson & J. Hansen (Eds.), *Reading: Disciplined inquiry in process and practice,* Twenty-Seventh Yearbook of the National Reading Conference (pp. 233–236). Clemsen, SC: National Reading Conference.

Hudgins, B. B., Phye, G. D., Schau, C. G., Theisen, G. L., Ames, C., & Ames, R. (1983). *Educational psychology.* Itasca, IL: F. E. Peacock.

Heimlich, J. E., & Pittelman, S. D. (1986). *Semantic mapping: Classroom applications.* Newark, DE: International Reading Association.

Johnson, D. D., Toms-Bronowski, S., & Pittelman, S. D. (1981). *A review of trends in vocabulary research and the effect of prior knowledge in instructional strategies for vocabulary acquisition* (Theoretical paper no. 95). Madison, WI: Wisconsin Center for Education Research.

Langer, J. A. (1982). Facilitating text processing: The elaboration of prior knowledge. In J. A. Langer & M. T. Smith-Burke (Eds.), *Reader meets author/bridging the gap.* Newark, DE: International Reading Association.

Manzo, A. V. (1974). The group reading activity. In *Forum for Reading.* College Reading Special Interest Group. Newark, DE: International Reading Association.

Manzo, A. V., & Manzo, U. (1990). *Content area reading: A heuristic approach.* Columbus, OH: Merrill.

Mathewson, G. C. (1994). Model of attitude influence upon reading and learning to read. In R. B. Ruddell, M. R. Ruddell, & H. Singer (Eds.), *Theoretical models and processes of reading* (4th ed.) (1131–1161). Newark, DE: International Reading Association.

Newman, F. M. (1991). Linking restructuring to authentic student achievement. *Phi Delta Kappan, 72,* 458–463.

Pittelman, S. D., Heimlich, J. E., Bergland, R. L., & French, M. P. (1991). *Semantic feature analysis: Classroom applications.* Newark, DE: International Reading Association.

Raphael, T. E. (1986). Teaching question answer relationships revisited. *The Reading Teacher, 39,* 516–522.

Rosenblatt, L. (1994). The transactional model of reading. In R. B. Ruddell, M. R. Ruddell, & H. Singer (Eds.), *Theoretical models and processes of reading* (4th ed) (1057–1092). Newark, DE: International Reading Association.

Ruddell, M. R. (1993). *Teaching content reading and writing.* Boston: Allyn & Bacon.

Ruddell, M. R-H. (1992). Integrated content and long-term vocabulary learning with the vocabulary self-collection strategy. In E. K Dishner, T. W. Bean, J. E. Readence, & D. W. Moore (Eds.), *Reading in the content areas: Improving classroom instruction* (3rd ed.) (pp. 190–196). Dubuque, IA: Kendell/Hunt.

Ruddell, R. B. (1980). Literacy achievement profiles and literacy use of high and low achievers. In M. L. Kamil & A. J. Moe (Eds.), *Perspectives on reading research and instruction,* Twenty-Ninth Yearbook of the National Reading Conference (pp. 292–302). Clemsen, SC: National Reading Conference.

Ruddell, R. B., & Haggard, M. R. (1982). Influential teachers; Characteristics and classroom performance. In J. Niles & L. A. Harris (Eds.), *New inquiries in reading research and instruction,* Thirty-First Yearbook of the National Reading Conference (pp. 227–231). Rochester, NY: National Reading Conference.

Ruddell, R. B., & Kern, R. G. (1986). The development of belief systems and teaching effectiveness in influential teachers. In M. P. Douglass (Ed.), *Reading: The quest for meaning,* Fiftieth Yearbook of the Claremont Reading Conference (pp. 113–150). Claremont, CA: Claremont Reading Conference.

Rumelhart, D. E. (1984). Understanding understanding. In J. Flood (Ed.), *Understanding reading comprehension* (pp. 1–20). Newark, DE: International Reading Association.

Russell, D. H. (1956). *Children's thinking.* Boston: Ginn.

Sadoski, M., Goetz, E. T., & Fritz, J. (1992). The impact of concreteness on comprehensibility, interest, and memory for text: Implications of dual coding theory for text design. Manuscript submitted for publication.

Sharan, S., & Sharan, Y. (1986). *Small-group teaching.* Englewood Cliffs, NJ: Prentice-Hall.

Slavin, R. E. (1990). Cooperative learning: Theory, research and practice. Englewood Cliffs, NJ: Prentice-Hall.

Smith, C. B., & Elliott, P. G. (1979). *Reading activities for middle and secondary schools.* New York: Holt.

Tierney, R. J., & Pearson, P. D. (1992). Learning to learn from text: A framework for improving classroom practice. In. E. K. Dishner, T. W. Bean, J. E. Readence, & D. W. Moore (Eds.), *Reading in the content areas: Improving classroom instruction* (pp. 87–103). Dubuque, IA: Kendell/Hunt.

Torrance, E. P., & Myers, R. E. (1974). *Creative learning and teaching.* New York: Dodd, Mead.

Vygotsky, L. V. (1986). *Thought and language* (Trans. & Ed., A. Kozulin). Cambridge, MA: MIT Press.

Chapter 9   Carl Smith

Bunstingly, J. J. (1992). *Schools of quality: An introduction to total quality management in education.* Alexandria, VA: Association for Supervision and Curriculum Development.

Deming, W. E. (1987). *Out of the crisis.* Cambridge, MA: Massachusets Institute of Technology.

Edmonds, R. (1982). On school improvement interview. Edited by R. S. Brandt for *Educational Leadership, 40* (3), 12–15.

Fruston, K. R. (1992) Getting started with TQM. *Educational Leadership, 50,* 14–17.

Garvin, D. A. (1988). *Managing quality.* New York: Free Press.

Kounin, J. S. (November, 1982). Classrooms, individuals or behavior settings? Bloomington: Indiana University, School of Education, 1983 (Monographs in Teaching and Learning. General Series. ISSN 0193-4740; No. 1). Lecture given at Indiana University.

Smith, C. B. (1986). Teachers speak out about success. *Early Years, 17,* 54–56.

Chapter 10   Eleanor W. Thonis

Archambeault, B. (1992). Personalizing Study Skills in Secondary Students. *Journal of Reading, 35,* 468–472.

Asher, J. (1977). *Learning Another Language Through Actions.* Los Gatos, CA: Sky Oaks Productions.

Jewell, M., & Zintz, M. (1986). *Learning to Read Naturally.* Dubuque, IA: Kendall-Hunt.

Krashen, S. (1985). *Input in Second Language Acquisition.* Oxford: Pergamon Press.

Merino, B., & Coughran, C. (1991). Lesson Design for Teachers of Language Minority Students. In M. McGroaty & C. Faltis (Eds.), *Language in School and Society: Politics and Pedagogy.* Berlin: Mouton de Gruyter.

Thonis, E. (1983). *The English Spanish Connection.* Compton, CA: Santillana.

Chapter 11   Laura R. Roehler

Conley, M. (1992). Teacher decision-making: How can teachers use information about students, textbooks, and instruction to facilitate learning from secondary school textbooks? In D. Alvermann, D. Moore, & M. Conley (Eds.), *Research within reach: Secondary school reading.* Newark, DE: International Reading Association.

Doyle, W. (1984). Academic work. *Review of Educational Research, 53* (2), 159–199.

Duffy, G. G., Roehler, L. R., Meloth, M., & Vavrus, L. (1986). Conceptualizing instructional explanation. *Teaching and Teacher Education, 2* (3), 197–214.

Goodlad, J. (1983). *A place called school: Prospects for the future.* New York: McGraw-Hill.

Pearson, P. D., Roehler, L. R., Dole, J. A., & Duffy, G. G. (1992). Developing expertise in reading comprehension. In S. J. Samuels & A. E. Forstrup (Eds.), *What research has to say about reading instruction.* Newark, DE: International Reading Association.

Pearson, P. D., & Tierney, R. (1984). On becoming a thoughtful reader: Learning to read like a writer. In A. Purves & O. Niles (Eds.), *Becoming readers in a complex society.* Eighty-Third Yearbook of the National Society for the Study of Education, Part I. Chicago: University of Chicago Press.

Roth, K., Anderson, C., & Smith, E. (1986). *Curriculum materials, teacher talk and student learning: Case studies in fifth grade science teaching* (Research Series No. 171). East Lansing: Michigan State University, Institute for Research on Teaching.

Smith, E., & Anderson, C. (1984). *The planning and teaching of intermediate science study: Final report* (Research Series No. 147). East Lansing: Michigan State University, Institute for Research on Teaching.

Wade, S. (1983). A synthesis of research for improving reading in the social studies. *Review of Educational Research, 53,* 461–497.

Winne, P. (1985). Steps toward promoting cognitive achievement. *Elementary School Journal, 85,* 673–673.

Chapter 12   Larry Mikulecky

Diehl, W., & Mikulecky, L. (1980). The nature of reading at work. *Journal of Reading, 24,* 221–227.

Kirsch, I., & Jungeblut, A. (1986). *Literacy: Profiles of America's young adults.* Princeton, NJ: National Assessment of Educational Progress at Educational Testing Service.

Mikulecky, L. (1982). Job literacy: The relationship between school preparation and workplace actuality. *Reading Research Quarterly, 17,* 400–419.

Mikulecky, L., & Ehlinger, J. (1986). The influence of metacognitive aspects of literacy on job performance of electronics technicians. *Journal of Reading Behavior, 18,* 41–62.

Mikulecky, L., & Winchester, D. (1983). Job literacy and job performance among nurses at varying employment levels. *Adult Education Quarterly, 34,* 1–15.

Office of Educational Research and Improvement. (1993). *What's Wrong with Writing and What Can We Do Right Now?* Washington, DC: U.S. Department of Education.

Mullis, I., & Jenkins, L. (1990). *The reading report card, 1971–1988.* Princeton, NJ: National Assessment of Educational Progress, Educational Testing Service.

U.S. Department of Labor, Secretary's Commission on Achieving Necessary Skills. (1992). *Learning a living: a blueprint for high performance.* Washington, DC.: U.S. Department of Labor.

U.S. Department of Labor, Secretary's Commission on Achieving Necessary Skills. (1991). *What work requires of schools.* Washington, DC.: U.S. Department of Labor.

Chapter 13   Carol Minnick Santa, Lynn Havens, Shirley Harrison

Holliday, W. G. (1991). Helping students learn effectively from text. In C. Santa & D. Alvermann (Eds.), *Science learning: processes and applications* (pp. 38–47). Newark, DE: International Reading Association.

Pearson, P. D. (1985). Changing the face of reading comprehension. *The Reading Teacher, 38,* 724–737.

Santa, C., & Havens, L. (1995). *Creating independence through student-owned strategies: Project CRISS.* Dubuque, IA: Kendall-Hunt.

Santa, C., & Havens, L. (1991). Learning science through writing. In C. Santa & D. Alvermann (Eds.), *Science learning: process and applications* (pp. 122–133). Newark, DE: International Reading Association.

Slater, W., & Graves, M. (1989). Research on expository text: Implications for teachers. In D. Muth (Ed.), *Children's comprehension of text: Research into practice.* (pp. 140–166). Newark, DE: International Reading Association.

Chapter 14   Charles W. Peters

Beck, I. L., & McKeown, M. G. (1991). Substantive and methodological considerations for productive textbook analysis. In J. P. Shaver (Ed.), *Handbook of research on social studies teaching and learning* (pp. 496–512). New York: Macmillan.

Bradley Commission on History in Schools. (1988). *Building a history curriculum: Guidelines for teaching history in schools.* Washington, DC: National Council for the Social Studies.

Camperell, K., & Knight, R. S. (1991). In J. P. Shaver (Ed.), *Handbook of research on social studies teaching and learning* (pp. 567–577). New York: Macmillan.

Center for Civic Education and the Council for the Advancement of Citizenship. (1990). *CIVITAS. A framework for civic education.* Calabasas, CA.

Center for the Teaching of History. (1994). *National history standards.* Los Angeles: University of California at Los Angeles.

Joint Committee on Geographic Education. (1984). *Guidelines for geographic education: Elementary and secondary.* Lansing, Michigan: State Dept. of Education.

Joint Council on Economic Education. (1984). *Master curriculum guide in economics: A framework for teaching the basic concepts.* Lansing, Michigan: State Dept. of Education.

Kaltsounis, T. (1987). *Teaching social studies in the elementary school: The basic for citizenship.* Englewood Cliffs, NJ: Prentice Hall.

Newmann, F. M. (1992). Beyond common sense in educational restructuring: The issues of content and linkage. *Educational Researcher, 22* (2), 4–22.

Newmann, F. M. (1990). Higher-order thinking in teaching social studies: A rationale for the assessment of classroom thoughtfulness. *Journal of Curriculum Studies, 22,* 41–56.

Ogle, D. (1986). The K-W-L: A teaching model that develops active reading of expository text. *The Reading Teacher, 39,* 564–576.

Onosko, J. J., & Newmann, F. M. (1994). Creating more thoughtful learning environments. In J. N. Mangieri & C. C. Block (Eds.), *Creating powerful thinking in teachers and students: Diverse perspectives* (pp. 27–49). New York: Harcourt Brace.

Parker, W. C. (1991). *Renewing the social studies curriculum.* Alexandria, VA: Association for Supervision and Curriculum Development.

Parker, W. C., & Jarolimek, K. (1984). *Citizenship and the critical role of the social studies.* (NCSS Bulletin 72). Washington, DC: National Council for the Social Studies.

Perkins, D. (1992). *Smart schools: From training memories to educating minds.* New York: Free Press.

Peters, C. W. (1990). Content knowledge in reading: Creating a new framework. In G. Duffy (Ed.), *Reading in the middle school* (pp. 63–80). Newark, DE: International Reading Association.

Spoehr, K. T., & Spoehr, L. W. (1994). Learning to think historically. *Educational Psychologist, 29* (2), 71–77.

Tishman, S., Jay, E., & Perkins, D. N. (1993). Teaching thinking dispositions: From transmission to enculturation. *Theory into Practice, 32,* 147–153.

Chapter 15   *Nancy Farnan, Alicia Romero*

Applebee, A. N. (1977). ERIC/RCS report: The elements of response to a literary work: What we have learned. *Research in the Teaching of English, 1,* 255–264.

Baghban, M. (1984). *Our daughter learns to read and write.* Newark, DE: International Reading Association.

Beach, R., & Hynds, S. (1991). Research on response to literature. In R. Barr, M. L. Kamil, P. Mosenthal, and P. D. Pearson (Eds.), *Handbook of reading research, vol. 2* (pp. 453–489). New York: Longman.

Bleich, D. (1978). *Subjective criticism.* Baltimore, MD: Johns Hopkins University Press.

Cullinan, B. (1989). *Literature and the child* (2nd ed.). San Diego, CA: Harcourt Brace Jovanovich.

Durkin, D. (1984). Is there a match between what elementary teachers do and what basal reader manuals recommend? *The Reading Teacher, 37* (8), 734–735.

Farnan, N. (1988). *Reading and responding: Effects of a prompted approach to literature.* Unpublished doctoral dissertation. Claremont Graduate School and San Diego State University.

Farnan, N., & Fearn, L. (1991). *Developing writers: Process, craft, collaboration.* San Diego, CA: San Diego State University Developmental Writing Institute.

Farnan, N., Lapp, D., Flood, J., & Tregor, R. (1991). *Curriculum integration at the middle level.* Paper presented at the National Reading Conference, Palm Springs, CA.

Farnan, N., & Kelly, P. R. (1993). Response-based instruction at the middle level: When student engagement is the goal. *Middle School Journal, 25,* 46–50.

Farnan, N., & Kelly, P. R. (1991). Keeping track: Creating assessment portfolios in reading and writing. *Journal of Reading, Writing, and Learning Disabilities Quarterly, 7,* 255–270.

Farnan, N., & Kelly, P. R. (1988). Reader response: What kids think really counts. *Fifty-Second yearbook of the Claremont reading conference* (pp. 82–98). Claremont, CA: Claremont Reading Conference.

Flood, J., Lapp, D., Alvarez, D., Romero, A., RanckBuhr, W., Moore, J., Jones, M., Kabildis, C., Lundren, L. (1995). Teacher book clubs: A study of teachers' and student teachers' participation in a contemporary multicultural fiction literature discussion group (Research report no. 22). Athens, GA: National Reading Research Center, Universities of Georgia and Maryland.

Hawisher, G. E. (1990). Content knowledge vs. product knowledge: A false dichotomy. In G. E. Hawisher & A. O. Soter (Eds.), *On literacy and its teaching: Issues in English education* (pp. 1–18). Albany: State University of New York Press.

International Reading Association. (1988). *New directions in reading instruction.* Newark, DE: International Reading Association.

Kelly, P. R., & Farnan, N. (1991). Promoting critical thinking through response logs: A reader response approach with fourth graders. In J. Zutell & S. McCormick (Eds.), *Learner factors/teacher factors: Issues in literacy research and instruction* (pp. 277–284). Fortieth yearbook, National Reading Conference, Chicago, IL: National Reading Conference.

Langer, J. A. & Applebee, A. N. (1987). *How writing shapes thinking.* Urbana, IL: National Council of Teachers of English.

Little, J. (1990). *Hey world, here I am!* New York: Harper Trophy.

Many, J. E., & Wiseman, D. L. (1992). The effects of teaching approach on third grade students' responses to literature. *Journal of Reading Behavior, 24,* 265–287.

Mailloux, J. M. (1982). *Interpretive conventions: The reader in the study of American fiction.* Ithaca, NY: Cornell University Press.

McGee, L. (1992). An exploration of meaning construction in first graders' grand conversations. In C. K. Kinzer and D. J. Leu (Eds.), *Literacy research, theory and practice: Views from many perspectives.* Forty-First yearbook of the National Reading Conference. Chicago, IL: National Reading Conference.

Newkirk, T. (1989). *Critical thinking and writing: Reclaiming the essay.* Urbana, IL: National Council of Teachers of English.

Norris, S. P., & Phillips, L. M. (1994). The relevance of a reader's knowledge within a perspectival view of reading. *Journal of Reading Behavior: A Journal of Literacy, 26,* 391–412.

Paulsen, G. (1989) *The Winter Room.* New York: Orchard Books.

Petrosky, A. R. (1980). The inferences we make: Children and literature. *Language Arts, 57,* 149–156.

Probst, R. E. (1990). Literature and literacy. In G. E. Hawisher & A. O. Soter (Eds.), *On literacy and its teaching* (pp. 100–110). Albany: State University of New York Press.

Rosenblatt, L. M. (1991). Literature—S.O.S.! *Language Arts, 68,* 444–448.

Rosenblatt, L. M. (1982). The literary transaction: Evocation and response. *Theory into Practice, 21,* 268–277.

Scott, J. E. (1994). Literature circles in the middle school classroom: Developing reading, responding, and responsibility. *Middle School Journal, 26,* 37–41.

Squire, J. (1983). Composing and comprehending: Two sides of the same basic process. *Language Arts, 60,* 581–589.

Stotsky, S. (1983). Research on reading/writing relationships: A synthesis and suggested directions. *Language Arts, 60,* 589–599.

U.S. Department of Education. (1986). What works: Research about teaching and learning. Washington, DC: Office of Educational Research and Improvement.

Chapter 16   Joan F. Curry

Ciani, A. J. (1981). Mastering word and symbol language in mathematics. *School Science and Mathematics, 81,* 371–377.

Clarke, J. H. (1991). Using visual organizers to focus on thinking. *Journal of Reading, 34,* 526–534.

Farnan, N., & Fearn, L. (1993). Writers' workshops: Middle school writers and readers collaborating. *Middle School Journal, 24,* 61–65.

Fay, L. (1965). Reading study skills: Mathematics and science. In J. Allen Figurel (Ed.), *Reading and inquiry.* Newark, DE: International Reading Association.

O'Leary, P. W., & Dishon, D. (1985). Cooperative learning. In A. Costa (Ed.), *Developing minds.* Alexandria, VA: American Association for Supervision and Curriculum Development.

Pachtman, A. B., & Riley, J. D. (1978). Teaching the vocabulary of mathematics through interaction, exposure, and structure. *Journal of Reading, 22,* 240–244.

Robinson, F. P. (1946). *Effective study.* New York: Harper and Row.

Singer, H., & Donlan, D. (1980). *Reading and learning from text.* Boston: Little Brown.

Chapter 17   Lance M. Gentile, Merna M. McMillan

Blanton, W. E., Black, K., & Moorman, G. (1990). The role of purpose in reading instruction. *The Reading Teacher, 43,* 486–493.

Duffy, G., Roehler, L., & Hermann, B. A. (1988). Modeling mental processes helps poor readers become more strategic readers. *The Reading Teacher, 42,* 762–767.

Gentile, L. M., & McMillan, M. M. (1992). Literacy for students at risk: Developing critical dialogues. *Journal of Reading, 35,* 636–641.

Gentile, L. M., & McMillan, M. M. (1994). Critical dialogue: The road to literacy for students at risk in middle schools. *Middle School Journal, 25* (4), 50–54.

Graves, D. H. (1983). *Writing: Teachers and children at work.* Exeter, NH: Heinemann.

Joyce, B. R., & Clift, R. (1984). The Phoenix agenda: Essential reform in teacher education. *Educational Researcher, 13* (4), 5–18.

Langer, J. A. (1984). Examining background knowledge and text comprehension. *Reading Research Quarterly, 19,* 468–481.

Ogle, D. M. (1986). A teaching model that helps develop active reading of expository text. *The Reading Teacher, 39,* 564–570.

Ross, C. P., & Lee, A. R. (1983). *Suicide in youth and what you can do about it.* Burlingame, CA: Suicide and Prevention Crisis Center of San Mateo County.

Palinscar, A. M., & Brown, A. L. (1984). Reciprocal teaching of comprehension-fostering and comprehension monitoring activities. *Cognition and Instruction, 1,* 117–175.

Palinscar, A. M. (1986). The role of dialogue in providing scaffolding instruction. *Educational Psychologist, 21,* 73–98.

Ralph, J. (1988). Improving education for the disadvantaged: Do we know whom to help? Phi Delta Kappan, 70, 395–401.

Tharp, R. G., & Gallimore, R. (1976). Basketball's John Wooden: What a coach can teach a teacher. *Psychology Today, 9* (8), 74–78.

Tompkins, G. (1994). *Teaching writing: Balancing process and product.* New York: Macmillan.

Vygotsky, L. (1962). *Thought and language.* Cambridge, MA: MIT Press.

Chapter 18   Michael F. Graves, Wayne H. Slater

Anderson, R. C., & Nagy, W. E. (1993). *The vocabulary conundrum.* (Technical Report No. 570). Urbana: University of Illinois, Center for the Study of Reading.

Anglin, J. M. (1977). *Word, object, and conceptual development.* New York: Norton.

Beck, I. L., & McKeown, M. G. (1983). Learning words well: A program to teach vocabulary and comprehension. *The Reading Teacher, 36,* 622–625.

Beck, I. L., McKeown, M. G., McCaslin, E. S., & Burkes, A. M. (1979). *The rationale and design of a program to teach vocabulary to fourth-grade students.* Pittsburgh: University of Pittsburgh, Learning Research and Development Center.

Beck, I. L., McKeown, M. G., & Omanson, R. C. (1987). The effects and uses of diverse vocabulary instructional techniques. In M. G. McKeown & M. E. Curtis (Eds.), *The nature of vocabulary acquisition* (pp. 147–164). Hillsdale, NJ: Erlbaum.

Buikema, J. A., & Graves, M. F. (March 1993). Teaching students to use context cues to infer word meanings. *Journal of Reading, 63* (6), 450–457.

Calfee, R. C., & Drum, P. A. (1986). Research on teaching reading. In M. D. Wittrock (Ed.), *Handbook of research on teaching* (3rd ed., pp. 804–849). New York: Macmillan.

Carroll, J. B. (1956). Introduction. In J. B. Carroll (Ed.), *Language, thought, and reality* (pp. 1–34). Cambridge, MA: The MIT Press.

Carroll, J. B., Davies, P., & Richman, B. (1971). *The American heritage word frequency book.* New York: Houghton Mifflin.

Dale, E., & O'Rourke, J. (1981). *The living word vocabulary.* Chicago: World Book—Childcraft International.

Duin, A. H., & Graves, M. F. (1988). Teaching vocabulary as a writing prompt. *Journal of Reading, 22,* 204–212.

Fielding, L. G., Wilson, P. T., & Anderson, R. C. (1986). A new focus on free reading: The role of trade books in reading instruction. In T. E. Raphael (Ed.), *The contexts of school-based literacy* (pp. 149–160. New York: Random House.

Frayer, D. A., Frederick, W. D., & Klausmeier, H. J. (1969). *A schema for testing the level of concept mastery* (Working Paper No. 16). Madison: Wisconsin Research and Development Center for Cognitive Learning.

Graves, M. F. (1987). The role of instruction in vocabulary development. In M. G. McKeown & M. E. Curtis (Eds.), *The nature of vocabulary acquisition* (pp. 165–184). Hillsdale, NJ: Erlbaum.

Graves, M. F. (1985). *A word is a word.* New York: Scholastic.

Graves, M. F., Watts, S. M., & Graves, B. B. (1994). *Essentials of classroom teaching: Elementary reading methods.* Needham Heights, MA: Allyn & Bacon.

Jenkins, J. R., Stein, M. L., & Wysocki, K. (1984). Learning vocabulary through reading. *American Educational Research Journal, 21,* 767–787.

Jensen, A. R. (1980). *Bias in mental testing.* New York: Free Press.

Johnson, D. D., & Pearson, P. D. (1984). *Teaching reading comprehension* (2nd ed.). New York: Holt, Rinehart & Winston.

Klare, G. R. (1984). Readability. In P.D. Pearson (Ed.), *Handbook of reading research* (pp. 681–744). New York: Longman.

McKeown, M. G., & Beck, I. L. (in press). Ongoing vocabulary instruction in reading and language arts. In B. C. Konopak & A. J. Moe (Eds.), *Vocabulary instruction for content area learning.* Newark, DE: International Reading Association.

Petty, W. T., Harold, C. P., & Stoll, E. (1968). *The state of knowledge about the teaching of vocabulary.* Champaign, IL: National Council of Teachers of English.

Ryder, R. J., & Graves, M. F. (1994). *Reading and learning in content areas.* Columbus, OH: Merrill.

Sapir, E. (1921). *Language.* New York: Harcourt Brace.

Stahl, S. A., & Kapinus, B. A. (1991). Possible sentences: Predicting word meanings to teach content area vocabulary. *The Reading Teacher, 45,* 36–43.

Terman, L. M. (1918). Vocabulary test as a measure of intelligence. *Journal of Educational Psychology, 9,* 452–466.

White, T. G., Slater, W. H., & Graves, M. F. (1989). Yes/No method of vocabulary assessment: Valid for whom and useful for what? *Cognitive and social perspectives for literacy research and instruction* (pp. 391–398). Chicago: National Reading Conference.

White, T. G., Sowell, J., & Yanagihara, A. (1989). Teaching elementary students to use word-part clues. *The Reading Teacher, 42,* 302–308.

Whorf, B. L. (1956/1940). Science and linguistics. In J. B. Carroll (Ed.), *Language, thought, and reality* (pp 207–219). Cambridge, MA: The MIT Press.

Chapter 19   Donna M. Ogle

Anderson, C. W., & Smith, E. (1984). Children's preconceptions and content area textbooks. In G. Duffy, L. Roehler, & J. Mason (Eds.), *Comprehension instruction: Perspectives and suggestions* (pp. 187–201). New York: Longman.

Anderson, T. H. (1980). Study strategies and adjunct aids. In R. J. Spiro, B. C. Bruce, & W. F. Brewer (Eds.), *Theoretical issues in reading comprehension* (pp. 483–502). Hillsdale, NJ: Erlbaum.

Anderson, T. H., & Armbruster, B. B. (1984). Studying. In D. Pearson et al. (Eds.), *Handbook of reading research* (pp. 657–679). New York: Longman.

Beane, J. (1990). *Middle school curriculum: Rhetoric to reality.* Columbus, OH: National Middle School Association.

Bragstad, B., & Stumpf, S. (1982). *A guidebook for teaching study skills and motivation.* Boston: Allyn & Bacon.

Carr, E., & Ogle, D. (1987). KWL Plus: A strategy for comprehension and summarization. *Journal of Reading, 30,* 626–631.

Devine, T. G. (1981). *Teaching study skills.* Boston: Allyn & Bacon.

Estes, T. H., and Richards, H. C. (1985). Habits of study and test performance. *Journal of Reading Behavior, 17,* 1–13.

Estes, T. H., & Vaughan, J. L. (1986). *Reading and learning in the content classroom: Diagnostic and instructional strategies.* Boston: Allyn & Bacon.

Hayes, D. A. (1989). Helping students GRASP the knack of writing summaries. *Journal of Reading, 32,* 96–101.

Langer, J. A. (1981). From theory into practice: A prereading plan. *Journal of Reading, 25,* 152–156.

Larson, C. D., & Dansereau, D. F. (1986). Cooperative learning in dyads. *Journal of Reading, 29,* 516–520.

Ogle, D. (1992). KWL in action: Secondary teachers find applications that work. In E. K. Dishner, T.

W. Bean, J. E. Readance, & D. Moore (Eds.) *Reading in the content areas* (pp. 270–281). Dubuque, IA: Kendall-Hunt.

Ogle, D. (1986). KWL: A teaching model that develops active reading of expository text. *The Reading Teacher, 39,* 364–370.

Palinscar, A. M. S., Ogle, D. S., Jones, B. F., & Carr, E. M. (1986). *Teaching reading as thinking: Trainer's manual.* Arlington, VA: Association for Supervision and Curriculum Development.

Paris, S., & Jacobs, I. (1984). The benefits of informed instruction for children's reading awareness and comprehension skills. *Child Development, 55,* 2083–2093.

Pauk, W. (1989). *How to study in college.* (4th ed.) Boston: Houghton Mifflin.

Piaget, J. (1970). *Structuralism.* New York: Harper & Row.

Readance, J., Bean, T., & Baldwin, S. (1989). *Content area reading: An integrated approach* (pp. 132–133). Dubuque, IA: Kendall-Hunt.

Robinson, F. (1970). *Effective study.* (Rev. ed.) New York: Harper & Row.

Roth, K. J. (1986). Conceptual-change learning and student processing of science texts. (Research series No. 167). East Lansing: Michigan State University, Institute for Research on Teaching.

Starks, G. A. (1980). New approaches to teaching study habits in high school and college. *Journal of Reading, 23,* 401–403.

Tomlison, T. (1992). *Hard work and high expectations: motivating students to learn.* Washington, DC: U.S. Government Printing Office.

Vygotsky, L. S. (1978). In M. Cole, et al., *Mind in society: The development of higher psychological processes.* Cambridge, MA: Harvard University Press.

Chapter 20   *Diane Lapp, James Flood, Robert P. Hoffman*

Faletti, J., Fisher, K., Lipson, J., Patterson, P., & Thornton, R. (1986). *SemNet®* [computer program]. San Diego, CA: SemNet® Research Group.

Fisher, K. M., & Faletti, J. (1993). *Promoting metacognition about knowledge organization skills in biology.* Paper given in the symposium on Metacogni-

tion and Conceptual Change at the American Educational Research Association annual meeting, Atlanta, GA.

Flood, J., & Lapp, D. (1988). Using conceptual mapping for improving comprehension. *The Reading Teacher, 41,* 780–783.

Novak, J. (1991). Clarifying with concept maps. *The Science Teacher,* October 1991, pp. 45–49.

Chapter 21   *Helene M. Anthony, Taffy E. Raphael*

Alvermann, D. E., & Hayes, D. A. (1989). Classroom discussion of content area reading assignments: An intervention study. *Reading Research Quarterly, 24* (3), 305–335.

Applebee, A. N., & Langer, J. A. (1983). Instructional scaffolding: Reading and writing as natural language activities. In J. M. Jensen (Ed.), *Composing and comprehending* (pp. 183–190). Urbana, IL: ERIC.

Armbruster, B. B. (1984). The problem of "inconsiderate text." In G. G. Duffy, L. R. Roehler, & J. N. Mason (Eds.), *Comprehension instruction: Perspectives and suggestions* (pp. 202–220). New York: Longman.

Armbruster, B. B., Anderson, T. H., Armstrong, J. O., Wise, M. A., Janisch, C., & Meyer, L. A. (1991). Reading and questioning in content area lessons. *Journal of Reading Behavior, 23* (1), 35–59.

Ciardiello, A. V. (1986). Teacher questioning and student interaction: An observation of three social studies classrooms. *Social Studies, 77* (3), 119–122.

Davey, B. (1989). Active responding in content classrooms. *Journal of Reading Behavior, 33* (1), 44–46.

Englert, C. S., & Raphael, T. E. (1990). Writing and reading: Partners in constructing meaning. *The Reading Teacher, 43*(6), 388–400.

Flood, J., Lapp, D., & Farnan, N. (1986). A reading-writing procedure that teaches expository paragraph structure. *The Reading Teacher, 39,* 556–562.

Garner, R. (1988). *Metacognition and reading comprehension.* Norwood, NJ: Ablex.

Gaskins, I., Benedict, J., & Elliot, T. (1991). How content and process are joined: The tales of two social studies teachers. In I. Gaskins & T. T. Elliot (Eds.), *Implementing cognitive strategy instruction across the school* (pp. 81–97). Media, PA: Brookline Books.

Hansen, J., & Hubbard, R. (1984). Poor readers can draw inferences. *The Reading Teacher, 37,* 586–589.

Harms, T., Woolever, R., & Brice, R. (1989). A questioning strategies training sequence: Documenting the effect of a new approach to an old practice. *Journal of Teacher Education, 40* (5), 40–45.

Jones, B. F., Pierce, J., & Hunter, B. (1988–1989). Teaching students to construct graphic representations. *Educational Leadership, 46* (4), 20–25.

Langer, J. A. (1982). Facilitating text processing: The elaboration of prior knowledge. In J. A. Langer & M. T. Smith-Burke (Eds.), *Reader meets author/ bridging the gap: A psycholinguistic and sociolinguistic perspective* (pp. 149–162). Newark, DE: International Reading Association.

Langer, J. A. (1984). Examining background knowledge and text comprehension. *Reading Research Quarterly, 19,* 468–481.

Mason, J. M., & Au, K. H. (1986). *Reading instruction for today.* Glenview, IL: Scott, Foresman.

McGee, L. M., & Richgels, D. J. (1985). Teaching expository text structure to elementary students. *The Reading Teacher, 38,* 739–748.

Niles, O. S. (1985). Integration of content and skills instruction. In T. L. Harris and E. J. Cooper (Eds.), *Reading, thinking, and concept development: Strategies for the classroom* (pp. 177–194). New York: College Entrance Examination Board.

Palincsar, A. S. (1986). The role of dialogue in providing scaffolded instruction. *Educational Psychologist, 21,* 73–98.

Palincsar, A. S., & Brown, A. L. (1986). Interactive teaching to promote independent learning from text. *The Reading Teacher, 39,* 771–777.

Palincsar, A. S., Lipson, M. Y., & Wixson, K. K. (1983). Becoming a strategic reader. *Contemporary Educational Psychology, 8,* 293–316.

Paris, S. G., & Winograd, P. (1990). How metacognition can promote academic learning and instruction. In B. F. Jones & L. Idol (Eds.), *Dimensions of thinking and cognitive instruction* (pp. 15–51). Elmhurst, IL: North Central Regional Educational Laboratory.

Pearson, P. D., & Johnson, D. D. (1978). *Teaching reading comprehension.* New York: Holt, Rinehart & Winston.

Raphael, T. E. (1982). Question-answering strategies for children. *The Reading Teacher, 36,* 186–190.

Raphael, T. E. (1986). Teaching question-answer relationships, revisited. *The Reading Teacher, 39,* 516–522.

Raphael, T. E., & Kirschner, B. W. (1985). *The effects of instruction in compare/contrast text structure on sixth-grade students' reading comprehension and writing products* (Research Series No. 161). East Lansing: Michigan State University, Institute for Research on Teaching.

Raphael, T. E., Englert, C. S., & Kirschner, B. W. (1989). Students' metacognitive knowledge about writing. *Research in the Teaching of English, 23* (4), 343–379.

Raphael, T. E., Kirschner, B. W., & Englert, C. S. (1988). Making connections between reading and writing. *The Reading Teacher, 41,* 790–795.

Roehler, L. R., & Duffy, G. G. (1991). Teachers' instructional actions. In R. Barr, M. Kamil, P. Mosenthal, & P. D. Pearson (Eds.), *Handbook of reading research* (Vol. 2, pp. 861–884). New York: Longman.

Rosenshine, B., & Meister, C. (1992). The use of scaffolds for teaching higher-level cognitive strategies. *Educational Leadership, 49* (7), 26–33.

Ryder, R. J. (1991). The directed questioning activity for subject matter text. *Journal of Reading, 34* (8), 606–612.

Taylor, B. M., & Samuels, S. J. (1983). Children's use of text structure in the recall of expository material. *American Educational Research Journal, 20,* 517–528.

Wedman, J. M., & Moutray, C. (1991). The effect of training on the questions preservice teachers ask during literature discussions. *Reading Research and Instruction, 30* (2), 62–70.

Winograd, P., & Hare, V. C. (1988). Direct instruction of reading comprehension strategies: The nature of teacher explanation. In C. Weinstein, E. Goetz, & P. Alexander (Eds.), *Learning and study strategies: Issues in assessment, instruction, and evaluation.* San Diego, CA: Academic Press.

Wixson, K. K. (1983). Postreading question-answer interactions and children's learning from text. *Journal of Educational Psychology, 30,* 413–423.

Wong, J. A., & Au, K. H. (1985). The concept-text-application approach: Helping elementary students comprehend expository text. *The Reading Teacher, 38,* 612–618.

Chapter 22   Patricia L. Anders, Carol V. Lloyd

Allen, R. V., & Allen, C. (1982). *Language experience activities* (2nd ed.). Boston: Houghton Mifflin.

Alvermann, D. E. (1991). The discussion web: A graphic aid for learning across the curriculum. *The Reading Teacher, 45,* 92–99.

Alvermann, D. E., Smith L. C., & Readence, J. E. (1985). Prior knowledge activation and the comprehension of compatible and incompatible text. *Reading Research Q Quarterly, 20,* 99–158.

Anders, P. L., & Bos, C. S. (1986). Semantic feature analysis: An interactive strategy for vocabulary development and text comprehension. *Journal of Reading, 29,* 610–616.

Anderson, R. C., Reynolds, R. E., Schallert, D. L., & Goetz, E. T. (1977). Frameworks for comprehending discourse. *American Educational Research Journal, 14,* 367–382.

Bean, T. W., Singer, H., & Cowen, S. (1985). Acquisition of a topic schema in high school biology through an analogical study guide. In J. A. Niles & R. V. Lalik (Eds.), *Issues in literacy: A research perspective,* Thirty-Fourth Yearbook of the National Reading Conference. Rochester, NY: National Reading Conference.

Bransford, J. D. (1979). *Human cognition: Learning, understanding and remembering.* Belmont, CA: Wadsworth.

Bransford, J. D., & Johnson, M. K. (1972). Contextual prerequisites for understanding: Some investigations of comprehension and recall. *Journal for Verbal Learning and Verbal Behavior, 11,* 717–726.

Chi, M.T.H., Hutchinson, J. E., & Robin, A. F. (1989). How inferences about novel domain-related concepts can be constrained by structured knowledge. *Merrill-Palmer Quarterly, 35,* 27–62.

Guzzetti, B. J., Snyder, T. E., & Glass, G. V. (1992). Promoting conceptual change in science: Can texts be used effectively? *Journal of Reading, 35,* 642–649.

Hayes, D. A., & Tierney, R. J. (1982). Developing readers' knowledge through analogy. *Reading Research Quarterly, 17,* 256–280.

Holmes, B. C. (1983). The effect of prior knowledge on the question answering of good and poor readers. *Journal of Reading Behavior, 15,* 1–18.

Klausmeier, H. J. (1980). *Conceptual mastery.* New York: Academic Press.

Lipson, M. Y. (1982). Learning new information from text: The role of prior knowledge and reading ability. *Journal of Reading, 14,* 243–261.

Lloyd, C. V., & Contreras, N. J. (1985). Effectively enhancing vocabulary knowledge and text comprehension of average and low ability readers. Paper presented at the annual conference of the National Reading Conference, San Diego, CA.

Macrorie, K. (1988). *The i-search paper.* Portsmouth, NH: Heinemann.

Nicholson, T. (1984). Experts and novices: A study of reading in the high school classroom. *Reading Research Quarterly, 19,* 436–451.

Peabody, M. B. (1984). *The effect of concrete examples on transitional and formal students in the instruction of chemical bonding.* Unpublished doctoral dissertation, Northern Arizona University.

Pearson, P. D., Roehler, L. R., Dole, J. A., & Duffy, G. G. (1992). Developing expertise in reading comprehension. In S. J. Samuels & A. E. Farstrup (Eds.), *What research has to say about reading instruction* (pp. 145–199). Newark, DE: International Reading Association.

Posner, G. J., Strike, K. A., Hewson, P. W., & Gertzog, W. A. (1982). Accommodation of a scientific conception: Toward a theory of conceptual change. *Science Education, 66,* 211–227.

Rumelhart, D. E. (1981). Schemata: The building blocks of cognition. In J. T. Guthrie (Ed.), *Comprehension and teaching: Research reviews.* Newark, DE: International Reading Association.

Smith, E. L., Blakeslee, T. D., & Anderson, C. W. (1993). Teaching strategies associated with conceptual change learning in science. *Journal of Research in Science Teaching, 30,* 111–126.

Spilich, G. J., et al. (1979). Text processing of domain-related information for individuals with high and low domain knowledge. *Journal for Verbal Learning and Verbal Behavior, 18,* 275–290.

Tierney, R. J., & Cunningham, J. W. (1984). Research on teaching reading comprehension. In P. D. Pearson (Ed.), *Handbook of Reading Research*. New York: Longman.

Townsend, M.A.R., & Clarihew, A. (1989). Facilitating children's comprehension through the use of advance organizers. *Journal of Reading Behavior, 21*, 15–35.

Zakaluk, B. L., Samuels, S. J., & Taylor, B. M. (1986). A simple technique for estimating prior knowledge: Word association. *Journal of Reading, 30*, 56–60.

Chapter 23   John F. O'Flahavan, Robert J. Tierney

Atwell, N. (1987). *In the middle*. Portsmouth, NH: Heinemann.

Fulwiler, T. (Ed.). (1987). *The journal book*. Portsmouth, NH: Heinemann.

Vacca, R. T., & Vacca, J. L. (1986). *Content area reading* (2nd ed.). Boston, MA: Little Brown.

Chapter 24   Richard T. Vacca, JoAnne L. Vacca, Nancy Prosenjak, Linda Burkey

Anno, M. (1989). Anno's math games II. New York: Philomel.

Anno, M. (1982). Anno's counting house. New York: Philomel.

Bong, M. (1991). Picture this. New York: Bullfinch.

Bunting, E. (1990). The wall. New York: Clarion.

Crafton, L. (1983). Learning from reading: What happens when students generate their own background knowledge. *Journal of Reading, 26*, 586–593.

Estes, T., & Vaughan, J. (1985). *Reading and learning in the content classroom* (2nd ed.). Boston: Allyn & Bacon.

Neal, J., & Moore, K. (1991). *The Very Hungry Caterpillar* meets *Beowulf* in secondary classrooms. *Journal of Reading, 35*, 290–296.

Pringle, L. (1982). Water: The next great resource battle. New York: Macmillan.

Sewell, G. (1988). American history textbooks: Where do we go from here. *Phi Delta Kappan, 69*, 552–558.

Vacca, R., & Vacca, J. (1993). *Content area reading* (4th ed). New York: HarperCollins.

Wood, K. (1987). Fostering cooperative learning in middle and secondary level classrooms. *Journal of Reading, 31*, 10–18.

Yolen, J. (1988). The devil's arithmetic. New York: Puffin.

Chapter 25   Robert E. Slavin

Aronson, E., Blaney, N., Stephan, C., Sikes, J., & Snapp, M. (1978). *The jigsaw classroom*. Beverly Hills, CA: Sage.

Johnson, D. W., & Johnson, R. T. (1994). *Learning together and alone: Cooperative, competitive, and individualistic learning* (4th ed.). Boston: Allyn & Bacon.

Kagan, S. (1992). *Cooperative Learning* (8th ed.) San Juan Capistrano, CA: Kagan Cooperative Learning.

Sharan, Y., & Sharan, S. (1992). *Group Investigation: Expanding cooperative learning*. New York: Teacher's College Press.

Slavin, R. E. (1994). *Using Student Team Learning* (4th ed.). Baltimore, MD: Johns Hopkins University, Center for Social Organization of Schools.

Chapter 26   Roger Farr, Robert Pritchard

Bormouth, J. R. (1966). Readability: A new approach. *Reading Research Quarterly, 1*, 79–132.

Bormouth, J. R. (1968). Cloze test readability: Criterion referenced scores. *Journal of Educational Measurement, 5*, 189–196.

Brown, R. (1986). Evaluation and learning. In A. R. Petrosky & D. Bartholomae (Eds.), *The teaching of writing*. Eighty–Fifth Yearbook of the National Society for the Study of Education (pp. 114–130). Chicago, IL: University of Chicago Press.

Burstall, C. (1986) Innovative forms of assessment: A United Kingdom perspective. *Educational Measurement: Issues and Practice, 5*, 17–22.

Cambourne, B., & Turbil, J. (1990). Assessment in whole language classrooms: Theory into practice. *The Elementary School Journal, 90* 337–349.

Conley, M. W. (1992). *Content area reading instruction: A communication approach.* San Francisco: McGraw-Hill.

Cunningham, J. W., & Cunningham, P. M. (1978). Validating a limited-cloze procedure. *Journal of Reading Behavior, 10,* 191–196.

Early, M., & Sawyer, D. J. (1984). *Reading to learn in grades 5 to 12.* San Diego, CA: Harcourt Brace Jovanovich.

Estes, T. H., & Vaughn, J. L. (1985). *Reading and learning in the content area classroom: Diagnostic and instructional strategies.* Boston: Allyn & Bacon.

Farr, R. (1990, May). *Think-alongs: Modeling reading comprehension.* Paper presented at the International Reading Association annual convention, Atlanta, GA.

Goodman, Y. (1991). Evaluating language growth: Information methods of evaluation. In J. Flood, J. Jensen, D. Lapp, & J. Squire (Eds.), *Handbook of research on teaching the English language arts* (pp. 502–509). New York: Macmillan.

Guthrie, J. T., Seifert, M., Burham, N. A., & Caplan, R. I. (1974). The maze technique to assess and monitor reading comprehension. *The Reading Teacher, 28,* 161–168.

Herber, H. (1978). *Teaching reading in content areas* (2nd ed.). Englewood Cliffs, NJ: Prentice Hall.

Jacobson, J. M. (1990). Group vs. individual completion of a cloze passage. *Journal of Reading, 33,* 244–250.

Jongsma, K. (1989). Questions and answers: Portfolio assessment. *The Reading Teacher, 43,* 264–265.

Madaus, G. F. (1985). Public policy and the testing profession: You've never had it so good? *Educational Measurement: Issues and Practice, 4,* 5–11.

Priestley, M. (1982). *Performance assessment in education and training: Alternate techniques.* Englewood Cliffs, NJ: Educational Technology Publications.

Purves, A. (1984). The challenge to education to produce literate citizens. In A. Purves & O. Niles (Eds.), *Becoming readers in a complex society.* Eighty–Third Yearbook of the National Society for the Study of Education (pp. 1–15). Chicago, IL: University of Chicago Press.

Readence, J. E., Bean, T. W., & Baldwin, R. S. (1992). *Content area reading: An integrated approach.* Dubuque, IA: Kendall/Hunt.

Richardson, J. S., & Morgan, R. F. (1990). *Reading to learn in content areas.* Belmont, CA: Wadsworth.

Roe, B. D., Stoodt, B. D., & Burns, P. C. (1990). *Secondary school reading instruction: The content areas.* Palo Alto, CA: Houghton Mifflin.

Rubin, D. (1992). *Teaching reading and study skills in content areas.* Boston: Allyn & Bacon.

Salmon-Cox, L. (1981). Teachers and tests: What's really happening? *Phi Delta Kappan, 62,* 631–634.

Saretsky, G. (1973). The strangely significant case of Peter Doe. *Phi Delta Kappan, 54,* 589–592.

Shepherd, D. L. (1982). *Comprehensive high school reading methods.* Columbus, OH: Charles E. Merrill.

Stiggins, R. J., Conklin, N. F., & Bridgeford, N. J. (1986). Classroom assessment: A key to effective education. *Educational Measurement: Issues and Practice, 5,* 5–17.

Taylor, W. L. (1953). Cloze procedure: A new tool for measuring readability. *Journalism Quarterly, 30,* 415–433.

Tonjes, M. J. (1991). *Secondary reading, writing, and learning.* Boston: Allyn & Bacon.

Vacca, R., & Vacca, J. L. (1989). *Content area reading.* Glenview, IL: Scott, Foresman.

Valencia, S. (1990). A portfolio approach to classroom reading assessment: The whys, whats, and hows. *The Reading Teacher, 43,* 338–339.

Wixson, K., Bosky, A., Yochum, M. N., & Alvermann, D. (1984). An interview for assessing students' perceptions of classroom reading tasks. *The Reading Teacher, 37,* 346–353.

Wolf, D. P. (1989). Portfolio assessment: Sampling student work. *Educational Leadership, 46,* 35–39.

Chapter 27   James Barton

Calfee, R., & Associates. (1981). *Project READ: The book.* Unpublished resource text. Stanford University.

Chambliss, M., & Calfee, R. (1989). Designing science textbooks to enhance student understanding. *Educational Psychologist, 24,* 307–322.

Moscarelli, D. (1991). *A lesson on AIDS awareness.* Lesson plan created for Reading in the Content Areas, a university class focusing on literacy instructional strategies for middle school and secondary teachers.

Tassinari, J. (1990). *A lesson on probability.* Lesson plan created for Reading in the Content Areas, a university class focusing on literacy instructional strategies for middle school and secondary teachers.

Chapter 28   Karen D. Wood

Anderson, R., Hiebert, E., Scott, J., & Wilkinson, I. (1985). *Becoming a nation of readers: The report on the commission on reading.* Washington, DC: National Institute of Education, U.S. Department of Education.

Bean, T., & Peterson, J. (1981). Reasoning guides: Fostering readiness in the content areas. *Reading Horizons, 21,* 196–199.

Beck, I., & McKeown, M. (1991). Conditions of vocabulary acquisition. In R. Barr, M. L. Kamil, P. B. Mosenthal, & P. D. Pearson (Eds.), *Handbook of reading research, Vol. 2* (pp. 789–814) New York: Longman.

Brandt, R. (1988). On students' needs and team learning. A conversation with William Glasser. *Educational Leadership, 45,* 38–45.

Brandt, R. (1987). On cooperation in schools: A conversation with David and Roger Johnson. *Educational Leadership, 45,* 14–19.

Brozo, W., & Simpson, M. (1991). *Readers, teachers and learners: Expanding literacy in Secondary Schools.* (2nd ed.). Englewood Cliffs, NJ: Merrill.

California State Department of Education. (1987). Caught in the middle: Educational reform for young adolescents in California public schools. Report of the Superintendent's Middle Grade Task Force. Sacramento: California State Department of Education.

Carnegie Task Force on Education of Young Adolescents (1989). *Turning points: Preparing America's youth for the 21st century.* New York: Carnegie Council on Adolescent Development of the Carnegie Corporation.

Cuban, L. (1984). *How teachers taught: Constancy and change in American classrooms 1890–1980.* New York: Longman.

Davey, B. (1988). How do classroom teachers use their textbooks? *Journal of Reading, 31,* 340–345.

Eccles, J., & Midgley, C. (1989). Stage-environment fit: Developmentally appropriate classrooms for young adolescents. In C. Ames & R. Ames (Eds.), *Research on Motivation in Education, Vol. 3, Goals and Cognitions,* New York: Academic Press.

Goodlad, J. (1984). *A place called school.* New York: McGraw-Hill.

Herber, H. (1970). *Teaching reading in the content areas.* Englewood Cliffs, NJ: Prentice-Hall.

Johnston, J., & Markle, G. (1986). *What research says to the middle level practitioner.* Columbus, OH: National Middle School Association.

Johnson, D., Maruyama, G., Johnson, R., Nelson, D., & Skon, L. (1981). Effects of cooperative, competitive and individualistic goal structures on achievement: A meta-analysis. *Psychological Bulletin, 89,* 47–82.

Larson, C., & Dansereau, D. (1986). Cooperative learning in dyads. *Journal of Reading, 29,* 516–20.

Lehr, F. (1984). Cooperative learning. *Journal of Reading, 27,* 458–60.

Readence, J., Bean, T., & Baldwin, R. (1992). *Content area reading: An integrated approach* (4th ed.), Dubuque, IA: Kendall-Hunt.

Readence, J., Bean, T., & Baldwin, R. (1981). *Content area reading: An integrated approach.* Dubuque, IA: Kendall-Hunt.

Resnick, L. (1987). *Education and learning to think report.* Washington, DC: National Academy Press.

Ryder, R. (1994). Using frames to promote critical writing. *Journal of Reading, 38,* 210–218.

Slavin, R. (1983). *Cooperative learning.* New York: Longman.

Stiggins, R., Griswold, M., & Wikelund, K. (1989). Measuring thinking skills through classroom assessment. *Journal of Educational Measurement, 26,* 233–246.

Wood, K. D. (1992). Fostering collaborative reading and writing experiences in mathematics. *Journal of Reading, 36,* 96–103.

Wood, K. D. (1991). Communal writing. *Middle School Journal, 22,* 54–58.

Wood, K. D. (1990). Meaningful approaches to vocabulary development. *Middle School Journal, 21,* 21–23.

Wood, K. D. (1987a). Fostering cooperative learning in middle and secondary level classrooms. *Journal of Reading, 31,* 10–18.

Wood, K. D. (1987b). Helping students comprehend their textbooks. *Middle School Journal, 18,* 20–22.

Wood, K. D. (1988). Guiding students through informational text. *The Reading Teacher, 41,* 912–920.

Wood, K. D., Lapp, D., & Flood, J. (1992). *Guiding readers through print: A review of study guides.* Newark, DE: International Reading Association.

Wood, K. D., & Mateja, J. (1983). Adapting secondary level strategies for use in elementary classrooms. *The Reading Teacher, 36,* 492–96.

Wood, K. D., & Muth, K. (1991). The case for improved instruction in the middle grades. *Journal of Reading, 35,* 84–90.

Chapter 29   Donna Alvermann

Baker, L., & Brown, A. (1984). Cognitive monitoring in reading. In J. Flood (Ed.), *Understanding reading comprehension* (pp. 21–44). Newark, DE: International Reading Association.

Dolan, T. (1979). Improving reading through group discussion activities. In E. Lunzer and K. Gardner (Eds.), *The effective use of reading* (pp. 228–266). London: Heinemann.

Herber, H. L. (1978). *Teaching reading in content areas.* Englewood Cliffs, NJ: Prentice-Hall.

Richek, M. A. (1987). DRTA: Five variations that facilitate reading narratives. *Journal of Reading, 30,* 632–636.

Rose, M. (1989). *Lives on the boundary.* New York: The Free Press.

Stauffer, R. G. (1969). *Teaching reading as a thinking-process.* New York: HarperCollins.

Index